Michaela Baur, Bettina Gransow,
Yihong Jin, Guoqing Shi (Eds.)

Labour Mobility in Urban China

Berliner China-Studien

46

Herausgegeben von
Mechthild Leutner

Redaktion: Jens Damm

Ostasiatisches Seminar
der Freien Universität Berlin

LIT

Michaela Baur, Bettina Gransow,
Yihong Jin, Guoqing Shi (Eds.)

Labour Mobility in Urban China
An Integrated Labour Market in the Making?

Bibliographic information published by Die Deutsche Bibliothek
Die Deutsche Bibliothek lists this publication in the Deutsche
Nationalbibliografie; detailed bibliographic data are available in the
Internet at http://dnb.ddb.de.

ISBN 3-8258-9385-5

A catalogue record for this book is available from the British Library

© LIT VERLAG Berlin 2006
Auslieferung/Verlagskontakt:
Fresnostr. 2   48159 Münster
Tel. +49 (0)251–62 03 20   Fax +49 (0)251–23 19 72
e-Mail: lit@lit-verlag.de   http://www.lit-verlag.de

Distributed in the UK by: Global Book Marketing, 99B Wallis Rd, London, E9 5LN
Phone: +44 (0) 20 8533 5800 – Fax: +44 (0) 1600 775 663
http://www.centralbooks.co.uk/acatalog/search.html

Distributed in North America by:

Transaction Publishers
New Brunswick (U.S.A.) and London (U.K.)

Transaction Publishers
Rutgers University
35 Berrue Circle
Piscataway, NJ 08854

Phone: +1 (732) 445-2280
Fax: + 1 (732) 445-3138
for orders (U. S. only):
toll free (888) 999-6778
e-mail:
orders@transactionspub.com

Contents

Acknowledgements	7
Contributors	8
Introduction	10

The Chinese Labour Market – Developments and Analyses

Jutta Hebel, Günter Schucher, *Flexibility and Security in China's Emerging "Socialist" Market Labour Regime*	19
Zheng Zizhen, *"Peasant Worker Shortages" in Guangdong Province – A Demographic Analysis*	50

Labour Mobility – Driving Forces and Adjustment Strategies

Shi Guoqing, Zhou Jian, *A Cost-Benefit Analysis of Rural Labour Migration*	65
Bettina Gransow, *Risk Employment and Social Risk Management – Job Searching Strategies of Rural-to-Urban Migrants*	75
Heike Schmidbauer, *The Myth of Entrepreneurship – Migrant Returnees between Urban and Rural Labour Markets*	89
Tan Shen, *Labour Services for China's Migrant Workers – New Ideas and Practises*	100

Rural Migrants in Urban Areas

Wang Wei, *Family Patterns of Rural Migrants in Urban Areas and Their Migration Choices*	113
Wang Yijie, *Socio-Economic Status, Social Networks and Settlement Choices of Rural-to-Urban Migrants*	126
Zhu Li, *Cultural Life of Rural Migrants and Urban Integration*	140
Yang Wenjian, Sun Youran, Wang Pinghua, *The Problem of Overdue Migrant Wages: Legal Framework and Government Policies*	153

Informal Employment

Anne J. Braun, *Informal Employment – Integration or Segregation of the Labour Market?*   161

Jin Yihong, *Informal Employment and Labour Market Segmentation – A Gender Perspective*   175

Peng Xizhe, Yao Yu, *Social Protection for Migrant Workers in the Informal Economy – Issues and Options*   195

Active Employment Policies

Michaela Baur, *Labour Market Policy – Conflict of Aims Between Quantity or Quality*   207

Chen Xiaojiang, Dang Tianhu, *Small Business Start-up Models by Chinese Women - Introduction to the Research Report*   220

Andreas Klemmer, *Business Development Services for Migrant Workers in China*   228

Zhong Xiaoyun, *Active Employment Policies – The Case of the Nanjing Labour and Social Security Bureau*   246

Vulnerable Groups in the Urban Labour Market

Du Fenglian, Dong Xiaoyuan, *Gender Disparities in Unemployment Duration in Urban China*   251

Chen Shaojun, Zhang Runsen, *Peasants Who Lost Their Land – Rehabilitation Options from the Perspective of Sustainable Development*   266

Han Zhenyan, Dong Liyi, Zhou Ying *Involuntary Resettlement in Urban Areas – Development of Human Capital*   277

Index   289

Acknowledgements

The idea of a workshop on labour mobility in urban China first came into being when Bettina Gransow was teaching at the School of Public Administration, Hohai University Nanjing, in Autumn 2004. Most of the contributions contained in this volume are revised versions of papers which were originally presented at the workshop held in September 2005 at Hohai University. The workshop was organized and sponsored by the following institutions: Freie Universität Berlin, Hohai University Nanjing, Gesellschaft für Technische Zusammenarbeit (GTZ), Friedrich-Ebert Foundation (FES), Nanjing Normal University and Nanjing Association of Sociology. Support for the workshop and the book was provided by FES and GTZ. The book was printed with funds provided by GTZ.

The editors would like to thank all those who supported the workshop and have helped to make this publication possible. Special thanks to Antje Pfeiffer, GTZ Office Nanjing, Katja Meyer and Wang Beimin, FES Office Shanghai, Roland Feicht, FES Office Beijing, as well as Heike Schmidbauer, FU Berlin, and Anne J. Braun, Stiftung Wissenschaft und Politik, Berlin, for all their efforts in realizing the project.

Simona Thomas helped edit the text, created one manuscript out of the many contributions, and prepared the index of the volume. Anna Mackay revised the English version of the articles. We should like to express our gratitude to all these persons and institutions. A Chinese edition is in preparation.

Contributors

Michaela Baur, German Director of the German-Chinese Project "Reintegration of Unemployed Women into the Labour Force," Deutsche Gesellschaft für Technische Zusammenarbeit (GTZ) in Nanjing, PR China.

Anne J. Braun, Research Assistant and PhD Candidate, SWP – German Institute for International and Security Affairs, Research Unit Asia, Berlin, Germany.

Chen Shaojun 陈绍军, Professor, Deputy Director of the National Research Centre for Resettlement, Hohai University, Nanjing, PR China.

Chen Xiaojiang 陈小江, Director of the International Liaison Department, Shaanxi Women's Federation, Xi'an, PR China.

Dang Tianhu 党天虎, Deputy Director of the Department for Employment Services, Labour and Social Security Administration, Shaanxi Provincial Government, Xi'an, PR China.

Du Fenglian 杜凤莲, Associate Professor, School of Economics and Management, University of Inner Mongolia, PR China.

Dong Liyi 董力毅, Graduate Student, School of Public Administration, Hohai University, Nanjing, PR China.

Dong Xiaoyuan 董晓媛, University of Winnipeg, Canada.

Bettina Gransow, Professor of Chinese Studies at the Seminar of East Asian Studies, Freie Universität Berlin, Germany.

Han Zhenyan 韩振燕, Deputy Director of the Department of Social Security, School of Public Administration, Hohai University, Nanjing, PR China.

Jutta Hebel, Senior Lecturer and Researcher, Institute of Rural Development, University of Goettingen, Germany.

Jin Yihong 金一虹, Professor, Department of Labour and Social Security, Nanjing Normal University, Nanjing, PR China.

Andreas Klemmer, Chief Technical Advisor to the "Start and Improve Your Business China Programme" (SIYB), International Labour Organization Beijing, PR China.

Peng Xizhe 彭希哲, Professor, Dean of the School of Social Development and Public Policy, Fudan University, Shanghai, PR China.

Heike Schmidbauer, Research Associate (Wissenschaftliche Mitarbeiterin) and PhD Candidate, Seminar of East Asian Studies, Sinology, Freie Universität Berlin, Germany.

Günter Schucher, Director, Institute of Asian Affairs (part of GIGA German Institute of Global and Area Studies), Hamburg, Germany.

Shi Guoqing 施国庆, Professor, Dean of the School of Public Administration and Director of the National Research Center for Resettlement and Social Development Institute, Hohai University, Nanjing, PR China.

Sun Youran 孙友然, School of Public Administration, Hohai University, Nanjing, PR China.

Tan Shen 谭深, Professor, Institute of Sociology at the Chinese Academy of Social Sciences (CASS), Beijing, PR China.

Wang Pinghua 王平华, School of Public Administration, Hohai University, Nanjing, PR China.

Wang Wei 王微, PhD and Lecturer, Department of Social Work and Management, China Youth University for Political Sciences.

Wang Yijie 王毅杰, PhD in Sociology, Associate Professor at the Department of Sociology, Hohai University, Nanjing; Postdoctoral Researcher of the Institute of Sociology, Chinese Academy of Social Sciences (CASS), Beijing, PR China.

Yang Wenjian 杨文健, School of Public Administration, Hohai University, Nanjing, PR China.

Yao Yu 姚宇, PhD, Institute of Economics, Chinese Academy of Social Sciences (CASS), Beijing, PR China.

Zhang Runsen 张润森, School of Public Administration, Hohai University, Nanjing, PR China.

Zheng Zizhen 郑梓桢, Professor, Guangdong Academy of Social Sciences, Guangzhou, PR China.

Zhong Xiaoyun 仲晓云, Municipal Administration of Labour and Social Security, Nanjing, PR China.

Zhou Jian 周建, PhD Candidate, National Research Center for Resettlement, Hohai University, Nanjing, PR China.

Zhou Ying 周莹, Student, School of Business Administration, Hohai University, Nanjing, PR China.

Zhu Li 朱力, PhD, Sociological Association Nanjing, Professor at the Department of Sociology, Nanjing University, Nanjing, PR China.

Introduction

At the beginning of the 21st century, China's urban labour market is facing major challenges. Despite high economic growth, the capacity of the Chinese economy to create new jobs seems to be limited. Problems such as the expansion of flexible/informal work, frail social security systems, rising unemployment, an influx of rural labour migrants, competition between and within different population groups and sectors and mismatches between labour supply and demand require enormous efforts and creative problem-solving strategies by state and non-state actors alike. The old balance between employment and social security limited to urban areas as part of a strict rural-urban divide has been ruled out and a new, all-inclusive balance has yet to be found.

The challenges of the reform of the labour market in China are not an isolated phenomenon which can be attributed to China's national transformation from a planned to a market society alone. These processes have also to be seen as embedded in the broader context of globalization, international mass migration, and urbanization trends. In China, the influx of global forces dovetailed neatly with the open door policy initiated by Deng Xiaoping. The intensification of foreign trade and foreign direct investment were attributes of an export-driven development. As globalization advances, manufacturing jobs are shifting more and more to less developed parts of the world. As part of this development, rising labour costs and real estate prices have led more and more businesses to move their production sites from Hong Kong and Taiwan to mainland China. The reform offensive of the 1990s reinforced this development and China's entry into the World Trade Organization (2001) further accelerated the process. The development of export processing industries has resulted in a process of land-use transformation, during the course of which, much farmland has been transformed for industrial land use. Although urbanization in China is proceeding at an exceedingly rapid rate and can be seen as offering an important way out of employment problems, the relative ratio of urban to total employment is, nevertheless, still low in China.

This volume introduces labour mobility issues through an examination of the question whether, after twenty years of labour system reforms, an integrated labour market is in the making. The chapters in this volume were originally presented as papers in a workshop at Hohai University Nanjing in 2005. Bringing together Chinese and foreign researchers, practitioners and donors, the discussion gained from synergies in exchanging ideas on theoretical discourses and practical experiences in the field of labour market developments and policies. The chapters are grouped around the study of six problems central to the explanation of labour mobility in urban China: (1) the reform of the urban labour market, its outcomes and current distortions in the employment regime, (2) the driving forces and migration strategies from the perspective of rural-to-urban migrants, (3) the challenges and choices facing rural migrants in urban settings, (4) the increasing role of informal employment and its consequences regarding the reform and shape of social safety nets, (5) active employment policies, such as small business start-up models, (6) vulnerable groups in the urban labour market, such as unemployed women, peasants who lost their land (*shidi nongmin* 失地农民) or involuntarily resettled people. A theme that runs through several chapters in this volume (Gransow; Schmidbauer; Tan; Jin; Peng/Yao; Baur; Chen/Dang; Du/Dong) is the gender dimension of labour mobility and employment issues.

The reform of the Chinese labour market has led to a new situation characterized by a certain mismatch of the underlying institutional set. In introducing the theoretical model of "employment regimes" and the new term of "flexicurity" (a combination of flexibility and security) *Jutta Hebel* and *Günter Schucher* see this incoherence as resulting from the overlap of those institutions that still follow the logic of the planning system and those that emerged with the market society. Using the analytical framework of a labour regime described as a set of institutions that are shaped by various policies such as family policy, educational policy, social policy etc., they conclude that mobility in the formal sectors is still restricted while there is a fast growing sphere of atypical and informal work in China. In their view, the incoherence of the institutional set is responsible for distortions in the employment regime and the exclusion of large parts of the labour force.

China's economic success has been ascribed to the inexhaustible supply of cheap and eager labour migrating from the countryside to the cities which is keeping wages unimaginably low, but since 2004, a new phenomenon of worker shortages has been emerging, not only in terms of highly qualified specialists, but also of migrants from rural areas who now exceed 60 per cent of the workforce in some sectors (in production industries, for example) or even 80 per cent (in the construction industry). Reports from export production strongholds such as the Pearl River Delta, and from the southeast areas of Fujian and Zhejiang Provinces, speak of people "voting with their feet" (*yong jiao toupiao* 用脚投票) that has led to a noticeable shortfall of labour. Estimates suggest that the labour market could use another 10 per cent of the total workforce. What are the reasons behind this "jam" in the flow of workers, and what are the strategies, considerations, and levels of information that lead rural Chinese to seek work in the cities? *Zheng Zizhen* discusses the shortage of labour migrants in Guangdong Province by looking at demographic developments. In his view, the phenomenon of an acute labour shortage is of a temporary nature only, and he predicts that China will have to cope with a labour surplus for a long time. Proposed solutions to the problem include strengthening the employment rights of migrant workers, improving their working conditions, and providing them with country-wide job information and placement services free of charge. These are clearly all reasonable proposals that would help create a unified labour market and promote the continued growth of the market economy in China. At the same time, these proposals could well equalize the rights of migrant labourers relative to those of urban Chinese citizens and thus create more favourable conditions for the former to make the transition from informal to formal employment.

An analysis of the driving forces behind labour migration as well as the strategies used by individuals and households in the process of migration reveals a broader variety of motivations to leave the countryside than those of a purely economic nature. Using the theoretical model of cost-benefit analysis, *Shi Guoqing* and *Zhou Jian* explore the economic and social factors influencing migration decisions. Improving development opportunities and learning new skills seems to be as important or even more important for many people than the desire to earn higher wages. This holds true for men and women but applies more to younger people than to the elderly. *Bettina Gransow* introduces the terms of "risk employment" and "social risk management" to present survey results and explain the broader context of the job-searching strategies of labour migrants. *Heike Schmidbauer* takes a look back at the sending regions of migrant labour. She contrasts dominant discourses on return migration with actual volumes of return and the delineated structural and institutional barriers encountered by migrant returnees and especially returnee entrepreneurs.

Looking at new activities and programmes offered by state and non-state actors in the field of services for migrant workers, the question arises as to whether these fit with the needs of the labour migrants. Government at all levels has dedicated public funds to the services of rural workers. This suggests a considerable shift in government policy which has offered a wealth of opportunities for various forces to enter the field of providing services for migrant workers and safeguarding their rights and interests. In addition, multi-national corporations have been greatly involved in the field; a growing number of NGOs for labour has emerged and other organizations have put more effort into projects for migrant workers' services. *Tan Shen* looks at the development and changes in this field over the past five years. She analyses the relationships between different forces, with the aim of profiling the motives of different practitioners involved in offering their services to migrant workers. Meanwhile, suggestions are put forward with respect to projects for migrant workers' services.

The social exclusion of migrant workers in urban areas may not only have consequences for their living conditions, but also for their attitudes to work and their work ethos. It is therefore necessary, also from the perspective of labour relations, to analyse these relations as embedded in the broader social and cultural environment. *Wang Wei* suggests that the percentage of migrant families is increasing year by year and that this finding is important for identifying future migration trends. Labour migrants in urban areas are confronted with a variety of challenges and choices. Their willingness and possibilities with regard to settling down in urban areas is linked not only to the prospects of employment, wages, labour conditions and workers' rights, but also to central and local government policies encouraging or restricting their residence in urban areas, to the social services available, including schooling for the migrant families' children, and other conditions. Why are some migrants eager to settle down in urban areas while others want to return to the countryside in the long term? *Wang Yijie* presents results of a survey on the willingness of rural migrants to settle down in the city of Nanjing. In his view, social networks are vital for gaining an understanding of their propensity to stay.

Analysing the integration prospects of rural labour migrants in urban society, *Zhu Li* develops a model of three levels of adaptation: economic, social and psychological adaptation. He then examines the remaining obstacles, especially with regard to cultural integration. *Yang Wenjian, Sun Youran* and *Wang Pinghua* look at the problem of delayed or withheld migrant wages and put forth policy recommendations for legal guarantees of payment.

In recent years, informal labour has been growing rapidly in China. According to *Anne J. Braun* two groups of people are being employed in informal jobs: rural migrants and re-employed urban workers. Rural migrants have been employed in the informal sector since the very early days of economic restructuring in the early 1980s. The rigid system of household registration (*hukou* system) made it almost impossible for them to find employment in the formal sector. With the progression of labour market reforms in China's cities and growing unemployment, however, informal employment has also become an important employment channel for retrenched and laid-off urban workers. Jobs in the informal sector differ substantially from employment in the formal sector in terms of wages, job security and social benefits. She therefore assumes that the labour market is increasingly being divided between people employed in formal jobs and those migrants and re-employed urban workers employed in informal jobs, thus establishing a new kind of labour market segmentation according to status in employment that is increasingly replacing the "traditional" fragmentation of the labour market between urban workers and rural migrants. *Jin Yihong* looks at the rise in informal employment from a gender perspective. She warns that the promotion of the informal sector is likely to aggravate the situation of women by cementing existing gender inequalities. Focusing on the efforts of the Shanghai labour administration to "formalize" informal employment arrangements by integrating migrant workers, *Peng Xizhe* and *Yao Yu* point out the challenges awaiting local governments experimenting with social security net arrangements for rural migrants.

How are the challenges of labour mobility and the changes in the urban labour market addressed by the policies and measures of governmental and non-governmental actors? A policy-oriented perspective is put forth by *Michaela Baur* who concentrates on current labour market policies, questioning the dominant approach which focuses on quantity alone. Her specific perspective is based on the experiences of the Chinese-German cooperation project "Reintegration of Unemployed Women into the Labour force," which was implemented in cooperation with the Nanjing labour administration. On the one hand she describes the labour market situation in China as facing the typical problems of a transforming economy. On the other hand, she identifies certain problems and challenges which make the Chinese example a special one. She raises the question of whether the Chinese government's answer to these challenges is appropriate and will be able to relieve the pressure on the labour market.

Laid-off and unemployed women workers have been the subject of much debate in China, while the country has been experiencing a period of social transformation and the adjustment of its economic structure. The issue has attracted attention throughout society in China, because of its crucial links to the lives and development of individuals and families. For a number of reasons, Chinese urban women workers who have been made redundant or are unemployed, have exceeded more than 50 per cent of the total numbers of the laid-off and unemployed workers. Such high levels of unemployment among women may have a serious negative impact on both their own welfare and also on their marriages and families. Since society can only provide a limited number of new job opportunities, setting up a business has become a major avenue of re-employment, and a popular choice both for laid-off workers and those newly entering the labour market. As a result, job creation and re-employment through women's business start-ups has come to be seen by private individuals, society and government as an important economic reform strategy.

The Chinese government began its policy of creating jobs through business start-ups in 1998, attracting widespread interest in China. Implementation of this policy has been of great significance: it is seen as epitomizing a positive attitude towards economic globalization, as well as helping to reduce the tensions created by unemployment and encourage the establishment of individual businesses and the development of small and medium-sized enterprises. The Ministry of Labour and Social Security has focused on setting up an integrated business start-up service system, incorporating advice, training, and the gathering of project proposals, microfinance and follow-up activities. Local governments and non-governmental organizations have accumulated a wealth of data and practical experience in using a range of flexible approaches to support and assist laid-off and unemployed women in setting up small businesses. *Chen Xiaojiang* and *Dang Tianhu* focus on the use of women's small business start-up models in the non-state sector, as a means of tackling redundancy and unemployment. The research reveals that women involved in small business start-ups differ in many respects from those working in large or medium sized enterprises; there are also differences resulting from the social and economic situation in different cities. *Andreas Klemmer* looks at the business development services designed for migrants in China who have become an attractive target group for entrepreneurship development. In his view, the efforts of the government in this direction could pave the way for the successful integration of the migrants into their local host society. However, the current demand of the target group for business support services seems to be limited, partly due to their ignorance of their own training needs and partly due to a lack of knowledge on the part of training suppliers. A survey is presented covering 3,000 migrants working in the urban construction industry and the gastronomy sector in Sichuan Province. The purpose of the research was to assess the intrinsic demand of these domestic migrants for entrepreneurship development services. The author concludes that the demand of migrants for business support services needs to be stimulated in order to unlock their entrepreneurial development potential. To this end, he recommends that a policy should be developed to promote the concept of entrepreneurship among migrant workers by way of the mass-media, and then that classroom-based training and related business support services should be offered as a concrete follow-up. *Zhong Xiaoyun* reports on the experience of the Nanjing Labour and Social Security Bureau and gives an overview of local labour market policies which aim to achieve a gradual integration of urban and rural labour markets in the region.

In the past decade, China's public enterprises have undergone dramatic ownership reforms and labour retrenchment. While industrial restructuring is an inevitable feature of market transition, it has affected men and women differently. Studies show that women have borne a disproportionate share of the costs of adjustment. Women are more likely to be unemployed than men and have more difficulty in finding re-employment in the private sector. In consequence, women endure higher unemployment rates and their periods of unemployment are longer. The deterioration of the employment status of women makes the feminization of urban poverty a real possibility in post-restructuring China. The rising gender inequality in paid employment affects the well-being of not only women themselves but also their families; evidence obtained from a diverse set of countries has revealed that increasing a woman's contribution to the household income significantly increases the share of the household budget allocated to children's education, health and nutrition-related expenditures. Despite the significant impacts, the gender implications of industrial restructuring have not received adequate attention from economists and policy-makers in China. *Du Fenglian* and *Dong Xiaoyuan* focus on gender disparities in periods of unemployment. The authors study the determinants of gender differences in periods of unemployment in urban China using a nation-wide household survey undertaken in 2003. They apply a duration regression model to investigate the main reasons for women's periods of unemployment being longer than men's and evaluate the extent to which the gender disparity in unemployment duration is attributable to labour market structure and other institutional factors. Using an econometrical model, they come to the conclusion that institutional factors, not the individual characteristics of women, are decisive. They argue that a better understanding of the causes of gender disparities in unemployment is of critical importance for designing gender-sensitive public policies and seeking gender-equitable solutions for urban unemployment.

Preferential policies are not only needed for the unemployed, especially women, young people and the elderly, but also for new emerging vulnerable groups in the urban labour market such as involuntary resettlers and so-called peasants who have lost their land and who are at risk of impoverishment. In China, involuntary resettlement caused by development interventions is on the rise. Massive economic construction programmes have resulted in forced resettlement in rural and urban areas. It is necessary to establish the appropriate mechanisms to enable the involuntary resettlers to secure their livelihoods. *Chen Shaojun* and *Zhang Runsen* analyze the effects of different resettlement options based on a survey in Jiangning

County (Jiangsu Province). The authors create a sustainable development evaluation index system consisting of several subsystems. *Han Shenyan* looks at involuntary resettlers from the perspective of human capital theories. The Chinese concept of involuntary resettlement (*fei ziyuan yimin* 非自愿移民) includes the loss of land caused by development interventions. Peasants who lose their land are confronted with the risk of impoverishment when their conditions for making a living changes due to sudden landlessness. The essential issue is to relocate them in a way that will result in their gaining a sustainable livelihood.

Michaela Baur, Bettina Gransow, Jin Yihong, Shi Guoqing
Berlin and Nanjing, March 2006

The Chinese Labour Market –

Developments and Analyses

Flexibility and Security in China's Emerging "Socialist" Market Labour Regime

Jutta Hebel and Günter Schucher

Introduction

Flexibility and security are central parameters of modern labour markets. Both are highly important in China's labour market reforms. The planned labour system has been extremely inflexible but has provided comprehensive social security, at least to the urban population. The initial reforms aimed to smash the "iron rice bowl" of lifelong employment and enterprise-based comprehensive social security.

From the very beginning, labour market reforms aimed to eliminate all that chained the development of the productive forces (Hu 1986). China witnessed strong economic growth for more than 20 years, but accepted a steady increase in urban unemployment, new urban poverty and an increase in the numbers of uprooted rural migrants without any security provisions. The greater flexibility of the Chinese labour market eroded workers' rights, and reduced employment and income security as well as the stability of working and living conditions. As has been stated in recent studies carried out by Chinese think-tanks, the reform of the social security system has not yet been carried out successfully. The old balance between flexibility and security has been rejected and the idea of a new sort of balance has become one of the key issues in labour market policy.

The extension of labour intensive industries and the enlargement of the service sector are two main items, intended to reduce unemployment, on the policy agenda of the Chinese government (Information Office of the State Council of the PRC 2004). Even though the potential for labour intensive industrialization in China's inland provinces is still considerable, a one-dimensional "retro-strategy" in labour market policy will not solve the problems of a rapidly modernising economy. In its coastal provinces, despite all the structural and developmental differences, China's economic development is by-passing certain stages of Western industrialization. The increase in foreign investment and the pressure of world market competition have had a deep impact on production processes, employment and work organization as well as on security matters. There will not be any fundamental change in the tight labour market situation in the foreseeable future, particularly since the new labour market policy aims to increase the numbers of rural migrants, as opposed to urban migrants, in order to raise rural incomes.

Some parallels to this labour market imbalance can be found in Europe. This does not, however, mean that the Chinese model will become a globally valid institution. At least three arguments can be put forward regarding this: first of all, institutional change is not determined by current constellations; rather, changes are contingent and path-dependent. The process develops its own dynamic. Secondly, labour market policy is constantly faced with conflicting political aims, such as social harmony, family policy or the socio-political control of the population, which may restrict reforms aiming at a higher employment rate. And lastly, labour market inclusion is not the result of one single institution but stems from a set of institutions, varying in different countries and historical periods as well as for different groups of people (men-women, young-old).

In other words, various policies, such as family policy, social policy, educational policy, labour policy, and economic policy, shape the social institutions that structure employment and the labour market. A set of institutions and their mutual influences form what, in this paper, will be called a "labour regime." The different outcomes of labour market policies and different grades of labour market inclusion are related to the prevailing employment regime. The boundaries between the labour market and other social institutions may be either too high or not open enough, the employability of labourers may be inadequate, the effectiveness of labour market measures too limited or mobility too low.

In this paper, we will use the analytical framework of a *labour regime* to analyse ongoing labour market reforms in China. Particular attention will be paid to the balance of labour market flexibility and security in China. For the theoretical basis, we will review the literature on labour regimes in the second section and try to draw some conclusions for China as a transition economy which have been widely neglected in research so far. In chapter three, we will briefly characterize the *socialist labour regime* (SLR in what follows) and scrutinize the emerging new *"socialist" market labour regime* (SMLR in what follows). Empirical and statistical data on flexibility and security in the Chinese market labour regime, on transitions[1] from unemployment to employment and between different employment statuses are presented in chapter four. We will show that mobility in the formal sectors is still restricted while there is a fast growing sphere of atypical and informal work in China. Finally, we will draw some conclusions regarding the emerging socialist SMLR.

Labour regimes

Different labour market theories agree that the supply and demand of labour should match and that a mismatch creates unemployment. The reasons for such mismatches and unemployment may be found on either side, supply or demand. Changing job offers and demands of work result from a number of factors such as the restructuring of the economy, technological change and the rationalisation of production processes, demographic development, the level and type of qualification of the labour force and the degree of mobility and flexibility of the labour force.

Labour market theorists come up with different explanations of the labour market process, of mismatches and unemployment based on their different basic

---

[1] Note that "transition" in this context means the change of employment status in contrast to the transition from one to another economic system.

premises and assumptions. Economic theories dominated the mainstream of the labour market discussion for a long time, although, during the 1980s, new institutionalist concepts were developed which challenged the pure economic perspective. Broadly speaking, neoclassical economic theories focus on prices (on wages and income) and unemployment is explained as a failure to harmonise income demand and prices for work. In clear contrast to economic theories, sociological approaches emphasize the specific features of labour markets in each country. They bring into play a set of institutions that emerged during extended periods resulting from trade-offs between different values, goals and processes in society, that shape the present labour process and define labour participation. The new focus of labour market research is to decode the national particularities of labour markets and to highlight them by comparing them with the solutions found for similar problems in other countries.

Unlike Eastern European countries, China did not follow a "big bang" approach in order to erase the inherited institutional order, but favoured incremental change, building on institutional legacies. Although in both cases a transition from a planned to a market economy occurred, the labour markets differed. The path dependency school emphasizes the influence of the past and strictly refutes the idea of an institutional vacuum. It argues that a series of structured innovations over time will finally result in the complex reconfiguration of existing institutions.

During the 1970s and 1980s, a number of American academics (namely Doeringer/Piore 1980) started to investigate the national characteristics of labour markets. They developed new labour market concepts that underlined the dual character of labour markets. Their basic assumption was that labour markets are split up into different segments that absorb dissimilar groups of the workforce. The different segments are called *primary and secondary segments,* which represent different quality levels of jobs (contract security, work safety, wage level and qualification), or *internal and external segments*, which highlight processes of closure towards outsiders. Amending the latter concept, Lutz (1987) and Sengenberger (1978) paid special attention to the problems of qualification and used the term *firm-centred labour market* to describe the internal labour market segment. The insights offered by the various versions of segmentation theory proved to be very fruitful for the analysis of labour markets.

Since the 1980s, the concept has also been used as an analytical tool for the investigation of labour systems in transition countries, namely Eastern European countries (Grünert/Lutz 1994) and the PR China (Hebel/Schucher 1992). The driving forces behind the segmentation process and the outcomes in former centrally planned economies differed completely from those in Western societies. In market economies, explanations for segmentation processes draw on production regimes, human capital and training, job idiosyncrasies and the nature of work, whereas in planned economies, state regulations as well as the production strategies of state enterprises and their management of human resources are seen as crucial for the process of segmentation. Chinese scientists also opposed the economic assumption of one single labour market and made use of a *dual market approach*. Yang (2002: chapter 6) described the administrative division of the labour market as being due to the system of residential registration (*hukou* 戶口) as well as the interests of local governments and government departments. Its most prominent feature is multiple discrimination against rural labourers.

In addition to these valuable insights, current scientific contributions transcend the idea of segmentation. Recent concepts single out some new ideas from a broader debate on the institutional embeddedness of employment and the labour process. The labour market situation in any particular society is understood as the result of an interplay between various institutions each with a particular rationale and history. Pries (1998) described several major social institutions – the market is one of them – which shape labour allocation and employment conditions. Inspired by the discourse on *welfare regimes* and *varieties of capitalism* the new terms *labour regime* or *employment regime* were suggested to express the idea that the labour market is formed by a set of institutions in their entirety.

The labour market debate parallels some other strands of academic discussion, namely the welfare state typology (or *welfare regime*), *production regime* or *gender order*. We can also make reference to the discussion on the East-Asian welfare system (White 1998). The concept of labour (employment) regime shares, with the other strands, the concerns about the diversity, the differences and the divergence of a particular labour market in comparison with conditions in other countries or the labour market in an earlier period. Changes in the labour market, adaptations to new challenges (e.g., globalization) and the extent of work inclusion are *path-dependent*, i.e., framed by history, former solutions to labour exchange and the interplay of institutions. In other words, labour markets follow a unique (national) trajectory supported by a particular set of institutions.

Labour regime can be used as a generic term allowing us to decipher the entire set of institutional arrangements. *Regimes* or *orders*, in contrast to systems, are not stable. They can be understood as patterns of traditions, past experiences and problem solutions as well as of current expectations, perceptions, behaviour and relations. The institutional patterns change continuously, and, under normal conditions, changes are hardly noticeable (Heidenreich 2000).

But which institutions matter? Certainly, there is no definite answer to this question. In different countries the roles of different institutions vary, e.g., the role of labour unions which may act as political powers, as partners in corporatist arrangements or as institutions with social obligations. Following Schmid (1996), we highlight the interconnectedness of five institutions with the labour market: (1) the production regime, (2) the industrial relations, (3) the welfare regime, (4) the (private) household, family, kin and gender order, and (5) the education system. For the analysis of the Chinese labour regime we add (6) the institutions of socio-political control. Figure 1 displays the framework we will use to analyse the Chinese labour market reforms.

Fig. 1: Institutional setting of the Chinese labour regime

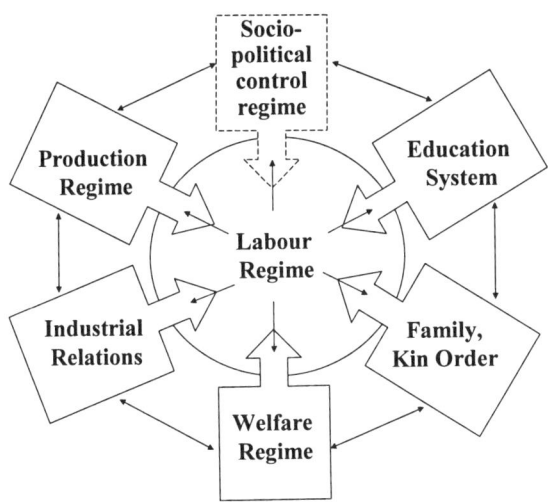

The literature on labour regimes makes reference to the welfare regime typology. Heidenreich (2000, 2004) reduced orders or regimes to two ideal types: an *order of high productivity* and an *order of high employment*. The first is characterized by the concentration on highly productive activities in secondary and tertiary industries and on a male dominated employment pattern. It is based on stable employment relations with full-time jobs as well as unlimited contracts for a qualified industrial labour force, the exclusion of "marginal" groups and the containment of precarious types of work. The second shows a high level of employment with the active inclusion of women, young people and elderly people; it accepts wide differences in wages, and focuses on labour intensive services. In doing this, it promotes an increase in precarious employment relations (self-employment, mini firms, and atypical jobs).

Muffels et al. (2002) explored the relations between *employment regimes* and performance indicators with respect to flexibility and security. They defined *flexibility* in terms of the opportunities for transitions or the likelihood of these between various employment statuses (i.e., from flexible into permanent or from part-time into full-time employment). *Security* is characterized as the likelihood of transitions from unemployment into part-time and permanent employment as well as vice versa. They found that regimes differ in their performance to safeguard flexibility and security, but that no employment regime has a monopoly on either flexibility or security, let alone on both. Variations originate in particular traditions and sets of institutions.

Flexibility in modern labour markets is not restricted to mobility and job transitions, but includes the end of a full employment model and the emergence of new forms of atypical employment as well as new mobile forms of labour relations. Security is supposed to act as a buffer against social exclusion and to close the gap between insiders and outsiders. It can be attained either by welfare systems, regulations and employment security (at the expense of high unemployment or, in the planned economy, of adaptability) or by a highly flexible and efficient labour market with low unemployment and a high share of atypical employment.

The key issue, as is mentioned above, is to redress the balance between flexibility and security. Wilthagen called it the "flexibility-security nexus" and offered a new policy model: *flexicurity*. In his definition, *flexicurity* is

a policy strategy that attempts, synchronically and in a deliberate way, to enhance the flexibility of labour markets, the work organization and labour relations on the one hand, and to enhance security – employment security and social security – notably for weaker groups in and outside the labour market on the other hand (Wilthagen/Tros 2003: 4).

Decisive elements of the strategy are synchronisation, coordination and security for weaker groups. That means it is not sufficient to enhance flexibility and security either consecutively or separately, nor would it suit the concept of stronger groups to meet security concerns. According to Wilthagen and Tros *flexicurity* involves a different attitude towards flexibility and security. Flexibility is no longer the monopoly of employers, but should enable unemployed people to reintegrate into the labour market and facilitate transitions within the domain of employment itself. Security needs are no longer exclusively met by income or job security, but also by the "maintenance of a good position in the internal and external labour market (e.g., in terms of training, employability, flexible organisation of work, et cetera)" (Wilthagen/Tros 2003: 16).

Insights from the various contributions on regimes and their trajectories mentioned above help us to analyse and understand ongoing changes in the Chinese labour market. In the next chapter, we will outline some characteristics of the old SLR and highlight present changes.

Socialist labour regime and labour market reforms

In our analysis of the Chinese labour market reforms, and, in particular, the present mobility and flexibility of labour, we will draw on the concept of labour regimes. As necessary background information, we will give a brief outline of the pre-reform SLR. Both endogenous and exogenous factors have driven the changes occurring during the reform period. At the behest of the Chinese Communist leadership, institutions should have special "Chinese characteristics" like the "market economy with Chinese characteristics." The idea underlying this expression is very much in line with our primary assumptions which are based on the labour regime concept. It paraphrases the embeddedness of the Chinese labour market in a unique institutional setting and on a particular pathway to change. Traditional cultural and socialist elements inspire the logic of diverse institutions, such as the kinship and family system, trade unions or the social security system.

Characteristics of the socialist labour regime (SLR)

A description of the characteristics of the SLR should start by mentioning the distinct differences between the urban and rural employment conditions in China, which are upheld by the *hukou*-system. In contrast to the rural areas, urbanites have been included in a labour regime based on what we call - using the term *Normalarbeitsverhältnis* from the German labour discussion – a socialist normal work pattern (SNWP in what follows). The SNWP is considered to be a normative pattern which has been institutionalised as a life course model for the urban population, including work training, work assignment by the labour bureaus, a normal work life as a member of a work unit (*danwei* 单位), related social security and benefits (such as housing, education, subsidies), regular retirement at a pre-scheduled age and retirement benefits provided by the *danwei*. This type of work relationship structures the life courses of Chinese individuals into three phases: work-preparation, full and stable employment and an old age period beyond the working life. The Chinese express the pattern in the picture of the "iron rice bowl."

The socialist employment regime has been upheld by a set or, in other words, a mix of institutions. All these institutions follow a specific logic based on tradition, ownership structure, and various factors including the socialist ideology which stems from Western ideas based on Marx's fundamental analysis of capitalism.

First, the institutions of socio-political control have been crucial for the Chinese SLR. Social control has dominated the logic of employment relations and has taken its toll on mobility and flexibility in the labour process. Political institutions such as the *hukou*-system, work units and rural collective units (communes, production brigades and teams) have established the rural-urban divide. They have given rise to a segmented labour system dividing the Chinese workforce into the urban part with access to the socialist labour system and into the rural majority chained to rural areas. The aim of these institutions was to control population mobility and they have caused the nation-wide inequality. They have been interrelated with all the other institutions. The influence of the *hukou* cannot be underestimated.

Second, the SLR has been in line with production planning and the production process. The state has held a monopoly on work allocation and employment as well as on wage setting within its planning system. The public sector has been funded by the state and has absorbed most of the urban labour force. The process has resulted in the well-known, large-scale labour redundancy. The socialist planned economy was based on the so called "soft budget constraints," and enterprises organized their labour process relying on the extension of their work force. State owned enterprises followed a policy of labour allocation without any consideration of efficiency. We have sound evidence that personnel policies in state owned enterprises have pursued labour consuming production strategies and gained prestige and resources by increasing the numbers of their workforces (Hebel 1997; Tomba 2002).

Third, trade unions have played a special role in the socialist labour regime. The role of trade unions has been inspired by socialist ideology. Workers, considered as the owners of the means of production and masters of the enterprise, do not need any particular protection from the employer. On the one hand, the trade union in China is a political institution, transmitting the policies of the party state (e.g., the idea of a "transmission belt") and, on the other hand, the union is a social institution responsible for the welfare arrangements at the grassroots. The basic rationale of this institution is not directed towards contracted work and the adjustment of the relationship between a powerful employer and a powerless employee.

Fourth, the system of employment has been coupled with the social security system. The strong connection between *danwei*-membership and social security entitlement has created the comprehensive inclusion of the urban population in society without any alternatives. Due to the imperfections of the market, individual risks and shocks could not be cushioned by individual spending or private insurance policies. The SLR did not rule out the family and kin networks as fail-safe systems of security, based on traditional "filial piety," kin reciprocity and the family law. In rural areas with little collective support and no developed social security system, the family net buffered all hardships. Despite state monopoly and *danwei* based social provision, the social security of urbanites also continued to depend on families.

Fifth, the Chinese SLR established and promoted a dual earner family/ household model. Inspired by a socialist gender concept, it enabled women to participate in the labour process by providing day care and schooling for children as well as by procuring a small degree of financial independence (i.e., pensions) for the elderly. Moreover, young people were almost all included in the workforce, since periods of training were short and the cohorts of students in tertiary education, small. Inclusion of women, however, did not mean the end of discrimination. Even though planned allocation did not differentiate between genders, the majority of women worked in lower ranked and less well paid positions.

Six, education and professional training is an important institution related to the labour market. The former education system was closely connected to the production sector, professional training being mostly provided by the enterprises themselves. It took the characteristic of job-preparatory training and served the specific needs of a particular enterprise with very special jobs. The education system did not provide the individual with marketable qualifications that could have been used elsewhere. It proved to be a very important source of immobility, at least for that section of the workforce with lower and middle level training.

The above-mentioned set of institutions quite clearly formed a highly inclusive work regime, producing full employment and a high female employment participation rate. It represented a trade-off between the goals of socio-political control, (in particular by means of risk reduction and migration control), and state-led industrialization in the urban regions, based on the extraction of resources from the rural areas using unfavourable terms of trade between countryside and cities. In the rural areas, the SLR relied, among other aspects, on land collectivisation and local commune institutions, which chained the farmers to the rural areas. Urban labourers, male and female, young and old, were included in the workforce by labour planning and administrative allocation.

The deep and almost insurmountable rural-urban divide separated urban people from rural competition. But this "invisible Great Wall" (Knight/Song 2005) was only one prominent feature segmenting the pre-reform labour system. The other characteristic that sharply distinguished China from market economies was the Chinese "work-unit," the *danwei*. State and large collective enterprises included the majority of urban workers in the SNWP. These enterprises were not employers in the Western sense, but social institutions, so-called "mini welfare-states" or "small societies." Employees, in accordance with the SNWP, enjoyed comprehensive security but had no flexibility or mobility. Chinese urban workers were much more tightly bound to internal, firm-centred labour markets than their colleagues in other socialist countries.

Even though the SLR preserved a small degree of flexibility by recourse to a small external segment of non-permanent – "extra-plan" and "non-planned" – employment, this external labour market existed only in a rudimentary form and the essential prerequisites for a functioning external labour market were not existant. These would include institutions and regulations that supplied workers with the information necessary for employment change, protection against the loss of income in case of unemployment, as well as enterprise external training and re-training institutions with standardised curricula.

Towards a "socialist" market labour regime (SMLR)

It is obvious to every Chinese and foreign observer that fundamental changes in the SLR took place during the reform period. A labour market has been emerging in China since the mid 1980s. The various steps and measures that have been undertaken will not be examined here; we have already discussed these elsewhere, as have several other Chinese and western researchers. Instead, we are going to try to elucidate the changes in the SLR and its interrelatedness with the above mentioned social institutions. We will argue that there is continuity (in the sense of a particular regime trajectory) and discontinuity (due to various factors, such as privatization, globalization etc.).

The particular model of a SNWP has been rapidly dismantled during the last two decades. In the public sector, the former lifelong job tenure and work unit membership has been challenged and in the private sector contracted work has become the rule. An informal sector of employment – within the public and private industry – has come into being and meanwhile has absorbed a considerable proportion of the work force. Self-employment has become an important option for the young or laid-off work force and, in particular, the rural population. Mobility has been growing during the early 1990s, covering processes of regional migration (rural-rural, rural-urban etc.) and job mobility (up- and downward mobility). The most important instrument of socio-political control, the *hukou* system, has lost its overwhelming importance.

The most decisive step in this process of regime change was the withdrawal of the state from labour allocation and employment. This step is in line with the transition towards a "socialist" market economy and includes the restructuring of the public sector and admittance being granted to private economic activities.

The Chinese labour market has been shaped by the division of jobs between a decreasing public sector and an increasing private sector, declining formal and increasing informal work and the expansion of self-employment at the expense of dependent work. The increase in mobility and flexibility in the workforce is due to the restructuring of the public sector and the expansion of the private sector. Yet, many of the detrimental effects of the transitional labour process from which many Chinese people suffer these days cannot be explained as only being due to privatization; these effects also result from the new fluidity of a whole set of institutions today.

Table 1 gives an overview of the main changes from the pre-reform socialist labour regime to the present "socialist" market labour regime. All these changes have been described in detail by several authors. We argue that they have not resulted in the emergence of a new and coherent ensemble of institutions so far. The new situation is characterized by a certain mismatch of the underlying institutional set. The above-mentioned institutions have become fluid and no longer support the old regime, nor are they appropriate for the new regime.

First, socio-political control has been relaxed, at least with respect to the *hukou*-system, although rural migrants to the cities still face discriminatory treatment in a number of different ways (Wang 2005). Most of the migrants are only integrated into the urban labour market at its margins of inferior, badly remunerated and insecure jobs.

Second, the decrease of the state's role in labour allocation and employment has given way to a new type of dependent and contracted work.

Third, despite the spread of contracted work in the private sector, only embryonic attempts at worker representation at different levels have been undertaken. The admittance of free trade unions is not on the reform agenda. The Chinese Labour Law of 1995 protects part of the formal workforce but lacks implementation and control.

Fourth, the renewal of the welfare system is taking place according to different goals: on the one hand, the new system has to comply with the entitlements of employees and workers under the old labour regime and, on the other hand, new guidelines have to be established to cover new groups of the work force.

Fifth, a considerable proportion of the Chinese labour force is left alone with the risks and shocks occurring during the course of their lives or they have to fall back on their family and kin networks. The Chinese family policy worked (and still works) against the family as a fall back position for people in need. The nuclear family and dual-wage-earner models may conflict with the new type of dependent work (beyond the *danwei*).

Six, the education system and professional training has become more sophisticated and better adapted to general labour market demand. Nevertheless, a low return to higher education can be observed as well as a mismatch between the offers and demands regarding qualifications.

Table 1. Overview of the pre-reform and present Chinese labour regime types

(Pre-reform) Chinese socialist labour regime - SLR -	(Present) Chinese "socialist" market labour regime - SMLR -
Socio-political control regime	
Hukou-based residence control	*Hukou* reform
Rigid rural-urban divide	Rural-urban migration
Danwei-based social controls	Reform of state-owned enterprises (socialisation of *danwei*-based services)
Rural collective commune system	Abolition of the rural collective organizations and responsibility of households
Production regime	
State-led industrialization and industrial planning	Market-led industrialisation; Opening policy; FDI
Monopoly of the public sector	De-monopolization of state labour (self-employment, private business, foreign-owned companies)
Labour intensive production processes	Productivity-oriented production
Supply-driven central labour planning, planned wage setting	Demand-driven job placement, market exchange on wages and the price of labour, labour mobility
Labour consuming enterprise policies (enlargement of the workforce)	Efficiency in labour use: quantity and quality of recruited employees and workers
Permanent and full-time employment	Contracted labour, atypical and informal employment, unemployment
Industrial relations	
Trades unions as political transmission belt and social institutions	Diminished importance of trades unions with unchanged functions
	Embryonic features of (politically independent) workplace representation; Corporate governance induced by international organizations (ILO)
Welfare regime	
Work unit related welfare system	New (national) welfare system, detached from the enterprise administration, with individual accounts; private insurances Monetarization of fringe benefits

Welfare regime (continued)	
Collective rural support	Local experiments with collective welfare in rural areas
Family as a (fall-back) safety net	Family as a (fall-back) safety net
Family, kin order	
Dual earner family model	Dual earner family model
High female work participation	(High) female work participation
	Family planning and one-child policy
Education system	
Enterprise specific and job preparatory training	Qualification as a personal property for market exchange
	National system of professional training (accreditation of certificates, quality control)
	Expansion of education system (knowledge based economy)

Source: Authors' own compilation.

Economic reforms and labour market reforms have led to a variety of employment conditions. In order to raise its economic efficiency and productivity, China has opened up to the world market, invited foreign investors, encouraged massive technological transfers and – facing international competition – started the reform of state-owned enterprises. As a consequence, a high-productivity work regime has evolved which excludes especially the unqualified, older and female workers. At the same time, the Chinese leadership is trying to maintain the image of a socialist inclusive system by enlarging (mainly "flexible") employment opportunities, regardless of whether they correspond with legal provisions, while also giving the formerly privileged groups of *danwei*-workers special treatment. The incoherence of the institutional set is responsible for distortions in the employment regime and for visible as well as invisible boundaries which have led to the exclusion of large parts of the work force – not only in the countryside, but also, increasingly, in urban areas.

Flexibility and security in the Chinese "socialist" market labour regime (SMLR)

In this chapter, we will provide some evidence to support our hypothesis on the prevailing incoherence of labour market institutions. This incoherence results from the overlap of those institutions that still follow the logic of the planning system and others that have emerged with the market economy (Hebel/Schucher forthcoming). Our hypothesis still has to be tested in subsequent empirical research. First we will take a look at the massive redistribution of labour. Then we will present some realistic calculations on unemployment and transitions into employment. In a third step, we will show that despite labour redistribution, the mobility of labour between enterprises and jobs is still extremely low. The prerequisites for a functioning labour market are not fully developed. One decisive reason for this can be found in the Chinese *danwei* institution that shapes other relevant institutions, e.g., the welfare system. The most prominent feature, however, seems to be the handling of redundancies in urban state-owned enterprises. Nevertheless, atypical (flexible) jobs are increasing and there is almost no security for this weak group of workers.

Redistribution of employment

The employment population almost doubled between 1978 and 2003. In 1978, the number of those in total employment stood at 401.52 million, by 2004 it had risen to 752 million.[2] Labour participation increased from 41.7 to 57.6 per cent (2003), that means labour force growth outpaced demographic expansion. In international terms, these figures are unusually high, especially for female workers, whose participation rate reached 45.7 per cent in 1995 (Rawski 1999: 2).

Table 2. Employment growth and elasticity, 1978-2000

Year	Growth rate per year in %			Elasticity coefficient of employment	
	GDP (a)	Net investment (b)	Employment (c)	Employment growth (c/a)	Employment investment (c/b)
1978-1989	9.51	12.32	2.96	0.31	0.24
1990-1995	11.98	9.14	1.23	0.10	0.13
1996-2000	8.27	13.87	0.93	0.11	0.07

Source: Hu/Yang 2003: 246.

The growth rate of employment, however, slowed down during this period and the growth elasticity of employment declined (see Table 1). Hu and Yang (2003: 246f.) characterize this development as a "high growth, low employment" type and explain the gap in employment creation with the industrialization pathway of "more capital and less labour."

From 1978 to 2003 labour was massively redistributed. The main factor of growth in employment was the increase in urban employment. The urban labour force almost tripled from 95 million to 256.39 million, rural employment rose from 306.38 million to 487.93 million. Compared with other countries, even those at similar levels of development, the ratio of urban to total employment was still low. As Hu and Yang stated (2003: 249) the relative speed of restructuring was significantly higher than in the 1980s, but absolute growth in the urbanization rate was slowing down continuously. They concluded that accelerating the urbanization process would be an important way out of employment problems.

---

[2] Figures – when not proved otherwise – are drawn from China Statistical Yearbook 2004, electronic version, Information Office of the State Council of the PRC 2004 and Green Book 2005.

In addition to urbanization, major changes in the employment structure took place in three more dimensions:

First, the employment share of the primary sector decreased continuously, while the shares of the secondary and tertiary sectors amplified. While employment in the primary sector dropped from more than 80 per cent in 1970 to 49.1 per cent in 2003, the shares of the secondary and tertiary sectors doubled or even tripled from 10.2 per cent to 21.6 per cent and from nine per cent to 29.3 per cent during the same period. This indicates the transfer of labour resources from low-productivity to high-productivity sectors of the economy. The tertiary sector's growth-elasticity was the highest from 1978 onwards and this sector became the main source of increased employment.

Second, comparing the period from 1990 to 1995 with the period from 1995 to 2000, Hu and Yang perceived a rapid and intense restructuring by industry. Employment in traditional industries, such as mining and quarrying, was downsized while social services, real estate trade, finance and insurance attracted additional workers (ibid.: 255).

Third, the period from 1978 onwards experienced a reduction in state labour and an increase in self-employment and private businesses as well as in employment in foreign funded units. While in 1978, state and collective-owned units covered almost the whole urban workforce, its share was reduced after the mid-1990s. The number of formal workers (*zhigong* 职工) in the state sector dropped to 66.21 million in 2003. As a result, the proportion of the former privileged segment of state workers in urban employment was reduced from 78.3 per cent in 1978 to 25.8 per cent and it accounted for only 9.4 per cent of all Chinese labourers in 2003.

From 1995 to 2003, the total number of workers in the traditional formal sector,[3] including state owned and urban collective owned units, decreased sharply by 65.32 million, so that they only comprised 39.7 per cent in urban employment. In parallel, the proportion of workers in the new emerging formal sector, including joint ownership units and foreign funded units etc., rose to 11.5 per cent. And the share of the informal sector, including privately-owned enterprises and self-employed individuals, increased to 19.2 per cent. This meant that the informal sector became the main source of urban employment creation even though industrial and financial policies obstructed its development for a long time and to a great extent.

The same holds true for the enterprises in rural China that have mushroomed since the beginning of rural reforms. The majority of employment opportunities are supplied by the private economy. 23 per cent of non-farm labourers are self-employed or work for private firms. 61.5 per cent (1998) of the town and village enterprises (TVE) are registered as private. This leads us to the highly astonishing

---

[3] Note that the informal sector is defined differently by different authors. Rawski (1999: 5), e.g., includes self-employed peasants, unemployed persons, and casual workers. Hu/Yang (2003) count employment in privately-owned enterprises and self-employed individuals as informal work.

conclusion that, at present, 90 per cent of the Chinese labour force (including household workers) work outside the state sector.

"True" unemployment and transitions into employment

Unemployment has become a prominent political issue in China. Although the Ministry of Labour and Social Security (MOLSS) considered employment policy in 2004 to have been rather successful since it was able to stabilise the official unemployment rate at 4.2 per cent (Renmin Ribao 20 July 2005), the Chinese leadership is still worried about under-employment in state-owned enterprises and in rural areas, open and hidden unemployment, problems of job allocation to high school graduates, and increasing urban poverty. The reduction of unemployment is not only one of the aims of the labour market policy; it has turned out to be a precondition for social stability.

The unemployment statistics of the National Bureau of Statistics (NBS) in China have not kept pace with the recent changes in the labour market. The official unemployment rate is not only confined to urban China, it also excludes the large numbers of those without any official status as unemployed. In particular, laid-off workers and the rural labour force working in the cities fall into this category. On the other hand, a considerable number of officially laid off or registered unemployed workers have found work on a full-time or part-time basis or opted out of employment (Giles et al. 2005: 151).

Due to systemic distortions and a lack of reliable data which is consistent with standard international practice, some researchers deny the possibility of counting unemployment in China (Solinger 2001). Others compare different data sets for alternative estimates. Using NBS-data, but including laid-off workers and rural migrants, Hu and Yang (2003: 261) calculated that there were 17 million urban unemployed in 2000, which amounted to an unemployment rate of about eight per cent against the then official rate of 3.1 per cent. Whereas the unemployment of rural labourers had remained rather small and stable since the mid-1990s, laid-off workers then became the main group of China's urban unemployed.

Knight and Xue compared NBS-data with that drawn from the household sample survey and the population census. Adjusting administrative data by including the laid-off workers, they calculated an unemployment rate of 7.1 per cent in 2000. But official data excluded several types of unemployment such as young people waiting for jobs and other people taking early retirement. Household survey data and population census data enabled Knight and Xue (n.d.) to broaden the definition of unemployment which resulted in their estimating an overall unemployment rate of 11.5 per cent in 1999. Roughly half of the unemployed were laid-off workers.

Giles et al. (2005) drew on sample survey data from 2002 and 2001 which included internationally comparable questions on unemployment. According to their calculations, the "true unemployment rate" among urban permanent residents increased from 6.1 per cent in January 1996 to 11.1 per cent in September 2002. They agreed with other calculations and concluded that unemployment among permanent residents was much higher than among temporary residents. Consequently, the unemployment rate including temporary residents increased over the named period from 4.0 per cent to 7.3 per cent.

The inconsistent and sparse data do not allow calculations of transitions from employment into unemployment or vice versa. Lay-offs, dismissals, and re-employment figures can be interpreted as rough indicators (see Table 3). In their analysis of the steadily rising overall unemployment rate, Giles et al. found the absence of any cyclical pattern to be striking. An explanation for this unexpected phenomenon is found in the continuous restructuring of state industries and the large numbers of laid-off workers over the age of 30. In 2002, 4.19 million workers were made redundant and 2.11 million workers were laid-off. During the same year, 6.89 million registered unemployed were placed and 1.94 million laid-off workers were re-employed. Placement agencies placed 13.5 million job-seekers, 12 per cent of them were laid-off workers and 34 per cent unemployed (National Bureau of Statistics in China 2003a: 155).

The re-employment of laid-off workers in the formal sector, however, is only one side of the coin. Many more of them are engaged in informal work. According to Giles et al. (2005: 160), in November 2001, only 31 per cent of officially laid-off workers and 28 per cent of the registered unemployed were actually unemployed. The others were either working or out of the labour force and the absolute and relative size of these "unofficial" unemployed increased steadily over time. This might explain the growing gap between the laid-off workers whose number decreased during the year and those actually re-employed. Official statistics are lacking in information about the whereabouts of the majority of these "decreased" laid-off workers. Some became registered unemployed or terminated their labour relations, but most of the others probably took up informal work. This coincides with the findings of Yang Yiyong (2002: 91) who, using official data, showed that in 1997 6.4 million laid-off workers were placed and that 35 per cent of the total became self-employed and 26 per cent retired early. Again, a survey from 1999 reveals that most of the re-employed were placed in atypical positions (ibid.: 108ff.).

In 2004, because of high economic growth, 9.8 million employees could be placed, 800.000 more than previously estimated. Governments at all administrative levels were called upon to take special care of the re-employment of laid-off workers. As a result, 5.1 million were able to find jobs, among them 1.4 million so called "40, 50s," that means hard to be placed workers aged 40 to 59. Researchers at the Chinese Academy of Social Sciences are convinced that the reform of state owned enterprises has basically been completed. That is why the number of lay-offs has gone down to 1.53 million. In contrast, the number of workers with atypical work conditions has increased to more than 40 per cent of the urban labour force (CA 1/2005: Dok 20).

The evaluation of data from employment agencies in 117 cities for the fourth quarter of the year 2004 shows that among the people looking for jobs the proportion of laid-off workers and those made redundant was declining while the proportion of unemployed young people was increasing. Within the group of registered job-seekers, those made redundant made up 24.2 per cent, unemployed youth 19.9 per cent, and laid-off workers only 5.9 per cent. Another subgroup consisted of rural migrants, whose numbers increased by 6.4 per cent compared with 2003 to make up a total of 26.1 per cent (Cai 2005: 28-30).

Table 3. Transitions into unemployment and from unemployment into employment, 1990-2004 (various years)

1990	1995	1998	1999	2000	2001	2002	2003	2004
Registered unemployed (mio)								
3.83	5.20	5.71	5.75	5.95	6.81	7.70	8.00	8.27
# unemployed youth (mio)								
3.13	3.10	n.a.	n.a.	n.a.	n.a.	n.a.	n.a.	
Unemployment from employment (mio)								
	0.99	1.75	1.92	2.59	3.61	4.19		
Employment from unemployment (mio)								
	4.31	4.13	4.39	4.79	5.70	6.89		
Registered unemployment rate (%)								
2.5	2.9	3.1	3.1	3.1	3.6	4.0	4.3	4.2
Laid-off workers at end of year (mio)								
	5.64	8.71	9.42	9.11	7.42	6.18		
# in state-owned enterprises (mio)								
	3.68	5.95	6.53	6.57	5.15	4.10	2.60	1.53
# in collective-owned enterprises (mio)								
	1.82	2.50	2.63	2.34	2.06			
# in other units (mio)								
	0.13	0.29	0.26	0.20	0.21			
# laid-off workers newly added during this year (mio)								
		7.39	7.82	5.12	2.83	2.11		
# laid-off workers decreased during this year (mio)								
		8.57	7.16	5.45	4.52	3.35		
# re-employed								
		7.84	6.07	3.62	2.41	1.94		5.1
Ratio of re-employed to total decreased (%)								
1990	1995	1998	1999	2000	2001	2002	2003	2004
		91.48	84.78	66.42	53.32	57.91		

Sources: National Bureau of Statistics in China 2003b; ibid. 2004: Tab. 5-1; ibid. 2003a: data from 1994, 1996-2003; Information Office of the State Council of the People's Republic of China 2004; Cai 2005: 25, 27.

As we can see, most of the transitions are involuntary and caused by industrial or enterprise restructuring. Looking at transitions into formal employment the majority are new labour market entrants, while the laid-off workers move into informal jobs or out of the labour market. Figures on the long-term unemployed - defined by the Chinese government as those who are unemployed for six months and longer – illustrate the problem of getting unemployed people back into jobs.

According to Yang Yiyong (2002: 50), the proportion of long-term unemployment compared with total unemployment was increasing and reached 59.6 per cent in 1998, more than half of the unemployed being women. Figures for the different provinces in 2002 varied between 19.6 per cent (Heilongjiang) and 85 per cent (Tianjin), the average figure was 44 per cent (National Bureau of Statistics in China 2003a: 131).

The expansion of the external labour market and limits of mobility

Economic growth and structural changes have driven the restructuring of employment. This, however, is not tantamount to an increase in inter-enterprise mobility or the voluntary movement of labour across ownership sectors. To a great extent, restructuring has been generated by the growth of the labour force and rural-to-urban migration. Furthermore, the changing ownership figures reflect the changing ownership status of firms rather than the movement of workers. From 1996 to 2001, only one fifth (female) or one fourth (male) of job separations was voluntary (Cai et al. 2004: 32f.).

Table 4. Changes in the labour force, 1980-2000

	Millions		Percentage of labour force	
	1980-1989	1990-2000	1980-1989	1990-2000
Labour force	128.1	86.5	100	100
Urban	37.1	74.2	29.0	85.8
Unemployed	-1.6	13.1	-1.2	15.1
Employed	38.7	61.1	30.2	70.6
State	20.9	-22.5	16.3	-26.0
Urban collectives	10.7	-20.5	8.4	-23.7
Other employment	7.1	104.1	5.5	120.3
Rural	91.0	12.2	71.0	14.1
TVE	63.7	35.5	49.7	41.0
Private and individual enterprises	--	24.7	--	28.6
Household workers	27.3	-48.0	21.3	-55.5

Source: Knight/Song 2005: 33.

Table 4 shows how the increase in the labour force has been absorbed into the economy, in millions and as percentages of the labour force (Knight/Song 2005: 31ff.). Above, we have already mentioned that the growth rate has decreased due to demographic change and family policy (one-child policy). In this context, it is noticeable that in the 1980s, 71 per cent of the new labour force were employed in rural China, with the emerging rural industry (TVE) accounting for no less than 50 per cent. In contrast to that, in the 1990s, no less than 86 per cent of the increment to the labour force went into the urban economy where new enterprises or old enterprises with new forms of ownership ("other employment") accounted for the entire addition.

In the 1990s the urban labour force grew by 3.6 per cent per annum, the rural by only 0.2 per cent. This was caused, amongst other reasons, by rural-to-urban migration that became a growing phenomenon in the Chinese labour market during the period of economic reform. Quantitative estimates of migration, however, were still difficult to arrive at due to *hukou* registration and statistical problems. The latest official figures, at that time, ranged from 110 to 140 million person, accounting for ten per cent of the Chinese population or one quarter of rural employment (CA 11/2004: Ü19; 05/2004: Ü22).

The increase in rural migrants in the cities can be seen as one of the causes of the expansion of the external labour market. Other components of the emerging external labour market are workers in the informal sector, atypical employment, and the urban unemployed. More than half of the classified urban employees are working in enterprises with private and mixed ownership or are self-employed.

Restrictions on rural employment in urban areas indicate different treatment even within the external labour market segment. The urban unemployed are protected against their rural competitors. But there are more indicators of segmentation, such as different conditions for inclusion into welfare programs and, not least, the problems of assessing the numbers of unemployed workers. Segmentation is also a pattern of job placement institutions. In addition to rather informal institutions that serve the external market of rural workers, the official institutions are still constructed according to the old administrative dividing lines of the planned labour system. Different categories of workers fall within the spheres of responsibility of different ministries (personnel, labour and social security, agriculture, civil affairs) or the party's organization department and different agencies (Hebel/Schucher forthcoming).

In comparison with the 1980s, the individually motivated mobility of urban workers has increased significantly. Young and qualified employees, in particular, strive for social advancement by changing jobs or employers. The administrative boundaries of the planned economy have lost their force. The spread of information on occupational trends and labour demand has been continuously improved. Nevertheless, traditional mechanisms are still in place. *Guanxi*-networks are still playing a decisive role for job entries – at least for the less qualified labour force – or chain-migration (e.g. Zang 2003: 125).

Analyzing data for the period from 1988 to 2000, Knight and Song stated that there was an enduring low rate of urban labour mobility, even though there might be "pockets of high labour mobility," e.g. for those workers with scarce skills and demand in the growing private sector or in the most dynamic provinces. The general rise in urban wages was not the result of market forces nor was the labour turnover among urban workers high enough to generate labour market forces. Collusion between employers and employees, seniority considerations and *danwei*-related welfare provisions resulted in long job duration for urban residents by international standards (on average 19.9 years in 1999) and a lack of labour mobility between employers. Among the respondents of a survey in 1999, no less than 74 per cent with 30 and more years of employment experience were still in their first jobs (Knight/Song 2005: 135f.; see also Wang/Zhao 2003).

Knight and Song explain this phenomenon of extremely low mobility as being due to the continuing influence of the *danwei* and a still highly segmented labour market (Knight/Song 2005: 41 f.). Several other empirical studies which analysed wage setting or asked for returns to education have confirmed these findings. On the one hand, competition has increased and individual performance has paid off to a much higher degree than before labour and wage reforms. On the other hand, wage differences among those holding the same qualifications (and with statistical control of personal characteristics like age or sex) can rather be explained by a segmented than a competitive labour market. This holds especially true for the steadily widening gap between urban and rural incomes regardless of the magnitude of labour flows out of agriculture and rural areas. China's persisting *hukou* system creates barriers to labour mobility and, "with imperfect mobility, any policy that treats rural and urban areas differently could affect income differences" (Cai et al. 2004: 21).

Wage setting within segments can also be shown for different categories of urban workers as well as enterprises. Permanent workers still enjoy the best wage conditions whereas re-employed urban workers and rural migrants earn less. And even though the wage levels of the last two groups are getting closer, they are conditioned by different institutional settings (Appleton 2004). Wages in state-owned enterprises and foreign funded enterprises are much higher than those in collective-owned enterprises. The considerable income gap between the state and the private sector is down-levelled in cases where non-monetary contributions in the state-owned sector are included in the income (Zhao 2002). Rural migrants are paid wages below their level of qualification and below that of comparably qualified urban workers. In comparison with the latter, they are given poorer jobs (Knight et al. 1999; Meng/Zhang 2001).

Moreover, surveys show that individual investment in education does not pay off despite China's long tradition of education and the scarcity of qualified persons. Once again, the explanation can be found in the low level of labour mobility (Fleisher/Wang 2001). In accordance with the recent "knowledge-based development strategy," the Chinese government has been expanding the tertiary educational sector since 1999 and stresses the importance of life-long education. As an unexpected result, many graduates face difficulties in finding jobs – to some extent because of inadequate expectations, but rather more because of the segmentation of the labour market and barriers to mobility.

The reform of the SNWP under the continuing influence of the danwei
One of the most significant results of the labour reforms is the dismantling of the socialist normal work pattern (SNWP). In 1986, the Ministry of Labour promulgated the introduction of labour contracts in order to make labour relations more flexible. In contrast to the life-long employment of permanent workers (*gudinggong* 固定工), the employment relationships of contract-system-workers (*hetong zhigong* 合同制工)[4] were supposed to end with the final date on the contract. At first, however, contracts were only implemented in state-owned enterprises and for newly employed workers. Consequently, in 1990 only 12 per cent of the workers in state-owned enterprises had signed labour contracts (Yu/Fu 1998: 44). Only when the National Labour Law was passed in 1994, which made contracts obligatory for all categories of firms and labourers, did the number of labour-contract-workers rise significantly. By the end of 2000, officially 98.9 per cent of the 107.05 million formal employees in urban enterprises had signed labour contracts. More than half of the workforce is said to have signed contracts in private enterprises (Yang 2002: 80).

In practice, "the labor contract system was more successful on the hiring than the firing side" (Cai et al. 2004: 6). Parallel to the introduction of termed labour relations, direct allocation and reallocation of workers and students by the government was gradually phased out and job placement agencies came into being. According to the principle of "mutual choice" (*huxiang xuanze* 互相选择), employers and employees were free to select their contract partner, but especially the individual workers – were also removed from the former state support system.

The introduction of the labour contract system revealed a certain pattern of reform that could be explained as "past-dependency," as Gu (2003) names it. By restricting the need to sign contracts to the newly employed, the party-state continued to grant privileges to the traditional formal employees. All attempts to make their labour relationships more flexible (like the "labour optimization" at the end of the 1980s) remained unsuccessful. The decisive turn came with the introduction of the *xiagang* concept (下岗) which, since the mid-1990s, has allowed state-owned enterprises to lay-off permanent workers. In contrast to the unemployed, however, laid-off workers still have a labour relationship with the enterprise, receive small living allowances, are administered by special institutions, are given retraining and preferential treatment so that they can be re-employed (Gu 2003; Chiu/Hung 2004). Thus, *xiagang* – or former permanently employed workers – enjoy a special status and do not directly compete with unemployed and rural migrants. Moreover, local governments are said to have intervened in personnel decisions in state enterprises and to have stipulated when, how many and even who should be

---

[4] This term has been used in order to distinguish workers with official labour contracts from "contracted" low-paid workers on a temporary basis (合同工, 临时工).

dismissed. Subsidies for the re-employment of laid-off workers belong to the instruments of the governments' active labour policy. Lay-offs – as Gu (2003: 7f.) concludes – "are structured by the transitional institutional context" and "constitute an institutional arrangement between formal employment and formal unemployment."

For several years, the government has been announcing that the *xiagang*-programme would be phased out, but obviously this could not be put into action. MOLSS is now planning that 2007 will be the last year when laid-off workers will be given preferential treatment. Without "merging the two tracks" (*binggui* 并轨) of lay-offs and unemployment, the government would not feel enough pressure to go on with labour reforms and establish a unified labour market (CA 11/2004: Ü20).

Since most laid-off workers have refused to terminate labour relations with their work-units for fear of losing their social security entitlements, the reform of the welfare regime seems to represent a decisive step towards a unified labour market. Welfare reforms, however, also show the continuing influence of the *danwei* and pre-reform urban-rural-segmentation. The reform of the pension and health insurance systems as well as the introduction of unemployment insurance was intended to set workers free from the *danwei* dependency and to open up social mobility between enterprises and jobs. Nevertheless, the reform followed the lines of the planning system. Coverage is restricted to urban residence and to formal employment. Rural welfare institutions are still embryonic. Consequently, coverage is still limited and locally diverging social welfare provisions have become an additional hurdle for cross-regional mobility (personal interviews 2004). The legacy of traditional arrangements also surfaces when enterprises on the verge of bankruptcy have to submit a plan to show how they will provide for their employees by setting aside enough funds.

Moreover, the unemployment, pension and health insurances are under a heavy financial strain due to the deteriorating ratio between labourers and receivers of payments for at least four reasons: (a) the generally low retirement age, (b) the former policy of replacing parents with their children, (c) strategies of early retirement in order to avoid dismissals, and (d) demographic change and the aging population. When the old pension system was implemented in the early 1950s, the average retirement age was 51.7 years and life expectancy, 39 years. Life expectancy, today, has risen to 70 years but female workers, for example, retire as early as the age of 45. The ratio between retirees and workers deteriorated from 1:3.2 in the year 2000 to 1:2.6 at the beginning of 2005. In Shanghai, the ratio is only 1:1.53 (CA 2005/4).

Strategies for early retirement exclude large sections of the able-bodied workforce. But, as Giles et al. emphasize, older workers, who are in their prime earning years and often the key breadwinners for their families, are most adversely affected. They often lack marketable skills, have to weather the largest employment shocks and are least likely to find new jobs or, if they do, only low paid jobs (Giles et al. 2003: 35).

China will not be able to succeed in establishing a nation-wide, unified welfare program under these conditions. It also seems unlikely that China will adopt the West European welfare models, using high income tax as a central solution for welfare distribution. The Hu-Wen leadership, however, has announced its clear intention of constructing a "harmonious socialist society." The practicability of both strategies, the dis-embedding of social protection from the labour market and the local embedding of security principles, will be put to the test in the future (see Herrmann-Pillath 2005: 32).

Atypical employment and flexibility in the Chinese labour market

During recent decades, the normal work pattern in Western societies has steadily lost its significance and has been gradually replaced by a diversity of atypical forms of employment. Labour market research has attributed this development not only to the requirements of modern production processes and the expansion of the service sector, but also to the needs and voluntary decisions of modern citizens aiming to balance their work and family life.

In China, atypical employment is also gaining ground. Definitions remain vague, however, and exact figures are almost unobtainable. Even the MOLSS does not seem to have a clear concept, since it uses the synonymous terms: "temporary employment," "informal employment" or "flexible employment" to describe "non-standard employment." Consequently, figures vary between 50 and 70 million atypical jobs or even more (Wang 2005; Ding 2004).

In official statistics, the total sum of formal and informal urban employment is, surprisingly, lower than the whole urban labour force. In 2003, the gap amounted to 99.08 million workers or 38.6 per cent of the urban labour force. Some suggest that the discrepancy in the figures displays the greater employment of temporary migrant workers in spite of government intentions and efforts (Johnson 2003: 28 f.). Others attribute the gap to statistical flaws, grossly underestimated private employment or inadequately assessed atypical employment (ADB 2004: 98; Cai 2004: 160ff.).

MOLSS (2005) emphasized, in a recently published analysis, that the actual figure of "flexible workers" was only 47 million in 2003 and 50 million in 2004. Official statistics on formal employment do not include workers in village enterprises or in agricultural activities within the cities' boundaries – and some formal employees are not reported by their employers. Among the 47 million flexible workers, 34 million are self-employed and freelancers, 6 million are household helpers, and 7 million are "others." Surprisingly, this official source does not include rural migrants and laid-off workers who account for the biggest component in atypical employment.

Cheng (2004) provided a more accurate picture, reporting a drastic expansion of the informal sector. In accordance with internationally used definitions for atypical employment, he states that informal flexible employment differs from typical forms of employment in at least one of the following criteria: working hours, income, workplace, insurance, labour relations, etc. The radical change in the labour market is giving rise to increasingly diversified forms of employment. The 145 million people comprising this group consists mainly of migrants, redundant workers from state and collectively owned enterprises, unemployed workers, the self-employed and others, such as home-based workers. While the majority of the flexibly employed work in small and micro businesses, a still considerably high number of them labour for large and medium-sized enterprises. Whereas the majority of flexible work is linked to unstable and insecure labour conditions, a small group of freelancers or tele-workers is related to modern production and emerging knowledge industries.

Migrants are usually given jobs at the lower end of the wage scale. They are hired and fired without any restrictions and enjoy almost no social security although the Labour Law of 1995 covers all kind of employment. The massive problem of outstanding wages, a topic that the central government has taken into account since 2004, is only the most obvious indicator of their irregular treatment. The overwhelming majority of the workers still registered as laid-off workers is currently employed in the informal sector. Even those re-employed are likely to work in disadvantageous ownership categories and receive lower wages than their never retrenched colleagues (Knight/Song 2005: 143ff.; Appleton 2004). Surveys reveal that human capital ceases to have an influence on their income and that therefore individuals who previously changed jobs and occupations enjoy greater success in moving to a new type of employment (Li/Zhang 2004). There are still restrictions to prevent migrants from competing with the laid-off urban workers on equal terms. Both groups, however, occupy segments of the labour market that are close to each other.

A survey carried out in 66 cities by MOLSS in 2002 showed that most of the new labour market entrants find jobs in the formal sector. Those who had experienced the hardships of unemployment entered atypical jobs to a great extent. This holds true no matter whether "atypical" is defined in terms of ownership (self-employed, private), working hours, community work, or contract relations. The authors of the Green Book have analysed this survey (Cai 2005: 179-203) and predict a new dualism in Chinese cities between typical and atypical workers. In all respects, workers in the formal sector are better off even those who are re-employed. The tendency towards a dual urban labour market might be strengthened by the migrants' distinctive views of work that bear few traces of nostalgia for the urban-centred employment systems because they were excluded from these in the past. According to Lei (2005) they have no feeling of solidarity with laid-off workers and little sense of entitlement to security: unemployment is seen as an episode in the employment career or even as a form of freedom. This contributes to the high mobility of migrants; especially those with low qualifications are able "to follow itineraries within the urban labour market" and "move from one province to another" (Roulleau-Berger/Lu 2005: 6f.). Atypical workers and rural migrants can be seen as weak groups that suffer from low income, lack social security, and have almost no legal protection.

Conclusion

Summarizing the main features of the emerging SMLR, we can record the impressive restructuring of employment in line with economic reforms aimed at transforming China into a highly productive competitor in the global economy. Flexibility and security have to be rebalanced. Restructuring can only be partly traced back to labour exchanges; the changes in the employment structure have resulted from the placement of new labour market entrants and involuntary dismissals. Flexibility and mobility have increased with the emergence of an external labour market and the erosion of the former SNWP. However, mobility is still very low due to the continuing influence of the *danwei* and political endeavours. In addition to a small group of highly qualified people in management positions and a number of high-tech jobs, the mobile work force consists of weak groups, such as migrants and laid-off workers in atypical jobs.

Central and local governments are willing to increase migration even further. They stress the importance of rural migrants for the urban economy and are afraid of rising social instability due to low rural incomes. They are therefore calling for the abolition of all restrictions, for equal treatment by enterprises and are even considering awarding urban citizenship to migrants. Minimum wages rules and other regulations have already been adjusted to the distinctive features of atypical employment. And for the moment at least, even trade unions are feeling the need to embrace migrant workers since "their existence is no longer a short-term phenomenon."[5]

Security, however, is still mainly confined to formal urban employment. Existing boundaries between rural and urban areas, cities and enterprises seem to have been reinforced. Social security regulations as well as labour legislation have been designed on the basis of formal and typical employment. Retirement regulations have led to the exclusion of a large section of the labour force that is supposed to be "old," whereas young people, such as high school graduates are excluded as a consequence of structural flaws in the economic system.

The pre-reform SLR, at least with respect to urban areas, was highly consistent. Central labour planning and the socialist SNWP were in accordance with the state-led production regime and industrial relations, with the social security and education systems and, finally, with the family order. The comprehensive participation of women as workers complied with two goals, the excessive labour demand of the state-owned enterprises and the politically induced emancipation of women. Low, but egalitarian wages corresponded with the socialist ideal of a proletarian society. Economic productivity was low and the economy did not require specialised qualifications. In sum, the whole set of institutions maintained the old labour regime. Low flexibility went hand in hand with basic security for urbanites. Mobility was

---

[5] Chen Hao, president of Shanghai Municipal Trade Union, Xinhua News Agency 16 September 2005.

reduced to the marginal event of administrative labour transfer. By administrative means, unemployment was rendered non-existent for the major part of the socialist period. Comprehensive welfare provisions compensated for low wages and a modest level of consumption. The whole arrangement was upheld by the socio-political control regime and its ideological underpinning at the expense of the rural section of the population.

The hoped-for increase in economic productivity and in living standards paved China's way towards a policy for opening up the country and the economy as well as towards a policy for fundamentally restructuring its basic social institutions. The Chinese economy had to be freed from the chains of the planning system and the constraints of an immobile workforce. Symbolically, the label of a "socialist market economy," propagated since 1992, stands for this transition process. A key element of the process is the emergence of an appropriate "socialist" market labour regime (SMLR) which does not copy any blueprint. Within the new context of liberalization, industrialization, technical modernization, and, not least, globalization, the various institutions shaping the former labour regime have been eroded step by step. Yet, the SMLR is path-dependent in the sense that the relevant set of institutions is strongly shaped by the features of the rural-urban divide and the internal (*danwei*) labour system of the earlier SLR; the traditional and the new institutions overlap.

China has chosen a production strategy, visioning itself as a global competitor in highly-productive and technologically sophisticated sectors. Its present active employment strategy promotes labour intensive industries and supports the expansion of flexible employment in order to reduce the growing employment pressure without changing the structural foundation of social security provisions. At the same time, the political protection of formerly privileged segments of the labour force still prevails. These and other factors have led to a labour regime, where the various components do not fit very well. Labour market reforms still face the challenges of reconstructing institutions and policies and getting away from urbanites' class prerogatives. China still has a long way to go towards developing a new coherent set of institutions to shape its SMLR and it might be necessary, as Gu (2003: 18f.) concludes, to invent certain transitional arrangements to bridge old and new institutions. Weak groups, in particular, need more legal and social security and should be supported by free trade unions.

References

ADB (2004) *Poverty Profile of the People's Republic of China*, Asian Development Bank.

Andreß, Hans-Jürgen and Heien, Thorsten (2001) "Four Worlds of Welfare State Attitudes? A Comparison of Germany, Norway, and the United States," in *Euro-pean Sociological Review*, 17, 4, pp. 337-356.

Appleton, Simon (2004) "Contrasting Paradigms: Segmentation and Competitive-ness in the Formation of the Chinese Labour Market," in *Journal of Chinese Economic and Business Studies*, 2, 3, pp. 185-205.

Aubert, Claude and Li, Xiande (2002) "Agricultural Underemployment and Rural Migration in China: Facts and Figures," in *China Perspectives*, 41, May-June, pp. 47-58.

Brooks, Ray and Tao, Ran (2003) "China's Labor Market Performance and Challenges," IMF working paper, WP/03/210. Online. Available HTTP: <http://www.imf.org/external/pubs/ft/wp/2003/wp03210.pdf> (accessed 21 January 2004).

CA = *China aktuell*, Hamburg.

Cai, Fang (2004) "Renkou zhuanbian zhong de laodongli shichang: xianzhuang and zhanwang" [Labour Market under Demographic Changes: Situation and Perspective], in G. Liu; L. Wang; J. Li (eds) *Zhongguo jingji qianjing fenxi - 2004 nian chunji baogao* [Analysis on the Prospect of China's Economy(2004)], Beijing.

Cai, Fang 蔡昉 (ed) (2005) *Zhongguo renkou yu laodong wenti baogao* 中国人口与劳动问题报告 [Greenbook of Population and Labor], 2005.6, Beijing.

Cai, Fang; Park, Albert; Zhao, Yaohui (2004) "The Chinese Labor Market," Chapter prepared for the second conference on China's Economic Transition: Origins, Mechanisms, and Consequences, Pittsburgh, preliminary draft.

Cheng, Duosheng (2004) *A Preliminary Study of the Flexible Forms of Employment in China*, Online. Available HTTP: <http://www.kli.re.kr/iira2004/pro/papers/ChengDusheng.pdf> (accessed 3 January 2005).

Chiu, Stephen W.K. and Hung, Eva P.W. (2004) "Good governance or muddling through? Layoffs and employment reform in socialist China," in *Communist and Post-communist Studies*, 37, pp. 395-411.

Clarke, Simon and Lee, Chang-Hee (n.d./2002) *Towards a System of Tripartite Consultation in China?*, Online. Available HTTP: <http://www.warwick.ac.uk/~syrbe/china/Tripartism%20paper.pdf> (accessed 29 December 2004).

Clarke, Simon; Lee, Chang-Hee; Li, Qi (2004) "Collective Consultation and Industrial Relations in China," in *British Journal of Industrial Relations*, 42, 2, pp. 235-254.

Ding, Saier (2004) "Normalize Labor Relation of Temporary Employment," Online. Available HTTP: <http://www.kli.re.kr/iira2004/pro/papers/DingSaier.pdf> (accessed 3 January 2005).

Doeringer, Peter B. and Piore, Michael J. (1980) *Internal Labor Markets and Manpower Analysis*, Lexington, Mass, (7th printing).

Esping-Andersen, Gøsta (1990) *The Three Worlds of Welfare Capitalism*, Cambridge: Cambridge University Press.

Esping-Andersen, Gøsta (1994) "Welfare States and the Economy," in Neil J. Smelser and Richard Swedberg (eds) *Handbook of Economic Sociology*, Prince-ton, pp. 711-732.

Esping-Andersen, Gøsta and Regini, Marino (2000) *Why Deregulate Labour Mar-kets?*, Oxford et al.: Oxford University Press.

Fleisher, Belton M. and Wang, Xiaojun (2001) "Skill Differentials, Return to Schooling, and Market Segmentation in a Transition Economy: the Case of Mainland China," Cerdi-Idrec International Conference on the Chinese Economy, Clermond-Ferrand.

Giles, John; Park, Albert; Cai, Fang (2003) "How has Economic Restructuring Affected China's Urban Workers?," Online. Available HTTP: <http://www.msu.edu/~gilesj/gilesparkcai.pdf> (accessed 5 January 2004).

Giles, John; Park, Albert; Zhang, Juwei (2005) "What is China's true unemployment rate?" in *China Economic Review*, 16, pp. 149-170.

Goodman, Roger; White, Gordon; Kwon, Huck-ju (eds) (1998) *The East Asian Welfare Model. Welfare Orientalism and the State*, London, New York: Routledge.

Grünert, Holle and Lutz, Burkart (1994) "Systems Transformation and Labor Market Structure: The Case of East Germany," 1 April 1994, Institute of Industrial Relations, Institute of Industrial Relations Working Paper Series, paper iirwps-060-94. Online. Available HTTP: <http://repositories.cdlib.org/iir/iirwps/iirwps-060-94> (accessed 19 August 2005).

Grünert, Holle (1997) "Starrheit und Mobilität im Beschäftigungssystem der DDR," in *Der Hallesche Graureiher*, 1997-5.

Gu, Eward (2003) *Labour Market Insecurities in China*, International Labour Office, Geneva; Online. Available HTTP: <http://www.ilo.org/ses>.

Hebel, Jutta (1997) *Chinesische Staatsbetriebe zwischen Plan und Markt. Von der "Danwei" zum Wirtschaftsunternehmen*, Hamburg: Institut für Asienkunde.

Hebel, Jutta (2004) "Transformation des chinesischen Arbeitsmarktes: Gesellschaftliche Herausforderungen des Beschäftigungswandels," working pa-per, No. 41, Göttingen: Institute of Rural Development.

Hebel, Jutta (2005) "Konturen einer neuen Arbeitsgesellschaft: Transformationsprozess in der VR China," in *Soziale Welt*, 56, 1, pp. 17-38.

Hebel, Jutta and Schucher, Günter (1992) *Zwischen Arbeitsplan und Arbeitsmarkt. Strukturen des Arbeitssystems in der VR China*, Hamburg: Institut für Asien-kunde.

Hebel, Jutta and Schucher, Günter (forthcoming) "Beschäftigungsstrukturen und Arbeitsmärkte: Chinas Übergang zur marktvermittelten Erwerbsarbeit," in Doris Fischer et al. (eds) *Länderbericht China*, Bundeszentrale für Politische Bildung.

Heidenreich, Martin (2000) "Beschäftigungsordnungen in Europa," August 2000. Online. Available HTTP: <http://www.uni-bamberg.de/sowi/europastudien/ employlong.htm> (accessed 29 June 2005).

Heidenreich, Martin (2004) "Beschäftigungsordnungen zwischen Exklusion und Inklusion. Arbeitsmarktregulierende Institutionen im internationalen Vergleich," in *Zeitschrift für Soziologie*, 33, 3, pp. 206-227.

Herrmann-Pillath, Carsten (2005) "Vom Wirtschaftswunder zur Weltwirtschafts-macht: Chinas Wirtschaft in zwanzig Jahren," in *Wirtschaftspolitische Blätter*, 1, pp. 23-36.

Hu, Angang and Yang, Yunxin (2003) "From Planning to Market: Employment and Unemployment Trends in China," in Françoise Nicolas and Charit Tingsabadh (eds) *Unemployment in East Asia and Europe. A CAEC Task Force Report*, Paris: Ifri, pp. 243-283.

Hu, Qili (1986) "Zhengque renshi laodong zhidu de gaige" [Understand the labour system reform correctly], in *Hongqi* [Red Flag], 19, pp. 10-15.

Information Office of the State Council of the People's Republic of China (2004) *China's Employment Situation and Policies*, White paper, Beijing: April 2004. Online. Available

HTTP: <http://www.china.org.cn/e-white/20040426/index. htm> (accessed 16 August 2005).
Johnson, D. Gale (2003) "Provincial Migration in China in the 1990s," in *China Economic Review*, 14, pp. 22-31.
Kim, Yeon Myung (2005) "The Re-examination of East Asian Welfare Regime," paper contributed at the workshop on East Asian Social Policy, January 13-15, 2005, University of Bath, UK. Online. Available HTTP: <http://www.welfareasia.org/ws1/data/contribution_YM%20Kim2.doc> (accessed 29 June 2005).
Knight, John and Song, Lina (2005) *Towards a Labour Market in China*, Oxford: Oxford University Press.
Knight, John; Song, Lina; Jia, Huaibin (1999) "Chinese Rural Migrants in Urban Enterprises: Three Perspectives," in *The Journal of Development Studies*, 35, 3, pp. 72-104.
Knight, John and Xue, Jinjun (n.d.) "How High Is Urban Unemployment in China?" Online. Available HTTP: <http://econrsss.anu.edu.au/pdf/china-abstract-pdf/Xue Knight2.pdf> (accessed 1 June 2004).
Kocka, Jürgen (2001) "Thesen zur Geschichte und Zukunft der Arbeit," in *Aus Po-litik und Zeitgeschichte - APuZ*, B21/2001, pp. 8-13.
Lei, Guang (2005) "Guerilla Workfare: Migrant Renovators, State Power, and Informal Work in Urban China," in *Politics and Society*, 33, 3, pp. 481-506.
Li, Peilin and Zhang, Yi (2004) "The Professional Reintegration of the 'Xiagang,'" in *China Perspectives*, 52, pp. 32-43.
Liu, Minquan; Xu, Luodan; Liu, Liu (2004) "Wage-Related Labour Standards and FDI in China: Some Survey Findings From Guangdong Province," in *Pacific Economic Review*, 9, 3, pp. 225-243.
Lutz, Burkart (1987) *Arbeitsmarktstruktur und betriebliche Arbeitskräftestrategie: eine theoretisch-historische Skizze zur Entstehung betriebszentrierter Arbeits-marktsegmentation*, Frankfurt/Main.
Meng, Xin and Zhang, Junsen (2001) "The Two-Tier Labor Market in Urban China. Occupational Segregation and Wage Differentials between Urban Residents and Rural Migrants in Shanghai," in *Journal of Comparative Economics*, 29, pp. 485-505.
MOLSS (2005) *Guanyu woguo linghuo jiuye qingkuang de tongji fenxi* [Statistical Analysis of China's Start-up Business Situation], Online. Available HTTP: <http://www.molss.gov.cn/news/2005/0107a.htm> (accessed 27 January 2005).
Muffels, Ruud and Fouarge, Didier (2001) "Working Profiles and Employment Regiomes in European Panel Perspective," OSA working paper WP2001-12, Oc-tober 2001, Tilburg: OSA.
Muffels, Ruud; Wilthagen, Ton; van den Heuvel, Nick (2002) "Labour Market Transitions and Employment Regimes: Evidence on the Flexibility-Security Nexus in Transitional Labour Markets," WZB Berlin, discussion paper, FS I 02-204, März 2002.
National Bureau of Statistics in China (2003a) *China Labour Statistical Yearbook 2003*, Beijing.
National Bureau of Statistics in China (2003b) *China Statistical Yearbook 2003*, Beijing.
National Bureau of Statistics in China (2004) *China Statistical Yearbook 2004*, Beijing.
Nee, Victor (2003) *Organizational Dynamics of Institutional Change: China's Market Economy*, Ithaca, NY.
OECD (2002) *China in the World Economy. The Domestic Policy Challenges*, Paris, Organisation for Economic Co-Operation and Development.

Pries, Ludger (1998) "'Arbeitsmarkt' oder 'Erwerbsstrukturierende Institutionen'? Theoretische Überlegungen zu einer Erwerbssoziologie," in *Kölner Zeitschrift für Soziologie und Sozialpsychologie*, 50, pp. 159-175.

Rawski, Thomas G. (1999) "China: Prospects for Full Employment," in *Employment and Training Papers*, 47, Employment and Training Department, ILO.

Rehm, Philipp and Schmid, Josef (2001) *Die vier Welten der Beschäftigung. Eine explorative Analyse der arbeitsmarktpolitischen Performanz und politisch-ökonomischen Korrelate in 10 Industrieländern 1980-2000*, WIP Occasional Paper Nr. 13-2001, Institut für Politikwissenschaft, Universität Tübingen.

Roulleau-Berger, Laurence and Lu, Shi (2005) "Migrant Workers in Shanghai," in *China Perspectives*, 58, pp. 2-9.

Schmid, Günther (1998) *Transitional Labour Markets: A New European Employment Strategy*, WZB discussion paper, FS I 98 – 206, October 1998, Berlin: WZB.

Schmid, Günther (1996) "Beschäftigungswunder Niederlande? Ein Vergleich der Beschäftigungssysteme in den Niederlanden und in Deutschland," WZB dis-cussion paper, FS I 96 – 206.

Sengenberger, Werner (1978) *Der gespaltene Arbeitsmarkt: Probleme der Arbeitsmarktsegmentation*, Frankfurt/Main: Campus.

Solinger, Dorothy J. (2001) "Why We Cannot Count the 'Unemployment'," in *The China Quarterly*, 167, September 2001, pp. 671-688.

Tomba, Luigi (2002) *Paradoxes of Labour Reform*, London.

Wang, Fei-Ling (2005) *Organizing Through Division and Exclusion. China's Hukou System*, Stanford, Calif.: Stanford University Press.

Wang, Xia (2004) Improve Wages Policy to Stimulate Flexible Employment. Online. Available HTTP: <http://www.kli.re.kr/iira2004/pro/papers/WangXia.pdf> (ac-cessed 3 January 2005).

Wang, Fenyu and Zhao, Yandong (2003) "Labour market construction and labour mobility in urban China," in Catherine Jones Finer (ed) *Social Policy Reform in China. Views from Home and Abroad*, Hants: Ashgate, pp. 97-115.

White, Gordon (1998) "Social Security Reforms in China: Towards an East Asian model?" in Roger Goodman, Gordon White, Huck-ju Kwon (eds) *The East Asian Welfare Model. Welfare Orientalism and the State*, London; New York: Rout-ledge, pp. 175-197.

Wilthagen, Ton and Tros, Frank (2003) "The concept of 'flexicurity:' a new approach to regulating employment and labour markets." Online. Available HTTP: <http://www.tilburguniversity.nl/faculties/frw/research/schoordijk/flexi curity/publications/papers/fxp2003_4.pdf> (accessed 21 September 2005).

Xue, Jinjun and Zhong, Wei (2003), "Unemployment, Poverty and Income Disparity in Urban China," in *Asian Economic Journal*, 17, 4, pp.383-405

Yang, Yiyong (2002) *Zhongguo zhuangui shiqi de jiuye wenti* [The Employment in the Transition Period of China], Beijing.

Yu, Yunxia and Fu, Liu (1998) *Maixiang 21 shiji: Zhongguo jiuye xin gainian* [Towards the 21. century: new terms of China's employment], Beijing.

Zang, Xiaowei (2003) "Network resources and job search in urban China," in *Journal of Sociology*, 39, 2, pp. 115-129.

Zawadzki, Kamil (2005) *Transitional Labour Markets in a Transitional Economy. Could They Work? The Example of Poland*, WZB discussion paper, SP I 2005–102, February 2005, Berlin: WZB.

Zhang, Ya-li (2004): "Youth employment in China." Online. Available HTTP: <http://www.jil.go.jp/event/itaku/sokuho/documents/20040924/china.pdf> (ac-cessed 10 October 2005).

Zhao, Yaohui (2002) "Earnings Differentials between State and Non-State Enterprises in Urban China," in *Pacific Economic Review*, 7, 1, pp. 181-197.

"Peasant Worker Shortages" in Guangdong Province – A Demographic Analysis

Zheng Zizhen

In 2004, the "peasant worker[1] shortage" problem was the focus of attention over the whole of China and was the subject of intense discussion. Guangdong province, considered to be the place where the "peasant worker shortage" phenomenon arose, naturally bore the brunt of this attention and became the target of public criticism and fiery debates. This long-lasting dispute, which involved both practical issues and factors of theoretical significance, gave rise to many relevant propositions, and it is the objective of this essay to analyze and respond to these propositions from a demographic perspective.

"Peasant worker shortage" is not existing in China's population

Alone the phrase, "peasant worker shortage," carries different meanings. If the phrase is used to suggest, in the context of population structure, a scarcity of peasant workers or the scarcity of the labour force, then it can be said that, in fact, there is no real "peasant worker shortage" either in Guangdong or in China and neither is there any concrete data to support such assertions.

Four indicators are structured and combined in this essay to reflect and describe the current situations as well as the developing and changing trends of the working age population resource reserves in Guangdong and in China, and also to formulate concrete evidence and provide a basis for later discussions. These four indicators are: the ingoing working age population (aged 16); the outgoing working age population (males aged 60, females aged 55); the net increase in the working age population; and the working age population (males aged 16-59, females aged 16-54). More specifically, by using data from the fifth national census in 2000 as statistical data, the population structure by age as a basis, by using relevant data to develop a population mortality rate model, a short-run floating population and registered population age structure model, and by combining these with population birthrate data from the China Statistical Yearbook and the Guangdong Statistical Yearbook from 2001 to 2004, it is possible to compute and forecast the annual working age population of the nation and that within the Guangdong registered population as well as the future trends of the above four indices from 2000 to 2020 (See Figure 1 and Figure 2).
For the sake of simplicity, settings and assumptions which do not affect outcomes were made about the above four indicators:

---

[1] In this paper the term *nongmingong* 农民工 is translated as "peasant worker(s)." Please note that besides this translation the terms "migrant workers" and "worker-turned-peasants" are also used in this volume.

- China implements a nine-year compulsory education system, so that it is perfectly legitimate to set the age of 16 as the starting age of the ingoing working age population;
- The outgoing working age of the rural population is difficult to define, thus by considering population urbanization trends, the urban retirement age (for males, the age of 60; for females the age of 55) is used to unify the outgoing working age of both rural and urban sectors. This setting will not lead to an exaggeration of the working age population; on the contrary, the real working age population is much greater.
- Every year, a small proportion of the ingoing working age population defers or does not consider employment because of further education or training courses, but people who have deferred employment in previous years are, at the same time, seeking employment. As a result, an assumption was made that these pluses and minuses each year would cancel each other out, so that the whole ingoing working age population would be considered as seeking employment.

National situation of working age population supply

Recent year situations suggest that the growth rate of employment opportunities is, at most, nine million per annum. This supply of nine million new employment opportunities does not only have to "unravel" the increase in the urban population demand for employment, but also has to unravel the demand from the rural population that is participating in the urbanization process and should thus be given urban employment opportunities. According to this, if it were now supposed that the employment opportunity growth rate would be sustainable at nine million per annum, facts show that even such a high level growth rate of employment opportunity supply would still be incapable of meeting the ever increasing employment demands of the national labour force population.

Looking at Figure 1, it can be seen from the working age population indicator that every year from 2000 to 2007, the annual ingoing working age population was and will be over 20,000,000, with two peaks reaching 26,247,000 and 26,142,000 in 2003 and 2006 respectively. The figure for the year 2004, when the "peasant worker shortage" was much debated, reached 24,533,000. The number will only fall under 20 million in 2008 (18,685,000). However, from 2008 to 2020, most years will have more than 15 million new ingoing working age populations and the nine million per annum increase in employment opportunities is, therefore, far less than these 15 million are required to cover the increase in working age population.

Even if some of the assumptions were set aside, and it was supposed that, every year, the employment opportunities surrendered by outgoing working age population were all taken up by the ingoing working age population (note that this taking up of employment opportunities does not imply any population urbanization), then because the annual outgoing working age population is enormous and increases every year (peak value is 20,864,000 in 2018), the net annual increase of working age population after replacement (annual ingoing working age population minus annual outgoing working age population), which is depicted in the graph, suggests a positive net increase before 2012 and a negative net increase thereafter (Figure 1). The net annual increase in the working age population will exceed 10 million until 2006, when it will reach 13,972,000. This indicates that the nine million per annum increase in new employment opportunities will still be inadequate to satisfy the demand created by the net increase in the working age population until 2006.

Figure 1. National registered working age population change (2000-2020)

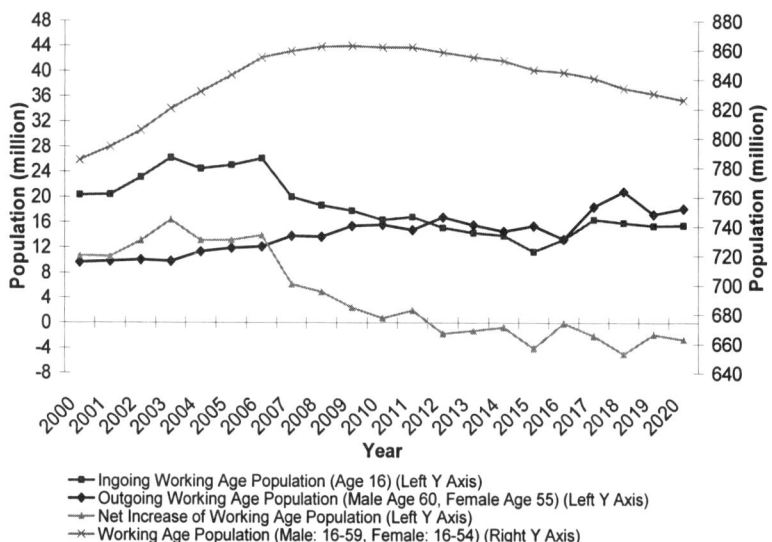

Source: Population Census Office under the State Council & Department of Population, Social, Science and Technology Statistics of the Bureau of Statistics of China, 2002.

This, however, does not necessarily mean that the situation will be more favourable after 2006 because although there will be a negative net increase in the working age population after 2012, the aggregate working age population will still be on an increasing trend within the first 20 years of the 21st century, from 785,368,000 in 2000 to 825,934,000 in 2020. Such an increase takes on a convex shape: at first it will increase rapidly, up to the peak value of 862,923,000 in 2009 – nearly 80 million over nine years; then it will decrease slowly, down to 825,934,000 in 2020 – no more than 40 million in 11 years. This implies that after 2006, a nine million per annum increase in employment opportunities will be incapable of satisfying the pressures brought about by the ever increasing but still somewhat sluggish aggregate working age population.

The preceding analysis is the result of computations and forecasts by the author, and is in line with the opinions of the relevant government departments. The

Ministry of Labour and Social Security has indicated that in each of the coming years, there will be more than 24 million urban populations per year needing employment. Under the current economic structure, only 12 million employment opportunities can be provided every year, out of which, nine million come from keeping the economy growing at eight per cent per annum and three million come from normal downsizing. Thus, there is a shortage of around twelve million urban employment opportunities.

To sum up, the labour and employment situation from 2000 to 2020 could be divided into two parts, representing two stages. In the first ten years (2000-2010), the huge numbers of the ingoing working age population, the rapid growth of the aggregate working age population, and the urbanization of the rural population are leading to significant pressure on employment. In the following ten years, the stagnant numbers of the aggregate working age population and the urbanization of the rural population will cause significant pressure on employment. In other words, in the first twenty years of the 21st century, at least, there will be no changes in the national supply and demand of the labour force population; labour redundancy and employment hardship will exist for a long time. Taking all this into consideration, how can the allegations of a "peasant worker shortage" be justified? Is there any demographic evidence on which assertions of a "peasant worker shortage" can be founded? It must be pointed out, that if it were not for the implementation of the family planning policy, the current labour force population would be even larger, the pressure of labour redundancy would be even higher, and such situations would last even longer. There is no doubt that the family planning policy is effective in controlling population growth and can lead to a reduction in the total population which includes the working age population; if, however, the aim is to decrease the population in China, to decrease the working age population in particular, so that its quantity will align with or even undersupply the labour demand which fits within the social and economic development context of China, this will only be possible after the 2040s at the earliest. Due to the inertia of population development, the total population of China will remain on an increasing trend until 2009, and then decrease, but for at least 20 years there will not be any shortage, only redundancy. To say that the family planning policy is one of the reasons for the "peasant worker shortage" is unscientific and disregards the actual facts.

Working age population supply of registered population in Guangdong

Looking at Figure 2, it can be seen that in the first twenty years of the 21st century, the trend of the working age population in the registered population of Guangdong shows similarities as well as differences to that of the nation. The similarities are that the Guangdong ingoing working age population also peak in 2006 (1,598,000), the outgoing working age population peak in 2018 (1,101,000), and the net increase in the working age population also peak in 2006 (1,028,000). One difference is that the growth rate and quantity differ greatly from that of the nation: the national net increase in the working age population is negative in 2012 and this trend continues; for Guangdong, however, the negative trends do not start to occur until 2017, five years later, the growth rate starts to be positive in 2019, and shows as an increasing trend. The other difference is that the national working age population peaks in 2009 and then decreases slowly, showing a convex shape when depicted in the diagram, whereas the working age population of Guangdong increases until 2016, when it reaches the peak (54,888,000), and then levels off. The tangency of the depicted curve of Guangdong decreases and then remains roughly constant when extending into the future.

Figure 2. Guangdong registered working age population change (2000-2020)

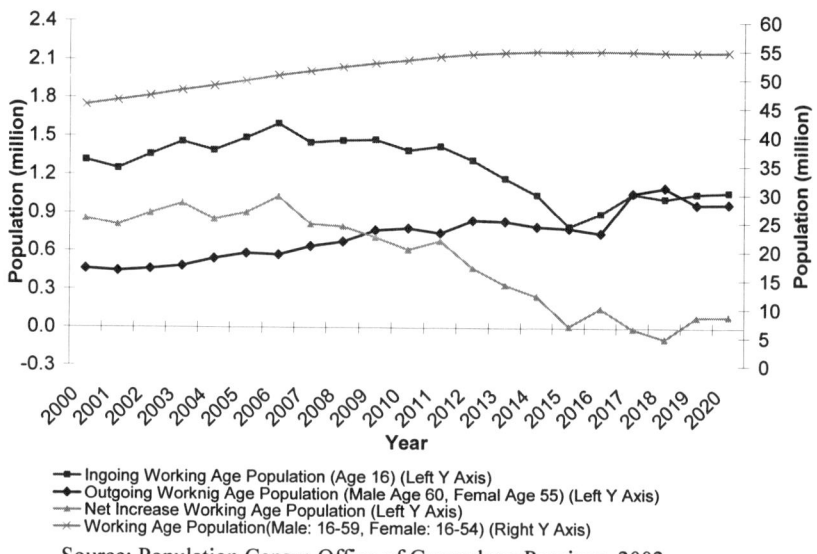

Source: Population Census Office of Guangdong Province, 2002.

Rationally speaking, Guangdong should not have any labour employment problems, because Guangdong has been importing labour from other provinces ever since the Reform and Opening period, which suggests the existence of a labour shortage. In fact, with regard to seeing employment as an important way for people to gain their livelihoods, in recent years, Guangdong has paid considerable attention to employment problems and made significant achievements. Compared with 2003, employment opportunities in Guangdong in 2004 increased by 1,050,000, resulting in an annual growth rate of 9.5 per cent. Moreover, new urban employment opportunities increased by 830,000, leading to a total of 12,880,000 urban employment opportunities at the end of the year and an annual growth rate of 6.9 per cent; new rural labour force transfer employment increased by 675,000, with an annual growth rate of 41 per cent; laid-off workers in state-owned enterprises decreased by 29 per cent annually to 320,000; the annual total of urban registered unemployment decreased by 7.7 per cent annually to 998,000; the end of year provincial urban registered unemployment rate decreased by 0.2 per cent annually to 2.7 per cent (Population Census Office of Guangdong Province, 2005). However, there are still about five million peasants who are urgently waiting for employment at the current time. The cultivated land area in Guangdong was 0.46 *mu* (unit of area equals to 0.0667 hectares) per capita, less than half of the national average (Population Census Office of Guangdong Province, 2005).

These facts suggest that, currently, in Guangdong, potential employees from other localities continue to flow in while the registered working age population is in a state of underemployment, and the rural surplus labour force within the province is far from completing the transfer process into non-agricultural employment. With regard to the developing trend of the Guangdong registered working age population, and supposing that Guangdong keeps adding 1,000,000 new employment opportunities (this is the highest standard achievable) annually, if the transfer of the rural labour force and the demand for the urbanization of the rural population were included in the plans and arrangements, Guangdong would still be in a situation of employment hardship and baffled by the fact that supply would be in excess of demand.

The "peasant worker tide" in Guangdong is still high

If the phrase "peasant worker shortage" does not have a meaning in the context of deficiencies in the population age and quantity structures of the total labour force in China, and does, in fact, have a meaning in the context of the labour shortage occurring in Guangdong, then the appropriate meaning should also be subjected to specific analysis.

If the term "peasant worker shortage" were used to indicate the receding of the "peasant-worker tide" in Guangdong, or to indicate that the flow of the "peasant worker tide" has changed direction and is no longer flowing into Guangdong, then it should be pointed out that the situation, in which the labour force population from other localities flowing into Guangdong, has not yet changed. The tide is still rising, or is, at least, still high, rather than falling. Although there is little comprehensive and complete statistical data like that obtained from the census, local data obtained through investigation and research is able to provide sufficient evidence. One source of such evidence is found in the statistical examples and evidence of Shenzhen, Dongguan and Guangzhou. Results from the fifth national census in 2000 showed that the population then flowing into Guangdong was about fifteen million, of whom 90 per cent belonged to the working age population.

The sum total of the population in Shenzhen, Dongguan and Guangzhou had already exceeded ten million. This means that to some extent, the proportion of the population from other localities in these three cities was enough to represent and reflect the aggregate trend of the population from other localities in Guangdong, and this could serve as a barometer to indicate changes in the population. In 2004, investigations and researches were conducted by several government departments and research institutions in Shenzhen and Dongguan; mainstream results suggested that the populations from other localities had exceeded 10 million in each of the two cities with the majority coming from outside the Guangdong province. Bao'an is one of the major population bearing districts of Shenzhen; its population from other localities, which consisted mainly of labour force inflow from outside of the province, doubled in 2004, compared with the year 2000, finally reaching four million. This means that, currently, the sum of population inflow from other provinces in Shenzhen and Dongguan has exceeded ten million. Since the statistics of Guangzhou will be at least at the same level with 2000, the conclusion that the current provincial population inflow exceeds 15 million is credible. The quantitative growth of out-of-province population inflow may become slower, but the total numbers will still be increasing.

Secondly, although the statistical coverage of the examples and evidence of the special investigations conducted by the Department of Public Security of Guangdong Province in the second half of 2004 was different to that of the national census, the published results showed that Guangdong had a floating population of over 24 million. During a public speech, Governor Huang Huahua pointed out that there were 13 million labour force inflows from other provinces in 2004; this was an increase of three million over 2003.

Although shortages in the labour force have arisen in some parts of Guangdong and in some industries, this is no justification for asserting that such a phenomenon is indicative of a reflux in the "peasant worker tide," or of a large scale slump in the numbers of peasant workers in Guangdong, or even of peasant-workers' migrating to other provinces nationally. Even if, as some investigations have concluded, there was a shortage of two million peasant workers in Guangdong, it would still be unjustifiable to suggest that the labour force population flow into Guangdong has changed. Quantitative changes do not necessarily mean qualitative changes.

With regard to the dynamics of such population movements, the preceding information and data, in addition to the out-of-province debates about the inflow of population from other provinces into Guangdong, suggest that the population will fluctuate by perhaps two million over and under around 15 million but the overall trend is still increasing.

The essence of the "peasant worker shortage" problem

There is no reason to deny the fact that in some parts of Guangdong, some of the industries have experienced labour recruitment difficulties and labour force shortages over recent years: recruitment difficulties have existed for years, for example, in Dongguan. The conflicts created by this problem and the differences in opinion over the causes, intensified in 2004, to become an issue of widespread public concern. The opinion expressed in this paper, however, is that the essence of the peasant worker shortage phenomenon in Guangdong does not derive from a "shortage" of labour, rather that it is found in the interaction of multiple factors from many different facets, as described below:

A lack of the scientific development perspective that is "putting people first"

Guangdong is in a leading position with regard to the development of a social security system. Year-end statistics from 2004, from the Population Census Office of Guangdong Province (2005), show that for the whole province, there were 12,255,000 basic pension insurance participants, (an increase of seven per cent compared with the year before); 10,342,000 medical insurance participants (an increase of 17.9 per cent); 12,151,000 work injury insurance participants (an increase of 8.5 per cent); 10,058,000 unemployment insurance participants (an increase of 5.4 per cent). These figures, of over ten million in each case, are the highest figures nationally. Although such achievements will definitely benefit migrant labour workers, significant problems such as overdue wages, overtime, poor working and safety environments, and some discriminatory social treatment still exist with regard to the protection and treatment of migrant workers compared with the rights and benefits of other workers. These negative factors have a significant impact on the admission and stability of the migrant labour work force. This is due to the lack of a "putting people first" philosophy. Labour is used in ways and according to philosophies which are now old-fashioned and obsolete, with the focus always on "labour" and to the detriment of "people." These ways have not been adjusted or updated under the strategic state philosophy of transferring rural labour, realizing urbanization, and establishing a harmonious society. As a result, conflicts have intensified among migrant workers, local governments, enterprises employing the workers and society, resulting in a highly distorted situation in which a labour shortage and a peasant worker surplus coexist.

Effects of industry restructure and upgrade

After more than twenty years of growth and development, it is natural, rational, and irrevocable that Guangdong should upgrade and restructure its industries. In fact, this is the only way Guangdong can promote its competitiveness, meet the requirements and face the challenges of economic globalization, and continue to achieve social and economic development. Industry structure adjustments involve one-off and fundamental turnarounds for Guangdong industry where labour intensive enterprises are in a majority, and these will certainly have an impact on the development and survival of such enterprises and hence, an influence on the market and employment. In recent years, the labour markets have been favourable for hi-tech, technology intensive, and capital intensive enterprises in Guangdong; there were, in general, few recruitment difficulties and labour was relatively abundant. The flourishing success of such industries has had an impact on the labour market, and this has resulted in the inclination of the labour force to enter these industries and to reject the labour intensive industries. It has also, however, led to hesitation on the part of the labour force, to the development of attitudes such as wait-and-see or merely waiting. This places labour intensive enterprises at a disadvantage when recruiting. The restructuring and upgrading of industry has given rise to fluctuations in the labour intensive industries, which once dominated the labour market.

Predicament of the labour intensive industries

The labour intensive industry in Guangdong is in a predicament. First of all, the costs of raw materials, energy fuels, and land resources are continuously increasing. Secondly, the pressures of international competition are becoming more and more intensive. Developing countries and regions, especially those in Southeast Asia and East Asia which are adjacent to Guangdong, also possess rich human resources. Their much less expensive labour forces pose a significant challenge to Guangdong. International capital and suppliers are making precise use of this situation to exert further pressure on the Chinese labour intensive enterprises and continue to demand lower prices as well as unreasonable conditions, passing the resulting negative impact on to those enterprises and the Chinese Government. Under such pressure, even if the labour costs were to remain unchanged, profits would be lower and would be unable to be increased. The competitiveness of wages, education and training courses, working environments, and the inputs and capacities of labour securities are diminishing. The low profitability of the industry has determined that, even if the situation were answered by the increasing of wages, this countermeasure would not be sustainable, and better measures for attracting labour would also be unavailable. Consequently, it is natural that the industry finds itself in this predicament, facing a labour shortage. The development of labour intensive industries in Guangdong is confronted with making critical choices with regard to future development and strategic turnaround. Against the background of the long-term existence of a huge amount of Chinese rural surplus labour and the accumulation of large numbers of the rural labour population from other provinces who are waiting for transfer employment in Guangdong, there would be significant negative consequences if the labour intensive industries were abandoned all at once. To adjust the production structure accordingly offers the best solution.

Labour employment market is more rationally and healthily market-oriented

The long-term existence of the huge amount of rural surplus labour in China is the cause of the inelasticity in labour prices and the unlimited labour supply situation in the low-level labour markets of cities and enterprises. This means that the development of urban industries and enterprises is able to maintain extremely low costs, because the prices of labour are insensitive in the labour market. This also indicates that the legitimate rights and benefits of the workers will be infringed without any scruples. Although labour and employment systems and regulations are becoming more and more market-oriented, there are still distortions and dissimilation, which cause the balance to weigh in favour of those representing capital. The positive side of a peasant worker shortage shows in the way that workers have awoken to their rights and benefits, and have started to "voting with their feet" in order to fight against such injustices as well as to vindicate their legitimate rights and benefits. It can therefore be proved that the self-adjustments of the labour market towards market-oriented operations and standardizations have started. By undergoing the impacts of the peasant worker shortage, the labour market will certainly develop more healthily and rationally.

Constraint of the low educational level of the Chinese population

It could be suggested that the underlying reason for the "peasant worker shortage" is the "skilled worker shortage", which means that the shortage consists in a lack of skilled workers rather than of labourers. This phenomenon also exists in other coastal cities and industrial regions. Its ultimate cause is the constraint of the overall low educational level. This is one of the major impediments to encumber the social and economic development of China in the 21st century. Indications and warnings of this were apparent from the situation at the end of the 20th century. The current shortage of skilled workers is merely one of the representations. There is no short-term solution to this serious problem, which will have a critical impact on the social and economic development of China for a long time.

Possible solutions to the problem

It is the intention of this paper to argue that the occurrence of a labour shortage does not constitute a denial of the hypothesis suggested by Lewis (1954; 1958) that there would be an unlimited supply of labour in developing countries under the rural-urban dual-sector model. China has an obvious work force surplus, the movement of the surplus population and the trend of its development are not yet clear and need to be observed and investigated. However, the rise of such a phenomenon is sufficient to indicate that the government and the society should take heed and start to look for possible solutions.

According to the preceding analysis, the following suggestions may be of use in finding effective solutions to the problems:

The concept of China as a country of immense population must be recognized and established. China is not a super power and should be thought of in these terms. However, in order for problems to be solved at national level, the concept of China as a country of immense population must be established. The vast population of China means that population pressures are extremely high and will continue to exist for a long time. Hence, in every matter that involves the national economy and the livelihood of the people, the constraints on the population must be taken into consideration. That is to say, the constraints on the population are never negligible and should never be overlooked. Failures will occur if the constraints are ever overlooked. Many of the phenomena that appear difficult to comprehend or explain turn out to be relatively simple if observed from the demographic perspective.

The concept of "putting people first" should be established in new ways of using labour in the enterprises by adhering to the scientific development perspective. The labour-using modes and philosophies of simply pursuing low cost labour and ignoring the legitimate basic rights and benefits of the workers are obsolete and should belong to the past. Not only do the old ways hamper the promotion of competitiveness and the sustainable development of enterprises, they also infringe the rights and benefits of workers, ultimately causing negative impacts on enterprise development and social stability. Therefore, a system and a mode for promoting labour and capital relationships in the socialist market economy context – that will lead to win-win outcomes – should be developed in order to create a favourable and harmonious labour and capital environment for social and economic development, and to ease the predicament resulting from the opposition of labourers towards enterprises, government and society.

Career training courses and education must be provided nationally, as rapidly as possible, particularly for the peasant workers. For peasants who have lost or left their land, moved into the cities, left their land but are still clinging to their hometowns, and laid-off workers, "40, 50 troops,"[2] large groups of people that are currently unemployed and the like, their weakness is that their career skills are narrow in scope, simple, and at a low level, which renders them unsuitable for urban or non-agricultural employment. Career training courses and education can help them to adapt easily to drastic social and economic transitions. Hence, to organize and push forward comprehensive career training and education should be one of the priorities of government at all levels. This is the only way, without differentiating between labour importing and exporting regions, to accomplish successfully the transfer of the rural labour force, especially to the cities.

The systems should be innovated and support systems should be developed for the urbanization of the rural population. The urbanization of the rural population is an important state strategy to deal with the transfer of rural surplus labour to the cities, which is a general trend. One of the reasons for the various negative encounters experienced by peasant-workers in the cities is that there are no clear laws, codes, or social policy support systems for the urbanization of the rural population or for peasant-workers who work in the cities. During their large scale movements towards cities, the rural population finds that little or non-standard support, if any, is available in terms of employment, career training, social insurance, social security, child education, and family life security and so on in urban systems. The ultimate solution to these problems is to innovate the systems. It would therefore be beneficial to go beyond the constraints of the household registration system, to develop comprehensive laws and social policies for the urbanization of the rural population. This involves strategic considerations of urban and rural

---

[2] These are workers of the age of 40 to 59 who are considered to be hard to be placed.

development as well as the rights and benefits of both the peasant workers and the urban citizens, in order to guide and push the rural labour populations towards forming and making rational decisions during their transfer to the cities.

The key to a support system for the urbanization of the rural population is social fairness. In developing a support system for the urbanization of the rural population, the relationship between efficiency and fairness must be handled first. Efficiency must not lead to the suppression of fairness, nor may fairness lead to the suppression of efficiency. The balance between efficiency and fairness is, in fact, the balance between the degree of economic development and the degree of social development. Efficiency cannot be the sole objective, but nor can fairness be pursued to the detriment of efficiency and the degree of economic development. Under certain phases of economic development, only certain degrees of social fairness can be enjoyed. Next, the relationship between equal opportunity and equal distribution of outcome should also be dealt with. At the current phase of development in Guangdong and China, the level of material wealth is still low, it will thus be impossible to provide equal outcomes. In fact, the emphasis should be on providing equal opportunities. To be more specific, this means equal rules, equal opportunities, and equal distributions. If the above two aspects are not given adequate consideration, the urbanization of the rural population will result in serious social conflicts, in social clashes as well as breaches in the concerted rural-urban development. Under these circumstances, the support system would exist in name only.

Such a support system, market-oriented but taking account of rights and benefits to offer social justice and fairness, since "policies are made by the government, and selected by market competition," must be seen as an essential tool for the strategic planning of rural-urban population development and for the urbanization of the rural population.

References

Lewis, W. Arthur (1954) "Economic development with unlimited supplies of labour," in *The Manchester School*, Vol. 22, No. 2, pp. 139-191.

Lewis, W. Arthur (1958) "Unlimited labour: further notes," in *The Manchester School*, Vol. 26, No. 1, pp. 1-32.

Population Census Office of Guangdong Province (2002) *Tabulation on the 2000 Population Census of Guangdong Province*, Beijing: China Statistic Press.

Population Census Office of Guangdong Province (2005) *Guangdong Statistical Yearbook*, Beijing: China Statistic Press.

Population Census Office under the State Council & Department of Population, Social, Science and Technology Statistics of the Bureau of Statistics of China (2002) *Tabulation on the 2000 Population Census of the People's Republic of China*, Beijing: China Statistic Press.

Labour Mobility –

Driving Forces and Adjustment Strategies

A Cost-Benefit Analysis of Rural Labour Migration

Shi Guoqing and Zhou Jian

Introduction

Since the reform period and opening up to the outside world, the rapid development of economy and society has speeded up the transformation of China's social structure and since the 1980s, the agricultural surplus labour force has been flowing from the agricultural sector to the secondondary and tertiary sector on a large scale. The flow has been moving from rural areas to urban areas; from the undeveloped middle-west areas to the developed eastern coast. It formed a great and grand "migrant worker tide" at the end of the 1990s. According to statistics obtained from the Ministry of Agriculture, the numbers of the rural labour force who moved away to obtain employment amounted to around 103 million in 2004, or 21 per cent of the total rural labour force. The "migrant worker tide" promoted both domestic rural and urban economic development, speeded up the state's economic restructuring and achieved the reasonable allocation and optimized combination of production factors.

However, although the "migrant worker tide" is moving actively, after the Spring of 2004, the "migrant worker shortage" phenomenon appeared unexpectedly in the Pearl River Delta, especially in Dongguan. According to statistics, in 2004, the shortage in migrant workers was up to 2 million in the Pearl River Delta. At the beginning of 2005, the "migrant worker shortage" reappeared in the Pearl River Delta, becoming bigger and bigger, and other large and medium-sized cities have also experienced, to various degrees, a shortage of migrant workers.

In recent years, many new features of the flow of migrant workers have emerged: the hot spot for the flow of migrant workers has changed, shifting from the Pearl River Delta to the Yangtze River Delta; some areas have seen the phenomenon of migrant workers "returning home" to farming at an increasing rate. Compared with the cross-provincial and cross-regional flow in the past, the most popular flow mode now is the "leaving the land but not the hometown" mode. What are the forces that drive peasants out to become migrant workers? What are the factors which affect their decisions regarding migration?

From the point of view of the traditional economic theory on development, the moving of population from rural areas to urban areas is a natural economic reflection of the fact that urban income is higher than rural income. The famous Todaro Population Migration Model supplements and develops this theory. Todaro thought that population migration was a reaction to the gap between different incomes, and mainly a reaction to the gap between different expected incomes.

Lee's (1966) Migrants Options Theory pointed out that migration has costs and benefits. The theory on the costs and expected benefits of the population migration put forward by Theodore W. Schultz, a representative of the American

Chicago economists' school, claimed that migration has monetary costs and non-monetary costs. The former include increased expenditure on transportation, accommodation, food and other aspects; the latter include a decrease in income caused by the migration, and the psychological costs. The expected benefits of migration refer to the fact that migrants expect to earn more money after migration. When the expected benefits of the migration are bigger than the cost of the migration, people are apt to migrate.

Cultural migration theories, however, emphasize different necessary relations between the migration activity and culture. Social civilization, identity and adaptation influence the whole process of migration.

The word "peasant worker" is not only a definition of an occupation, but also represents a combination of two forms of social status. They are "peasants" in terms of their inherent social status and they are, at the same time, "workers" in terms of their economic status. Under the dual economic structure, Chinese peasants are no longer controlled by that kind of narrow mind which describes them as "face the soil and back against the sky;" they are "economic people" who are seeking to gain their maximum individual and family economic benefits. They do some certain analysis on costs and profits of options in relation to areas, time, and methods of their moving.

As Schultz pointed out in his speech at the Nobel Prize-giving ceremony, when he was awarded the economics prize that all peasants around the world should be regarded as economic people who are calculating when they deal with costs, profits and risks. He also said that in the small, individual and resource distribution fields, they should be regarded as micro-regulating entrepreneurs, who do the regulation so delicately that many experts fail to find out how efficient they are.

This article uses the hypothesis of peasants as "economic people" as a premise to establish a model for the costs and benefits of the flow of migrant peasants to seek the mechanisms and influencing factors of the flow of migrant workers.

Calculation model of costs and benefits of the flow of migrant workers

How to calculate the costs and benefits of the flow of migrant workers who have left their hometown for jobs is still a question that is worth discussing. Generally speaking, the costs of migrant workers working away from their hometowns consist of monetary costs and non-monetary costs. The monetary costs are the expenditure on production and maintenance, the opportunity cost which is given up, and the expenditure on transportation during the moving process and so on. The non-monetary costs are mainly reflected in time, physical strength, mental labour and so on, including the psychological cost of entering unknown places. The motifs of migrants working away from their hometowns also consist of monetary benefits, which are economic benefits, and non-monetary benefits, which are social benefits and environmental benefits. For migrant workers, at present, the key and direct impacts promoting their short term actions are still economic costs and benefits. Non-economic costs and benefits affect them too, but they are not definitive. This article therefore offers an analysis of the costs and benefits of the flow of migrant workers mainly from the economic view, but also focuses on the social, cultural, psychological and other non-economic factors which affect the flow of migrant workers.

The outflow of migrant workers is essentially the outflow of human capital, and the value of maintaining the corresponding labour force. Costs, therefore, are the expenditures required to maintain the necessary labour force reproduction, and benefits are the value of the labour force.

Costs and benefits of rural production and living in a non-migratory situation

Even if the labour forces do not go away from their hometowns, and work and live in their original places, there will still be some subsistence expenditure. The costs and benefits of rural production and living in a non-migratory situation are represented by C1.

Compared with incomes earned from going away from the hometowns, the benefits of migrant workers staying in their original places is the opportunity cost that was given up. Influenced by William Arthur Lewis, many scholars in China point out that due to surplus rural labour force in China, the marginal rate of rural production is equal to or close to zero. Therefore, although peasants do not go away from their hometowns to look for jobs, they have no employment at home either; they have no direct monetary income. So the opportunity cost of going away from their hometowns is zero, or, it could be said, the benefit of staying in rural areas is zero. Despite the surplus in rural labourers, most of the migrant workers who go away are the best rural labour forces. Their ages are mostly from 20 to 45; most of them are young, middle-aged males with not too low a standard of education and market awareness. They constitute the labour force which is most needed for developing the agricultural and rural economy. The benefit of migrant workers in a non-migratory situation is made up of two parts: those who are working and those who are farming in their hometowns. This is represented by I1.

The net benefit of migrant workers in a non-migratory situation is represented by $\triangle$I1, and the cost-benefit-rate is represented by R1.

$$\Delta I1 = I1 - C1 \qquad (1)$$

$$R1 = \frac{\Delta I1}{C1} \qquad (2)$$

Costs and benefits after migration to urban areas

Costs after migration to urban areas consist of three parts: the first part is similar to that in the rural area, the expenditure of production and living in the urban areas. The second part is the extra expenditure caused by migration, mainly including employment information fees, skills training fees and the different regulation fees charged by the cities where the migrant workers move to. The third part is the expenditure during the migration journey itself of the migrant workers, including the transportation costs, the costs for missed work and so on. The costs of migrant workers after migration to urban areas are represented by C2.

In theory, the benefits obtained by migrant workers should correspond to the value of the labour force, which consists of monetary income and non-monetary income (wages in kind, corporation welfare, social security and so on). However, due to the dual economic structure, an integrated urban and rural system of welfare and social security has not yet been established. There is also some social discrimination against "migrant workers" and their unrecognized status as workers means that migrant workers' non-monetary income is almost zero (once in a while they receive some festival gifts/allowances which are very few and limited to a small number of people). Thus, the benefit of migrant workers after migration to urban areas is almost equal to their working income, and this is represented by I2.

The net benefit of migrant workers after migration in the urban area is represented by $\triangle I2$, and the cost-benefit-rate is represented by R2.

$$\triangle I2 = I2 - C2 \qquad (3)$$

$$R2 = \frac{\triangle I2}{C2} \qquad (4)$$

The net benefit of the outflow of migrant peasants and its formula

For the peasants who go away from their hometowns to work, it is only when their net benefit from working in the urban areas exceeds their net profit from staying in the rural areas that they like to leave their hometowns. Therefore, the net benefit ($\triangle I$) of the labour force flowing out is the most direct economic stimulus. It can be represented by the formula:

$$\triangle I = \triangle I2 - \triangle I1 = (I2 - C2) - (I1 - C1) \qquad (5)$$

Demonstration analysis

In order to validate the calculation model of costs and benefits for the outflow of migrant workers, the authors did a survey among migrant workers in Nanjing urban area and obtained clear data. The analysis is detailed below.

The investigation randomly selected 60 migrant workers to answer a questionnaire, including 30 migrant workers from the north of Jiangsu Province; the other 30 are from Henan Province. The contents of the questionnaire covered incomes from working and farming in the hometown; the production and living expenses of migrant workers in 2004; the wage income from working in the urban areas; every item of expenditure on production and living while job hunting; transportation and communication fees; all kinds of certification fees, medical expenses and other expenditure in Nanjing in 2005. There is a gathering effect in migrant peasants' job selection, which leads to peasants from the same towns and same villages tending to stay together. The authors therefore carried out a follow-up investigation and data collection with regard to the social and economic situation in the migrant workers' original villages – Henan Province and north of Jiangsu Province.

The investigation showed that the costs of production and living in a non-migratory situation in the rural areas (mainly subsistence cost) are 1,509.5 RMB, the annual profits are 2,173.5 RMB (including a working income of 264 RMB and a farming income of 1,909.5 RMB), the net benefit is 664 RMB, and the cost-benefit-rate is 44 per cent. After migration to the urban areas, the costs of production and living are 5,058.6 RMB, including subsistence costs of 3,667.6 RMB, extra expenses of 662 RMB (including all kinds of certification fees of 245 RMB, employment information fees of 128 RMB and skills training fees of 289 RMB), the travel expenditure for migration is 729 RMB (including the transportation costs of 389 RMB and costs for missed work of 340 RMB), profits are 7,922 RMB (including wages of 7,908.6 RMB and others 13.4 RMB), the net benefit is 2,863.4 RMB, the cost-benefit-rate is 57 per cent. The net benefit of the labour force of migrant workers in cities is 2,199.4 RMB.

Table 1. Comparison of the social and economic situation of two villages

	Village A in north of Jiangsu	Village I in Henan
The number of labour forces aged from 20-45	432	309
The number of farmers going out for jobs	194	197
The percentage of migrant workers to the total labour forces	45 %	64 %
The average net income of individual in a rural household in 2004	4,389	2,555
The main sources of peasants' incomes (following orders)	- working for village owned enterprise - going out of the hometown to work - agriculture	- going out of the hometown to work - agriculture - livestock raising

Findings and conclusions

The theoretical model and demonstration analysis provided the following findings and conclusions:

The principal factor which drives peasants to work in cities is the relatively higher income from working in the urban areas

Although the costs of production and living increase when migrant workers move to the urban areas – the costs on average increase from 1,509.5 to 5,058.6 RMB – their net benefit is raised by a wider margin. The cost-benefit-rate has increased from 44 to 57 per cent; the net benefit of the outflow of migrant workers is

2,199.4 RMB. This is the principal motivation for thousands of peasants leaving their hometowns to work in the urban areas. Although the costs of going away are very high, going away to work can result in higher comparative benefits; flowing is better than always staying in one place; working in the urban areas is better than farming in the rural areas. This validates the Migrants' Options Theory and the peasants as "economic people" hypothesis.

The wage income level and its change have important impacts on migrant workers' net benefit

The wage income is the main benefit resource of migrant workers in urban areas, and is also the basis of net benefit. The amount of wage therefore directly affects the net benefit and cost-benefit-rate of migrant workers. The higher the wage the higher the net benefit and cost-benefit-rate for the migrant workers.

Migrant workers always spend little money when they live in the urban areas and maintain minimum consumption levels; although there is a small difference in consumption in different cities, this has no big impact on migrant workers' living costs standard. When the cost difference of moving to different cities is not big, according to a rational economic comparison, the difference in wages becomes the principal reason for migrant peasants' migration. A shortage in migrant workers occurred in the Pearl River Delta in 2004, when large numbers of migrant workers moved to relatively better-paid areas – the Yangtze River Delta is the best illustration.

On the other hand, delayed payment of wages or reduced wages and other factors affect the benefits of migrant workers. If these circumstances occur, the net benefit of migrant workers will even become a minus figure, and severely affect the enthusiasm of migrant workers to go away to work. In order to promote the enthusiasm of migrant workers for going away to work, various approaches should be used to protect the rights of migrant workers, continuously increase migrant workers' wage levels, stop the monopolization of the labour force market, prevent delays in the payment of wages and so on.

Various increased costs have reduced the net profit of the outflow of migrant workers

The net profit is the balance of benefits minus costs; under the precondition of fixed profits, increased cost will reduce the benefits, this is a basic economic relationship. Costs of production and living have increased by a wide margin, the main reason being that the living costs are increased by the different market price level in the urban areas, which is much higher than that in the rural areas.

The investigation revealed that when migrant workers move to the urban areas, the extra cost is RMB 662, which is 13 per cent of the total living cost in the urban areas. Under the circumstances, that the wages of migrant workers have not been increased for several years, and that this kind of extra cost is raised, there will certainly be an increase in costs, and a decrease in the benefit and cost-benefit-rate, which is equal to raising the cost level for migrant workers working in the urban areas and limiting the flow of migrant peasants. The government therefore needs to take action to amend the unfair regulations and reduce the unreasonable charge items.

Increased peasants' rural incomes have a great impact on the migrant workers' decisions regarding migration

When they go to urban areas for jobs, peasant workers have to face a lot of risks and social, psychological and maladjustment problems, such as the feelings of loneliness which result from their leaving their families, and the discrimination or self-discrimination which can be experienced after they have separated themselves from their original social relations network to assume a low social position in the city. They also very often suffer accidental injury, delays in the payment of wages and so on.

If, in addition to the other potential risks faced by the migrant peasants, the expected benefits from agricultural production could not be increased continuously (although the degree of increase is limited), and the benefits from working outside their hometowns could not be improved for a long time, the surplus rural labourers would probably choose another way to earn a living; they would go back to farming in their hometowns, with its low risks, increased benefits and enjoyable family life. Since the recent implementation of the Central Government's policies to relieve the burden on peasants, the benefits from peasants' farming production have increased to a great extent, in other words, the opportunity cost of going away to work has increased correspondingly, and that is why, in some areas, many migrant workers have "flowed" back to their hometowns.

The different benefit levels of the migrant workers in their places of origin have a greater impact on their decisions regarding migration

As far as costs are concerned, the rural subsistence costs and benefits depend on the rural economic development level and consumption level; the urban living costs and benefits depend on the relevant city's economic development level, especially the wage level. Actually, the costs and benefits of migrant workers going away for employment are the embodiment and a reflection of the existing dual economic structure in China. The flow of migrant workers is from the rural areas to the urban areas, from the west to the east, and from the undeveloped areas to the developed areas.

At the same time, the diversities in social and economic development also exist among different rural areas. These diversities are shown directly in the different incomes from working and farming in rural areas: the lower incomes in peasants' places of origin, the lower costs of going away to work, the greater net benefits of the flow of migrant workers, and the greater motivation of the flow of migrant workers. Most of the economically undeveloped provinces, therefore, are the migrant workers' places of origin, such as Anhui, Henan and the western provinces. Compare, in this situation, village A from the north of Jiangsu and village I from Anhui: the percentage of migrant workers in village I, aged from 20 to 45, who have gone away to work, is much higher than that in village A. The reason is that village A is more developed and the main income of the peasants in village A is from village-owned enterprises and specialized farming, so the motivation to go away to work decreases, and also the need to move to the cities or other places is less.

Economic benefits of going away to work can offset the peasants' non-economic costs

Peasants leave their hometowns for an unfamiliar urban environment to seek work; in addition to the labour-intensive work and bad living conditions, their psychological costs are also considerable. These are mainly feelings of homesickness, described in terms of "it's hard to leave the native land;" fear of the unknown society and potential discrimination; worries about possible communication problems and whether they will be able to find a job. There are also worries about some external calamities, such as the risks involved with doing some dangerous jobs and so on. Although the migrant workers have a lot of psychological costs, they still enter cities without any hesitation; the reason is that the economic benefits from going away to work offset peasants' non-economic costs, such as social, cultural and psychological costs. When peasants find a stable job with a stable wage in a city, obtain safe accommodation and thus satisfy the psychological expectations they had when they left their hometowns, peasants adapt themselves to urban life psychologically; the economic benefits are a source of comfort for the migrant workers and make up for the great psychological costs of going away to work. In order to save up to cover the costs of a round trip home and back again, (the third part of the urban costs in the costs and benefit model), some migrant worker only go home once a year, some of them even give up going home so as to get the higher overtime rate during the Spring Festival.

The psychological costs of migrant workers going away to work occur along with the migration, they cannot be avoided. The provision of the means for economic adjustment is necessary, such as setting up a convenient employment information release system for migrant workers, and raising the wages of migrant workers step by step, etc.

Non-economic social benefits have a positive impact on the economic benefits for migrant workers

After migrant workers enter the city, their trust in the new living and working environment declines, the former social regulations and social networks are no longer intact or even lost, the social capital soon disappears. However, looking at the situation from a long-term perspective, the non-economic social benefits they get, along with the migration, will have positive impacts on the economic benefits.

The main non-economic benefits for migrant workers, which result from going away to work, consist in their making some new friends, extending the social and economic networks, gaining a vast amount of social and economic information, expanding their view of society, learning how to accommodate themselves with urban life and knowing the importance of education. These will all positively promote an increase in peasants' incomes in the long term. For example, in village A, north of Jiangsu, mentioned in this article, most of the village-owned enterprises have been established by some migrant workers who went away to work a couple years ago, quickly learnt some good market opportunities and then returned home to start factories.

References

Cheng, Guodong 程国栋 (2005) "Nongmin jincheng wugong xindong xiang jingjixue toushi" 农民进城务工新动向经济学透视 [New trends among the la-bour migrants from the perspectives of economics], in *Fujian luntan (Renwen shehui kexue ban)* 福建论坛（人文社会科学版）[Fujian Forum (Humanities and Social Science edition)], June 2005.

Huang, Chengwei 黄承伟 (2004) *Zhongguo nongcun fupin ziyuan yimin banqian de lilun yu shijian* 中国农村扶贫自愿移民搬迁的理论与实践 [Theory and prac-tice of voluntary resettlement in rural poverty alleviation in China], Beijing: Zhongguo caizheng jingji chubanshe 中国财政经济出版社 [Publishing House for Finance and Economy].

Lee, Everett S. (1966) "A theory of migration," in *Demography*, Vol. 3, pp. 47-57.

Liu, Fang 刘芳 (2005) "Jin nian lai guanyu chengshi nongmingong wenti de yanjiu zongshu" 近年来关于城市农民工问题的研究综述 [An overview of the re-searches on the migrant workers in recent years] in *Xibei shifan daxue bao (Shehui kexue ban)* 西北师大学报(社会科学版) [Northwest Normal University Gazette (Social Sciences Edition)], January 2005.

Liu, Zheng 刘铮 (2005) "'Mingong huang' chengyin de jingjixue fenxi - jiantan ruhe zujin nongcun shengyu laodongli de zhengxiang liudong" '民工荒'成因的经济学分析－兼谈如何促进农村剩余劳动力的正向流动 [Reasons and causes of the "migrant worker shortage" from the perspective of economics-and to pro-mote the positive flow of the rural surplus labour force], in *Changbai xuekan* 长白学刊 [Changbai Academic Paper], March 2005.

Sheng, Hong 盛洪 (2003) *Xiandai zhidu jingjixue* 现代制度经济学 [Contemporary Institutional Economics], Beijing: Beijing daxue chubanshe 北京大学出版社 [Beijing University Publishing House].

Wang, Zhe 王哲 (2005) "Chengxiang eryuan jiegou xia de nongmingong wenti tantao" 城乡二元结构下的农民工问题探讨 [Discussion of the issues concerning the migrant workers under the urban and rural dual structure], in *Nongcun zhanwang* 农村展望 [Prospect of the Countryside], June 2005.

Wu, Xinglu 吴兴陆 and Qi, Mingjie 亓名杰 (2005) "Nongmingong qianyi juece de shehui wenhua jingxiang yinsu tanxi" 农民工迁移决策的社会文化影响因素探析 [Analysis on the social and cultural factors influencing the migrant workers' decision on migration], in *Zhongguo nongcun jingji* 中国农村经济 [The Rural Economy of China], January 2005.

Xu, Qiaoxian 许巧仙 (2004) "'Mingongchao' xianxiang de jingjixue sikao" '民工潮'现象的经济学思考 [Consideration from the view of economics of the "migrant workers shortage"], in *Hehai daxue xuebao (zhexue shehui kexue ban)* 河海大学学报(哲学社会科学版) [Hohai University Gazette (Philosophy and Social Sciences Edition)]. June 2004.

Zhang, Guangyu 张广宇 and Du, Shuyun 杜书云 (2005) „Zhijie chengben, jihui chengban yu nongmin waichu dongli: lilun fenxi he moxing shizheng" 直接成本、机会成本与农民外出动力：理论分析和模型实证 [Direct cost, opportunity cost and driving force for migrant workers: theoretical analysis and model test], in *Zhongguo nongcun jingji* 中国农村经济 [China Agricultural Economy], January 2005.

Risk Employment and Social Risk Management – Job Searching Strategies of Rural-to-Urban Migrants

Bettina Gransow

Introduction

The labour market emerging in Chinese cities is highly segmented. People with urban household registrations monopolise jobs in state industry, government administration, education and the rest of the formal sector. Those with only a rural household registration, which includes most migrants, are formally excluded from these high-status jobs. Most migrants to the cities therefore work in manufacturing, the service sector, construction or commerce. In 2003, more than 100 million rural labourers were working in urban areas. In the service sector they made up more than 50 per cent of the labour force, in the manufacturing sector they accounted for more than 60 per cent, and in the construction sector they represented over 80 per cent (Fan 2005:320).

Migrant workers are restricted to jobs that local people would not want because the pay is too low or the work is too hard or dirty. In the major cities at least, catering and construction offer the most employment to migrants and therefore merit attention. Despite the barriers, migrants are increasingly breaking into industrial employment in some areas. Many state-owned enterprises continue to employ migrants on temporary contracts even when they lay off regular workers. Migrants are preferred not only because their wages are low but also because they are not entitled to the welfare benefits that impoverished state enterprises are finding increasingly difficult to pay. Nevertheless, with a high (and growing) income gap between rural and urban areas in China, the numbers of labour migrants (as well as their expectations) are still on the rise.

As migrant workers are often employed in the informal sector, without contracts, insurance and welfare programs, with minimal benefits, high rates of work-related accidents and little job security, their precarious working conditions may well be described as forms of risk employment – a concept that stresses the various risks of informal employment patterns related to self-employment, flexible forms of labour, and the lack of positive legislation to define labour standards (Krzeslo 2003). Under these conditions, migrant workers are in particular need of social services and social security measures.

Lacking a sound safety net, rural migrants mobilise personal networks, with individual and household strategies to cope with the varied risks associated with migration processes. Thus, the job-searching strategies of rural migrants are not only about acquiring job-specific information and finding employment, but are also embedded in systems of personal relations and social networks on which they can rely in the new and unknown surroundings. Drawing on the concept of social risk management (Holzmann/Jorgensen 2000; Schmid 2004), the job-searching strategies of rural-to-urban migrants can be defined as the informal social risk management strategies of individuals or households to prevent, mitigate and cope with migration and employment related risks.

The focus of this paper is on job-searching strategies from the perspective of rural migrants. Gender-specific differences may lead male and female migrants to develop different job-searching priorities. How do they find their jobs? What motivates them to work abroad and how do they decide to go? What are their information channels and what kind of information is needed? It is argued that job-searching strategies employed by rural-to-urban migrants (which may appear to be sub-optimal strategies from the perspective of supply and demand on the labour market) follow a complex logic of preventing, mitigating and coping with social risks. This paper looks into the role of social networks in job-searching strategies of rural migrants as well as into the reasons why labour agencies play only a minor role in these strategies. Special consideration is given to the question of job information and information channels for both initial and subsequent jobs. It is concluded that a redistribution of the social risk between the market, the state and society is urgently needed.

Motivation for leaving home and the decision-making processes

There is a huge volume of literature (regarding the situation both in China and elsewhere) on what determines individual migrants' choices to leave home and look for a job elsewhere. I will not repeat all the arguments here, but restrict myself to introducing some of our survey findings.[1] In answer to the question "What was the reason for leaving home and working elsewhere?," one would expect that the most frequent answer selected by rural migrants would be "earn more money by working elsewhere" (see Li/Zhang/Zhao 2000: 182).

However, in our survey, the answer to a more detailed query as to why migrants leave home for the city shows some deviation from a purely economic motive: 86.5 per cent of respondents cited a search for better development opportunities as the reason for migrating, 76.8 per cent replied that their motive was to acquire more skills, while "earn more money by working elsewhere" was only the third most popular response representing 76.3 per cent. This shows that a broad complex of interests underlies the motivation to migrate, and that especially high significance is accorded to education, qualification, and individual further development. In addition to the three most commonly cited reasons above, additional factors included a longing for urban life, a wish to leave rural life behind, a lack of activity at home, and a low labour-to-land ratio. Analyzed by gender, the "many people, little land" response was cited more frequently by male than female migrants – probably

---

[1] The data presented here are taken primarily from a social survey performed in 1999/2000 in which 600 migrants (377 male/223 female) in Beijing, Shanghai and Guangzhou were asked about their working and living conditions. Other results of this survey have been published in Ke/Li 2001.

because the young women normally leave home to marry. For both men and women, the most important reason for leaving home was "to look for more and better development opportunities." This was even more important than earning money. Both reasons, however, were chosen more often by men than by women.

Table 1. "What was the reason for leaving home and working elsewhere?" (in per cent)

	male	female	all
Nothing to do at home	49.3	53.2	50.8
Many people, little land	49.1	36.5	44.4
Famine caused by poor harvest	18.0	15.3	17.0
Earn more money by working elsewhere	79.8	70.4	76.3
Looking for more and better development opportunities	89.1	82.0	86.5
Longing for urban life	65.0	63.1	64.3
Want to learn skills	77.2	76.2	76.8
Do not like rural life	51.2	52.7	51.8

It is worth noticing that the reasons for migration clearly differ according to age. Among rural migrants, younger individuals placed a higher emphasis on seeking better development opportunities and acquiring new skills than their older counterparts. In contrast, a greater number of older migrants than younger migrants cited a shortage of land as a reason for migration. Most respondents between the ages of 36 and 45 believed migration could bring in more income and therefore gave this as the main reason for their actions (see Table 2).

Table 2. Comparison of reasons to migrate by age group (in per cent)

	Age groups				
	16-25	25-35	35-45	over 45	total
Nothing to do at home	56.6	50.8	38.9	33.3	50.8
Many people, little land	34.4	48.8	55.6	61.9	44.4
Famine caused by poor harvest	14.3	16.8	24.4	19.0	17.0
Earn more money by working elsewhere	69.1	79.1	90.0	71.4	76.5
Looking for more and better development opportunities	92.2	83.2	84.4	66.7	86.5
Longing for urban life	63.1	67.2	61.1	57.1	64.3
Want to learn skills	85.2	75.4	65.6	47.6	76.9
Do not like rural life	50.8	54.5	45.6	57.1	51.8

The different answers provided by different age groups also indicate the need to view motives for migration as not static, i.e. as changing over the years and from generation to generation. This is also indicated by Wang Chunguang, who compared the motives of the first generation of older rural migrants with those of their counterparts under 25 years of age. While the first generation's reasons focused on the hardships of working the fields, the shortage of land, and the poverty of life in the countryside, the younger respondents reported that they knew nothing about agriculture (because they had spent all their time at school), and that working or doing business elsewhere was viewed as a promising opportunity. In other words, while push factors exerted a comparatively dominant effect on the first generation (40 per cent), the pull factors played a much stronger role for the younger respondents, with only 25 per cent of them listing push factors (Wang 2003: 198f., 201). Wang sees generally higher and more varied expectations on the part of the younger generation[2] as well as a stronger orientation toward working away from home.

Who decides whether to migrate? What roles are played by general conditions, individual decisions, and family strategies? Hein Mallee has argued that

rather than being permanent migrants, rural workers circulate between their villages and the destinations in urban and peri-urban areas. They do not necessarily intend to settle down permanently at their destinations; as their dominant frame of reference remains their rural family and the village community, they are part of two worlds. Labour circulation is therefore firmly rooted in the strategies and dynamics of rural families (Mallee 1997: preface 1).

In this approach, spatial dispersion is viewed as part of the family's strategy. Following Stark and Lucas, Mallee argues that

the home tie serves as a form of protection against employment risk, while at the same time providing the migrant with a strong degree of identification, allegiance, and social connectedness (...) The main mechanism of self-enforcement of the 'contract' between migrant and family is, however, the different time profile of risks and profits for the two parties. Both can rely on the other at a time when assistance is needed, and this moment tends to be different for the migrant who can rely on support during the initial phase, and the family, which may profit from remittances later on. Thus "migration of a family member facilitates effective pooling of risks and insurance in both alleviating the size constraint and gaining access to independence of risks" [Stark and Lucas 1988] (Mallee 1997:12).

The main point for Mallee is that mobility is seen as part of a larger repertoire of household labour allocation strategies. The question of whether the actual decision is taken by the (potential) migrant, the head of household, or the entire household, is of less importance to Mallee.

In our survey, a very clear majority described the decision to migrate as their own individual decision. Here, however, we see a clear gap between the answers of men and of women. 79 per cent of male and 65 per cent of female respondents decided to migrate on their own. Spouses and parents have a greater say if their wives or daughters intend to migrate than in the case of husbands or sons.

---

[2] Of whom 90 per cent were not yet married – in contrast to the older respondents of the first generation of migrants, 81 per cent of whom were married.

Table 3. *"Who was responsible for the decision that you should migrate?" (in per cent)*

	male	female	all
Yourself	78.8	64.6	73.5
Your spouse	2.4	11.2	5.7
Your parents	2.9	9.4	5.3
Your children	-	0.4	0.2
Your friends	1.3	3.6	2.2
Your relatives	3.4	1.8	2.8
Result of family discussions	10.6	9.0	10.0
Result of discussions with friends	0.5	-	0.3

From a gender perspective, Louise Beynon has criticized the household strategy model. "This model ignores individual motivation and the complex process of conflict and compromise among household members"(Beynon 2004:133). She suggests that young rural women leaving for the city use labour migration as a way to evade early marriage and pressure from parents to control their marriage choices, and at the same time may see migration as an opportunity to make a better marriage. She assumes therefore that individual motives are more important for women than for men in contemporary rural migration. As a consequence, most female migrants leave home to gain economic independence, but most cannot establish a secure life in the city; they therefore work to postpone marriage, but this is a dangerous strategy, as marriage is (also) viewed as a way to secure one's future (ibid.: 148). If a young woman postpones her return home for too long, she runs the risk that most of the eligible young men in her home area will be "married off." Furthermore, with her horizons expanded by the experience of migration, her expectations for her future spouse will also rise, with the result that simple farmers may not be able to fulfil them.

Fan agrees with Beynon that for female migrants, push factors are more important than pull factors (more so than for men), because a greater number of non-economic reasons related to marriage considerations play a role here (Fan 2004: 199f.). However, Fan is of the opinion that most rural women consider it less risky to find a husband in their native area than in the city. In Shanghai, for example, a female migrant would probably find a husband with a Shanghai *hukou* only if he were twice her age, a widower, or disabled. Marrying other migrants is also described as risky, because their backgrounds are unclear.

The point here is that risk assessment regarding labour migration for young women is in many respects closely related to considerations regarding marriage plans. Especially in rural areas, women's life planning differs from men's because of the patrilocal marriage system. Thus men's life planning is characterised by continuity – the role traditionally ascribed to men in Chinese society is that of ensuring the continuity of their family – whereas marriage for women means discontinuity, a change from the familial relations in which she has grown up to those of her husband's family, and a spatial relocation as well. This has far-reaching implications for access to land and the different ways in which migration is perceived by and impacts on men and women. The majority of women engaged in farming activities are married. It is because of the fact that their husbands have migrated to find jobs elsewhere that they have to do the farming work left behind. Further research is needed on the migration patterns of married women, but it seems that the percentage of married female migrants is increasing.

Job-searching strategies for first placement

As confirmed by numerous other studies (e.g. Li 1999), our survey confirms the importance of social networks for migrants' job searches, especially for the first job outside the home area.

Table 4. "How did you find your job outside your home area?" (in per cent)

	male	female	all
Relatives facilitated connection	54.9	63.7	58.2
Migrant friends from home area	8.2	4.9	7.0
Migrated together with local companions	8.5	6.3	7.7
Job placement organization	2.1	2.7	2.3
Approached by a job contractor	1.1	-	0.7
Coordinated/organized by local government	0.5	-	0.3
Recruitment of migrants	0.5	2.2	1.2
No one helped, searched on my own	22.3	19.7	21.3
Other	1.9	0.4	1.3

55 per cent of male and 64 per cent of female respondents obtained their jobs with the help of relatives. This figure is significantly higher for women than for men. In contrast, more male than female migrants found their jobs with the help of friends from their home areas or because they migrated together with local companions. If one agrees with Marc Granovetter's finding that "the strong ties are the weak ties," i.e. that the stronger networks of family and relatives are closer and less suitable for establishing individual job careers than looser networks that extend further into different areas of society (Granovetter 1982), then the family connections of female migrants are less suitable for job searches than the more extended networks of male migrants. This is also reflected in the responses to the question on migrants' active role in facilitating job placement for others.

Table 5. "Since leaving home to work elsewhere, have you taken or introduced others to work opportunities?" (in per cent)

	male	female	all
yes	45.6	28.3	39.2
no	54.4	71.7	60.8

According to these answers, male migrants clearly introduce others to work elsewhere more often than their female counterparts. This indicates that male migrants are involved in networking activities to a greater degree. As Zhao Shukai points out, however, the core element of self-organized labour mobility is kinship networking. Only when almost all the members of a family circle have left home does the network expand to include non-relatives. He supports this argument as follows:

To take or introduce someone to external work opportunities also means that one is responsible for helping him settle in the new environment. Sometimes it also means sharing risks. In general, people are more willing to bear risks with close relatives (Zhao 2000: 234).

Those leaving their hometown for the first time usually do so with others. They have a common destination and can provide each other with mutual assistance. Zhao Shukai divides self-organized forms of labour mobility into small-scale (less than five people) and larger-scale (five and more people). Small groups of migrants are usually taken or introduced by their kinsmen. Usually these individuals get piece-work jobs in factories or employment in micro-enterprises in the commercial or service sectors; some may become self-employed. Mobility among larger groups is characterized by a leader (*lingxiu*) who serves as the core link among members. There are three different types of leaders in larger-scale groups. One type is the contractor (*baogongtou*) in the construction sector. They recruit workers from their hometown without any formal recruitment procedure. The second type is the middleman in industrial enterprises. They recruit labourers from less developed villages for factories in urban areas and charge a commission from applicants. Some charge a flat fee (100-300 RMB); others a certain percentage (five to eight per cent) from the successful applicant's wages for a fixed period of time. Recently, critics of these exploitative practices have become louder. A third type of leader is described as emerging naturally. They are normally more experienced in moving around and have better networks. They are also more capable at managing and negotiating affairs (Zhao 2000: 233).

Moreover, personal networks do not only play a job-finding role, they can also promote success on the job, especially for self-employed persons. Thus, in response to our questions in an extended interview regarding the working and living conditions of migrants to Chinese metropolises, a tailor reported that his circle of friends also played an important role in his acquisition of new customers:

Everything depends on the recommendations by friends. Friends are most important for a business man. If I can sell my goods in Harbin very well, then the friends will recommend my products.[3]

Job placement services clearly do not play a relevant role for rural migrants in their search for external employment. This is confirmed in a comparative study by Li Minghuan on the job-searching strategies of rural migrants and white-collar

---

[3] Exploratory interview Beijing July 1999.

employees. Taking the Xiamen labour market as an example, Li Minghuan examined the differences in job-hunting channels between rural-to-urban migrants (factory workers and workers in the informal economy) and white-collar employees (including mid-level administrators, technicians etc.). He found that the white-collar workers acquired their current occupation via advertisements in newspapers or the Internet, recruitment agencies or contractors, or by direct solicitation from employers. In contrast, his sample of factory workers and workers in the informal economy found their current occupation via family members or relatives, friends or co-villagers, or by their own efforts (Li 2004: 13).

The fact that official recruitment agencies play only a very small role in the job searches of rural migrants is due not only to the fact that certain labour markets are not open to rural migrants and that active recruitment programs frequently target only urban candidates. Rural respondents often cite low efficiency, high fees, and a fear of being cheated (Xin 2000; Li 2004). "One of the common concerns of rural-urban migrants in China is whether they are going to be paid regularly in the city as there are many cases where employers delay payment for a substantial period" (Xin 2000: 174). Xin Meng suggests that when deciding where to migrate, an individual must be sure that a job is waiting for her/him or that there is a very high possibility of obtaining a job in a very short period. The majority of rural labourers who leave their hometowns already have a confirmed job or know somebody who can help in obtaining employment (Zhao 2000: 233). Personal networks based on relationships of trust provide some protection against the risks associated with individual job searches.

Job information and information channels

As we have seen, most migrants find their first jobs through personal channels. "As such information is often obtained in an ad hoc manner, the efficient allocation of labour may be interrupted by the random nature of the information itself" (Xin 2000:175). This kind of information channel is considered rather inefficient for the purposes of a fully functioning labour market, in that the matching of demand and supply is an uncertain event. Efficient allocation of resources requires formal information channels. To eliminate the existing large regional wage differentials in China, it is essential to expand the channels through which specific job information may flow. Personal contacts are, however, viewed as much more efficient than official government agencies, not only by rural migrants, but also by employers, for the latter are also unwilling to use government channels due to the associated high fees and forms of control. Another reason why Chinese rural-to-urban migrants hesitate to search for jobs via official channels is their lack of trust in these institutions. "Getting information on specific job offers from personal contacts not only ensures a job opportunity, but also provides greater assurance to migrants about the trustworthiness of their prospective employers" (Xin 2000: 176).

Migrants' apparent aversion to risk may also be due to a lack of credibility regarding China's legal system. Therefore, Xin Meng argues, enforcing labour laws may alleviate migrants' fears of being cheated, and thus encourage them to use formal information channels.

What determines the individual migrant's choice of destination? More than half of the respondents were clear or very clear about the wage levels and recruitment conditions at their target destination before migrating (see Table 6). More male than female migrants had a very clear idea of the wage levels and recruitment conditions. This may correlate with the results showing that fewer women than men decide to migrate on their own. It may be assumed that in cases where parents or spouses have a considerable say in the decision of a (prospective) migrant to leave home, the migrant himself/herself might know less about the job situation than the actual decision-maker.

Table 6. "Did you know about the wage levels and recruitment conditions at your target destination before migrating?" (in per cent)

	male	female	all
Very clear	18.6	9.9	15.3
More or less clear	36.9	37.7	37.2
Not very clear	37.1	48.0	41.2
Does not matter	7.4	4.5	6.3

Xin Meng argues that a high proportion of rural-to-urban migrants have specific information before leaving home. Here wage distribution (as general information) seems to be less valued than specific information (such as the likelihood of getting a job). This type of specific information flows through personal contacts and not through formal channels. The importance of specific information and its flow through social networks is confirmed by other research (Knight/Song 2005: 210ff.). These personal contacts do not only function as information channels, they also serve to reduce individual risk. "A risk-averse person would rather choose to migrate to an area where he/she has a specific contact than to an area where the wage offer may be higher" (Xin 2000: 174).

Information about government policies relating to the labour market does not reach rural migrants easily. The commercial nature of government supervisory policy (outgoing employment registration card and incoming labourers' work permit) has raised the cost of mobility for migrants. Because of this expensive system, most outgoing labourers appear to disregard the rules and evade the permit system (Zhao 2000: 236).

Job changes and subsequent mobility

Job changes and subsequent mobility can include those who are changing their work units or acquiring new employment. It also comprises those who have lost their jobs and are returning home before embarking on another trip. Several factors influence job changes and subsequent mobility. The primary factor is a violation of labour rights, such as delayed wages, excessive working hours, poor working conditions, and so on. A second factor is comparative gain. Workers change jobs when they are offered higher wages, better opportunities, a rise in social position or otherwise more attractive positions. In our survey, 45.6 per cent of the men and 28.3 of the women had already migrated to work in other cities before they took up their current jobs in Beijing, Shanghai or Guangzhou. This included not only job changes, but also job-related mobility such as the activities of construction teams. Men had worked more often in other cities than women.

Table 7. "What did you do before you came to this city?" (in per cent)

	male	female	all
Migrant work in another city	45.6	28.3	39.2
Military service	6.6	-	4.2
Worked as local cadre	4.0	0.9	2.8
Worked in a TVE	15.9	17.9	16.7
Worked in the service sector	10.1	12.6	11.0
Went to school	43.2	44.4	43.6

Of the male migrants in our survey, 59.1 per cent had already worked away from their home areas for 6 years or more. This figure is nearly double that of 31.5 per cent for female migrants. Job changes are frequent occurrences for both male and female migrants. But five or more changes are significantly more frequent for male migrants (13.4 per cent) than for their female counterparts (6.2 per cent). Here it must be taken into account that more men have a longer history of migration than women. The high frequency of job changes among migrant workers has been confirmed by several studies and is seen as a reflection of the instability of migrants' employment (Li Qiang 2000: 33).

There seems to be a difference between the mechanisms of initial and subsequent mobility. Social networks established on the basis of co-worker relationships become the core element in subsequent labour mobility. Job-searching strategies here may also include publicly available information such as recruitment notices. "Subsequent mobility is mainly one's own reaction toward exterior job opportunities, not an outcome of one's social resources in the home village" (Zhao 2000:235). This is confirmed by Li Minghuan, who found that "when unskilled labourers intend to find access to a better job than the one they currently have they need the help of brokerage. We may, therefore, conclude, that brokerage contributes significantly to people's upward social mobility" (Li 2004: 15).

Migrants may also take new jobs with different types of institutions. In our survey, we asked respondents about the types of institutions in which they had started to work (Table 8), and compared these with the institutions in which they were currently working as well as the institutions in which they most wished to work. More than half of all migrants started their first jobs in the private sector. Female migrants (59.2 per cent) took their first jobs outside their home areas in privately or individually owned enterprises more often than male migrants (51.6 per cent). Men took their first external jobs significantly more often in state-owned (20.2 per cent) and collectively owned institutions (13.3 per cent) than women (12.6 per cent and 4.9 per cent, respectively).

Table 8. "Which type of institution describes your first job outside your home area?" (in per cent)

	male	female	all
State owned	20.2	12.6	17.4
Collectively owned	13.3	4.9	10.2
Street committee owned	2.7	3.1	2.8
Privately or individually owned	51.6	59.2	54.4
Three kinds of joint ventures	1.1	0.9	1.0
Foreign enterprises	1.9	2.2	2.0
Town and village enterprises	1.1	1.8	1.3
Village, private or individual	6.4	7.6	6.8
Other	1.9	7.6	4.0

A comparison of current jobs with first jobs reveals that the percentage of migrants working in the state-owned and collective sectors is declining, while the percentage of migrants working in the private sector is increasing (63.9 per cent versus 54.4 per cent). Male migrants changed from the state-owned and collective sectors to the private sector; female migrants show a similar tendency, but less significantly.

When asked "At which kind of institution would you most like to work?," 32.6 per cent of respondents chose state-owned institutions. Broken down by gender, the 31.4 per cent of male migrants who would like to work at state-owned institutions contrasts with the 16.5 per cent of the total male migrants who actually do, while 34.5 per cent of female migrants would like to but only 10.8 per cent actually do so.

This presents a very clear picture: state-owned institutions, and to a certain degree, foreign enterprises as well, seem to be attractive to both male and female migrants. More research may be needed as to why migrants are changing from state-owned enterprises to the private sector (are they leaving the state sector because they want to or because they have to?) and what makes the state sector so attractive to rural migrants. It may be assumed that the idea of the state-owned sector is closely connected with welfare benefits even if these are often not provided for migrant labourers. This finding might be interpreted as a wish on the part of the rural migrants to change to the formal employment sector. This finding requires further examination, especially when interpreting rural migrants' job-seeking strategies as individual or household risk management strategies.

Conclusion

Social risks associated with searching for jobs and working away from home are compensated for by the social ties within the family. Even when decisions to migrate are made by the individuals alone, family ties are retained in circular migration (the still dominant form in China) and function as a form of protection against the risks associated with migration and employment. This structure, however, manifests itself differently for men and women, because tradition in the patrilocal marriage system of rural China requires the bride to move in with her husband's family. For the young female migrants who are generally not yet married, risk assessment and social risk management of labour migration is thus linked in many ways to considerations regarding their marriage plans. For both unmarried and married women, labour migration can also serve in one way or another to help them to escape from the confines of the village and unwanted family influence.

The personal networks, which are so important in the search for employment, and especially for the first job outside the home area, serve the dual functions of providing mutual protection and support in overcoming initial hardships in new surroundings. As far as protecting others from risk is concerned, this is practised considerably more among family members and relatives than within looser relational frameworks. Networking functions clearly extend well beyond the provision of information. They help to manage social risks in complex ways, and in so doing, they serve not only to solve the immediate problems of job searches but also to handle contingent developments.

These individual and family strategies for dealing with social risk reveal the obstacles, in both legal and social terms, associated with insufficient job information and inadequate security for migrant workers. As it will take some time to establish a comprehensive social security system in China, it may be concluded that within the near future, a new division of labour for social risk management is needed among the market, the state and society. Social risk management needs to be redesigned to fit the dynamics and distribution of new risk employment and migration (Schmid 2004: 6). More detailed studies of individual and family strategies to manage social risks will undoubtedly yield valuable starting points for the design of policies and measures to redistribute the responsibility for social risk management among the state, the employer and the family.

References

Beynon, Louise (2004) "Dilemmas of the heart: rural working women and their hopes for the future," in Gaetano/Jacka, pp. 131-150.

Fan, Cindy (2004) "Out to the city and back to the village: the experiences and contributions of rural women migration from Sichuan and Anhui," in Gaetano/ Jacka, pp. 177-206.

Fan Ping 樊平 (2005) "2004 nian Zhongguo nongmin" 2004年中国农民 [Rural Laborers in 2004], in Rong Xin 汝信; Lu Xueyi 陆学艺; Li Peilin 李培林 (eds) *Shehui lan pi shu*

2005 nian: Zhongguo shehui xingshi fenxi yu yuce 社会蓝皮书 2005 年：中国社会形势分析与预测 [Blue book of China's society 2005: analysis and forecast of China's development], Beijing: Social Sciences Academic Press, pp. 315-327.

Gaetano, Arianne and Jacka, Tamara (eds)(2004) *On the Move. Women in Rural-to-Urban Migration in Contemporary China*, New York: Columbia University Press.

Granovetter, Marc (1982) "The strength of weak ties: a network theory revisited," in Peter Marsden and Nan Lin (eds) *Social Structure and Network Analysis*, Beverly Hills: Sage Publications, pp. 105-130.

Holzmann, Robert, and Jorgensen, Steen (2005) "Social risk management: a new conceptual framework for social protection, and beyond," social protection dis-cussion paper No. 0006, World Bank.

Ke, Lanjun 柯兰君 and Li, Hanlin 李汉林 (eds) *Dushi li de cunmin. Zhongguo da chengshi de liudong renkou* 都市里的村民。中国大城市的流动人口 [Villagers in the city. Rural migrants in Chinese metropolises], Beijing: China Central Translation Publishing House.

Knight, John and Song, Lina (2005) *Towards a Labour Market in China*, Oxford: Oxford University Press.

Krzeslo, Estelle (2003) "Is there an area of employment with 'social risk'? Synthesis of a European research on the deterioration of the conditions of employment in six European countries," paper presented to the Shanghai Conference on Em-ployment, Social Cohesion and Globalization, September 11-13. Online. Available HTTP: <http://www1.msh-paris.fr/reseauemploi/Shanghai/EstelleShangha.../EstelleShanghaiEN1.htm>, accessed 9 July 2005.

Li, Peilin 李培林; Zhang, Yi 张翼; Zhao, Yandong 赵延东 (2000) *Jiuye yu zhidu bianqian. Liang ge teshu qunti de jinzhi guocheng* 就业与制度变迁。两个特殊群体的求职过程 [Job searching, employment and institutional change], Hangzhou: Zhejiang People's Press.

Li, Peilin (1999) "Social network of rural-urban labor migration and social mobility in China," in Chinese Academy of Social Sciences (eds) (1999) *Current Trends and Thoughts. Perspectives in Some Fields of China's Social Sciences*. Foreign Affairs Bureau, Chinese Academy of Social Sciences: Social Sciences Documentation Publishing House: pp. 159-176.

Li, Minghuan (2004) *Labour Brokerage in China Today: Formal and Informal Dimensions*. Duisburg Working Papers on East Asian Studies, February 2004.

Li, Qiang (2000) "Occupational mobility of rural workers in Chinese cities," in *Social Sciences in China*, Vol. 21, No.4 (Winter), pp. 28-37.

Liu, Qiming and Kam, Wing Chan (1999) "Rural-urban labor migration process in China: job search, wage determinants and occupational attainment," CSDE (Center for Studies in Demography and Ecology) Working Paper No 99-16, University of Washington.

Mallee, Hein (1997) *The Expanded Family: Rural Labour Circulation in Reform China*, PhD Thesis, Leiden.

Schmid, Günther (2004) "Risikomanagement am Arbeitsmarkt: die Karriere eines Begriffs," in Günther Schmid; Markus Gangl; Peter Kupka (eds) *Arbeits-marktpolitik und Strukturwandel: Empirische Analysen*, Nürnberg: IAB – Institut für Arbeitsmarkt und Berufsforschung der Bundesagentur für Arbeit, pp. 3-18.

Wang, Chunguang 王春光 (2003) "Xin shengdai nongcun laodong renkou de waichu dongyin yu xingwei xuanze" 新生代农村流动人口的外出动因与行为选择 [Motivation to work outside and options of the new generation of rural mi-grants]，in Li, Peilin 李培林 (ed)

Nongmingong. Zhongguo jincheng nongmin-gong de jingji shehui fenxi 农民工。中国进城农民工的经济社会分析[Peasant workers. Socioeconomic analysis of peasant workers in Chinese cities] Beijing: Social Sciences Academic Press, pp. 196-205.

Xin, Meng (2000) *Labour Market Reform in China*, Cambridge: Cambridge Uni-versity Press.

Zhao, Shukai (2000) "Organizational characteristics of rural labor mobility in China," in Loraine A. West and Zhao Yaohui (eds) *Rural Labor Flows in China,* University of California: Berkeley, pp. 231-250.

The Myth of Entrepreneurship – Migrant Returnees between Urban and Rural Labour Markets

Heike Schmidbauer

Introduction

Internationally, the role of migration and return migration in rural development and poverty reduction is complex and much debated. While supporters of neoclassical or modernization theory claim that rural labour mobility is instrumental in developing source communities (through financial and human capital transfer, new investment, infusion of "modern" values and ideas), the structuralist school tends to highlight negative effects such as the "brain drain," increasing interregional inequality, and growing poverty in areas of origin (Ammassari/Black 2001).

In China, the preponderant attention focused on receiving areas has quickly resulted in a closer examination of the *sending regions* as the places of origin of this massive outflow. The Chinese government is certainly aware of the enormous potential of migration, not only for developing urban areas but also for transforming and "modernizing" rural China. At present, however, there is only scant understanding of the impact of large-scale return migration on places of origin (Zhao 2001; Murphy 2002).

This also holds true for the role models of enterprising peasants who head homewards, after several years of working in urban China, to invest and establish businesses, and thus contribute towards rural urbanization, industrialization, and the diversification of rural labour markets. In the mid-1990s, these pioneers began to be lauded as "phoenixes returning home to their nests" (*feng huan wo* 凤还窝), and so-called "stars of entrepreneurship" (*chuangye zhi xing* 创业之星) received widespread attention (e.g. Wang/Deng 1999; Chen 1996; Lin 2004).

My aim, in this paper, is to debate the "myth of entrepreneurship" (*chuangye shenhua* 创业神话) that still permeates discussions on return migration and development.[1] First of all, I will present the mainstream discourse and the general approaches of central and local governments. Then I will give an overview of the actual extent and composition of return flows and the main reasons for return, before looking at the volumes and special characteristics of returnee entrepreneurs as well as the institutional and structural barriers they are facing. In the last section, there will be a brief discussion of the implications of these findings for future policy.

---

[1] By using the term "myth of entrepreneurship," I follow Bai/Song et al. 2002: 12. For very positive assessments of the role of returnee entrepreneurship, see especially Murphy 2002, Ma 2002, Chen 1996, or Wang/Deng 1999.

Official discourses and initiatives – encouraging the "phoenixes to return to their nests"

When substantial return flows were recognized for the first time in the mid-1990s, general expectations were high that returned migrants would act as the motor of economic growth in the Chinese countryside. Articles in newspapers and academic journals praised migrant entrepreneurs as central agents of rural modernization and development, and speculation was rife about a large-scale transfer of capital, technology, modern management techniques, and talent. Commentators predicted an extensive "brain re-gain" as a result of skilled migrants going back to their homes to establish prospering business ventures or factories, and thus helping to expand township and village enterprises or TVEs (*xiangzhen qiye* 乡镇企业), absorb rural surplus labour, speed up the process of urbanization, establish links with developed coastal regions, and raise social welfare funds (e.g. Chen 1996; Zhang/Yang 1996; Wang/Deng 1999; Huang 1999). Often rather sketchy in style, these articles reported impressive success stories in regions as diverse as Fuyang District in Anhui (Zhang/Yang 1996), Huantai County in Shandong ("Nongmin liudong yu xiangcun fazhan" ketizu 1999), or Huaian City in north Jiangsu (Chen 1996).

Returnee entrepreneurship was actively encouraged at all levels of the state hierarchy. From 1994 onwards, national "Stars of Entrepreneurship" forums have been held on a bi-annual basis to identify outstanding achievers among the new social category of returning migrants. At the Fifth National People's Congress, even Li Peng, the Premier at that time, stated that experienced and skilled migrants should be encouraged to return and start new businesses and thus to contribute towards the overall objective of alleviating poverty in underdeveloped areas (Murphy 2000: 237).

Major labour-exporting provinces such as Anhui and Sichuan were not only pioneers in establishing representative offices for their migrant workers in destination areas, they were also very active in expanding their services and in locating and trying to lure back promising migrants. In some regions, at least, state actors at the local level took innovative steps to persuade migrants to "return to their roots" and create businesses. Sponsorship of various "bring back projects" (*huiyin gongcheng* 回引工程), extensive publicity campaigns, coordination of training, migration and return, preferential tax treatment and simplification of administrative procedures, building of infrastructure, help with land acquisition, information and credit, better access to small rural towns and county towns, and even integration into the local political system were among the various measures taken to entice migrant talent to return (Murphy 2000: 236-240, 2002: 124-195; Bai/Song et al. 2002: 5-9, 351-358; Wang/Deng 1999: 598-604).

In short, central and local governments in the vast rural hinterland viewed return migration and the promotion of returnee entrepreneurship as a viable and low-cost alternative to a continuing rural exodus with its manifold social, economic, and administrative problems for China's already overburdened cities. The primary fundamental question, however, is: who actually returned, and why?

Volumes of return flows, demographic characteristics, and reasons for return

As it is calculated that by the year 2000 almost 20 per cent of the rural labour force were working as migrants (de Brauw/Rozelle 2003: 9), the potential reverse stream to the villages of origin is certainly having immense consequences for the development of rural China. According to a rough official estimate, approximately one third of migrant workers have returned to their homes since 1995 (Murphy 2002: 2). A more precise estimate is almost impossible, because quantifying return migration is an even thornier issue than calculating out-migration. And it is extremely difficult to ascertain whether a person is returning permanently or just for the time being.

Many authors claim that the bulk of the so-called "workers-turned-peasants" (*nongmingong* 农民工) follows the patterns of circular or seasonal migration and that the majority of these will thus finally return to their home regions after a few years. Contrary to these predictions, some recent studies maintain that increasing numbers are not willing to go home at all (Tan 2004: 218; Wang 2003: 165). Their ties to the land become weaker, evidenced by the fact that returnees do not go back to their original home villages, but settle down in nearby county towns or small rural towns where they become involved in non-agricultural ventures (Murphy 2002: 126; Zhang 2005: 60).[2]

Compared with earlier migration phases, there is a clear tendency to stay as long as possible in urban China (e.g. Li 2003: 146). In addition, an ever increasing proportion of married farmers and even whole families choose to leave their villages (Zhou et al. 2002: 73; Woon 1999: 489). And finally, the older generation is much more eager to head homewards than the younger generation which is vehemently opposed to the drudgery of farm work. There are indications that an entirely new generation of migrant workers, better educated and much more demanding than the pioneers of the 1980s, is on its way to China's urban areas (Wang 2003: 162).

On the whole, the few existing large-scale studies on return migration conclude that it is currently rather limited. The most comprehensive study to date, the Sichuan and Anhui Survey of 5,484 households by the Research Center for the Rural

---

[2] Gender-specific differences should be stressed here. Rural women normally leave their home villages upon marriage, thus unmarried migrant women may return "home" for a very short period of time only before moving to the domiciles of their spouses. All are eager to "marry up" into more prosperous villages or regions, and some even dream of finding an urban husband. For the specific marriage problems of migrant women, see Schmidbauer 2003: 52-55. For an overview of the general situation of young female migrants, see Schmidbauer 2001.

Economy under the Ministry of Agriculture, found that the number of returnees made up only 6.3 per cent of the total rural labour force and 28.5 per cent of the current and former migrants (Bai/Song et al. 2002: 15). Another study of 824 households in six provinces showed that only 30.4 per cent of all migrants who started to migrate before 1996 had returned by the end of 1998. Return migration has evidently increased in recent years, but so has out-migration (Zhao 2001: 4). In all studies, the actual rate of return varied greatly from county to county and even from village to village – returnees comprising from two per cent of the total labour force up to more than 30 per cent of the total migrant labour (Bai/Song et al. 2002: 15; Zhao 2001: 4; Ma 2002: 1770).

With regard to *demographic characteristics*, the prototypical returnee seems to be more often female than male; to be older than current migrants and slightly younger than non-migrants, to average 37 years in age, to have an above-average educational level (junior high school), and to be married. The mean duration of absence from the home village varies in different surveys between 2.9 years and 5.2 years (Bai/Song et al. 2002: 26; Zhao 2001: 4; Ma 2002: 1770). Not surprisingly, the propensity for return is higher in villages where non-farm employment is available. In general, the likelihood that former migrants will work outside agriculture might be greater than it is for non-migrants, nevertheless most returnees go back to cultivate their family land. This holds especially true for regions where migrant labour is concentrated in destination areas in specific sectors such as coal mining, because acquired skills are not transferable after return (Zhang 2003: 109).[3] In the Anhui and Sichuan Survey, it was found that 11.2 per cent of returned migrants worked as labourers, 1.6 per cent undertook large-scale specialized farming, and 2.7 per cent were engaged in non-agricultural businesses (1.4 per cent in retail, 0.6 per cent in services, 0.3 per cent in transport). Only a tiny minority of 0.3 per cent were rural entrepreneurs (Bai/He 2003: 156).[4] In other studies, the percentage of rural entrepreneurs is considerably higher with up to 9.1 per cent (Ma 2002: 1770), but this seems to be an exception rather than the rule.

The *reasons* for the flowing back of rural migrant workers to their places of origin are manifold and often a complex mixture of "push" and "pull" factors. A shortage of household labour, marriage, childbirth, the need to care for aging parents or small children, old age, illness and injury, discrimination in urban society and the urban labour market are among the most important reasons for leaving cities and coastal regions. Interestingly, only a small minority seems to come back specifically for the purpose of investment, even if the dream of starting a business and becoming

---

[3] And this holds true also for the millions of (mostly female) assembly-line workers in South China whose chances to learn some skills are limited at best. In her study in the Pearl River Delta, Yuen-Fong Woon (1999: 501) correctly notes: "Not many technological or management skills are transferred to temporary migrants."

[4] The service sector mentioned here comprises mainly restaurants, dance halls, *karaoke* halls, and the like.

a boss (*zuo laoban* 作老板), a small one at least, is a powerful personal driving force while working away from home. Overall, the proportion of those who cite difficulties in finding a city job has tended to increase in recent years whereas the likelihood of return for family reasons has declined (Bai/Song et al. 2002: 29).[5] Factors such as gender, age, marital status, education, family composition and household cycle, work experience, local conditions, or government policies are instrumental in decisions about an eventual return to the countryside.[6] And these factors are also of crucial importance for prospective re-migration, since a very high percentage of returnees, in one study up to 52.8 per cent (Bai/Song et al. 2002: 32), shows a strong desire to venture out again if circumstances permit.

Returnee entrepreneurs and rural development – structural and institutional constraints

As shown above, returnee entrepreneurs constitute a tiny minority of between less than one per cent and 9.1 per cent of the migrant labour force that heads home. It is not possible, at present, to estimate the actual number of peasants who establish businesses after their return as research on this new social group is mostly small-scale and is thus hardly representative statistically (e.g. Zhang/Yang 1996; Lin 2001, 2004; Wang/Deng 1999). It should however be emphasized that the overwhelming majority of these "phoenixes" starts relatively small-scale business ventures in sectors such as services, retail, transport, food processing, or specialized farming. The businesses are predominantly individually owned (*getihu* 个体户), family-based, with limited financial resources, and a small number of employees, if any. Huge, capital-intensive private enterprises (*siying qiye* 私营企业) with large numbers of workers are rare (Bai/Song et al. 2002: 137f.; "Nongmin liudong yu xiangcun fazhan" ketizu 1999: 65). Numerous small-scale businesses are in constant flux – they are set up, they function for a few months, they fail, and their owners are forced back to the cities (Murphy 2000: 236).

A certain consensus has been reached on the key characteristics of *really* successful business creators. They are nearly exclusively male, mostly in their mid-thirties to mid-forties, they have higher levels of formal education (junior high school at least, but many have senior high school certificates), and they have acquired special skills and/or considerable management experience (Bai/Song et al. 2002: 129-143; Zhang/Yang 1996: 43f.; Lin 2001: 65f.; Ma 2002: 1779). As rural "aristocrats," they possess a fair amount of financial as well as social capital, and social capital does play a critical role in overcoming capital and risk constraints in

---

[5] Nevertheless, family needs or marriage remain the key motives of migrant *women*.
[6] It is too early to assess the impact of local government initiatives that try to lure back migrant labour. As far as I know, no systematic research has been done on this question, there are only a few reports on individual returnees who profited from such projects (e.g. Bai/Song et al. 2002: 351-358).

the formation of large-scale businesses, especially in undeveloped areas (Ma 2002: 1781). The widely cited case of Fuyang District in Anhui Province where the entrepreneurial activities of returnees have become a driving force in the local economy is but one example. By the mid-1990s, they had established more than 700 sizable TVEs, using acquired skills, technology, and connections with urban destinations. In Fuyang, as in many other places, the majority of these new factories are labour-intensive branches or processing factories for companies where these returned migrants were previously employed (Ma 2001: 251; Murphy 2000: 234). Unfortunately, this renders them extremely vulnerable to fluctuations in the world market, as their "parent companies" are mainly export-oriented.

For many enterprising returnees, the main hurdle to be overcome is the shortage of capital. Not everybody has earned enough while working away to be able to establish a large business or factory from scratch. Loans from friends and family are the most important sources of investment, given the imperfect credit markets in rural China. Predictably, insufficient credit is cited by 90 per cent of the returnees as a major obstacle to expansion (Murphy 2000: 245). Another quandary is the availability of skilled labour. In some regions, at least, a sort of reverse chain migration has emerged where other ex-migrants are recruited by returned migrant entrepreneurs due to their work experience in urban industry (e.g. Murphy 2002: 161). The trend is to employ skilled co-migrants, not local surplus labour, as enthusiastic commentators on the "wave of business creation" (*chuangyechao* 创业潮) would like to have it. Furthermore, the development of businesses is hampered by the backward infrastructure, inadequate transport systems, shortage of market information, and lack of reliable energy and raw material supplies. Low productivity, outmoded technology, poor product quality, pollution problems, the reduplication of booming enterprises by newcomers, fierce competition with privileged state-owned or urban companies, and, last but not least, the dominant presence of the local state renders the situation even worse for prospective investors in rural China.

The sponsorship of the local state described in section one is, at best, a mixed blessing. Fiscal reforms and political decentralization have placed increasing pressure on local governments to raise their own funds for social welfare expenditure and administrative wages, causing cadres to act as revenue maximizers. It was found that in Jiangxi Province, for example, large signs were posted outside sizable migrant returnee enterprises in order to protect them against the arbitrary fines, fees, and levies imposed by local cadres (Murphy 2000: 244). Capable business owners are seen as veritable "cash cows," keen and able to finance road construction, offer free dining and entertainment, and donate to much-neglected areas such as school building. "Getting eggs by killing the chicken" is a term often used by entrepreneurs to describe such claims (Ma 2002: 1782). Certainly, it is not the greediness of corrupt officials, striving only to advance their careers, that brings about hardship; it is, rather, a structural problem – given the present situation in rural China where many cadres are at a loss to find new avenues for economic development and ways of filling empty tax coffers in order to comply with directives from higher levels.

Policy implications

Despite quite successful examples in several regions, the overall numbers of returnee entrepreneurs whose activities have a measurable socio-economic impact on their home communities is much too small for reliance to be placed entirely on a strategy of promoting return migration and business creation. The nature of business opportunities varies enormously across China, and the famous "Wenzhou model" where thousands and thousands of former migrants transformed their home region into a booming development zone is hard to replicate (Ma 2001: 251).

This is not to say that returnee entrepreneurship has no potential at all with regard to the overriding goal of rural development in regions where conditions, at least, allow for that but structural and institutional obstacles are currently impeding progress. The vigorous support of the local state at all levels (village or *cun* 村, township or *xiang* 乡, county or *xian* 县) for enterprising returnees is certainly essential, but cooperation between different government levels, vertically as well as horizontally, is often shaky at best. The dilemma is exemplified by the unwillingness of township governments to consent to a physical relocation of larger firms to the county seat where economic conditions are much better, because they fear to loose control over scarce resources and their most precious "cash cows" (e.g. Murphy 2000: 242). Unfortunately, decentralization has weakened the power of the central state to negotiate conflicting local interests. To prevent excessive claims by local state agencies on businesses formed by returned migrants, reliable policy mechanisms have to be enacted (Ma 2002: 1782). Furthermore, current ownership structure and the resulting privileges have placed a high percentage of the so-called "phoenixes" at a distinct disadvantage. Although discrimination against the private sector has diminished in recent years, state-owned or collective enterprises in rural areas still have much better access to valuable resources such as land, energy, raw materials, marketing and information channels.

Reform of the rural credit market is another field of utmost importance, since the shortage of credit is the most pressing problem for many returnees. In rapidly developing coastal and suburban areas around growing cities, farmers have access to formal lending institutions, but this is not the case in more remote and undeveloped locations (de Brauw/Rozelle 2003: 3). Dependent as they are, for the most part, on small informal loans, returnees have difficulties in expanding their businesses, paying wages, or investing in new machinery. In view of the fact that most returned migrants are small-scale business owners, it could be useful to link business formation more directly to anti-poverty schemes as already practiced effectively in several areas (e.g. Murphy 2002: 185).

On the whole, rural fiscal and policy reforms, state sponsorship of migrant entrepreneurs, assistance in small-scale business formation, opening of small rural towns, and expansion of township and village enterprises (TVEs) are not sufficient to stop massive labour outflow. In the 1980s, the key rural development strategy to retain peasant labour under the slogan "leaving the land, but not the village; entering the factory, but not the city" (*litu bu lixiang, jinchang bu jincheng* 离土不离乡, 进厂不进城) was only temporarily successful as the development of TVEs soon began to spiral downwards, a trend which became even more marked in the 1990s. The capacity of the rural secondary sector, not to speak of the underdeveloped rural tertiary sector, to absorb the future mass of surplus labour is obviously limited (Nongyebu ketizu 2000: 8).[7]

This is why a comprehensive two-way approach appears to be much more promising. As migrant workers will continue to leave their home communities in search for jobs and a better life in urban China, there is no alternative to continuing with *hukou* (户口) reforms. Cities have to design policies giving due recognition to the fact that peasants will stay for even longer periods of time. Part of this migrant labour pool has to be integrated more completely and *long-term* into urban society where local conditions will allow this. With regard to the return flows to the countryside, the skill levels and the entrepreneurial acumen of migrants at urban destinations have to be enhanced in order to facilitate a real "brain re-gain" for rural areas. The provision of low-cost training programmes before, during, and after migration and more opportunities to work in skilled and managerial positions are instrumental in increasing the competitiveness of rural migrants in rural *and* urban labour markets (Ma 2002: 1781f.).

Conclusion

At present, return migration is on a limited scale only, and the prospect of re-migration by huge numbers of returned migrant workers looms large. Overly optimistic, many observers proclaimed that the "tide of peasant workers" (*mingongchao* 民工潮) would be followed by a corresponding "tide of business creation" (*chuangyechao* 创业潮) in rural China. In many regions, this wave has not yet materialized and perhaps it is time to re-evaluate the "myth of entrepreneurship" (*chuangye shenhua* 创业神话). The role model of returning "phoenixes" might be appealing for migrant youth because this seems to offer opportunities for social mobility on their home soil; for the vast majority, however, this will not be a viable option in the near future. So the exodus from the countryside will continue, and the new generation of so-called "working sisters" (*dagongmei* 打工妹) and "working sons" (*dagongzai* 打工仔) is likely to be much more ambitious than their predecessors were in the 1980s.

In response to these developments, the Chinese government has shown an unprecedented determination in recent years to tackle not only the notorious "three

---

[7] This is not to deny the vital role played by rural industry in generating new employment opportunities for substantial numbers of surplus labourers in agriculture nor the importance of TVEs for migrant returnees and the interrelationship between an expansion of the rural secondary sector and migration.

rural problems" (*san nong wenti* 三农问题), i.e., problems encompassing the rural economy, rural areas, and rural people, by pushing forward various tax and price reforms. The central state has also gradually relaxed the household registration system (*hukou zhidu* 户口制度) and given the legal rights (labour protection, first experiments with social security schemes, expansion of services, better access to health care and education) of rural migrant workers in cities and special economic zones a prominent position on the political agenda. It remains to be seen whether this more integrative approach to the bifurcation of Chinese society into rural and urban segments yields results that make the daunting task of building a "relatively well-off society" (*xiaokang shehui* 小康社会) for *all* citizens much easier.

References

Ammassari, Savina and Black, Richard (2001) "Harnessing the potential of migration and return to promote development: applying concepts to West Africa," Sussex Migration Working Papers 3, Sussex Centre for Migration Research, July. Online. Available HTTP: <http://www.gapresearch.org/production/migration.html> (accessed: 24 October 2004).

Bai, Nansheng 白南生 and He Yupeng 何宇鹏 (2003) "Huixiang, haishi jincheng? Zhongguo nongmin waichu laodongli huiliu yanjiu" 回乡，还是进城？中国农民外出劳动力回流研究 [Back to the village or out to the city? A study of rural-urban return migration in China], in Li Peilin 李培林 (ed) *Nongmingong: Zhongguo jincheng nongmingong de jingji shehui fenxi*农民工：中国进城农民工的经济社会分析[Peasant workers: a socio-economic analysis of China's peasant workers in the cities], Beijing: Shehui kexue wenxian chubanshe, pp. 4-30.

Bai, Nansheng 白南生 and Song Hongyuan 宋洪远 et al. (eds) (2002) *Huixiang haishi jincheng? Zhongguo nongcun waichu laodongli huiliu yanjiu* 回乡，还是进城？中国农村外出劳动力回流研究 [Back to the village or out to the city? A study of rural-urban return migration in China], Beijing: Zhongguo caizheng jingji chubanshe.

Chen, Ru 陈如 (1996) "Dangqian qingnian nongmin huiliu xianxiang tanxi" 当前青年农民回流现象探析 [Discussion of the current phenomenon of young peasants' return flow], in *Nongye jingji wenti* 农业经济问题 [Problems in Agricultural Economy], 10, pp. 26-30.

de Brauw, Alan and Rozelle, Scott (2003) "Migration and household investment in rural China," Department of Economics Working Papers 200, Williams College, December. Online. Available HTTP: <http://www.williams.edu/Economics/wp/debrauwmiginv_jce_initial.pdf> (accessed: 24 October 2004).

Huang, Yuguo 黄余国 (1999) "Guanyu huiliu nongmingong wenti de yanjiu" 关于回流农民工问题的研究 [Research on the problem regarding the return flow of peasant workers], in *Huadong jiaotong daxue xuebao* 华东交通大学学报 [Journal of East China Jiaotong University], 16/4, pp. 94-97.

Li, Peilin 李培林 (2003) "Social Network of Rural Migrants in China," in *Social Sciences in China*, 24/4, pp. 138-148.

Lin, Fei 林斐 (2004) "Dui 90 niandai huiliu nongcun laodongli chuangye xingwei de shizheng yanjiu" 对90年代回流农村劳动力创业行为的实证研究 [Positive research on the entrepreneurial behaviour of the returning rural labor force in the 90s], in *Renkou yu jingji* 人口与经济 [Population and Economics], 2, pp. 50-54.

Lin, Fei 林斐 (2001) "Dui baiming 'dagong' huixiang chuangye nongmin de wenjuan diaocha ji zonghe fenxi" 对百名'打工'回乡创业农民的问卷调查及综合分析 [A survey and summarized analysis of one hundred returned peasant entrepreneurs], in *Jianghuai luntan* 江淮论坛 [Jiang-Huai Forum], 4, pp. 64-67.

Ma, Zhongdong (2002) "Social-capital mobilization and income returns to entrepreneurship: the case of return migration in rural China," in *Environment and Planning,* A34, pp. 1763-1784.

Ma, Zhongdong (2001) "Urban labour-force experience as a determinant of rural occupation change: evidence from recent urban-rural return migration in China," in *Environment and Planning,* A33, pp. 237-255.

Murphy, Rachel (2002) *How Migrant Labor Is Changing Rural China.* Cambridge: Cambridge University Press.

Murphy, Rachel (2000) "Return migration, entrepreneurship and local state cor-poratism in rural China: the experience of two counties in South Jiangxi," in *Journal of Contemporary China,* 9/24, pp. 231-247.

"Nongmin liudong yu xiangcun fazhan" ketizu "农民流动与乡村发展" 课题组 [Working group on "peasant migration and rural development"] (1999) "Nongmingong huiliu yu xiangcun fazhan: Dui Shandongsheng Huantaixian 10 cun 737 ming huixiang nongmingong de diaocha" 农民工回流与乡村发展：对山东省桓台县10村737名回乡农民工的调查 [The peasant workers' return flow and rural development: yurvey on 737 returned peasant workers in 10 villages in Huantai County, Shandong Province], in *Zhongguo nongcun jingji* 中国农村经济 [China's Rural Economy], 10, pp. 63-67.

Nongyebu ketizu 农业部课题组 [Working group of the ministry of agriculture] (2000) "21 shiji chuqi woguo nongcun jiuye ji shengyu laodongli liyong wenti yanjiu" 21世纪初期我国农村就业及剩余劳动力利用问题研究 [Research on China's rural employment problem and the usage of surplus labour at the beginning of the 21st Century], in *Zhongguo nongcun jingji* 中国农村经济 [China's Rural Economy], 5, pp. 4-16.

Schmidbauer, Heike (2003) "Living on the fringes: urban experiences of rural migrant women in reform China," in *Berliner China-Hefte,* 25, pp. 44-57.

Schmidbauer, Heike (2001) *Aufbruch aus den Dörfern: Chinesische Migrantinnen zwischen Modernisierung und Marginalisierung (Leaving the Villages: Chinese Migrant Women between Modernization and Marginalization)*, Münster: LIT Verlag.

Tan, Shen 谭深 (2004) "Waichu he huixiang: nongcun laodong nüxing de jingli" 外出和回乡：农村流动女性的经历 [Leaving home and coming back: experiences of rural migrant women], in *Women zai yiqi* 我们在一起 [Together with migrants]. A UNESCO Project for Poverty Reduction: Pairing Art, Research and Action against Poverty. Catalogue, Beijing: UNESCO Office Beijing, pp. 216-221.

Wang, Chunguang (2003) "The social identities of new generations of migrants from China's rural areas," in *Social Sciences in China,* 24/4, pp. 160-167.

Wang, Yuzhao 王郁昭 and Deng Hongxun 邓鸿勋 (eds) (1999) *Nongmin jiuye yu Zhongguo xiandaihua* 农民就业与中国现代化 [Peasant employment and China's modernization]. Chengdu: Sichuan renmin chubanshe.

Woon, Yuen-Fong (1999) "Labor migration in the 1990s: homeward orientation of migrants in the Pearl River Delta region and its implications for interior China," in *Modern China*, 25/4, pp. 475-512.

Zhang, Luwen 张露文 (2005) "Nongmingong huiliu wenti de lilun he anlie fenxi" 农民工回流问题的理论和案例分析 [Theoretical and case study analysis of the problem of peasant workers' return flow], in Zhang Shuguang 张曙光 and Deng Zhenglai 邓正来 (eds) *Zhongguo shehui kexue pinglun 3* 中国社会科学评论 3 [China Social Sciences Critique 3], Beijing: Falü chubanshe, pp. 48-63.

Zhang, Mei (2003) *China's Poor Regions: Rural-Urban Migration, Poverty, Econ-omic Reform, and Urbanisation*, London: RoutledgeCurzon.

Zhang, Shanyu 张善余 and Yang Xiaoyong 杨晓勇 (1996) "'Mingongchao' jiang dailai 'huixiang chuangyechao': Yi Anhuisheng Fuyang diqu wei li" '民工潮' 将带来'回乡创业潮'：以安徽省阜阳地区为例 [The tide of peasant-workers will bring about a wave of return entrepreneurship: the example of Fuyang Dis-trict in Anhui Province], in *Renkou yu jingji* 人口与经济 [Population and Economics], 1, pp. 43-47.

Zhao, Yaohui (2001) "Causes and consequences of return migration: recent evidence from China," CCER Working Paper E2001010, Peking University, Oc-tober, 26pp. Online. Available HTTP: <http://old.ccer.edu.cn> (accessed: 24 October 2004).

Zhou, Weiwen 周伟文; Yan Xiaoping 严晓萍; Liu Zhongyi 刘中一 (eds) (2002) *Shengcun zai bianyuan: Liudong jiating* 生存在边缘：流动家庭 [Existence at the margins: migrant families], Shijiazhuang: Hebei renmin chubanshe.

Labour Services for China's Migrant Workers – New Ideas and Practises

Tan Shen

In recent years, thanks to the state's macro-policies, the problems facing migrant workers and services provided to migrant workers have now become mainstream societal topics. In the past 12 to 24 months, in particular, government at all levels has dedicated public funds to the services of migrant workers. This suggests a considerable shift in government policy, regarding the question of migrant workers. Such a shift has offered a wealth of opportunities for various forces to enter the field of providing services to migrant workers and safeguarding their rights and interests. In addition, multi-national companies have been greatly involved in the field; a growing number of NGOs targeting migrant labour has emerged and other organizations have put more effort into projects for migrant workers' services.

This article will be largely devoted to a summary and analysis of the development and changes in this field over the past five years, as well as an analysis of the relationships between different forces, with the aim of profiling the driving forces behind the different practitioners involved in offering their services to migrant workers. Meanwhile, suggestions will also be put forward with respect to projects for migrant workers' services.

Government: from administration to services

Since 2003, substantial progress has been made in the state policies on population migration, from eliminating unreasonable restrictions on the migration of migrant workers and creating a favourable employment environment, to supporting and promoting the migration of rural labour forces and facilitating their settling into cities. These are aspects directly related to the state's urbanization strategy, an understanding of the problems facing agriculture, rural areas and peasants, and the employment and rights of migrant workers. The foremost considerations for rural workers included in the fiscal budget of government at all levels are allowances for vocational training, children's education, labour security, and other services, as well as administration. This marks the state's thinking evolution on the issues of population migration and migrant workers, from control to administration and finally to services.

With the dynamics of the state macro-policies, all the related departments under the central government and all local governments (including places of sending and receiving labour forces) have taken action with regard to serving the migrant workers. The Ministry of Labour and Social Security, for example, have launched a nationwide public employment service known as "Spring Wind Action" (*chunfeng xingdong* 春风行动), asking all public employment service institutions in large and medium-sized cities to include migrant workers in the scope of public-welfare service and provide various free employment services and training for migrants entering cities for employment (MOLSS 2005). The Ministry also required all cities to hook up to Hotline 12333 for labour security consulting, with expenses to be borne by local labour and social security departments. The Sunshine Project, jointly advocated by six ministries,[1] and the Training Program for Labour Transfer in Poverty-Stricken Areas,[2] advocated by poverty-alleviation departments, enjoy government public financial subsidies, remain under the supervision and management of government at all levels in labour-supply places, and provide training for the rural labour force who intend to leave the countryside and work in cities. The Ministry of Construction has set forth a plan for training five million rural workers in the following five years, aiming for improvement in the quality of construction projects and the level of safe production. The expense of training is shared by government, enterprises, and peasants, and enterprises are requested to draw a training outlay on the basis of 1.5 to 2.5 per cent of the employees' total salaries.[3] The Ministry of Education conducted reforms in vocational and adult education to cater to employment and strengthen short-term training and practical skills training, and the decision was made to provide training for 16 million rural workers each year (*Zhongguo qingnian bao* 25 February 2004). The Ministry of Labour and Social Security took their impetus from the "Sino-US Labour Legal Cooperation Project," which is sponsored by the US Department of Labour and primarily devoted to the services and rights of migrant workers. In close coordination with the International Labour Organization (ILO) (MOLSS 2003),[4] the Ministry of Labour and Social Security will soon carry out the training program, "Start and Improve Your Business,"[5] to benefit peasants working in urban areas, The above-mentioned projects involve international cooperation to some extent and, in my opinion, as

---

[1] The six ministries are: Ministry of Agriculture, Ministry of Finance, Ministry of Labour and Social Security, Ministry of Education, Ministry of Construction, and Ministry of Science and Technology. The Ministry of Agriculture, however, is the major organizer and player of the project, and in local areas the project is mainly implemented by agricultural departments. Further information on the "2003-2010 National Migrant Workers Training Plan" worked out by the six ministries and the "Sunshine Project" (*yangguang gongcheng* 阳光工程) of the Ministry of Agriculture can be found under <http://www.nmpx.gov.cn>, and also see Yang shi guoji [CCTV International] 2004.
[2] The author participated in the prophase investigation and research of the Training Program.
[3] The Ministry of Construction worked out five measures for training 5 million rural workers in five years (see Xinhuanet 2004, Zhongguo xinwen wang 2004a, Wang 2004).
[4] The training service program of the Project was sponsored by The Asia Foundation, and the author took part in the prophase investigation.
[5] Materials about the ILO's "Start and Improve Your Business" (SIYB) programme which in China is run with the Ministry of Labour and Social Security (MOLSS) can be found at the SIYB's Chinese website under <www.siyb.com.cn>. See also the contribution of Andreas Klemmer in this volume.

migrant workers' service has been included in the work of government at all levels, the government's demand for exterior support will increase and the space for international governmental cooperation will expand accordingly.

Projects in labour supply areas

The Sunshine Project, which targets labour supply places, is an example of government action in labour supply areas and relationships between all departments concerned.

In 2003, based on the central government's guideline of offering training for rural labour forces, the General Office of the State Council issued the "2003-2010 National Migrant Workers' Training Plan," as laid out by the six ministries. According to the plan, training programs for the rural labour force comprise three primary training levels: introductory training before labour transfer and employment (namely, Labour Law, general knowledge about working outside the hometown, etc.), short-term vocational and skills training, and re-training for peasants who have been employed in non-agricultural sectors. The Sunshine Project, a short-term vocational and skills training program, is being carried out in phases: 2004 and 2005 encompass the demonstration phase of the project, targeting training for five million peasants in certain areas who intend to work in cities; in the period from 2006 to 2010 the project will be spread nationwide, aimed at 30 million trainees; after 2010 the training of the rural labour force will be included in the national educational system.

In respect of training funds, the Sunshine Project took the lead in conducting vocational and skills programs for the rural labour force before their transfer was supported and sponsored by public finance. In 2004, a total of 250 million RMB from the revenue of the central government and 300 million RMB from local government (funds provided by government in different areas vary) were subsidized to the training program, averaging 100 to 200 RMB per trainee. In the form of organization, an integration of government guidance and market operation has been adopted. This means the government organizes, monitors and administers the program and through public bidding designates some schools as bases for training, employment, and tracing service. At present, trainees mainly enjoy such allowances as "training certificates"[6] and lowered tuition fees.

The Sunshine Project and "training certificates" are both carefully designed and have taken into consideration many factors such as government management, capital usage, training institutions' interests and benefit, and migrant workers'

---

[6] This is a successful experience of Changshan County in Quzhou City, Zhejiang Province, deriving from the "education certificate system" of the United States, which was fundamentally operated thus: establish certain certificates, based on the amount of the government subsidy, and allocate the certificates to beneficiaries in exchange for training of equal values; then the training institutions cash in the collected training certificates with the government.

demands. In order to guarantee that the state financial subsidies would be expended to benefit trainees, the allocated funds exclude office outlay, and the roster of beneficiaries and subsidy amounts are required to be shown to the public. To avoid beneficiaries using subsidies for purposes other than training, the use of training certificates is advocated, rather than the cash being simply handed over to the peasants. To ensure good results, the "order-form training" mode will be adopted.

However, implementation of any comprehensive system is a process. To achieve an ideal result from any system, it should be required that all work and each step in the process is fully carried out and that all players involved in each step shall understand and strictly abide by all requirements of the system. This is not an easy proposition. In many cases, the cause of the unsatisfactory effects of a system lies not only in design, but also in practice. Essentially, systems are instituted and implemented by human beings. Therefore, all problems with systems are actually human problems. For local government, the transition from charging rural workers management fees to providing services is not just a change in their work content, but, more meaningfully, it is also a change in attitude and mode of working. How to effect such a transition in the process actually determines whether the project will achieve the desired goals. Thus, training is recommended for government and project participants at all levels.

Since the state changed its policies towards the rural areas and agricultural workers, local government, especially grassroots government below county level, have been faced with capital difficulties. In view of this alone, the local governments mostly are probably in the need of external support. In addition, a transition from administration to service requires government to make great changes in their mode of working, and to be able to adapt to such a transition and finally achieve their goals, government needs assistance from external experts.

Labour services in labour demand areas

The projects mentioned above are mainly projects based in labour supply areas. Labour projects in the past, however, were mostly carried out in labour demand areas. The migrant status of the migrant workers, however, makes it difficult to trace the effects or results in labour demand areas. Service to migrant workers is virtually human-oriented service. For the migrant workers, working away from their hometowns is a kind of process, where both the starting points and end points are their hometowns. Therefore, projects based in labour supplying areas can be supportive to the entire working process of the farmers and it is comparably easier to obtain support for these from local government. Of course, the best way is to link up the labour supplying and demanding areas. At present, labour-supply activities organized by government and various institutions are adopting the link-up mode.

Whether in labour supplying areas or in the link-up mode, the success of a project will depend upon whether the peasants themselves are supportive. An investigation into labour-supply activities carried out by organizations shows that the working efficiencies of the organizations are usually moderate, due to the fact that peasants generally best believe in and depend on their own social networks and seek help from formal organizations only when they have no other choice. Therefore, how to obtain the peasants' trust remains an important pending issue for such projects. In my perspective, making use of non-government relations, such as personal relationships, as well as farmers' social networks is probably an effective solution. I will discuss this afterwards.

The experience in the government section at the seminar "Service and Innovation: Seminar on Social Policies for Migrant Workers"[7] in 2000 mainly came from labour-demand areas, which are primarily located in the Pearl River Delta. According to the researchers, Guangdong Province, back then, had already stayed ahead of the nation in the management, systemization, standardization, and innovation of the labour market. It was characterized by its transition in managing migrant labourers as social members of local communities or local areas.[8] Such a transition started from the role migrant workers had played in the local economy. The government realized that migrant workers were not a response to the labour-lacking period, but a long-term phenomenon. The influence of migrant workers on local society was not limited to the labour market but was all-inclusive. To some extent, therefore attention was paid to the peasants' social rights and interests besides their rights and interests as labourers. Back then, however, coastal areas were faced with conditions featuring a limitless labour supply and a shortage of capital, and the "territoriality principle" in social administration was only oriented towards local permanent residents. Therefore, the services for migrant workers were mainly subject to the goals of economic development and social stability.

In recent years, labour-demand areas have put in place measures and service projects beneficial to migrant workers. Through my investigations, I have discovered that these measures and service projects mainly include constructing residential quarters for the migrant population; establishing labour rights maintenance centers, amusement centers, and specialized service centers; hooking up government hotlines; giving migrant workers the right to stand for election as candidates of the National People's Congress (NPC) delegates and for advanced posts; rewarding outstanding rural workers with permanent residence; and reducing or exempting migrant workers' children from tuition.

---

[7] The seminar was organized by Tsinghua University's Research Center for Contemporary China and the Development Research Center of Guangdong Provincial Government and funded by The Asia Foundation. Invited to the symposium were government officials from the Ministry of Labour and Social Security, the Ministry of Public Security, related departments of Guangdong Province, and related department of six cities in the Pearl River Delta; NGOs from Beijing and the provinces of Henan, Sichuan, and Guangdong; domestic researchers; representatives from Guangdong-based enterprises; as well as representatives from some international organizations and multi-national companics.

[8] Here, I refer to the speech by Prof. Wang Hansheng at the seminar.

Beginning in 2004, the central government effected a series of orders abolishing irrational charges, abolishing restrictive policies, establishing a social insurance and social security system that covers the migrant population, and including the management and services for the migrant population within the local government' financial budgets. Whether in finance or management mode, these are great challenges which are facing the governments of labour demand areas. Although the elementary prerequisites of local government' attitudes towards migrant population are still maintaining the competitiveness of the local economy and the stability of society, the concept of "putting people first" has gradually found its way into the thoughts of labour-demand-area governments, as is shown in the following example:

The 16th National Congress of the Communist Party of China put forward a plan to balance the urban and rural economy, and one of the key points in this plan is the relationship between rural migrant workers and local societies. In respect to this issue, I once carried out an investigation. According to the survey, the so-called migrant workers can be divided into three categories. One of the categories is rural workers in the vicinity of cities and towns. Belonging to the permanent residents of the cities/towns, this group is more easily accepted by local society and thus regarded as "new citizens" (*xin shimin* 新市民). Another category is composed of migrant farmers within the province. In most of the developed provinces, "geared assistance and support" is practiced between developed and undeveloped areas. Thanks to the coordination of provincial governments, these migrants usually enjoy priority in being accepted by the labour-demand areas and viewed as "new social members" (*xin de shehui chengyuan* 新的社会成员). The third category is devoted to trans-provincial migrant workers. In labour-demand cities, they exist simply in the capacity of labour, subject to separate management as the "outside population" in the local government plans. In view of this, it would seem to be still too early at the moment to simply propose a "fusion." The more important things right now should be how rural workers can gain from government the protection of their fundamental rights and interests and more impartial, more humanized policies and how various welfare systems and service measures can be further promoted.

In view of this, a transition of labour-demand area government is mainly attributed to the impetus of the central government's macro-policies. The voice for a "migrant worker shortage," which has grown louder each passing day since last year, put forward, from a market perspective, the issue of migrant workers' rights and interests in labour-demand areas. All this has provided a broader space for the support of migrant workers and the legalization of services provided to them. In terms of exterior support, there is a difference between labour supplying areas and labour demanding areas. In terms of capital, labour-demand areas do not have dynamics as intense as labour supply areas in foreign cooperation. Because the direct influence of the rights-and-interests issues of rural workers to labour-demand areas is complicated, local government would find it difficult to construct a favorable investment environment while giving attention to both labour cost and political image, so as to maintain the competitiveness of the local economy. Nor is it an easy proposition to make non-government and exterior powers provide migrant workers with supporting services that government is unable to take into account without impacting on social stability. Cooperation with half-official non-government organizations, however, will greatly increase the legitimation of the supporting projects. And for the projects solely undertaken by non-government organizations, timely communications with the administrative department concerned will equally increase the trust of the government, thus reducing unnecessary misunderstandings.

Labour services provided by non-government organizations (NGO)

During the last decade, non-government organizations (NGOs) in China have witnessed a rapid development. By the end of 2002, a total of 142,000 mass organizations and 124,000 non-state non-profit enterprises had been established across the country (Zhongguo xinwen wang 2004b), but according to researchers' estimation, plus a large number of self-governing social organizations, the existing NGOs are ten times the figure actually registered (Xie 2004).

The appearance and development of NGOs are undoubtedly an important historical and social phenomenon in China which has attracted attention from all sides. The study of NGOs has found its way into the important research agenda of universities, scientific research institutes, and government, and has even become a growth point of theoretical research. So far, the study has been mainly concentrated on the relations between NGOs and government – the legal and policy environments of NGOs, government's administration of NGOs, the influence of NGOs upon government decisions and policies; relations between the state (state institutions, or the government) and society – the growth of civil society and civil spirit, the credibility and justness of NGOs; the relations between media and NGO; the capacity building of NGOs; etc.

This article is mainly devoted to an analysis of the NGOs committed to working in the field of migrant workers' services. What we will discuss is how to offer migrants the services they need as much as possible within the framework of the existing system.

In recent years, labour unions, youth leagues, and women's federations have carried out some work in the field of migrant workers' services. Thanks to the leadership of the CYL Central Committee, for example, the Community Training Project for Young Migrant Workers (1997-2000) (Without author: n.d.), the Development Project for Young Migrant Workers (2001) (Renmin ribao 2001), the "Peaceful Working" Campaign for Migrant Workers (2000) (Zhong qing lian 2000), and Project Hope's educational fund-raising campaign for the children of migrant workers were launched across the nation. The All-China Federation of Trade Unions set up the "12351" Hotline for assistance on workers' rights (Li 2004). The All-China Women's Federation is currently carrying out the training, policy, information, and rights maintenance services for the transferred employment of rural women

(Jiangsu nongye xinxi wang 2004), and is about to establish a website for the transfer of rural women labourers.

At the local and grassroots levels, such projects as labour supply, rights maintenance, and labour service have also been carried out. The "bi-directional rights maintenance" experience of the Labour Union of Xinyang City, Henan Province, was a good attempt by a labour-supply area to maintain the rights of migrant workers. The Women's Federation of Chifeng City, Inner Mongolia, has also gained experience in labour training, supply, and service. At present, because of an increasing demand for nursemaids, the labour transfer of rural women by women's federations has become more and more active. According to the superior requirements, both the labour supplying and demanding areas are obligated to maintain the legal rights and interests of the migrant women. Therefore, theoretically, service should be offered along with the supply of labour. Thanks to the support of charity groups, the Women's Federation of Chifeng has done a great job in this respect. Another example is the Asia Foundation, which has launched a labour service project in Guangdong Province, in cooperation with women's federations and labour unions.

The following example of Jintang County, Sichuan Province, can help explain how the Chinese women's association can serve the migrants and how they offer the services: the project in Jintang County consists of several programs, of which the latest two were funded by the Asia Foundation – one is to pay a visit to the migrant workers who returned home due to injuries suffered on the job and the other is a supporting campaign for migrant workers carried out at railway stations and on coaches. These two programs have both been successful, which should be largely credited to the county's comparatively "strong" women's federation. One of the reasons for their saying that the federation is "strong" is because it has put much effort into this project. Based on other projects in previous years, the women's federation of the county has viewed labour services as one of their routine works. Another reason is that through communications, the capable cadres of the federation have won the support and participation of leaders and institutions at all levels in the county. They have also attracted young cadres of different institutions to act as volunteers, who later mobilized another group of volunteers among railway station workers and bus drivers. The current service projects are all carried through by using volunteers. Although the projects are not perfect and their results are not steady, it is indisputable that they have become a process of social mobilization, during which the women's federation gave a full play to its advantage and informally mobilized and connected resources in and outside system. As long as this exploration continues, we will gain more experiences.

Although the government is not the only player, it remains the major player, recognized by the system. In addition, the interactions among social, domestic, and international acceptance and recognition will also influence the government's attitude. In order to attain a higher level of legitimacy, civil NGOs have made painstaking efforts, including dialogues and cooperation with all circles of society, especially the government. For instance, at the 2000 conference (as mentioned at the beginning of this article), Chinese active civil NGOs for labour services conducted effective dialogues with the governments at different levels in Guangdong Province. Successful meetings like these have been numerous in recent years (Zhan/Han 2004).[9] At present, it is common for the government to invite NGOs to participate in government activities, and vice versa.

Generally speaking, the government has projected a supportive attitude towards civil organizations' work in public-welfare and has also recognized and worked in cooperation with NGOs which are committed to environmental protection. Since the SARS epidemic in 2003, the government has become increasingly aware of the positive effect of civil forces, including NGOs, in public issues. The environment for NGOs has been loosened, and the bottom line for a loose environment is "political correctness." This means "no violation," or "playing a constructive role" to express it more positively (see also Gao 2005). The bottom line, however, is controlled by certain departments and people, based on common understandings, and is therefore not so specific and clear. Compared with the abovementioned fields, the labour issue is a more sensitive field, involving the interests of a larger number of groups. NGOs therefore need to be clear and make sure that all activities are carried out within a legal framework.

References

Gao, Bingzhong 高丙中 (2005) "Shehui tuanti de hefaxing wenti" 社会团体的合法性问题 [The legitimacy issues of social groups], in Shehiuxue renleixue Zhongguo wang 社会学人类学中国网 [China network on sociology and anthropology], Beijing daxue Zhongguo shehui yu fazhan yanjiu zhongxin 北京大学中国社会与发展研究中心 [The center for sociological research and development studies of China], 30 November 2005. Online. Available HTTP: <http://www.sachina.edu.cn/Htmldata/article/2005/11/666.html> (accessed 21 January 2006).

Gongyi shibao 公益时报 [Public Welfare Times] (2004) "Nongmingong weiquan, yikao ziji de zuzhi" 农民工维权，依靠自己的组织[Rural workers' rights maintenance depends on their own organizations], in *Gongyi Shibao* 公益时报 [Public Welfare Times], 23 June 2004.

Jiangsu nongye xinxi wang 江苏农业信息网 (2004) "Quanguo nongcun funü zhuanyi jiuye xianchang peixunhui zai ning zhaokai" 全国农村妇女转移就业现场培训会在宁召开

---

[9] The Beijing-based "Home of Migrant Women," for example, held symposiums on the rights and interests of migrant women in 1999, 2001, 2003, and 2004, and each of the symposiums was attended by officials from the governmental departments concerned. In June 2004, The Beijing Collaborators Cultural Communications Center and the State Administration for Safe Production Supervision jointly held the First Symposium on the Vocational Safety and Health of Rural Workers, which achieved a success and was later described by the media as a "cooperation of a civil organization, a governmental institution, and a medium" (Gongyi Shibao 2004).

[The training program for the transfer and employment of rural women held in Nanjing], in *Jiangsu nongye xinxi wang* 江苏农业信息网 [Jiangsu agricultural information network], 29 September 2004. Online. Available HTTP: <http://news.aweb.com.cn/2004/9/29/8530547.htm> (accessed 21 January 2006).

Li, Honghong 李江泓 (2004) "Quanguo gonghui '12351' zhigong weiquan rexian jiang kaitong" 全国工会'12351'职工维权热线将开通 [The All-China Federation of Trade Union to open '12315' hotline for assistance on workers' rights], in *Anhuinews.com*, 13 October 2004. Online. Available HTTP: <http://law.anhuinews.com/system/2004/10/13/001014296.shtml> (accessed 21 January 2006).

MOLSS [Ministry of Labour and Social Security] (2003) "Zhong Mei laodong falü xiangmu shu qianshu" 中美劳动法律项目书签署 [The signing of the agreement on China-US Labour Legal Cooperation Project] Online. Available HTTP: <http://www.molss.gov.cn/news/2003/1118.htm> (accessed 12 December 2005).

MOLSS [Ministry of Labour and Social Security] (2005) "Laodong baozhang bu zai quanguo kaizhan 'chunfeng xingdong' wanshan nongmingong jiuye fuwu" 劳动保障部在全国开展'春风行动'完善农民工就业服务 [The Ministry of Labour and Social Security carries out the nationwide campaign, 'Spring Wind Action,' aiming at an improvement of the employment service for migrant workers.] Online. Available HTTP: <http://www.molss.gov.cn/news/2005/0121a.htm> (ac-cessed 12 December 2005).

Renmin Ribao [People's Daily] (2001) "Quanguo 'jiangcheng wuwu qingnian fazhan jihua' jidong" 全国'进城务工青年发展计划'启动 [National 'development project for young migrant workers'], in *Renmin ribao* [People's Daily], 20 July 2001. Online. Available HTTP: <www.people.com.cn/GB/paper464/3823/462757.html> (accessed 21 January 2006).

Wang, Guangshou 汪光焘 (2004) "Yu shi ju jin - kaituo kuangxin - zuohao xinshiqing jianshe rencai gongzuo – zai quanguo jianshe rencai gongzuo huiyi shangde zongjie jianghua" 与时俱进 - 开拓创新 - 做好新时期建设人才工作 - 在全国建设人才工作会议上的总结讲话 [Progressing with every hour – Opening up to new ideas – Complete a new period of building up qualified personnel – Summary speech at the Work Conference on Building Qualified Personnel for the Whole Country], Speech of Wang Guangshou, 29 October 2004. Online. Available HTTP: <http://www.cin.gov.cn/indus/speech/2004111501.htm> (accessed 21 January 2006; *Originally cited* HTTP: <http://www.mochr.com/news/2004-10-26/jinyan/jyjl.asp>.

Without author (n.d.) "Shequ 'qianxiao bai wan' wai lai wugong qingnian peixun jihua" 社区'千校百万'外来务工青年培训计划 [Community training project for young migrant workers]. Online. Available HTTP: <http://www.xjbz.gov.cn/ bztw/gzhd/wlwg.htm> (accessed 21 January 2006).

Xie, Haiding 谢海定 (2004) "Zhongguo renjian zuzhi de hefaxing kunjing" 中国民间组织的合法性困境 [The legitimacy difficulties of Chinese NGOs], in *Faxue yanjiu*, 2004, No. 26(02), pp.17-34. Online. Available HTTP: <http://www.iolaw.org.cn/paper/paper280.asp> *Zhongguo faxue wang* 中国法学网 [China Law Study Network] (accessed 21 January 2006), *Originally cited* HTTP: <http://www.tylf.net/shehui/minjian zuzhi.html>.

Xinhuanet (2004) "Jianshe bu jiang da li kaizhan nongmingong jineng peixun" 建设部将大力开展农民工技能培训 [The Ministry of Construction uses great efforts to develop technical training for migrants]. Online. Available HTTP: <http://news.xinhuanet.com/zhengfu/2004-11/01/content_2162822.htm> (accessed 21 January 2006; *Originally cited HTTP*: <http://sq.cein.gov.cn/home/jskx/news_show.asp?rec_no=4394>.

Yang shi guoji 央视国际 [CCTV International] "'Yangguang gongcheng xia yue qidong' guojia chuxian peixun nongmingong"'阳光工程下月启动' 国家出钱培训农民工 [,The Sunshine Project started last month' the state spends money on the training of migrants]. in *Yang shi guoji* 央视国际 [CCTV International], 18 February 2004. Online. Available HTTP: <http://news.fjii.com/2004/02/18/204664.htm> (accessed 31 March 2004).

Zhongguo xinwen wang 中国新闻网 [China News Network] (2004a) "Jianshe bu weichu wu xiang cuoshi wu nian jiang peixun wu bai wan nongmingong" 建设部推出五项措施5年将培训500万农民工 [The Ministry of Construction worked out five measures for training 5 million rural workers in five years]. Online. Available HTTP: <http://finance.sina.com.cn/g/20041102/14151126336.shtml> (accessed 21 January 2006).

Zhong Qing Lian 中青联 [Chinese Federation of Youth] (2000) "Guanyu zai jincheng wugong renyuan zhong kaizhan 'ping'an dagong' huodong de tongzhe" 关于在进城务工人员中开展"平安打工"活动的通知 [A notification on "peaceful working" campaign for migrant workers], Notification Nr. 58, 2000.

Zhongguo Qingnianbao 中国青年报 [China Youth News] (2004) 25 February 2004.

Zhongguo xinwen wang 中国新闻网 [China News Network] (2004b) "Woguo yi you 26 yu wan ge minjian zuzhi zuoyong huo gongfang chongfen keding" 我国已有26余万个民间组织 作用获官方充分肯定 [China has so far more than 260,000 NGOs, whose effects have been fully recognized by the government], in *Sina.com.cn*, 10 December 2004. Online. Available HTTP: <http://news.sina.com.cn/c/2004-12-10/18214490055s.shtml> (accessed 21 January 2006).

Zhan, Shaohua 占少华 and Han, Jialing 韩嘉玲 (2005) "Zhongguo de nongmingong fei zhengfu zuzhi: jingyan yu tiaozhan" 中国的农民工非政府组织：经验与挑战 [China's non-governmental organizations for migrants: experiences and challenges]. Online. Available HTTP: <http://203.93.24.66/shxw/shzc/t20050624_6321.htm> (accessed via <www.usc.cuhk.edu.hk/wk_wzdetails.asp?id=4282> 21 January 2006).

Rural Migrants in Urban Areas

Family Patterns of Rural Migrants in Urban Areas and Their Migration Choices

Wang Wei

Background

The rural economic reforms in 1978 stimulated the labour market in China. The reforms have given peasants relative autonomy in land cultivation and operation as well as the right to control their own productivity. The two policies allowing peasants to operate and choose jobs freely and to do business in cities generated about 125 million township enterprise workers in rural areas and 80 to 100 million migrant workers in urban areas. The migrant farmers have already become an important component of the urban labour market in China.

It should be noted that there are fundamental differences between migrant workers and urban workers in their working purpose and attitude. It seems that the migrant peasants pay more attention to short term benefits and objectives. A survey has shown that migrants are not pursuing career development and promotions when they go out to work; they are rather more willing to accept boring and hopeless jobs for low pay (Sabel 1982: 101). In other words, the only requirement for the migrant workers is to be able to earn money without considering career development. Such a money-driven employment attitude will hamper the further development of their productivity quality.

One earlier study showed two differences between those workers who were formerly peasants and hereditary urban workers: the former have no interest in their jobs and only work to get a salary; they also despise their work and do not see it as a life-long means of earning a living but only as a temporary situation and a way of acquiring possessions. A good job, for these workers, only means a good opportunity to gain as many benefits as possible, whereas, for people who are psychologically prepared to be workers or have such a development tendency, a good job can be a final goal or a means to obtain a better job. What Max (a case in this study) finally did, is totally contrary to the peasants' psychology: he decided to invest all his money in education and to go to university, which indicated that property was no longer a concern in his life and was replaced by employment. His peasant's mentality changed to a typical worker's mentality with regard to economic issues (Thomas/Znanieski 1984/2000: 50).

When peasants enter the urban labour market, an important issue to consider for the labour market is whether or not they can be changed from peasants into urban workers. And this issue has much to do with whether they are able to migrate to the city. Two processes are involved when peasants migrate to cities: one process is to move away from rural areas and the other is to settle down in cities, so peasants have only completed the first process in their rural-to-urban migration when they move away from rural areas. Further study is required to decide whether they are then willing to settle in their chosen locations.[1] If they cannot settle, they will always have the status of floaters and will finally return to rural areas. In such conditions, they will always remain peasants instead of real workers for the urban labour market. The research on peasants' migration will expand and deepen the research on the labour market.

Many researchers have stressed the social exclusion of migrant workers by a series of urban social institutions with the household registration system at its core. Under such circumstances, migrant peasants will always have the status of floaters and will not settle in cities, let alone become urban residents. "When labour transfer is no longer restricted by systems, the two processes of immigration will be able to be completed simultaneously" (Cai 2001). Cai Fang stressed the social exclusion of peasants but could not explain the fact that quite a lot migrant peasants have been working and living for a long time in the cities and have expressed the desire to stay in the cities for good; some of them have even moved their families from rural areas to the cities.

Earlier research showed that the majority of peasants who went to the cities only wanted to earn some money to send back home and were not prepared to stay in the cities for good (Solinger 1999: 186f.), but a large scale survey in 2001, in Beijing, Wuxi and Zhuhai revealed that 50 per cent of them wanted to stay in the cities where they lived and only 10 per cent of them wanted to go back to where they came from (the place stated on their residence permit). 60 per cent of the floating population living together with their family members hoped to stay on and peasants with their spouses living elsewhere hoped to bring their families to the cities rather then go back (Wang/Li 2001). A survey in Shanghai among female migrants in cities also revealed that the overwhelming majority of them are potential permanent residents rather than a floating population (Roberts 2002).

The macro-social system only serves as a background for actions and cannot totally determine the actions. All social actors are able to make use of this background and make their own decisions. At the same time, their actions are constantly changing the action background. Why, against the same social background, are some migrant peasants willing to stay in the cities for good and others determined to go back to their place of origin in the future? For those who are willing to stay on in the cities, what are their priority considerations? What actions will they undertake? Answers to these questions require detailed, in-depth research and investigation.

A new phenomenon is quietly emerging in the population structure of the migrant workers: the number of migrant couples is increasing. According to the results of the relevant surveys, in 1994, only nine per cent were migrant couples (survey of 100 villages with rural migrants in China); in 1997 there were 75.5 migrant families among the 2.299 million floating population in Beijing, which amounted to 30 per cent. (Song/Gu 1999). A survey in 2001 revealed that in Beijing, 17 per cent of the

---

[1] See also the contribution of Wang Yijie in this volume.

migrant workers lived with their spouses and 18 per cent with their extended family members, whereas in Zhuhai, 32 per cent of the migrant workers lived with their spouses and 41 per cent in Wuxi (Wang/Li 2001: 281). This data proves that the population structure with single migrant workers as the main body during the "migrant workers' tide" is changing and the proportion of floating migrant families is increasing year by year.

This kind of floating migrant family represents a shift in the family barycenter from rural areas to urban areas. This phenomenon has raised a new issue for the migration of the migrant peasants, which is the final consideration for those migrant peasants: the migration of the whole family rather than a single member. It is hard to imagine that a single family member would settle in a city and leaves his/her family behind in rural areas; the whole migrant family is an important element that can not be left out in the research on migrant workers. Discussions about the migrant family, family structure and its changes should give more attention in migration research.

This paper will look into: 1) current family patterns of the migrant workers and the changing trend; 2) impacts of different family patterns on the migrant workers' decisions on whether to settle in cities or not.

Review of relevant research

Some scholars believe that research on peasants' migration should be conducted at four levels: macro social level; community level; household level and individual level. Factors at each level may have independent impacts or combined impacts on behavior. It is only when research is conducted at these four levels at the same time that we shall be able to gain a complete and accurate understanding of peasants' migration, and construct a convincing migration model compatible with the Chinese situation (Hong 1996).

The research on the reasons for peasants' choosing to work away from home has paid enough attention to factors at household level. Many researchers have pointed out that decisions made by peasants regarding their actions are normally rooted in their households and their autonomy is influenced by their households. Their household decisions determine individual behavior patterns; this is particularly obvious among married women. For instance, the obligations connected with married life have encouraged men to go away to work, but have restricted women from going away to work (Tan 1997). With the changes in family responsibilities, the migrant peasants' lives move in a cycle: they go away to work in order to pay for their new houses, marriage and children's education and return home once they have completed their missions. Family ethics and unwritten family agreements have forced a great number of migrant workers to remit their income to their parents at home mainly for their children (Li 2001). These researchers mainly considered the family as a whole.

When an individual peasant goes away to work on his own, we can not unilaterally stress individual independency in peasants' decisions about their migration. By the same token, peasants in cities will not forget their families when they make decisions on their future development.

Once a peasant moves to a city, his/her family will be separated into two parts, one part in the rural area and the other in the city. As some research has already shown, long-term separation of family members is characteristic for the migrant peasants' family, namely the separation of the migrant workers from his/her other family members. Families of migrant workers can be categorized into the following five types according to the family members who go away to work:
- single child leaves home;
- brothers and sisters leave home;
- either husband or wife leaves home;
- a couple leaves home and their children stay behind;
- whole family leaves.

Family separation is the result of a voluntary decision by migrant workers; this family type will have a reduced birthrate and migrant workers will be more inclined to go back home when they start to make their decisions on migration (Li 1996). This type of separated family has brought about great challenges for sociological research; the families of migrant peasants can no longer be considered as a whole.

From the point of view of research, the families of migrant workers should not be treated as a whole nor be pre-determined as existing in a static and unchangeable situation. The separation of family members may be ended with either the migrant worker returning home and settling down in rural areas or with the family members who had remained in rural areas migrating to cities and settling down in cities.

Research has revealed that the whole family is more likely to migrate when married women go away to work, since women have to fulfill their commitments of raising the young and looking after the elderly even when they are not at home; this has led to a flow of accompanying non-working migrants (Zhongguo nongcun 1998). Almost all married rural women in cities are willing to stay in the cities when there are no great changes in their existing conditions (Roberts 2002).

The family modes of migrant workers are constantly changing and research on these changes needs to focus on all members of the migrant peasants' families. Who are the first, second and last migrant labourers? Will they all move to the cities? If this is not possible, where might they stay? Answers to all these questions require a comprehensive review of all family members and a thorough study of the specific elements they take into consideration, when family decisions are made.

Explanation of research data and materials

In July, 2000, the task force dealing with "migrant workers in Chinese cities"[2] conducted a survey among the floating population in Chengdu, Sichuan. 662 valid answers were collected through structured random sampling among those migrant

---

[2] This task force was funded by the Ford Foundation and headed by the author.

workers who are in a job or between jobs and have been living in the city for over half a year. 330 of them were employed, 174 were looking for jobs in labour market and the other 158 were self-employed. The purpose of this research was to seek for relations between variables rather than to make statistical judgments. Relevant information about all family members (the operating definition was based on whether they live apart), including their relationship with the interviewee, age, current residence and job, etc. was collected through a questionnaire. The total number of people was 2,523 including the 661 respondents and 1,862 family members associated with them. The average size of the 661 families surveyed was then worked out to be 3.82 people. The following data analysis is based on these figures.

Family modes of migrant workers, changes in these modes and their impacts on migration choices

The categorization of family mode is related to the structure of family members, for instance, the nuclear family, stem family and extended family. When peasants move to cities, their families are separated into two parts, some family members are in rural areas and the others are in cities. Any investigation of the family mode of migrant peasants needs to consider whether their family members are in rural areas or in cities, this provides the basis of their relationship. Another reason for the difficulties in defining the family modes of migrant workers is the fact that their family members move to the cities one by one; this changing trend needs to be considered as well.

Description of current family modes of migrant workers

According to the survey of migrant peasants and their family members, their working and living conditions are as shown in Table 1. In situations where cities or rural areas can be clearly identified as the living or working sites, the ratio between family members in rural areas and cities is 1.2 to 1, with that in rural areas being a bit higher. Even so, it can certainly be concluded that the family focus of migrant workers is still in rural areas.

Table 1. Working and living conditions of migrant workers and their family members

Current situation of family members	Frequency	Percentage
Farming	1,199	47.5
Working in cities	1,021	40.5
Living together without work	85	3.4
Going to school in rural areas	166	6.6
Going to school in cities	27	1.1
Others	4	0.1
No answer	21	0.8
Total	2,523	100.0

Due to the great diversity in the age and marital status of the migrant peasants, the nature of their families is also diverse. For those who are married, their existing families will remain their life-long families if no thunderbolts occur, whereas those who are unmarried may separate from their families after their marriage. The following table uses marital status as a dominant variable to show the family modes of interviewees in cities with four marital statuses: married; unmarried; divorced; widowed. Since the two latter have too few samples, they are not included.

Table 2. Family modes for married migrant workers in cities

Family modes in cities	Frequency	Percentage
One person	187	48.1
With spouse	75	19.3
With children	44	11.3
With spouse and children	49	12.6
Whole family (including parents and other members)	18	4.6
With other family members	16	4.1
Total	389	100.0

Table 3. Family modes for those unmarried migrant workers in cities

Family modes in cities	Frequency	Percentage
One person	166	72.5
Whole family (including parents and other members)	14	6.1
With other family members	49	21.4
Total	229	100.0

The figures on the tables show that the proportionate number of single married migrant workers is much lower than that of unmarried workers in the cities. Married migrant workers tend to have more family members in the cities. This situation may be due to their strong sense of responsibility for other family members. They are willing to share urban life with their family members when the conditions are right.

Study of the changes in family modes among migrant workers in cities

The family modes of migrant workers living in the cities are subject to changes over time; these changes are brought about by family members either moving to cities or staying in rural areas. Under what circumstances do the family members of migrant workers move to cities and what is the order of these events?

The future of the unmarried workers is rather uncertain and once they are married, they will probably separate from the families currently being surveyed; the following analysis, therefore, only aims at the family modes of married migrants and looks into how their family modes are changing.

First of all, there are the impacts of the migrant workers' floating experience on their family modes in the cities. Logically speaking, the earlier the peasants move to the cities for the first time, the longer they will work and live in the cities and the more family members there will be in the cities. A correlation analysis of the total length of time migrant workers have stayed in the cities and the number of family members (including themselves) living in the cities, shows a correlation coefficient between the two of r=0.41 which is a positive middle degree of correlation; that is to say, the longer the migrant workers live in the cities, the more family members they have in the cities. The migrant workers also tend to have more family members as their stay in the cities is prolonged. Compared with single migrant workers in the cities, the peasants living together with their spouses and children tend to stay 3 years longer in cities. This indicates that migrant workers do not necessarily return home once they have earned money in the cities; they might also bring their family members to the cities one by one. The longer they stay in the cities, the more they are likely to do this.

The correlation between the type of employment and the family mode of the migrant workers is very obvious. The family mode is strongly linked with the type of employment of the migrants, that is, whether they are employed or self-employed (X2=68.1, p<0.001); a much higher proportion of the self-employed migrants stay with their family members. 58 per cent of the self-employed migrants live with their spouses and only 24 per cent of migrants work as hired labour. The majority of the self-employed migrants in the cities usually undertake small scale business activities, such as running a small store or a stall that needs the support of two or more people. It is, therefore, quite common to see a couple working side by side. In comparison, as many as 62 per cent of the migrants working as hired labour, but only 34 per cent of self-employed migrants are living alone in the cities. The self-employed migrants enjoy a higher social status than those working as hired labourers in the cities. Special conditions, such as funds, stock and sales channels, are necessary to enable the migrants to become self-employed. Migrant workers often become self-employed many years after they move to the cities. Once they are self-employed, they will have a relatively stable means of living in the cities and their economic stability will promote the migration of their family members to the cities. The conditions of the self-employed migrant workers and the migration of their family members impact on and supplement each other.

The above analysis is about the general changing trend of the family modes of the migrant peasants. More family members will gradually join the migrants in the cities, but who will go first, and who will follow on afterwards?

A substantial amount of research has shown that migrant workers are not surplus but main rural labourers. The leading bread-winner in a family will go away to work before anyone else, mainly to earn money. The more competent peasants are likely to be employed in the labour market. This line of reasoning also tells us that the second family member to go away to work will be another leading labourer. Statistics have proven that the labourers in a family go away first and those family members who need to be supported will follow later on. Normally, the male adults in a family will migrate first of all and leave their parents, wives and children at home. If a second migration opportunity arises, it will still be given to a family labourer, but there could be diverse results, with the choice falling upon the wife or the grown-up children.

The age of the migrant workers is the basis of their family life cycle. Since there are wide age differences among the migrants, the structure of family labourers varies. The following table demonstrates the inter-relationship between the age of the interviewees (married) and their family modes in the cities.

Table 4. Relationship between the age of the married migrant workers and their family modes in the cities

Family mode in cities	18-25	26-35	36-49	Over 50	Total
Alone (187)	10.2	46.5	31.0	12.3	100.0
Stay with spouse (65)	16.9	55.4	23.1	4.6	100.0
Stay with children (40)	0.0	15.0	40.0	45.0	100.0
Stay with spouse and children (49)	8.2	44.9	32.7	14.3	100.0
Whole family (incl. parents and other members) (18)	11.1	33.3	38.9	16.7	100.0
Stay with other family members (16)	18.8	50.0	18.8	12.5	100.0
Total (N=375 people)	10.4	44.0	30.7	14.9	100.0

Statistically, it has been revealed that the families of migrant workers in different age cohorts have different family members. Among those in a low age cohort with no children or very young children, a large number stay with their spouses; among those in a high age cohort, a higher proportion of them stay with their children. The older the migrant workers are, the more unlikely they are to migrate with their spouses. The transition towards non-agricultural occupations is a kind of active orientation strategy of social change, especially when these peasant families lack the necessary resources for such opportunities to go to the cities. With regard to the sequence of migration among family members, main labourers and their grown-up children will migrate first; if they do not have any grown-up children, they will migrate with their spouses, then they will bring their children and lastly their parents over to the cities.

Among those migrant workers in a low age cohort, the children are not grown-up and their children's growth will be affected enormously whether they are brought over to the cities or left behind in rural areas. If the mother works or lives in a city, this will lead to the migration of the non-working family members and most of these are children. Among the 389 migrant workers who were surveyed, there were 353 children, including 118 aged below 6; 78.8 per cent of them stayed in the rural areas and 21.2 per cent lived in cities. Among the 235 children aged between 6 and 15, 67.2 per cent go to school in the rural areas and 3.4 per cent in the cities; the others do not go to school and these amount to 17.9 per cent in rural areas and 4.7 per cent in the cities.

Family modes of the migrant workers and their migration choices

The collective returning home by the migrant workers during the Spring Festival is largely due to the fact that they do not have a "home" in the cities. If they do have a home in the cities, what difference will this make?

The current family mode of the migrant workers is related to their choice of settlement in the cities. The more willing they are to remain in the cities, the more inclined they are to move their main family members to the cities and as more family members move into the cities, the migrant workers become more resolute when making their choices.

The focus of the survey was on the second aspect, the link between the current family mode of the migrant workers in the cities and their future plans. The aim was to find out which was the more decisive variable in the migrant workers future choices: the individual variable or the family variable. The following analysis is based on a matrix of regression equation which allows the assessment of impact on a causal variable from the change of a variable while keeping other variables in the matrix constant.

Table 5. LOGISTIC regression analyses of migration choices among migrant workers

Independent variables	Causal variables (remain in cities=1)
Basic individual variable:	
Sex	-0.006
Age	-0.006
Education	
Middle school	0.293
High school	0.122
Monthly income (LN)	-0.114
Year of first migration	0.053**
Length of time in cities	0.005**
Family mode in cities	
Stay with spouse	0.618*
Stay with children	-0.264
Stay with spouse and children	0.683*
Whole family (incl. parents and other members)	0.808*
Stay with other family members	-0.180
Constant	-105.642**
Correspondence between expected value and observed value	62.01%
Number of samples	361

(Note: *$p<0.1$; **$p<0.05$; ***$p<0.01$; ****$p<0.001$; numerical values in the form are standardized regression coefficients)

Two indicators were found to be notably influential in migrant workers' choices. The first is their floating experience: the earlier their first migration is, the more inclined they are to remain in the cities; the longer they stay in the cities, the more apt they are to settle in the cities. The second indicator is the family mode of the migrant workers in the cities. There are three influential types: "staying with spouse;" "staying with children;" "staying with the whole family." If the family mode of the migrant workers falls into one of these three types, the migrants concerned tend to stay in the cities as well. What should be noted is that the spouse is included in all these three types of family mode and not in the other two indistinctive types; therefore, whether the couple who form the family core is included or not in the family mode of the migrant workers in the cities will play a decisive role in their future choices. Because their spouse fails to join them, some elderly migrants may choose to go back to the rural areas after a few years in the cities even though all their children are in the cities. The analytical variable is the future planning of the peasants' migration: that is, to remain in the cities or to return to rural areas. The numerical values in the form are standardized regression coefficients; their magnitude shows the influence on choices. We can see that although two types of floating experience are notable, their standardized regression coefficients are as low as 0.053 and 0.0005 respectively; this means that their impact on causal variables is weak. The three standardized regression coefficients of family modes in the cities are 0.618, 0.683 and 0.808 respectively, with a great impact on causal variables. These three numerical values increase along with the increase in family members. This shows that when more family members work or stay in the cities, the migrant workers are more inclined to remain there.

Preliminary conclusion and discussion

The research on migrant workers should take more factors into consideration, such as changes in the system and social structure, the community situation and the social networks of the migrant workers, etc. This paper has discussed migrant peasants' choices of migration from the perspective of their families; all the conclusions still need to be tested by empirical research.

The above data analysis has validated two assumptions in the research on migrant workers at family level: the first is that the family modes of the migrant workers do not remain unchanged; the modes change all the time. Under certain conditions, the general trend is for more and more family members of the migrant workers to migrate to the cities. In this process of migration, labour forces among family members have the priority; the second is that variables related to the families of the migrant workers are more decisive than variables related to individual migrants' decisions on future development. The most influential element is whether their spouses are in the city or not. Those migrant workers with their spouses in the cities tend to settle in the cities.

Migrant peasants should not be treated as a sweeping whole. Floating and immigration are totally different in terms of urbanization and changes in social structure and they should therefore be treated differently. It is only when peasants' behaviour has shifted from floating to migration that it will be more meaningful to discuss their merging with urban society. Migrant workers who are prepared to remain in the cities care more about their colleagues and the communities in which they live (Li 2003). Other studies have indicated that migrant workers who have been living in the cities for a long time have actually become part of the new urban migrants who share strong feelings of identity with the city and can actively mix with urban society (Wen 2005).

Migrant workers who just want to earn money may have different choices, with regard to their career development, from those who are willing to settle in the cities. This is an important element for the urban labour market to consider. Those who are prepared to return to their hometowns will not spend their money on education and career development, whereas those who are planning to remain in the cities will pay attention to their future development and have a long-term perspective of their status in the urban labour market. In our interviews with individual peasants, they did not know what to say when they were asked about their next jobs; most of them have adopted a wait-and-see attitude and only few of them even mentioned that they will return to their hometowns if there is no way out. Migrant workers often only consider temporary employment in cities; this has led to the absence of career development plans among them. If they were pressed to answer questions about what they want to do in the future, a large number of them would mention running a small business. This answer is merely an imaginary idea of the future rather than a concrete plan.

Education is an important precondition for further development in the urban labour market. In China, only those who have received a senior high school education will have the opportunity to become white collar workers. In an interview, Xiao Jiang, a youngster from a rural area, mentioned that she regrets not attending senior high school with her friend, and that this has led to differences between the two in their career development:

in Chengdu, I worked in a tea house with a monthly salary of 400 RMB and the tea house paid for my food and accommodation. She (Xiao Jiang's friend who received a senior high school education) worked in a small company as a secretary with a monthly salary of 500 RMB, but the company did not cover the cost of her food and accommodation. I spent more when we went out to have fun. She finished her senior adult education last year and moved to another company as a secretary. Her monthly salary has increased to 700 RMB and her company does not cover the cost of her food and accommodation, but she is now better off and engaged in an honorable job with a promising future, while I am still working in a tea house and will continue like this in the future. I cannot take part in senior adult education but I may go to a vocational high school, but that will not change my current situation.

The migrant workers, especially the young ones, can feel that they are selected by the urban labour market for their work and can make choices about their future career development. One of the key influencing factors is, if they are prepared to remain in the cities. Family migration is a yardstick to measure whether the migrant workers have completed their migration. More in-depth and valuable research should be done on the different choices on career development between migrant workers with and without their families in the cities.

References

Cai, Fang 蔡昉 (2001) "Laodongli qianyi de liangge guocheng jiqi zhidu zhang'ai" 劳动力迁移的两个过程及其制度障碍 [Two Processes of the labour migration and the institutional impediments], in *Shehuixue yanjiu* 社会学研究[Study of Sociology], Issue 4，pp. 44-51.

Hong, Dayong 洪大用 (1996) "Guanyu jiating yu nongmin qianyi jincheng zhi guanxi de yanjiu" 关于家庭与农民迁移进城之关系的研究 [Research on the relations between households and migration of peasants to cities], in *Guowai shehuixue* 国外社会学 [Sociology Overseas], Issue 3，pp. 6-14.

Li, Qiang 李强 (1996) "Guanyu 'nongmingong' jiating moshi wenti de yanjiu" 关于'农民工'家庭模式问题的研究 [Research on family mode of the migrant peasants], in *Zhejiang xuekan* 浙江学刊 [Zhejiang Study], Issue 1，pp. 77-81.

Li, Qiang 李强 (2001) "Zhongguo waichu nongmingong jiqi huikuanzhi yanjiu" 中国外出农民工及其汇款之研究 [Research on Chinese migrant workers and their remittance], in *Shehuixue yanjiu* 社会学研究 [Sociological Research], Issue 4，pp. 64-76.

Li, Qiang 李强 (2003) "Yingxiang Zhongguo chengxiang liudong renkou de tuili yu lali yinsu fenxi" 影响中国城乡流动人口的推力与拉力因素分析 [Analysis on the push and pull factors affecting Chinese urban and rural floating population], in *Zhongguo shehui kexue* 中国社会科学 [Chinese Social Sciences], Issue 1，pp. 125-136.

Song, Guochen 宋国臣 and Gu, Chaolin 顾朝林 (1999) "Beijing nüxing liudong renkou de jiating leixing jiqi xingcheng yinsu" 北京女性流动人口的家庭类型及其形成因素 [Family mode of the female floating population in Beijing and its shaping factors], in *Renwen dili* 人文地理 [Humanities Geography], Issue 2, Volume 14，pp. 11-14.

Roberts, Kenneth D. (2002) "Female labour migrants to Shanghai: temporary 'floaters' or potential settlers?" in *International Migration Review*, p. 36.

Sabel, Charles F. (1982) *Work and Politics: the Division of Labour in Industry*, Cambridge: Cambridge University Press.

Solinger, Dorothy J. (1999) *Contesting Citizenship in Urban China: Migrants, the State and the Logic of the Market,* Berkeley: University of California Press.

Tan, Shen 谭深 (1997) "Nongcun laodongli liudong de xingbie chayi" 农村劳动力流动的性别差异 [Gender difference in the flow of rural labourers], in *Shehuixue yanjiu* 社会学研究 [Sociological Research], Issue 1，pp. 42-47.

Thomas, William J. and Znanieski, F. 托马斯、兹纳涅茨基（USA） (1984/2000) *Shenchu Ou-Mei de Bolan nongmin* 身处欧美的波兰农民[The Polish peasant in Europe and America], Beijing：Yilin chubanshe 译林出版社[Yilin Press].

Wang, Fenyu 王奋宇 and Li, Lulu 李路路 (2001) "Beijing nüxing liudong renko de jiating leixing jiqi xingcheng yinsu" 中国城市劳动力市场——从业模式·职业生涯·新移民

[Urban labour market in China—employment mode, occupational career and new migrants], Beijing: Beijing chubanshe 北京出版社 [Beijing Publishing House].

Wen, Jun 文军 (2005) "Lun Woguo chengshi laodongli xin yimin de xichong goucheng jiqi xingwei xuanze" 论我国城市劳动力新移民的系统构成及其行为选择 [On the system structure and behavior choice of the new migrants among urban labourers in China], in *Nanjing shehui kexue* 南京社会科学 [Nanjing Social Sciences], Issue 1, pp. 54-58.

Zhongguo nongcun laodongli liudong baicunzhuizong diaocha ketizu 中国农村劳动力流动百村追踪调查课题组 [The task force of a tracing survey among 100 villages with migrant labourers in China] (1998) "Zhongguo nongcun laodongli liudong de qushi fenxi" 中国农村劳动力流动的趋势分析 [Trend analysis of the flow of Chinese rural labourers], in *Jingji yanjiu cankao* 经济研究参考 [Economic Research Reference], Issue 6, pp. 33-48.

Socio-Economic Status, Social Networks and Settlement Choices of Rural-to-Urban Migrants[1]

Wang Yijie

Raising the problem

The social reforms and restructuring which have been implemented since the late 1970s and early 1980s have created "free migration resources" and "free migration space" for peasants, who have been migrating to cities at an unprecedented speed. They have migrated from the countryside and have made a hard living in cities, but this does not mean that they are willing or able to stay and settle in the cities. Only when rural migrant settlement in cities is achieved will urbanization and social transformation truly start, without sacrificing rural development.

According to the individual migration and settlement conditions in M.P. Todaro's Population Migration Model, if the product of expected income and the probability of employment in the cities outweigh the actual costs, opportunity costs and psychological costs of migration and settlement, individuals will migrate and settle in the cities, otherwise they either do not migrate or they return to their hometowns after migration. The hypothesis for this model is that the actors are free to make decisions about their activities in the labour market.

Some domestic research, however, seems to show that although the income gap between city and countryside is increasing, most rural migrants are unwilling or unable to settle in the cities. The basic reason given for this is that the rural migrants are still in a binary labour market which is segregated from urban labour, and that they are also trapped in the inertia of the household registration system and the associated "townspeople preferred" welfare systems as well. Only when these systems are abolished permanent settlement in terms of citizenship will be possible for rural migrants instead of marginal residency.

However, these arguments cannot explain why there are differences in rural migrants' settlement in the cities, why some rural migrants are willing to settle in the cities and others are not. These arguments ignore the microcosmic dynamics of rural migrant settlement, which is independent of the structure of the system, which has household registration as its nucleus.

Hypothesis on settlement choices

There has been some research on the microcosmic settlement occurrence mechanism that pays attention to the influence of factors such as gender, age, education, time spent living in the cities and income. The basic conclusion of this

---

[1] This research is being aided financially by the National Social Sciences Funds (04BSH034) and the National Postdoctoral Research Funds (2005037265).

research is that elderly rural migrants with low educational attainments, short periods of residence in the cities, a low income and humble occupations are likely to want to return to their places of origin and will also do so (Bai/He 2002; Li 2004: 63-68; He/Guo 2004; Wu 2005).

All this research has been carried out from the perspective of individualism; the actor's position in the social structure is based on concepts such as gender, age, education, time spent in the cities, income, etc. and describes the restrictions and the effects on the individuals in the social system.

Due to the fact that the existing research seldom pays attention to the influence of social networks upon the rural migrants' willingness to settle in the cities, the individual is likely to be assumed to be rational and self-interested in economic terms. As Granovetter (1985) said:

A fruitful analysis of human action requires us to avoid the atomization implicit in the theoretical extremes of under-socialized and over-socialized concepts. Actors do not behave or decide as atoms outside a social context, nor do they adhere slavishly to a script written for them by the particular intersection of social categories that they happen to occupy. Their attempts at purposive action are instead embedded in concrete, ongoing systems of social relations.

The importance of the social networks for rural migrants cannot be emphasized too much, because every linkage in migration relates closely to the social networks (Alba/Nee 1997; Portes 1995; Sanders/Nee 1996).

The research into social networks offers a view of network structures, but not a view of status structures. Social networks form a comparatively stable system through the social interaction of the actors. The perspective of this stable system helps us to understand the positions of the actors in the social structures, but does not reduce them to intrinsic attributes and normative characteristics of the actors. It emphasizes the actors' ability to take up or mobilize the social resources, but not their relation to the resources. It is complementary to the mainstream individualism method (Wellman 1994).

The willingness of rural migrants to settle in the cities is influenced by both the variables of the actors' socio-economic status and the social networks which enable the actors to take up or mobilize various resources when living in cities. This is the key hypothesis of this paper. To test the hypothesis, the following variables will be used:

Dependent variables: the willingness of rural migrants to settle in the cities. This is calculated from answers to questions such as, "Are you going to settle in the city?" in the questionnaire. The possible answers are: "agreed very much," "agreed," "not clear," "not agreed" and "not agreed at all." In the model analysis, the first two answers are combined as "agreed" and the last two answers are combined as "not agreed."

According to the previously mentioned hypothesis, there are *two types of independent variables*. The first is the "socio-economic status" variable. Based on existing research, the economic status of the rural migrants will be defined in terms of the following factors:

- *Age.* The rural migrants usually take up dirty, demanding and dangerous work with high labour intensity and poor living conditions. They suffer from a lack of essential labour protection and nutrition. It is highly likely that they will be injured or fall sick, but they have no medical insurance, and they can not bear the cost of the medical expenses in the cities by themselves. It is therefore assumed that as they grow older, they will not be able to undertake so much physical labour as when they were young. In addition, the main family expenditures such as weddings, house maintenance and children's education will have been dealt with. These rural migrants are likely to return to their places of origin and not stay in the cities.
- *Education.* It is assumed that the rural migrants with a high level of education are likely to adapt to city life and that they will be willing to settle in the cities.
- *Time spent in the cities.* Inkeles thinks that experience in factories, in the public media, in city life and school education are the most important factors for individuals if they are to adapt to modernity (Inkeles 1992: 7). The time rural migrants spend in the cities helps them to transfer the human capital acquired in the countryside by school eductation into the human capital required for city life, helps them learn the labour experience and language skills required for city life, and helps them to adapt themselves to city life. Due to the differences between the city and countryside in school education, the human capital accumulated in the countryside must be transformed before it is possible to profit from city life (Zhao/Wang 2002). Meanwhile, the time spent in the cities offers an indication of the individual's objective settlement behavior to some extent. It is assumed that the longer the rural migrant has been living in the cities, the more social capital they will acquire. This is not correct. It is therefore assumed in this article that the longer the time they spend living in the cities, the more likely the rural migrants are to settle there.
- *Income.* Some research has revealed that if rural migrants earn a high income in the cities and they can afford various expenditures, such as housing, children's education, medical expenses, etc., they are likely to settle in the cities. The rural migrants with a low income are likely to return to their places of origin, because they can not afford the necessary living costs. This article will test this hypothesis.
- *"Gender."* This is introduced to the model as a control variable.

The second type is the "social networks in city life" variable. Considering the accessibility of this resource for the actors, this paper will study the influence of social networks upon rural migrants. There are three types of social network variables:

- According to *the types of ties*, the "social networks in city life" are classified as relatives, friends and acquaintances. To some extent, these classifications refer to the strength of the tie. According to Granovetter, the strength of a tie is a combination of the amount of time spent together, the emotional intensity, the intimacy and reciprocal service. In China, however, the source of the tie is much more important than other factors. Although there would not be much reciprocal service or intimacy between lineal relatives, it is the most reliable and strong tie at times of crisis. (Luo 2005: 50f.) Some researchers were inspired by the Taiwanese researcher, Huang Guangguo, and proposed that ties should be classified into "strong ties," "moderate ties" and "weak ties," which correspond to "emotional ties," "emotional-instrumental ties" and "instrumental ties" respectively and replace the previous dichotomy of "strong and weak ties"(Wang 2003). The rural migrants may not possess a particular resource, but a wide network of relatives, friends and acquaintances in the cities will enable them to take up and mobilize more material and spiritual resources from the network, and further prompt their willingness to settle there. It is thus assumed in this paper that the wider the networks of relatives, friends and acquaintances, the more likely the rural migrants are to settle in the cities.

- *Spouses*. It is assumed that among married people, those living together with their spouses are likely to settle in the cities.
- Scale of the network with urban households living in the cities, that is, the *"townspeople."* According to Peter Blau, "the communications with other groups and strata propel people to migrate to those groups and strata" (Blau 1991: 394); it can thus be concluded that communication with "townspeople" will propel rural migrants to migrate to the strata of the townspeople. This paper therefore assumes that in the rural migrants' social networks, a larger network of "townspeople" will prompt the migrants to settle in the cities.

The materials used in this article come from the questionnaire which I used to carry out interviews in the Hongshan Sub-district of Xuanwu District and the Saihongqiao Sub-district of Yuhua District, Nanjing City in the summer of 2002. The interviewees were selected from the registered temporary resident population of Nanjing City and, in accordance with the existing research the samples were allocated under consideration of gender structure, age structure, occupation structure and employment structure. 410 questionnaires were distributed and all were collected; of these questionnaires, 383 are valid and the validity rate is thus 93.4 per cent. Details of the interviewees and the variables are given in Table 1.

Table 1. Social network: interviewees and variables

Gender	Male: 236, 61.6%	Female: 147, 38.4%	
Age	Average value: 32.43 years	Standard deviation: 9.783	
Education	Elementary education: 104, 27.2%	Junior high school education: 207, 54.0%	Higher education: 72, 18.8%

Duration of residence in Nanjing	Average value: 6.65 years	Standard deviation: 4.938	
Income per month	Average value: 917.5 RMB	Standard deviation: 1004.116	
Scale of relatives in city	Average value: 1.14	Standard deviation: 1.200	
Scale of friends in city	Average value: 1.90	Standard deviation: 1.946	
Scale of acquainttances in city	Average value: 1.09	Standard deviation: 1.630	
Living with spouse	Living together: 214, 55.9%	Not living together: 66, 17.2%	No spouse: 103, 26.9%
Scale of "townspeople"	Average value: 0.86	Standard deviation, 1.252	
Willingness to settle	Agree: 130, 33.9%	Not clear: 140, 36.6%	Not agree: 113, 29.5%

Findings of the Analysis

I introduced the previously mentioned independent variables to different models using multivariate regression analysis. All of them passed the significance test. This method of analysis linearizes the dependent variables probability function with the independent variables mathematically. By reviewing the odd ratio of each independent variable in the equation, it defines, if other variables are controlled, the change to a dependent variable odd ratio when a variable changes by one unit. From this, it is possible to show the effects of the independent variables on the dependent variables. This method of analysis is therefore better than the correlation and variance analysis method.

In addition, Models II, III and IV are better than Model I. The three groups of social network variables contribute significantly to the models (Wang/Guo 2001: 153). In other words, not only the socio-economic status variables, but also the social network variables are needed in the analysis.

In Model I, the socio-economic status variables were introduced. It was found that when other variables were controlled: Firstly, the older the rural migrants are, the more unlikely they are to agree to settle in the city. However, the influence of age is complicated: it does not have a simple linear relation to the dependent variables. Secondly, rural migrants with only an elementary education are more likely to return and not settle in the city than those migrants with higher levels of education. There is, however, no difference between those with a junior high school education and those with higher levels of education. Thirdly, the longer they live in the city, the more likely they are to settle there. Fourthly, income does not make a difference; and finally, there is no significant difference between the "not clear" and "not agreed" rural migrants on these variables.

Table 2. Multivariate regression analysis: willingness of rural migrants to settle

	Model I		Model II		Model III		Model IV	
	Agree	Not clear	Agree	Not clear	Agree	Not clear	Agree	Not clear
Gender (Male as reference group)								
Female	-.063 (.939)	-.360 (.697)	-.177 (.838)	-.590 (.554)	-.202 (.817)	-.528 (.590)	-.091 (.913)	-.367 (.693)
Age								
	-.248 (.780)**	-.159 (.853)	-.250 (.778)**	-.158 (.854)	-.176 (.839)!	-.144 (.866)	-.250 (.779)**	-.156 (.856)
Age square								
	.003 (1.003)*	.001 (1.001)	.003 (1.003)*	.001 (1.001)	.002 (1.002)	.001 (1.001)	.003 (1.003)**	.001 (1.001)
Education (higher education as reference group)								
Elemen. Edu.	-1.267 (.282)**	-.173 (.841)	-1.188 (.305)*	-.170 (.844)	-1.224 (.294)**	-.125 (.883)	-1.213 (.297)**	-.180 (.835)
Junior high school	-.317 (.728)	.077 (1.080)	-.330 (.719)	-.006 (.994)	-.281 (.755)	.085 (1.089)	-.251 (.778)	.077 (1.080)
Duration of residence in Nanjing								
	.100 (1.105)**	.049 (1.050)	.090 (1.094)**	.028 (1.028)	.098 (1.103)**	.044 (1.045)	.093 (1.098)**	.049 (1.050)
Logarithm of income per month								
	.351 (1.421)	.010 (1.010)	.350 (1.420)	.051 (1.053)	.359 (1.433)	-.006 (.994)	.312 (1.367)	.006 (1.006)
Scale of relatives in city								
			.204(1.226)		.286(1.331)*			
Scale of friends in city								
			.075(1.078)		-.027(.973)			
Scale of acquaintances in city								
			-.074(.929)		-.176(.839)*			
Living with spouse ("living together" as reference group)								
No spouse					.381(1.464)		-.069(.933)	
Not living together					-.833(.414)*		-.847(.429)*	
Scale of "townspeople"								
							.172 (1.188)	.005 (1.005)
-2LogLikehood								
	737.704		728.879		728.908		735.613	
Chi square (variance)								
	58.552 (14)***		70.149 (20)***		67.348 (18)***		62.029 (16)***	
Number of sample								
	365		365		365		365	

Note: value outside parentheses is non-standard regression coefficient; value inside parentheses is standard regression coefficient; ***p<.001, ** p<.01, *p<.05.

In Model II, the socio economic status variables and the variables of numbers of relatives, friends and acquaintances in the city were introduced. Under the calculation that other variables are controlled, the data shows that, firstly, the influence of social economic status variables on dependent variables is in the same direction as that in Model I; only the specific value was changed. Secondly, regarding the social network variables, the three different types of variables did not show any difference between migrants who want to settle down and migrants who want to return home, nor between those who want to settle down and answered "not clear." Two variables, however, showed a difference between "not clear" and "return." When other variables fed into the model were controlled, the larger the scale of relatives, the more likely the rural migrants were to be "not clear" but not "return;" the larger the scale of acquaintances, the more likely they were to tick "return" but not "not clear."

In Model III, the rural migrants' socio economic status variables and living with spouse condition variables were introduced. Under the calculation that other variables are controlled, the data shows that, firstly, some socio economic status variables changed compared with Models I and II. The age and education variables did not pass the significance testing. Only the duration of residence in the city variable revealed that the longer the time spent there, the more likely the migrants are to settle in the city and not to return to the countryside. Secondly, regarding the living with spouse condition, whether they had "no spouse" or were "living together with spouse," this did not make any difference to their willingness to settle. Compared with "living together with spouse", the "not living together" category of rural migrants is likely to return and not settle in the city. They are not "not clear" about their future. The living with spouse condition did not show any difference between "not clear" and "willing to settle."

In Model IV, the socio economic status variable and the "scale of townspeople" variable were introduced. According to the statistics when other variables were controlled: Firstly, the influence of socio economic status variable was the same as that in Model I. Only the specific value was changed. Secondly, the difference in "scale of townspeople" vs. "willingness to settle" did not pass the significance test.

From the above analysis, it was revealed that when other variables were controlled, the age, education, duration of residence in the city variables of "socio-economic status" had a significant influence on willingness to settle. None of the models provided evidence to support the income variable. The hypothesis that a higher income produces willingness to settle in the city could therefore not be verified by this research.

In the variance analysis, the average income per month of the rural migrants who agreed to settle in the city was RMB 1,090.79. The income of the "not clear" category was RMB 854.15. The income of the "not agreed" category was RMB 794.04. The integral difference between groups passed the significance test (F=3.016, df=2, significance is 0.05). Why, however, was the hypothesis verified in the models? From the linear regression analysis with "income per month" as a dependent variable (see table 3), it was found that the older the peasants and the higher the level of their education, the higher the income they can earn. The relation between the two variables reflected in the variance analysis was decided by age and education.

When other variables were controlled, we found that the scale of relatives, scale of acquaintances and the living with spouse condition in the social network variables have a significant influence on willingness to settle. The scale of friends and scale of "townspeople" did not pass the significance test.

The first step here is to review the "scale of friends in the city" variable. In the variance analysis, the average scale of friends for rural migrants who agreed to settle in the city was 2.32; that of the "not clear" category was 1.82; the "not agreed" category was 1.50. The integral difference between groups passed the test (F=5.654, df=2, significance is 0.004). Why, however, did it not pass the significance test in Model II? According to the linear regression analysis with "scale of friends in the city" as a dependent variable (see table 3), it was found that in Model II, gender and education restricted the "scale of friends in the city." In other words, the scale of friends as "moderate ties" or "emotional-instrumental ties" does not have an independent influence on willingness to settle in the city.

Table 3. Settlement willingness: linear regression analysis of relevant variables

	Income per month	Towns people scale	Relative scale in city	Friend scale in city	Acquaintance scale in city
Gender (female as reference) Male	156.714 (.076)	-.148 (-.057)	-.614 (-.247)***	.427 (.106)*	.161 (.048)
Age	67.530 (.658)*	.004 (.033)	.039 (.313)	-.038 (-.188)	.089 (.530)
Age square	-.706 (-.509)	.000 (-.128)	.000 (-.216)	-7.7E-005 (-.028)	-.001 (-.481)
Education (Elementary as reference) Junior high school	368.362 (.183)**	-.039 (-.015)	.148 (.061)	.704 (.180)**	-.397 (-.121)
Higher education	921.875 (.362)***	.375 (.117)	-.190 (-.062)*	1.050 (.213)***	.331 (.080)
Duration of residence in Nanjing	.161 (.001)	.038 (.149)**	.042 (.171)**	-.006 (-.016)	-.059 (-.178)**
Logarithm of income per month		.247 (.128)*	.190 (.103)	.206 (.069)	.409 (.163)**
F (variance)	8.407 (6)***	3.852 (7)***	6.426 (7)***	8.578 (7)***	3.273 (7)**
Correction Factor	.107	.052	.094	.127	.042

Note: value outside parentheses is non-standard regression coefficient; value inside parentheses is standard regression coefficient; ***p<.001, ** p<.01, *p<.05.

The next step is to review the "scale of relatives in the city" and the "scale of acquaintances in city." In the variance analysis, the rural migrants' average scale of relatives "agreed" to settle in the city was 1.18; that of "not clear" was 1.20; of "not agreed" was 1.02. The integral difference between the groups did not pass the test (F=0.823, df=2, significance is 0.440). That means, with regard to the scale of relatives in the city, there was not much difference between interviewees. In the variance analysis, with regard to the rural migrants' average scale of acquaintances those who "agreed" to settle in the city amounted to 1.05; the "not clear" category came to 0.89 and the "not agreed" category was 1.41. The integral difference between groups passed the test (F=3.324, df=2, significance is 0.037). In the linear regression analysis taking "scale of relatives in the city" and "scale of acquaintances in the city" as dependent variables (see table 3), there were some socio-economic status variables influencing them, but in Model II, they were separate from socio economic status variables and had an independent influence on willingness to settle in the city.

The penultimate factor to review is the "living with spouse" condition. In the binary logistic regression analysis, taking the living with spouse factor for married peasants as a dependent variable, two variables of gender and age passed the significance test. In Model III, however, although these variables were controlled, this condition still had a significant influence. The influence of "no spouse" did not pass the test because the age variable, which is closely related to marital status, was controlled.

Finally, we shall review the "scale of townspeople" variable. In the variance analysis, the average "scale of townspeople" for rural migrants "agreed" to settle in city was 1.12; that of the "not clear" category was 0.74; that of the "not agreed" category was 0.71. The integral difference between the groups passed the test (F=4.223, df=2, significance is 0.05). Why, however, was the hypothesis not verified in Model IV? From the linear regression analysis with "scale of townspeople" as a dependent variable (see table 3), it was found that the longer the time the rural migrants live in Nanjing and the higher the income they earn, the greater is their "scale of townspeople." Therefore, the relation between the two variables reflected in the variance analysis is the result of education, duration of residence in Nanjing and income. In other words, the "scale of townspeople" does not have an independent influence on the willingness of rural migrants to settle. The hypothesis regarding the scale of townspeople is thus not verified.

So who are the "townspeople" in the social networks of rural migrants? What sort of social support can they provide? Is there any difference between the "townspeople" and "non-towns people" living in the cities? Calculated from the types of tie, of the 329 "townspeople" mentioned by 383 interviewees, 12.8 per cent were relatives, 52.0 per cent were friends, 35.3 per cent were acquaintances. The corresponding percentages of "non-townspeople" were 31.4 per cent, 44.4 per cent and 24.2 per cent respectively. The difference passed the significance test. Calculated from the type of support, 21.6 per cent of "townspeople" provided mutual "emotional support" opportunities, 14.9 per cent provided advice, 24.0 per cent provided financial aid, 24.3 per cent provided employment opportunities, 33.8

per cent provided assistance to deal with "troubles," 12.5 per cent were companions, and 25.8 per cent provided communication support. The corresponding percentages of "non-town people" were 35.6 per cent, 27.9 per cent, 23.3 per cent, 18.0 per cent, 10.1 per cent, 33.7 per cent, and 33.5 per cent. The statistical analysis revealed that in comparison with "non-townspeople", the "townspeople" were able to provide better instrumental support for employment opportunities and risk avoidance, but were not able to provide emotional support such as confiding opportunities, advice, companionship and communication. There was, however, no difference with regard to financial aid. Regarding the degree of intimacy, rural migrants had a higher degree of intimacy with "non-townspeople" than with "townspeople." Those having "very close" and "close" relationships with "townspeople" amounted to 66.9 per cent. Those having "medium" relationships amounted to 30.4 per cent. The corresponding percentages for "non-townspeople" were 81.1 per cent and 16.6 per cent. With regard to the length of communication time, this was shorter with "townspeople" than with "non-townspeople." Those with over five years' communication time with "townspeople" amounted to 52.6 per cent. Those with between one to five years amounted to 38.0 per cent. Those with less than one year amounted to 9.5 per cent. The corresponding percentages with "non-townspeople" were 61.2 per cent, 29.1 per cent and 9.7 per cent. It is therefore the "middle ties" or "instrumental ties," and weak ties or "instrumental ties" that dominate the relationships between rural migrants and "townspeople". It is the "middle to weak" network that does not have any actual influence on the willingness of rural migrants to settle settlement.

In the members of the social networks of rural migrants, it would appear that there is a continuous spectrum with, at one end, the spouse, representing the strong ties, and at the other end, all the various people met at work and during their daily lives, representing the weak ties. All the network members can be found in these positions on this continuous spectrum. They also keep changing their positions with the variation of circumstances. On this continuous spectrum, the strong ties provide advice on important issues concerning decision-making and financial aid, and the weak ties provide assistance with risk avoidance and give communication support (see Table 4). In other words, one end provides emotional support and the other end provides instrumental support.

Table 4. Type of ties and type of support

	Relative	Friend	Aquaintance	Chi sqare
Comfort	30.5%	33.4%	27.4%	5.028
Advice	61.0%	15.0%	9.1%	515.227***
Financial aid	34.0%	29.1%	16.1%	44.333***
Employment opportunities	8.8%	23.0%	18.4%	57.004***
Risk avoidance	6.1%	11.4%	24.1%	84.095***
Companionship	24.7%	23.0%	22.9%	.796
Communication	8.3%	31.6%	44.0%	206.353***

Note: ***p<.001, ** p<.01, *p<.05.

In this social network, it is the two ends of the continuous spectrum that influence the rural migrants' willingness to settle. The strong ties or "emotional ties" encourage rural migrants to settle. The weak ties or "instrumental ties" result in rural migrants being not clear about their future. The "middle ties" or "emotional-instrumental ties" sector does not have much influence on migrants' willingness to settle.

The two driving forces behind the rural migrants' social activities in the city are the maintaining of the resources in their possession and the desire to acquire resources which they do not yet possess. The strong ties or "emotional ties" help rural migrants to maintain their existing resources. The weak ties or "instrumental ties" help them to acquire resources which they do not yet possess (Lin 2005). From the transfer of employment information to going along with companions, from the acquisition of the first job to mutual assistance in the city, reliance upon "emotional ties" can be found among rural migrants. It lowers the migration costs and risks for rural migrants whose circumstances are uncertain. Subsequently, while living in the city, in addition to the extensive connections with strong ties, they start to seek new business ties networks and various market information, and start to establish instrumental ties with city officials and residents as well (Peng 1996; Xiang 2000; Liu 2001; Qu 2001; Cao 2003; Wang/Tong 2004). Rural migrants expect to acquire more resources. However, with their need for respect and equality, they are liable to feel pressurized and nervous when social reciprocal services with weak ties are established. They seldom or never experience such feelings when participating in reciprocal services with strong ties. This results in rural migrants being "not clear" about their future direction.

Conclusion

With regard to the questionnaire and interviewing of rural migrants in Nanjing in 2002, I carried out research on the rural migrants' willingness to settle, in the contexts of both socio-economic status and social networks. The analysis revealed that the "socio economic status" variables of age, education and duration of residence in the city and the two extremes of the social networks, i.e. "emotional ties" and "instrumental ties" will all produce differences in the rural migrants' willingness to settle. The influence of other factors could not be verified in this research.

Some research has revealed that since the 1990s, there has been a trend towards family migration. From the perspective of the social networks, the migrant spouses have adopted a "survival strategy" to cope with the separation. When the "survival strategy" takes effect, they will make an effort to live together in the city. Moreover, rural migrants with a strong desire to settle will bring their children with them to the city. In the survey, the living-in-city ratio of the children of rural migrants who "agreed" to settle in the city is 0.5823; that of the "not clear" is 0.4978 and that of the "not agreed" is 0.3395 (by variance test, the difference between groups passed the significance test, F=5.613, df=2, significance is 0.004). Therefore, although they are still "rural migrants", the nuclear family has "moved" to the city. It is undoubtedly helpful for them to stay in the city and undertake substantial settlement action instead of following the previous circular migration pattern.

When they have solved their survival problems with the assistance of "emotional ties" and "emotional-instrumental ties," the rural migrants, in order to acquire more valuable resources and seek better development, start to establish and rely on the "instrumental ties" and "emotional-instrumental ties." What is the actual result of the reliance on the "emotional-instrumental ties" and "instrumental ties" between rural migrants and "townspeople?" Unlike the "emotional ties" which enable them to settle in the city, instrumental ties lead the interviewees to be "not clear" about their future or to return home when they have earned enough money.

In the social networks, with the pulling force of "emotional ties" and the pushing force of "instrumental ties," there is a strong willingness to settle and substantial settlement activity at one end, and segregation and isolation from "townspeople" at the other end. Even when they live in the same "village in cities," they live separately and in different spiritual worlds (Li 2003). There will therefore be segmented assimilation among rural migrants and townspeople.

References

Alba, Richard and Nee, Victor (1997) "Rethinking assimilation theory for a new era of immigration," in *The International Migration Review* 31(4), pp. 826-874.

Bai, Nansheng 白南生 and He, Yupeng 何宇鹏 (2002) "Huixiang, haishi waichu? Anhui Sichuan er sheng nongcun waichu laodongli huiliu yanjiu" 回乡，还是外出？——安徽四川二省农村外出劳动力回流研究 [Return or migration? – Research on reflow of emigrant labour of Anhui and Sichuan], in *Shehuixue yanjiu* 社会学研究 [Sociology Research] 3, pp. 64-78.

Blau, Peter (彼得•布劳) (1991) *Bupingdeng yu yizhixing* 不平等与异质性 [Inequality and heterogeneity], Beijing: Zhongguo shehui kexue chubanshe 中国社会科学出版社 [China Social Sciences Press], p. 394.

Cao, Ziwei 曹子玮 (2003) "Nongmingong de caijiangou shehuiwang yu wangnei ziyuan liuxiang" 农民工的再建构社会网与网内资源流向 [Peasant-workers social network restructure and network resource tendency], in *Shehuixue yanjiu* 社会学研究 [Sociology Research] 3, pp. 99-110.

Granovetter, Marc (1985) "Economic action and social structure: the problem of embeddedness," in *American Journal of Sociology* 91(3), pp. 481-510.

He, Pichan 和丕禅 and Guo, Jinfeng 郭金丰 (2004) "Zhidu yuesu xia de nongmingong yimin qingxiang tanxi" 制度约束下的农民工移民倾向探析 [Analysis of peasant-worker immigrant tendency under system restriction], in *Zhongguo Nongcun Jingji* 中国农村经济 [Chinese Rural Economy] 10.

Inkeles, Alex 阿列克斯•英格尔斯等 et al. (1992) *Cong chuantongren dao xiandairen* 从传统人到现代人 [From traditionalist to modernist], Beijing: Zhongguo renmin daxue chubanshe 中国人民大学出版社 [China People's University Press], p. 7.

Li, Hanlin 李汉林 (2003) "Guanxi qiangdu zuowei yizhong shequ zuzhi fangshi" 关系强度作为一种社区组织方式 [Strength of ties as a community organization method], in Li Peilin 李培林(Ed) Nongmingong: Zhongguo jincheng nongmingong de jingji shehui fenxi 农民工：中国进城农民工的经济社会分析[Peasant-worker: economic and social analysis of Chinese peasant-work entered cities], Beijing: Shehui kexue wenxian chubanshe 社会科学文献出版社 [Social Sciences Academic Press].

Li, Qiang 李强 (2004) Nongmingong yu Zhongguo shehui fenceng 农民工与中国社会分层 [Peasant-worker and social hierarchy in China], Beijing: Shehui kexue wenxian chubanshe 社会科学文献出版社 [Social Sciences Academic Press], pp. 63-68.

Lin, Nan 林南 (2005) Shehui ziben: guanyu shehui jiegou he xingdong de lilun 社会资本：关于社会结构和行动的理论 [Social capital: theory about social structure and action], Shanghai: Shanghai renmin chubanshe 上海人民出版社 [Shanghai People's Press].

Liu, Linping 刘林平 (2001) Wailai renqun benzhong de guanxi yunyong 外来人群体中的关系运用 [Ties operation in migrant groups], in *Zhongguo Shehui Kexue* 中国社会科学 [Social Sciences in China] 5.

Luo, Jiade 罗家德 (2005) Shehui wang fenxi jiangyi 社会网分析讲义 [Social network analysis teaching materials], Beijing: Shehui kexue wenxian chubanshe 社会科学文献出版社 [Social Sciences Academic Press], pp. 50-51.

Peng, Qingen 彭庆恩 (1996) "Guanxi ziben he dili huode" 关系资本和地位获得 [Relationship Capital and status acquisition], in *Shehuixue yanjiu* 社会学研究 [Sociology Research] 4.

Portes，Alejandro (ed) (1995) "Economic Sociology and Sociology of Immigration: A Conceptual Overview" in Alejandro Portes (ed.) *The Economic Sociology of Immigration*. New York: Russell Sage Foundation.

Sanders, Jimy and Nee, Victor (1996) "Immigrant self-employment: the family as social capital and the value of human capital as social capital and the value of human capital," in *American Sociological Review* 61, pp. 231-249.

Qu, Jingdong 渠敬东 (2001) "Shenghuo shijie zhong de guanxi qiangdu" 生活世界中的关系强度 [Strength of ties in life worlds], in Ke Lanjun 柯兰君and Li Hanlin 李汉林 (eds) Dushi li de cunmin 都市里的村民 [Villagers in city], Beijing: 中央编译出版社 [Central Compilation & Translation Press].

Wang, Hejian 汪和建 (2003) "Renji guanxi yu zhidu de jiangou" 人际关系与制度的建构 [Human relations and institution structure], in *Shehui lilun xuebao* (Xianggang) 社会理论学报(香港) [Journal of Social Theory (Hong Kong)] 1.

Wang, Jichuan 王济川 and Guo, Zhigang 郭志刚 (2001) *Logistic huigui moxing – fenxi yu yingyong* Logistic回归模型——分析与应用 [Logistic regression model – analysis and application], Beijing: Gaodeng jiaoyu chubanshe 高等教育出版社 [Higher Education Press], p. 153.

Wang, Yijie 王毅杰 and Tong, Xing 童星 (2004) „Liudong nongmin shehui zhichi wang tanxi" 流动农民社会支持网探析[Research on rural migrants support networks], in *Shehuixue yanjiu* 社会学研究 [Sociology Research] 2.

Wellman, Barry 巴里·韦尔曼 (1994) "Wangluo fenxi: cong fangfa he yinyu dao lilun he shizhi""网络分析：从方法和隐喻到理论和实质 [Network analysis: from method and metaphor to theory and essence], in *Guowai shehuixue* 国外社会学 [Foreign Sociology] 4.

Wu, Xinglu 吴兴陆 (2005) "Nongmingong ding juxing qianyi juece de yingxiang yinsu shizheng yanjiu" 农民工定居性迁移决策的影响因素实证研究 [Research on influencing factors on peasant-worker settlement migration decision], in *Renkou yu jingji* 人口与经济 [Population and Economics] 1.

Xiang, Biao 项飚 (2000) Kuayue bianjie de shequ 跨越边界的社区 [Community beyond border], Shanghai: Sanlian shudian 三联书店 [Sanlian Bookstore].

Zhao, Yandong 赵延东 and Wang, Fenyu 王奋宇 (2002) „Chengxiang liudong renkou de jingji dili huode yi jueding yinsu" 城乡流动人口的经济地位获得及决定因素 [Rural migrant economic status acquisition and determinative factor], in *Zhongguo renkou kexue* 中国人口科学 [Chinese Journal of Population Science] 4.

Cultural Life of Rural Migrants and Urban Integration

Zhu Li

The social policy for the floating population in China saw a turning point in 2003 when the National People's Congress and China's People's Political Consultative Conference (CPPCC) passed a series of motions to protect the rights of the floating population, such as, to dun overdue salary for rural migrants and to address schooling problems for their children in cities. Quite a number of local People's Congresses have promulgated local rules and regulations to protect rural migrants' rights. Such protection from social policies is unprecedented. The "Opinions on the policies of increasing peasant's income from the Central Government and the State Council" issued in the No. 1 circular of the Central Government on 8 February 2005 clearly stipulated that "rural migrants employed in cities have already become an important part of the industrial workers." The social policy at central level has, for the first time, clarified the class attributes of the rural migrants and their rights in cities. As part of the working class and urban residents, problems of the migrant workers in cities should naturally be considered by the city administrators with regard not only to their basic working and living rights but also to a higher level of need and rights in their vocational training, spiritual and cultural life. Issues concerning migrant workers, their spiritual condition, their survival and development are closely linked with the development of the cities they live in.

Theory: urbanization and rural migrants' adaptability of urban life

A great deal of research on migrant workers has been conducted from economic perspectives, for the increased income of the migrants has had an obvious impact on the economic development of the city. In fact, research on migrants from the cultural and social perspectives is equally important. The migration of peasants to cities is not merely the spatial migration of the rural population; it is also a "cultural migration" in modern sense. It is more of a transformation process for the individual, from a rural person to a city person, which deals with changes in peasants' life styles, values and social psychology.

Urbanization is closely linked with modernization. From the perspective of individual adaptability, modernization means "a process of changing the traditional life style for an individual and adopting a complicated, technologically advanced and constantly changing life style" (Rogers/Burdge 1988: 309), "urbanity" is one of these life styles. Due to the differences in size, population density and social complexity, the city has its own set of social and cultural features which are different from those in rural areas (Wirth 1938: 1-24). A city is an organic whole consisting of city people, city material facilities and city culture.

"The final products of the city environment are various new pattern personalities" (Park et al. 1987: 273). The city is not just an area where people live together, it is also an "urban" state of mind and lifestyle. The filtration and influence of the city culture play a vital role in the urbanization of peasants. The urbanization is not just the modernization of material facilities but also "a general reflection of the modernization of social productivity and social relations; human being's spiritual world and lifestyles" (Zheng 1987: 343).

Rural people are confronted with a multicolored world when they arrive in cities; they try to adapt themselves to the great changes actively or passively and start their transition from being rural people to becoming urban people. Urbanization is a "comprehensive concept oriented towards the human being and involving many factors, levels and variables"(Xin 1994: 15). The urbanization of migrants involves primarily the process of identifying themselves with the city and adapting to urban life when they move to cities. Modernization is not the merely spatial migration of the rural population, it is also a "cultural migration" in the modern sense. It is more of a transformation process for the individual from being a rural person to becoming a city person, which deals with changes in peasants' life styles, values and social psychology.

"Adaptability" and "socialization" are closely related. The term "socialization" is used to refer to the educating function of society, where the emphasis lies on the educating process exercised by the various institutions of socialization; the term "adaptability" is mainly used to refer to the individual socialization, where the emphasis lies on the individual's acceptance of the surrounding environment and the socializing process in social life. "Socialization is a social interaction enabling people to acquire the individuality and lifestyles of the society they live in (…), socialization allows people to learn rules, criteria of values, language, skills, religions and other indispensable thinking and acting models in their social lives"(Robertson 1990). Adaptability has resulted in the behaviour of individuals or a group of people complying with some or all rules and standards of the group they belong to or those commonly accepted social and cultural rules and standards. Socialization is a complicated processes involving the individual's efforts to adapt to and construct, to re-adapt to and re-construct society (Zheng 1989: 99).

Rural migrants are a special new social stratum. They have moved from rural areas to cities where they have found the living environment totally different from that in rural areas and have taken on a new social role. Such a variation in the living environment and social role has forced the migrants to adjust themselves and change their economic life, social intercourse and values in order to better fit into the new urban environment. The adaptation of the migrants is clearly reflected in their ongoing socialization in the new environment.

We have classified the adaptation of rural migrants into three levels in ascending order: economic, social and cultural adaptation. Adaptation at the economic level looks into rural migrants' occupations, income and accommodation; adaptation at the social level looks into their lifestyles and social intercourses; adaptation at cultural level examines concepts, psychology and wills.

When the rural migrants move to urban areas, they need, first of all, to find a job that will give them a relatively stable income and accommodation so that they are able to survive. Adaptation at the economic level is the basis for their being able to stay in the cities. Once they have finished the preliminary adaptation necessary for survival, the migrants will look for new lifestyles and social intercourse as their next requirement, which reflects the degree of identification with urban life.

Adaptation at the cultural level is spiritual; it shows the recognition of urban lifestyles among rural migrants. The profound changes of the inner spiritual factors, such as new concepts, attitudes and desires are the natural result of long-term adaptation to the living environment, which shows the depth of the rural migrants' involvement in urban life. Only when adaptation has occurred in cultural psychology, can we say that urbanization has been effected, has shaped and raised the migrants' personalities and that the socialization process from their being rural people to becoming urban people has been completed. These three aspects are interrelated, interactive and inseparable.

Reality: rural migrant peasants' lifestyle in their spare time

Lifestyle is the summation of the fixed styles and typical features in acquiring consumed subsistence materials (including labour), controlling free time and daily activities. The lifestyle has a distinctive group character. Economic conditions are normally decisive in shaping the lifestyles. In addition, the social conditions and the natural environment are all influencing factors. Rural life and urban life are entirely different. When the migrants move from rural areas to cities, their lifestyle is naturally changed towards becoming an urban lifestyle; this can also be called the urbanization of the rural migrants' lifestyle. While living in cities, the migrants limit their consumption to "necessities" and have rather low living requirements. Such a relatively low economic frame of reference is helpful for the economic adaptation of the migrant peasants, but this kind of adaptation remains as an adaptation for survival.

The migrants' consumption is characterized by austerity: apart from those necessities of food, clothing, accommodation and transportation, they economize wherever possible and spend very little on recreation each month. According to the survey carried out by Nanjing University in 2000, the monthly salary of the migrants at that time was RMB 680.7 and their consumption was RMB 319.6. Among their consumption, the largest amount they spent was on food amounting to RMB 177.9 on average, followed by RMB 52.5 on clothing, RMB 42.5 on accommodation, RMB 22.9 on articles of daily use, RMB 22.3 on transportation and only RMB 1.5 on others. More than half of the salary was sent home. We can see that the majority of rural migrants spent little except on daily necessities. Cultural life is almost a luxury for them. "Having painstaking job and going to bed when there is nothing to do" depicts the monotonous and deficient pastimes of many migrants. In comparison, "the proportion of the entertaining and developmental consumption on education, leisure and recreation among urban residents is on the rise, from 12.6 per cent in 2000 to 14.6 per cent during January to September of 2001 with the average per capita consumption increased from RMB 628 to over RMB 800" (Zhu Qingfang 2002: 156). The average monthly expenses spent on education and recreation among urban citizens increased from RMB 52.3 in 2000 to RMB 66.7 in 2001.

An important part of the lifestyle is the arrangement of spare time. In the survey conducted by Nanjing University (Zhu Li 2002: 263), there was a question on "what you do in your spare time" and there were several possible answers to this question. The top six answers were: 38 per cent of the respondents play cards, 37 per cent watch TV, 36 per cent listen to radio, 35 per cent chat, 30 per cent go for a stroll and 20 per cent read newspapers. Other answers chosen were sleeping (most of the spare time of those working on shifts is spent sleeping), doing family chores, looking for jobs, going to a dance hall and meeting fellow countrymen.

According to another survey (Chen 2005), the spare time recreational life is rather monotonous among the rural migrants: 67 per cent of male migrant peasants have nothing to do; 40 per cent chat with their fellows countrymen; 19 per cent play cards or mah-jong; 19 per cent call their families; 11 per cent drink and five per cent admitted that they visit prostitutes. 52 per cent of the female migrants call their families, 35 per cent go window shopping; 28 per cent visit their fellow countrymen; 27 per cent read books or newspapers and 20 per cent go to bed after meals. The arrangement of the spare time activities may vary among individuals with regard to the nature of their jobs.

The social intercourse of the rural migrants is related to their occupations and places of residence. Since most of the migrant peasants are involved in jobs with strong sectoral and regional natures, the circle of their social life is relatively small and making contact with urban people is difficult. Apart from the work place, the place of residence is the main area for their social intercourse. The location and community environment of their places of residence greatly impacts on their social intercourse. At the same time, their jobs also determine their working time and work intensity, thus influencing the amount of spare time and energy that they have at their disposal and which are important conditions for social intercourse. The rural migrants spend most of their spare time on internal group recreational activity or simply kill the time themselves.

The several recreational ways ranked top do not involve any expense and are also relaxing, which accommodates both austerity and practicality. Even though some practices which are particular to urban inhabitants have been adopted by some migrants, the utilization of spare time among most of them still does not bear any of the strong characteristics of urban life. The recreational activities among the married migrants are evidently few; some of them kill time by listening to the radio. The pressure of life on single migrants is relatively light and they tend to have more recreational activities, but these are only limited to chatting, playing cards, playing chess, reading newspapers, writing letters and watching TV in shops or along the street. Some peasants in their twenties have started to imitate urban inhabitants by going to Karaoke, dancing and playing in parks. Female migrants have one more recreational activity, that is window shopping. The most common characteristic of the leisure consumption among the migrants is the cost-free activities. Many of them feel bored in their spare time; even though there are more places for entertainment and recreational activities in urban areas than in rural areas, they seldom take part in these.

We can see that the spare time among migrants is scarce and monotonous. There are some obvious reasons for this: firstly, their income is relatively low and therefore they normally stay away from ballrooms, swimming pools, tea houses, Internet bars and coffee shops where entertainment can easily cost them dozens of RMB. Secondly, their educational level is low and they do not feel the need to read books, go to museums, listen to music and watch dancing. Thirdly, there is insufficient guidance on cultural consumption. The rural migrants do not have much contact with local residents and their recreational activities are basically inherited from friends and relatives who moved to cities earlier on. Information on TV is mainly for urban residents and only very little is useful to the migrant peasants. TV is only used to watch soap opera. Fourthly, the work unit where migrants work apparently pays little attention to the spare time activities of the migrants. Most of the employers believe that spare time activities are the business of the migrants themselves and that the company does not need to interfere. They do not consider this to be in the companies' interests. The big gap between the exorbitant cultural consumption in cities and the mean income of the migrants is the main obstacle to their merging with mainstream urban culture. They are very cautious about spending their hard-earned money on cultural consumption. Fundamentally speaking, the way to change the migrant peasants' poor spiritual and cultural life would be a universal increase in their income. At the same time, this is related to working hours and labour intensity. There is a grouping of isolated people in cities, although they are physically close to others, they are very far apart from a social point of view. This is particulary true of the migrant peasants.

Our attention has been drawn to the damage to the migrants' external interests. We should also note the sacrifice of their invisible interests. They pay huge amounts in hidden costs. Nearly 80 per cent of migrants are alone in cities; only a few have brought their family members along with them. That has left them unable to enjoy many family protective functions, which is difficult for urban people to comprehend. For instance, leisure time is an important family function and urban people have so many different ways of spending their leisure time, such as travelling, shopping, body building and recreation or simply watching TV and reading at home. These very common leisure pastimes for urban people are a kind of luxury and only exist in the wild dreams of rural migrants. In addition, they cannot get those common but indispensable protections they have when they are at home, such as emotional communication, family enjoyment, concern and spiritual comfort from their relatives. All these are the hidden costs paid by the migrant peasants. And these are also needs they hope to get fulfilled. Some of the family functions are irreplaceable, but others can be made available through the city's cultural life.

Do some of the migrants spend their spare time on further education? The survey carried out by Nanjing University showed that 14.48 per cent of the migrant peasants in cities were engaged in further education (Zhu Li 2002: 264), which was mainly the technical training organized by their employers. We have learnt from the survey in enterprises that, first of all, some of the migrants wanted to continue their education, but their wishes were rather disoriented and influenced by popular employment trends in society. Secondly, their desire to learn is restricted by their level of education. Thirdly, some of the enterprises want the migrant peasants to use their further education to better serve the enterprise and are willing to cover the costs of this. Some of the migrants have realized that in order to adapt to urban life and develop their lives in the cities, they have to continue improving their competences in order to be able to take advantage of new opportunities. A small number of rural migrants even sit the self-study examination.

The healthy and scientific pastime will relax the migrants in body and mind, amuse their hearts, increase their feelings of identity and assimilation with the cities in which they live and help develop friendly communication with urban citizens. Our interviews showed, however, that even though the migrants can keep in step with the urban population during the eight working hours, they drift away from the urban population. After their eight working hours; this has led to the problems with migrant peasants' leisure time in the cities. The insufficient cultural life is not the main reason for the confused mentality among the migrant peasants, but the monotonous cultural life is a factor which affects their mental adjustment. Most of the rural migrants are not happy with their cultural life: "no TVs, no books to read, no place to sing, no internet bars and no videos to watch." They are suffering from cultural thirst. Negative impacts from this situation are emerging:

- There is no cultural life and there are no channels to disseminate the information that rural migrants love to see and hear. Therefore, they cannot learn about party and government policies. This is not helpful in protecting their legal rights;
- Cultural issues are not merely related to pastimes; they are also related to psychological matters. If the spare time cultural life for this group of people remains boring and monotonous for ever, some people will inevitably become listless or even go mad. The unsatisfactory cultural life and the sluggish information flow will lead to degradation and an inability to improve their quality of life;
- The rural migrants can create problems for society if they feel bored. The physical tiredness will be mediated through recreational activities. The absence of colourful pastimes will make the energetic youngsters wander around and try things like gambling and whoring, thus leading to dangers for local social security. How to enrich the pastimes of the migrant peasants is a piece of "virgin soil" in community management that needs to be tapped and developed;

- Rural migrants do not have an urban lifestyle and they are roving on the periphery of mainstream urban life, "their rural life style in cities," "the rural ways of communication in cities" plus the "pastime of cultural desert in cities" have made them feel like always drifting aimlessly "outsiders" or "transients;" it is difficult for them to produce an attitude of assimilation, namely to love the cities. This has made urbanization difficult for them. At present, the management and services for rural migrants' leisure time is zero: This should be looked after by enterprises and communities in order to ensure migrants have healthy pastimes.

The cultural adaptation among the migrants is actually psychological adaptation which is the highest level of adaptation. It is only when the rural migrants have completed their cultural adaptation that they will really finish the process of adapting to city life. To properly address the question of an adequate cultural life for the migrant peasants is crucial to safeguarding social stability and urban modernization. Last year, a migrant in Beijing jumped into a septic tank and killed himself after watching pornographic videos; his death attracted the attention of society and indicates that the spiritual and cultural life of the 100 million migrant peasants cannot be neglected.

Suggestions: how to improve the cultural life of rural migrants

Recognize the importance of enriching cultural life for the rural migrants
By 2020, according to the indicator for the well-off society in China, the urbanization rate will be 56 per cent. If the annual growth rate is one per cent, this means that there will be 13 million peasants moving to cities each year. The issue of an adequate cultural life for these rural migrants will become more prominent. Currently, this issue is regarded as trivial for the following reasons:
- A static view of the rural migrants. They are seen as just making some hard-earned money in the cities and do not need a cultural life. Actually, the needs of the migrants nowadays are different from what they were ten years ago. Earlier on, most of the rural migrants simply wanted to earn money to support their families, but nowadays most of them have received a middle school or high school education and they come to cities not only for money but for the urban civilization and because they think there are more opportunities for development. As a new generation of migrants, they have much higher levels of education and faith. Like most of the urban citizens, they long for colourful spiritual and cultural lives. They are more open-minded than the previous generation of migrants.
- Their cultural lives are the personal affairs of the migrant peasants and government does not need to interfere. It is not possible for more than one hundred million of rural migrants to meet their cultural needs. This is not only a personal issue for the migrants; it is also related to the protection of spiritual

rights and the normal needs of human beings. It is an issue for the enterprises, for the communities and also for the government to consider. To address the cultural deficiency among the rural migrants is the common responsibility of society, the country, enterprises and the migrants themselves.
- The migrant workers are everywhere and the absence of cultural activities will not affect recruitment. In the last two years, the Pearl River Delta has experienced a shortage of migrant workers. This is not only due to low incomes and poor welfare but also to the respect they received and how their various needs were met. The migrant workers will soon become seller's market from current buyer's market. Precautions need to be taken in order to attract migrants and to create a social environment for them to work and live in. We should pay attention not only to the protection of their survival and working rights but also to their cultural and spiritual life. We should also make good use of the complete and modern facilities in the cities to provide cheap or even free quality services pertinent to the migrants' needs in order to allow them to enjoy the advanced cultural products. They will then become not only the masters of urban economic construction but also the masters of the urban spiritual civilization and actively participate in the healthy urban cultural life.

Strengthen the social responsibility of the enterprises

In the process of enriching rural migrants' cultural lives, the government can only serve as a first driving force. In the long run, employers should play a leading role. Some of the well-situated enterprises should be urged to properly organize the training and cultural lives of the migrant workers. More attention should be paid to other activities, such as subscribing to newspapers, providing TV sets and organizing some colourful spare time activities for them. If possible, evening schools may be set up by enterprises or by industrial associations. The government should also invest some in addressing the inadequate cultural life of the migrants.

Increase the knowledge content in cultural activities

The cultural education of the migrant workers should be linked with the needs of the enterprise development. The key element in changing the inferior position of the migrants is to increase their human capital. The training should be pushed forward by the government and operated by enterprises. The technical training system should be set up and improved in order to make good use of the factory schools, vocational schools and various industrial technical training centers to provide training for the migrant workers. A "competent worker" campaign should be organized and skilled workers and qualified technicians should be asked to help them. Sports meetings should be held for technical operations and a foundation should be set up for those talented migrant workers so as to motivate them to commit to their work and learning., In this way, we will not only be able to attract the migrants but also keep them in the cities.

Positive spiritual contents should be incorporated in the cultural activities

The organization of cultural activities is just a means of concentrating on their work and lives; the ultimate goal is to inspire them with the enthusiasm to build and love the city. Organize a cultural activity of "my second hometown" with investment from the government, people's organizations and communities. For instance, a series of activities has been organized, such as "loving my second hometown and building my second hometown" and how to be a civilized citizen. Carry out publicity on legal information with the rural migrants as the main target. The party and youth leagues at various levels should properly handle the transfer of the party and league relations and recruit more members. A party committee and youth league committee should be set up in enterprises with a large number of rural migrants. Select "progressive migrant workers" and "distinguished worker in building the second hometown" and make TV programs about these people.

Set up trade union among the migrant workers

As a part of the working class, the rural migrants should naturally be included in the trades unions. Compared with urban workers, they are a disadvantaged group and need more care and support from the trades unions. Trades unions at various levels should treat the migrants as the fresh blood of the working class and try to bring them into the trade union and protect their legal rights. Trade unions should also be established in private enterprises. According to the figures from the Shanghai Trade Union, there are 3.8 million rural migrants among the 7.7 million industrial workers, which amounts to nearly 50 per cent, and most of these are working in the new economic organizations. The non-public enterprises are a missing link in the trade union management. The absence of the trade union is one of the reasons for the liable damage of the legal rights of the migrant workers and the migrants in the non-public enterprise are people who need the support from the trade union the most. The involvement of the trade union could get twice the result with half the effort. The trade union will urge the enterprise to fulfill its commitment in protecting the employees' rights and with regard to their cultural lives will, for instance, help the enterprise with purchasing TV sets, setting up libraries and organizing mobile film-playing team etc. The Youth League and Women's Federation will use their own channels to carry out educational and cultural activities.

Bring into play the self-organizing role of the migrants

Currently, the protection of the migrants' legal rights depends mainly on the government and mass media and hardly on themselves. This is not an effective long-term strategy. The ultimate goal is to enable the migrants to protect their own rights with their own power. The self-organization of the migrant workers has been a sensitive issue. There is a concern about certain force running against the government. The self-organization among the migrants is similar to the function of of trade unions in protecting their various rights. It should therefore be allowed in order to mobilize the enthusiasm of the migrant workers in protecting their own rights so long as they follow the relevant regulations on social organizations. It is both a pressure group and a relieve group. It will be a long-term approach rather than a horrible thing to allow the self-organization of the migrant workers. The elite among the migrant workers should be allowed access to political channels (as members of the People's Congress or Political Consultative Committee) so as to speak on behalf of the migrant workers and solve issues for them as well. In addition, the migrants can also organize some recreational activities on their own to enrich their spare time activities. Organize artistic troupe and home of female migrants. Supports are needed for these organizations. The self-directed and self-performed programs about the life of rural migrants will dissolve their mental distress. Of course, due to financial and technical limitations, it is not possible for these organizations to fundamentally address the barrenness of the spiritual and cultural lives of the masses of migrant workers. Support is still needed mainly from the government and society at present.

Mobilize social resources to enrich cultural life of the migrants

It is not the responsibility of an individual unit to enrich the cultural lives of the migrant peasants; it is the responsibility of the whole of society and requires a common effort and support from the working units, communities, government agencies, social organizations and all members of society. At the moment, quite a lot of social resources need to be explored. Free cultural consumption is mostly welcomed by the migrant workers, but the facilities for cultural consumption in China are basically home-based, such as TV, VCD and computer etc. The migrant workers can neither bring these things with them nor can they afford them. However, quite a lot of these electrical appliances are idle or need to be replaced in urban residents' home. This is proved by the flourishing second-hand market in every city. We can adopt the idea of the charity supermarket to establish something like a migrants' supermarket. So long as someone organizes it, many families will be quite willing to donate their used TV sets, VCD and computers to the migrants. Many film copies are stored for many years and can be shown to the migrant workers free of charge. Libraries in the enterprises and community reading rooms should also be open to the migrants free of charge. It may be possible for the sports bureaus to organize sports meetings for the migrant workers or invite them to participate in the city sports meeting. We can also mobilize retired scholars, technicians and volunteer university students to work for the migrant workers' schools organized by the communities and train them in skills, scientific knowledge, social morality, laws and regulations as well as in technical skills demanded by the labour market. We can also win financial support from the national and international donors such as Canadian NGOs, HK Amity Foundation and Oxfam HK, etc. We can also run a hotline providing psychological consultation for the migrant peasants. We should make good use of the idle human and material resources in the cities to provide cheap and free quality cultural products to allow the rural migrants to enjoy the advanced urban cultural achievements.

Pay attention to institutional innovation

In Jinhua City, the relevant department invited public bids for free films for the migrant workers. The free evening film market operates like this: they attract enterprises to pay for tile through the advertising effect from the big square and masses of people. The enterprise which wins the bidding will show its advertisement before the film is played each evening apart from the fixed advertisement sign board and the enterprise will cover all the costs for film screen stands, film playing fees, cleaning fees and social order maintenance fees. The films and advertisements will be censored by the city propaganda department. This approach has attracted funds from many enterprises;[1] it is a mechanism combining government function with market operation and can last forever. The government can only be an initial driving force and is not able to cover all the administrative issues. When there is an innovative system, there will be a lasting driving mechanism and the services for the migrants will be maintained.

The media should stress the open and tolerant nature of the city and close the gap between the "First Class citizens" and the "Second Class citizens"

It is inevitable that the peasants, with their awareness of the historical differences between the urban and rural areas will feel mental distress. It will also take some time for the city to accept them. The media can do quite a lot of meaningful work towards dissolving the prejudice against the migrants which can be found among some of the urban people. The media should cover more of the progressive action of the migrants so as to eliminate the hostility between the urban residents and the migrants. In China, there are no "First Class citizens" and "Second Class citizens," there are only equal members of the socialist society. The rural migrants should walk out of their isolated life and integrate themselves into the cities where they work and live.

It will be a long process to change the overall situation of the rural migrants. More attention is needed from the whole of society on the in-depth issues concerning migrants. This does not only requires policies and regulations to incorporate migrants' interests into the urban interest system; a lot of good and practical actions are required to deal with the difficult situation and unfair treatment of this

---

[1] The Jinhua Branch of the Zhejiang Mobile Telecom won the bidding recently. The manager Mr. Wang said: "It is really a value for money." According to him, each night there are 2000 audiences, there should be 500,000 people each year not counting rainy days and big public events. For such a large number of audiences, the annual cost is no more than RMB 200,000, this is a most welcome opportunity for a enterprise, which can generate long-tern return with limited input.

disadvantaged group in cities and allow them to blend successfully into mainstream urban life so as to realize the harmonious development of urban society.

References

Castles, Stephen and Miller, Mark J. (1993) *The Age of Migration, International Population Movement in the Modern World*, New York.

Chen, Chaobing 陈朝兵 (2005) "Bangzhu nongmingong zouchu wenhua shamo" 帮助农民工走出文化沙漠 [Help the migrant peasants walking out of the cultural desert]. Online. Available HTTP: <http://www.cnhubei.com/200502/ca689405.htm> (accessed 15 October 2005).

Goldscheider, Calvin (1983) Boulder: *Urban Migrants in Developing Nations: Patterns and Problems of Adjustment*, Westview Press.

Ke, Lanjun 柯兰君 and Li, Hanlin 李汉林 (Eds) (2001) *Dou shi li de cunmin: Zhongguo da chengshi de liudong renkou* 都市里的村民－－中国大城市的流动人口 [Villagers in cities: rural migrants in Chinese metropolises]，Beijing：Zhongyang bianyi chubanshe 中央编译出版社 [China Central Translation Publishing House].

Li, Peilin 李培林 (Ed) (2003) *Nongmingong: Zhongguo jincheng nongmingong de jingji shehui fenxi* 农民工－－中国进城农民工的经济社会分析[Migrant peasants - social and economic analysis of the migrant peasants in China], Beijing: Shehui kexue wenxian chubanshe 社会科学文献出版社[Social Science and Cultural Heritage Publishing House].

Park, Robert E. (R•E•帕克) et al. (1987) *Chengshi shehuixue* 城市社会学 [Urban sociology], Beijing：Huaxia Chubanshe 华夏出版社[Huaxia Publishing House].

Robertson, Ian (伊恩·罗伯逊) (1990) *Shehuixue* 社会学[Sociology]，translated by Zhao Minghua赵明华et al., Beijing: Shangwu yinshuguan商务印书馆[Commercial Publishing House].

Rogers, Everett M. (埃弗里特 M.罗吉斯) and Burdge, Rabel J. (拉伯尔•J.伯德格) (1988) *Xiangcun shehui bianqian* 乡村社会变迁 [Social Change in Rural Societies], translated by Wang Xiaoyi 王晓毅 and Wang Dishan 王地山，Hangzhou: Zhejiang renmin chubanshe 浙江人民出版社 [Zhejiang People's Publishing House].

Wirth, Louis (1938) "Urbanism as a Way of Life," in *American Journal of Sociology*, 44(1938), pp. 1-24.

Xin, Qiushui 辛秋水 (1994) "Nongcun chengshihua lilun yanjiuhui zongshu" 农村城市化理论研究会综述 [Outline of the theoretical research society of rural urbanization]，in *Jianghuai luntan* 江淮论坛[Jiang-Huai Forum], 1994, Issue 5, p. 15.

Xu, Xinxin 许欣欣 (2000) *Dangdai Zhongguo shehui jiegou de bianqian yu liudong*当代中国社会结构的变迁与流动 [The change and flow of the contemporary Chinese social structure], Beijing: Shehui kexue wenxian chubanshe 社会科学文献出版社 [Social Science and Cultural Heritage Publishing House].

Yu, Depeng 俞德鹏 (2002) *Cheng xiang shehui: cong geli zouxiang kaifang. Zhongguo hukou jidu yu hukoufa yanjiu* 城乡社会：从隔离走向开放－－中国户籍制度与户籍法研究 [Urban and rural society: from isolation to opening up – Chinese household registration system and research on household registration law], Jinan: Shandong renmin chubanshe 山东人民出版社 [Shandong People's Publishing House].

Zheng, Hangsheng 郑杭生 (Ed) (1987) *Shehuixue gailun xinbian* 社会学概论新编 [New introduction to sociology], Beijing: Zhongguo renmin daxue chubanshe 中国人民大学出版社 [People's University Publishing House].

Zhu, Li 朱力 (2002) *Zhongguo mingong hu* 中国民工潮 [Migrant workers tide] Fuzhou: Fuzhou renmin chubanshe 福建人民出版社 [Fujian People's Publishing House].

Zhu, Qingfang 朱庆芳 (2002) "Chengxiang jumin shenghuo zhiliang he xiaocai shichang de xin dongxiang" 城乡居民生活质量和消费市场的新动向 [New trend of the living quality and consumption market of urban and rural people], in Ru Xin 汝信 et al. (eds) (2002) *2002: Analysis and Projection of the Chinese Social Situation*, Beijing: Shehui kexue wenxian chubanshe 社会科学文献出版社 [Social Science and Cultural Heritage Publishing House].

The Problem of Overdue Migrant Wages – Legal Framework and Government Policies

Yang Wenjian, Sun Youran and Wang Pinghua

Research background

In recent years, the phenomenon of delayed payment for migrants has become more and more serious: it has badly affected the personal interests of ordinary people, the development of the national economy, the market order and social stability. It has attracted the attention of the Central Committee of the Communist Party and the State Council. At the beginning of 2004, the State Council organized a telephone and television conference on the subject of liquidating the delayed payment for construction work and making specific arrangements for settling the delayed payments due to the migrant workers. General Party Secretary, Hu Jintao, and Premier, Wen Jiabao, issued important instructions to settle the delayed payment for construction work over the next three years. The Central Disciplinary Committee made it a priority this year to check and liquidate the delayed payment. In August of 2004, the State Council held another conference to arrange the next step of the task, with a focus on the delayed payment for construction work invested in by the government. This has been done to mobilize the society to clear other project funds and ensure that all the delayed payments will have been made in three years' time.

The national policies aim at settling the sustainable development of the national economy; it also protects the migrant peasants' interests. We therefore need to consider the theories and viewpoints linked with sustainable development and the protection of interests and start, first of all, by addressing the problem of overdue migrant wages and instituting safe mechanisms for their being paid.

Analysis of the impacts of overdue migrant wages

Once peasants move to cities, they become urban industrial workers and builders of the cities, but they are not able to enjoy the same rights and personal interests as urban people. The delayed payment of migrant workers has made a great impact on them and has led to many social problems:

The personal interests of the labourers suffer

Separated from their parents, wives and children, migrants have to work away from their homes for a long time in order to earn money to support their family; their payment for their migrant labour becomes their main source of income. Many migrant workers, however, do not receive the payment owed to them for their hard work. When they return home during festivals, they are not able to bring back the money needed by the family members for their food, clothing, medical treatment and education; the delayed payment also affects their return home. The migrant workers sweat and toil for their pay, subjecting themselves to the risk of physical injury or even death. Any delay in paying them for their labour is a direct infringement of their rights.

Effect on social stability

Usually, the migrant workers receive living allowances and their total payment at the end of the year; most of the dunning, therefore, happens during the Spring Festival and has an adverse effect on social order.

In recent years, there have been more and more cases involving the breaching of migrant workers' rights and interests, and the conflict between employees and employers has potentially changed into a conflict with society. In some places in China, some shocking social problems have arisen after many migrants, who had failed in their repeated efforts to get paid, resorted to extreme measures to try to get what was due to them. These actions had a serious impact on social and public order.

Progress towards becoming a "well-off" society has been affected

The objective of building a "well-off" society in China, guided by the concept of scientific development was put forward at the 16th National Congress of the Communist Party of China (CPC). This does not mean striving for "big iron rice bowl" nor for the elimination of gaps; it means building a society where the poor can survive, the rich can lead a good life, employers can earn money and labourers' rights can be protected. Part of the "three rural issues"[1] raised by the central government are especially the low employment rate among rural labourers, low income and slow income growth. There are still many poor people in rural areas nowadays and migrant labour is an important means of raising their income. The delay in payment has seriously affected their living standards and production levels. If the migrant families – a huge social group of more than 200 million – are not able to build well-off lives, the goal of striving too develop a well-off society in China is just empty words.

Macro mechanisms to secure migrant workers' payment

Reform the social administration system of the migrant workers

One important reason for the delayed payment of migrants is their unequal position and treatment in cities compared with urban residents. Society has not made good use of the floating employment potential of migrant workers from a strategic perspective nor treated them as a driving force for reform. In order to protect the

---

[1] The "three rural issues" (*san nong wenti* 三农问题) describe the situation of the peasants (*nong min* 农民), the development of rural areas (*nong cun* 农村), and role of agriculture related industry (*nong ye* 农业).

rights of the migrants, there is a need to start changing the closed and segmented social administration system.

Reform of the residential record management systems

The different household registration systems[2] in urban and rural areas acts like a great wall, preventing peasants from melting into the city and also hurts their feelings. It is also an important institutional factor for maintaining the unfair treatment of migrant workers in cities and a psychological barrier to their conforming in cities. The household registration system must be reformed, in line with the requirements of the socialist market economy, to change the situation in which the transformation of the migrants' status lags behind their professional development and thus create an institutional environment for them to become urban production workers and citizens. From a long-term perspective, it would be helpful to address the differences in status of urban and rural inhabitants as well as their unequal employment opportunities and treatment, and to encourage the migrant workers to decide independently on their jobs.

Establish a long-term and effective employment management mechanism for the migrants

The labour market is the main hub and site for human resource distribution, which should provide information and service for the full employment of peasants. The labour market in some towns, however, is not well developed, management is chaotic and discriminating policies are applied towards the employment of migrant workers, the information provided is inaccurate and service is poor.

At present, the migration of the peasants is spontaneous. They move to economically developed cities without any plan, mainly depending on help and guidance from relatives and friends. This has led to a degree of blindness among the migrants with regard to their employment opportunities and their choices are also limited. The places of origin and receiving cities of the migrants should therefore reform the employment management system for the migrants.

Change the prevention and restriction oriented administration of the government to service-oriented management

Due to the influence of the planned economy with its dual and preventive management system, the migrants are controlled and guarded against; this is one of the reasons for the migrant workers' employment rights and other social rights being infringed. Some units use their power optionally to restrict the employment freedom of the migrant workers; they charge them additional fees and pay insufficient attention to the appeals of the migrants regarding overdue wages and other injuries. This hints at disrespect for the personal well-being and rights of the migrants and indicated the unequal relations existing between the government as managers and the common people as being managed.

Institutional change and changes towards becoming a market economy and legal society should be implemented to reform the government management system.

---

[2] These different systems are known as *huji zhidu* 户籍制度, and *hukou zhidu* 户口制度.

In a market economy, it is up to the employees to decide on their employment and up to the employers to make decisions on recruitment. The main decision-making body is no longer the government, but rather the individual labourers or enterprises. The government should incorporate the management of the migrant workers' employment and other issues into the urban and rural employment management system. Social management is not a singular government behaviour separate from public management; the government has the main responsibility of training the self-management capacity of various groups and supporting their self-management, such as the self-regulation of the common people and enterprises, self-coordinated relations and self-organized management. The establishment of a good public social and economic order needs a combination of public management and the self-management of the common people, the concerted efforts of the government and the masses. This changes singular government administration to multi-centered social management including the participation of the citizens and autonomous governance.

The establishment of a legal system to secure the migrants' payment
Formulate laws and regulations for the migrants' payment

The action of delaying payment has to do with the lack of relevant legal prescriptions. China is now in a transitional period when a standardized, open and regulated competitive labour market has not yet been established. Under these circumstances, some enterprises and employers are tending to take advantage of the loopholes in the legal system with the intention of cutting down and delaying payment. In order to eradicate the practice of delaying payment and protect the legal rights of migrant workers, well-established laws and regulations are required.

Since the migrants form a special and large group in China, more compulsory regulations are needed to protect their rights. China has legislation which protects different groups of people, for instance, a law to protect the handicapped; a law to protect women's rights and interests. The migrants' group is not going to disappear in the near future, it is therefore necessary to promulgate relevant laws and regulations for their protection, such as laws to protect the interests and rights of migrants and regulations on the payment of migrants, which will clearly define the payment date and establish relevant units to monitor and examine the payment situation. The legal definition of "without reason" in the "delay of payment without reason" (*wugu tuoqian* 无故拖欠) should be narrowed down to leave no opportunity for the employee's working units to delay payment.

Look into the legal responsibilities of those who delay the payment of migrants

"The law has teeth and will bite if need be,"[3] but this does not happen often. In some legally well-established countries, however, the teeth of law are sharper. In Germany, for example, section 266 of the German Criminal Code (*Strafgesetzbuch – StGB*) stipulates the crime of criminal breach of trust: the employer is guilty of this if he/she does not fulfill his/her commitments to employees or misuses his/her power. The employer may be thrown into jail if he/she delays the payment of his/her staff. The protection of labourers' rights should be a high priority but this area has not been dealt with in China.

In Hong Kong, according to the relevant regulations, if the employer does not pay his/her staff in time, he/she can be sued. If convicted the employer may be fined as much as HKD 200,000 or sentenced to one year's imprisonment. According to the current inland "Administrative Criminal Law" (*xingzheng chufa fa* 行政处罚法), the highest penalty is RMB 50,000. The amounts with regard to delayed payment can range from hundreds of thousands to tens of millions of RMB but the penalty for non-payment is just tiny. Only by increasing the deterrent effect of punishment and the cost of violation will the employers be forced to adhere to the regulations and not dare to defy the law. It is therefore necessary to include the "crime of delayed payment" in the Criminal Law and use this law to punish those who are guilty of delaying payment so as to deter others from committing similar illegal actions. Only in this way, can the state show its determination to protect the legal rights of the disadvantaged groups.

With regard to the delayed payment of the migrants, it is not a matter of implementing countermeasures, it is a matter of wanting to tackle the issue and dealing with it consistently. So long as the government pays attention to protecting the migrants' rights and the necessary laws and regulations are in place, the employees' working units will not dare to defy the law.

Improve the laws and regulations relating to social security for migrant workers

The social security system should be based on the principle of equality and the government is the main body responsible for achieving social equality. The government should not find excuses to shrug off or avoid its responsibilities with regard to developing a social security system for the migrant workers. Even though conditions are not yet suitable for the formulation of complete social security regulations for migrants, it should be remembered that all laws are products of their times and can only be improved through modifications.

The migrant workers are a high risk group in our developing society. There is an essential need to extend social security to them. If they are offered basic social

---

[3] Here, the authors refer to the American scholar E. Adamson Hoebel who 1954 formulated this in his work "The Laws of Primitive Man: A Study in Comparative Legal Dynamics," New York: Atheneum, p. 26.

security or bottom line cover, the migrants themselves, their families and their future communities will pay for the various risks in the end. Although employers have managed to reduce their costs and, in the short term, have gained high economic returns as a result of using the migrant workers and not paying for their social security, they have also accumulated a big risk. The large number of accidents and occupational diseases as well as the subsequent disputes between employers and employees indicates that accidents at work and occupational diseases have become the main risk for production workers, especially the migrant workers at this stage. This kind of risk does not only directly damage the health and lives of the labourers and plunge them and their families into difficult living conditions; it also has a serious effect on the enterprises concerned. At the same time, the competitive edge gained at the cost of the migrant workers' rights will be weakened more and more by the increasing social civilization and the migrant peasants' increased awareness of equality. The migrant workers should also realize that occupational changes will also bring about changes in risks; they should increase their awareness of social security and consciously assume their individual responsibility. The establishing of laws and regulations on social security for the migrants, along with the intensification of publicity and guidance are the means which are necessary to complete the shift from the traditional concept of land-based security to the modern concept of social security.

Conclusion

In general, the issues related to the overdue migrant wages are historical phenomena resulting from social developments in China and they will gradually be resolved with the development and improvement of the market economy. At the moment, the tasks involved with addressing these issues are hard and arduous: the delayed payment of the migrants does not only closely correlate with the economic efficiency of enterprises and even of industrial sectors, but also with long-term social stability and overall development. To address the delayed payment of the migrants is a systematic process which involves many parties. No matter how difficult it may be, however, we need to eradicate this phenomenon that injures the basic rights of the migrants. China has already moved into a human-oriented development era which is characterized by comprehensive and coordinated development. The determination with which they tackle the issues related to the delayed payment of the migrants and the protection of their legal rights will be an important yardstick to prove the government's capacity to govern for the people and push forward social civilization.

Informal Employment

Informal Employment –
Integration or Segregation of the Labour Market?

Anne J. Braun

Introduction

Recent decades have seen a dramatic increase in informal employment in nearly all parts of the world, including industrialized countries. Contrary to earlier predictions, this can no longer be considered a temporary or residual phenomenon. In the last few years, the bulk of new employment has been in the informal sector, particularly in developing and transition countries (ILO 2002: 1).

As a consequence of labour market reforms and opening up towards the global market, this phenomenon can now also be seen in China. In recent years, informal employment has been growing rapidly in line with accelerating labour market competition. In China's cities, the ratio between employment in the informal sector and the formal sector increased from 1:4 in 1996 to more than 1:2 in 2001 (Cai/Wang 2004: 21). According to recent estimates given by the Ministry of Labour and Social Security, about 40 per cent of urban employment is currently informal (Schucher 2005: 36). These figures show that informal employment has become an important employment channel in urban China.

In the main, two groups of people are being employed in informal jobs: rural migrants and re-employed urban workers. Rural migrants have been employed in the informal sector since the very early days of economic restructuring at the beginning of the 1980s. The rigid system of household registration (*hukou* system) made it almost impossible for them to find employment in the formal sector. With the progression of labour market reforms in China's cities and growing unemployment, however, informal employment has also become an important employment channel for retrenched and laid-off urban workers. Today, not only rural migrants are forced to work in the informal sector but also formerly privileged urban citizens.

Those jobs differ substantially from employment in the formal sector in terms of wages, job security and social benefits. It may therefore be assumed that the labour market is increasingly being divided between people employed in formal jobs and those migrants and re-employed urban workers employed in informal jobs. My paper argues that this kind of labour market segmentation according to status in employment is increasingly replacing the "traditional" fragmentation of the labour market between urban workers and rural migrants.

The paper starts by defining and conceptualising informal employment. It then develops a model of employment-based labour market segmentation in urban China and considers the consequences of this model for the relationship between urban and rural workers in the cities.

Informal employment between integration, endangerment and exclusion

Definition and characteristics of informal employment

In the academic debates, there is a wide variety of definitions of the terms "informal sector," "informal economy" and "informal employment." The spectrum of interpretations for the term "informal employment" alone ranges from private and individual enterprises to illegal activities.

My definition of informal employment (*feizhenggui jiuye*) is closely related to the concept developed by the International Labour Organisation (ILO) (Hussmanns 2004: 3-7).[1] The ILO defines informal employment as all those jobs which have an employment relationship that is, in law or in practice, not subject to national labour legislation, income tax, social protection or entitlement to certain employment benefits. The point of reference is the informality of the status in employment, not the enterprise. This means that employment in the informal sector constitutes only one part of the definition. Informal employment can also be seen to exist in enterprises in the formal sector if the above mentioned characteristics are taken into account.

Informal employment comprises:

- *own-account workers* who are basically and mainly engaged in individual economic operations and activities (such as street vendors, cleaners or people engaged in various forms of so-called community services); *employers* employed in their own informal sector enterprises
- contributing *family workers*, irrespective of whether they work in formal or informal sector enterprises (often engaged in simple processing production and services)
- *employees* holding informal jobs in enterprises in the formal and informal sectors, and in private households (casual labour, seasonal or temporary work, part-time work, unregistered labour, etc.)
- members of informal *producers' cooperatives*

The ILO definition of "informal employment" is therefore a broader concept than that of "informal sector employment." According to this definition, informal employment is not only seen in the context of a rather dubious "shadow economy," emphasis is also placed on the idea of a continuum of formality and informality.

Conceptualising informal employment

How to conceptualize informal employment, how to classify it? In order to fit informal jobs into the wider context of employment as a whole, I am going to refer

---

[1] In contrast to the ILO, I limit my definition to market-based informal jobs. I therefore exclude own-account workers engaged in the production of goods exclusively for their own final use by their households (such as subsistence farming or do-it-yourself construction of their own dwellings). In addition, my research focuses on the urban labour market: this includes rural-urban migrants but not the rural labour market.

to the three-zone concept of employment based on a model by Castel (2000) which was further developed by Vogel (2003), Bartelheimer (2002) and Oschmianski/ Oschmianski (2003).

Figure 1. Three-zone concept of employment: integration, endangerment, exclusion

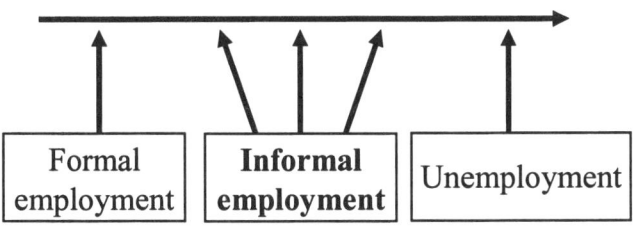

Source: Author's own creation, based on Oschmianski/Oschmianski (2003).

This model classifies the working part of society into three zones: "integration," "occupational and social endangering," and "exclusion." [2] The zone of "integration" consists of stable and secure employment relationships. Formal employment can be included in that zone. In contrast, the zone of "exclusion" means exclusion from work, i.e. joblessness. Informal employment is located between the two extremes and can be assigned to the zone of "endangerment." Castel attributes precarious jobs with lower employment security and lower employment standards to that zone.[3]

---

[2] The concept of integration and exclusion is based on the terms "exclusion" and "inclusion" used in Luhmann's systems theory (Luhmann 1995). In the (socio-)political debate, however, the term "integration" is preferred due to the French roots of the concept (see Hebel 2004: 3). Jutta Hebel points out that the term "exclusion" (*paichi* 排斥) is also used in the Chinese debate on social problems. There, it mainly refers to marginalization and is defined as exclusion "from the mainstream of society, by being pushed out of political arenas, economic networks or physical living and working spaces"(Zhongguo Guoji Gongcheng Zixun Gongsi 2004: 194f.).

[3] The classification is based on the premise that labour is a major mechanism for integration into the modern society, if not the only one. As Jutta Hebel puts it, labour is "not only a source of income, but also the basis of social status, power, recognition, social contacts as

Informal employment can therefore be described as an in-between position that implies neither integration into society nor complete exclusion. This classification is not static, but rather a continuum. Since informal employment is very heterogeneous, a ranking of different forms of informal jobs is not possible. Many factors – such as the limitation of employment duration, wages, job security, working conditions or job prestige – can be influential in deciding whether a job tends more towards integration or exclusion.

Transitions are possible between the three zones: an informal job can develop into a regular employment relationship (integration); it can, however, also be followed by a phase of joblessness (exclusion) (Oschmianski/Oschmianski 2003: 4). The risk of sliding down into unemployment seems to be especially high for seasonal or temporary workers. The same applies to the self-employed and micro-entrepreneurs, if their businesses fail. In contrast, opportunities for an upgrade into regular employment are considered to be best for informal workers in formal enterprises, such as employees with temporary work contracts. Labour authorities hope for "adherence" in this kind of enterprises, i.e., transfer into formal employment relationships by the hiring company. However, this still proves very difficult in China, as the Nanjing pilot projects for the support of socially acceptable temporary work have shown. Only in a few cases were temporary workers successfully and permanently re-integrated into the first labour market.[4]

Transitions within the zone of informal employment are possible as well. Informal workers can move closer towards the zone of "integration" through qualification or an upgrade of working hours, for example. To increase the upwards transition, the Chinese government has implemented labour policies that try to improve working conditions for informal workers, such as the pilot project for development of the informal economy in Shanghai.[5]

Informal employment – A new form of labour market segmentation in China?

Having developed a classification of the different forms of employment, I am now going to examine the implications of the enormous rise in informal employment for the structure of the Chinese labour market. Will this lead to a new form of labour market segmentation? Will it change old segmentation patterns? What are the consequences for the relationship between urban and rural workers in Chinese cities? Is there an integrated labour market in the making?

---

well as the meaning of life and individual characteristics. Labour is the basis of social production and reproduction" (Hebel 2004: 5).
[4] For experiences of socially acceptable temp-work, see Kühnert 2003.
[5] For an overview of the Shanghai Pilot Project, see e.g. Howell 2002 and the contribution by Peng Xizhe and Yao Yu in this volume.

Labour market segmentation between formal and informal employment

There is no doubt that the erosion of regular employment in China is having a significant influence on the structure of the urban labour market. It can be assumed that the urban labour market is becoming increasingly divided between formal and informal employment. This assumption is based on institutional approaches in labour market segmentation theory.[6] Segmentation theories are based on the recognition that the total (labour) market is divided into several submarkets (Henneberger/Kaiser n.d.: 6). The single labour market segments are characterized by certain features of workers and workplaces and differ in structure and mode of operation. Since access to the different segments is restricted by institutional and social barriers, income and employment conditions also differ in the submarkets.

Similar patterns can be detected in the Chinese labour market which is divided into a formal and an informal segment.[7] Workplaces and employment relationships differ in both in terms of status of employment, job characteristics, wage levels, social security benefits and legal protection.[8] It is true that informal employment is very heterogeneous as the term can be equally well applied to poor street vendors as well as to highly paid freelancers in software-design. However, highly skilled professionals engaged in information technology, consultancy and development who demand high fees (but do not necessarily have social insurance) constitute only a small minority in China (Research Group 2002: 2). In general, incomes in informal employment are low and very unstable. Most of the informal workers do not have labour contracts and are not covered by social security provisions. Operational activities are often *in the grey areas* of laws and regulations. Workers need to be very "flexible" and seldom have regular working hours. Additionally, the social prestige of informal jobs is low. Table 1 gives an overview of the typical characteristics of informal employment in comparison with formal jobs.

---

[6] Institutionalist segmentation theories criticize the assumption of neo-classical labour market theory that the labour market operates in the same way as any other market – based on prices (wages) and tending towards equilibrium.

[7] At the same time, this kind of segmentation co-exists with other fragmentations of the Chinese labour market that are widely discussed in (China-related) labour market literature. Other forms of labour market segmentation include fragmentation due to ownership (state/non-state sector) or administrative system (professionals/workers).

[8] In this article, I refer to only one level of labour market segmentation. One level below this, both the formal and the informal labour market are again divided into smaller sub-markets (according to education, sex, origin etc.) This phenomenon is already well-documented for the formal labour market, but it also appears in the informal labour market. In a case study in Quebec, Williams and Windebank (1998: 35) even suggested that the informal labour market is more heavily segmented than the formal market.

Table1. Characteristics of formal and informal employment

	Formal Employment	Informal Employment
Employment status	mostly wage-earners	own-account workers, micro-entrepreneurs, wage-earners in informal or formal enterprises
Job characteristics	permanent employment usually fixed working hours good working conditions	often temporary employment flexible working hours poor or dangerous working conditions
Remuneration	relatively stable wages medium/high income subject to income tax	unstable/unpaid wages often low income not subject to income tax
Social insurance	unemployment insurance, retirement pension, health insurance	no social insurance
Legal protection	directly or indirectly protected	low level/absence of protection
Skills	high and medium skills formal education	often low skills skills acquired through experience/apprenticeship/ self-taught

Source: Author's own compilation.

In China, this kind of labour market segmentation even cuts through enterprises (Li Qiang 2003: 128). Informal and formal employment often coexists within the same company. Informal workers are employed in enterprises of the formal sector; that is, not only in micro-enterprises but also in huge companies (Li/Tang 2002: 15). Even in the state sector, large numbers of jobs have been informalized by sub-contracting to the self-employed, and also by directly hiring informal workers (Liu/Chan 1999: 5). Those workers, however, are subject to a completely different employment and remuneration system to that of formal employees in the same enterprise (ibid.). The phenomenon which I call "one *danwei* – two (employment) systems" manifests itself in lower pay and benefits for the same work. In a survey conducted in a district of Beijing, Li Qiang (2003: 128) found that informal workers were being paid, on average, only half the amounts earned by their formally employed colleagues. In addition, legal ties were relatively loose, labour disputes occurred frequently and employment relationships between informal workers and their employers were more unstable. Dorothy Solinger (2002: 374) even reports cases where informal workers were only being given one fifth of the customary wage normally paid by the enterprise but did not dare to complain because they did not have labour contracts and could therefore easily be fired.

In accordance with segmentation theories, several barriers can be recognized between both sub-markets. As is widely discussed in the literature on rural-to-urban migration, the *hukou* system is one of the main institutional obstacles restricting access to the formal labour market segment for migrant workers. This issue will be further examined in the next chapter. But re-integration into the formal labour market is also difficult for urban informal workers. Increasing employment duration in informal jobs devalues qualifications and skills. Due to its low social prestige, informal employment can also lead to stigmatization and discrimination. As Sengenberger (1987) shows for the German labour market, job characteristics are by and by assigned to the workers holding the jobs: people employed in "insecure" jobs involuntarily become "unstable" workers in the eyes of their employers and are seen as unsuitable for employment in the formal labour market. These barriers can lead to permanent continuance in precarious occupational and social positions without financial, social and job security. In other words: informal workers often stay in the zone of endangerment and have only limited opportunities for re-integration into regular employment.

Shifting away from hukou-*based labour market segmentation*

Labour market segmentation is not a new phenomenon in Chinese cities. Up to now, however, the labour marked has been divided predominantly along the lines of "urban citizens" versus "migrants". The rigid system of household registration (*hukou*) prevented rural labourers from taking up regular employment in cities and made them dependent on informal jobs. Although differences in the status of rural workers and urban citizens continue to exist, these no longer serve as an adequate explanation of the differences in the labour market. I would argue that the "traditional" labour market segmentation is gradually being replaced by the division between informal and formal employment (Figure 2).

Figure 2. The shift of the segmentation border

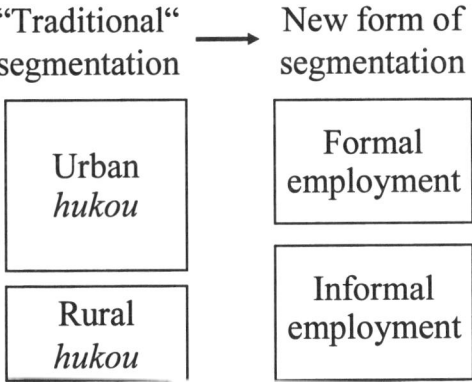

Source: Author's own creation.

This development can be explained by two factors: the "flexibilization" of urban employment and the gradual liberalization of the *hukou* system.

Firstly, employment reforms and especially the introduction of the system of labour contracts since the late 1980s have led to the successive flexibilisation and informalisation of urban employment. The shrinking of the protective state sector and the growing relevance of the private economy have changed the "rules of the game" in the urban labour market. Dorothy Solinger (2002a: 373) refers to those developments as a "process whereby formal rules regulating employment are greatly relaxed or eliminated altogether." She further argues that:

Employment thus becomes more "flexible," entailing the phasing out of entitlements and benefits, reduction of safety and other humane provisions at the workplace, and denial of job security, where all of these guarantees once existed. These cutbacks in welfare go along with a surge in short-term, temporary jobs having these features, and a marked upswing in very petty projects of brief self-employment. (ibid.)

As a result of extensive lay-offs and the lack of regular re-employment, more and more urban citizens have become dependent on informal jobs since the middle of the 1990s. According to estimates given by the Chinese Ministry of Labour and Social Security, more than 70 per cent of urban laid-off workers only find re-employment in informal activities (Xia Wang 2004: 2). Other sources give even higher estimates, listing figures as high as 80 to 90 per cent (see e.g. Cheng Duoshen 2004: 9). A study by the All-China Federation of Trade Unions carried out in 2000 found that 48.7 per cent of the "re-employed" were in fact self-employed. Of the other half that had succeeded in finding paid wage labour, another 59 per cent were employed in temporary – i.e. informal – jobs (Solinger 2002a: 374). Apart from laid-off workers, it is especially new job entrants – even university graduates – who are dependent on informal employment. The same applies to many retirees whose pensions are insufficient to grant them a living.

Secondly, during the last couple of years, the *hukou* system has gradually been liberalized. It is true that the system of household registration is still one of the central mechanisms for securing urban citizens' privileges and hindering the free flow of labour. Since the year 2000, however, several policy initiatives have been undertaken to liberalize the labour market across China and to guarantee more equal treatment for migrant workers. A 2003 document on labour migration issued by the State Council states that any excessively unfair restrictions on rural labourers seeking either temporary or permanent employment in urban areas are to be abolished. Rural migrants and urban residents are to be treated in the same way when they apply for jobs and no more extra fees are to be charged. Furthermore, the document aims at improving legal procedures (contracts, on-time payment of wages) and the working and living conditions of migrant labourers (health care and social security benefits) (Huang/Pieke 2003:17f.). These policy initiatives are striking, but there is still a significant lack of implementation. Particularly in cities and towns with a tight labour market, migrants are still facing tough restrictions. Some cities are even re-imposing migration quotas after a short period of liberalization. Nevertheless, despite these drawbacks, it can be expected that barriers between urban and migrant workers will be further relaxed as economic reforms progress. As some statistical labour market studies suggest, the traditional discrimination between urban residents and rural migrants in the labour market has already been significantly weakened (see e.g. Appleton et al. 2001; Yang/Chen 2001).

Both the liberalisation of urban employment and the *hukou* system are leading to a gradual shift of the segmentation border in the labour market. Migrants and the urban re-employed are more and more frequently holding jobs with the same characteristics, which in general differ substantially from the employment relationships of permanent workers.

On the one hand, this relates to wage levels, as a study by Cai and Wang (2004: 23) suggests. According to their research, which was based on census data, "the jobs for re-employment were usually low-paid ones, similar to the jobs that the migrant labourers held." This study reveals that the salary gap between re-employed and permanent workers is similar to that between migrants and permanent urban workers (ibid.). The argument presented by Appleton, Knight, Song and Xia (2001), which was based on a 1999 urban survey of 2500 households in 13 cities in 6 provinces, goes even further. They suggest that in terms of mean earnings, migrants are even paid more than re-employed urban workers (Appleton et al. 2001: 15).

On the other hand, re-employed urban workers are facing similar problems to those faced by migrants in their new jobs. Their employers do not usually offer social security benefits and refuse to sign formal labour contracts. Re-employed workers are often employed temporarily and have to accept low wages. Self-employed urban citizens are – very much like their rural counterparts – restricted by a lack of funding (Solinger 2002: 374, 379). That they are equally disadvantaged and vulnerable is illustrated by the fact that laid-off urban workers and rural labour migrants today account for an equally large proportion of the urban poor. Together, they represent 70 to 90 per cent of that part of the population which is living below the poverty line in the cities (Mo Rong 2002: 285).

All these changes indicate that the "traditional" *hukou*-based segmentation of the urban labour market in China is being replaced by a labour market segmentation based on status in employment. The formal segment is predominantly filled with urban workers that have never been hit by lay-offs and still have stable employment. In contrast, the informal sub-market employs migrants and laid-off urban workers, job entrants and retirees (Figure 3).

Figure 3. The new pattern of labour market segmentation

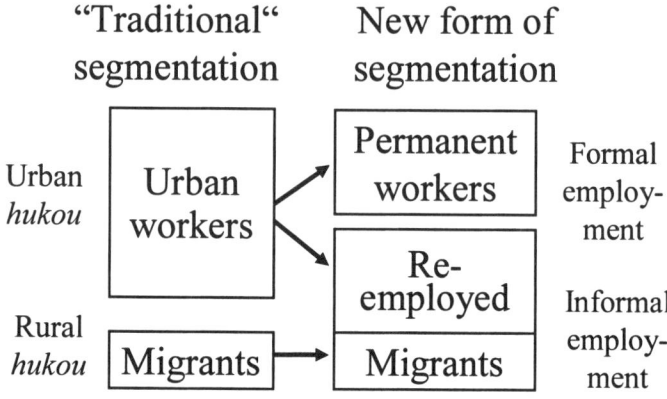

Source: Author's own creation.

Despite the changes in employment conditions, differences between urban residents and rural migrants persist. The urban unemployed are entitled to basic living allowances and the services of the labour offices. In addition, public authorities have set up projects to help the urban unemployed find re-employment or start their own businesses – even in the informal sector. This *de iure* preferential treatment of urban unemployed *de facto* often has few consequences. On the one hand, social welfare payments are often very low or not disbursed at all. On the other hand, re-employment projects are very limited in scope due to a lack of capital and personnel (Solinger 2002b: 317). In addition, changes in ways of thinking can also be perceived in terms of employment projects. As illustrated in the contribution by Zhong Xiaoyun in this book, recent labour market projects aim to include the rural population and offer help to migrant workers.

Integration or conflict between urban and rural labourers?

What are the consequences of this shift in the segmentation border? Will there be rivalry between laid-off urban workers and rural migrants in the informal labour market? Will both parties become involved in wage dumping? Will it come to open conflict between them over employment?

On the one hand, current labour shortages in Guangdong seem to indicate that – at least in economically prosperous regions – the demand for low-paid, informal workers is huge and growing.⁹ Many Chinese researchers and politicians believe that the informal sector possesses an enormous employment potential and that the demand for such jobs is far from being satisfied (see e.g. Zhang Xiaofeng 2003, Wang/Tan 2003). This would open enough employment opportunities for both laid-off urban workers and rural migrants.

On the other hand, there is some evidence that employment competition between migrants and urban workers is increasing in a wide range of industries. (Appleton et al. 2001) In sectors such as trade, services and construction, this competition is becoming particularly intense and it is mostly the urban unemployed and re-employed who are suffering as a result. Self-employed urban citizens have to compete with migrants who have market advantages such as longer market experience, better market connections or specialized craftsmanship skills (Solinger 2002b: 313). In contrast, the urban unemployed, after their dismissal from state-owned enterprises, usually lack the skills which would enable them to run businesses or to offer special services. They have usually been trained for very specific jobs in these enterprises and have done the same tasks for many years. Furthermore, for those laid-off urban workers looking for new wage work in the informal sector, it is difficult to compete with migrants' wage levels and their relatively high tolerance of bad working conditions (ibid.). The situation is especially severe for laid-off women workers. Not only are women more often subject to dismissal than men, but they also have below-average opportunities of finding re-employment. Since it is mostly middle-aged women who are laid off, they additionally have to compete with much younger migrant women for jobs.¹⁰ In Shanghai's textile industry, for example, it is not urban but mainly migrant women workers who are able to find employment (Wuellner 2001: 214).

This new situation offers certain potential for conflict. Whereas engaging in informal work in the city usually means an increase in wage and status for rural migrants, the opposite is true for city dwellers. As Dorothy Solinger puts it:

The startling thing is that the demeaned drudges practising these trades are city-born and registered citizens, members of the once celebrated factory proletariat, turned now into the cohort of the xiagang [off-post or laid-off] workers, and not second-class immigrating peasants, who had held such posts just a few years back (Solinger 2002a: 374f.).

The "old" segmentation of the labour market between urban and rural workers had been in place for a long time and was therefore accepted or at least tolerated by the public. But will this also apply to the "new" segmentation cutting right through the urban community? The potential for unrest that is connected to the informalization of employment and the growing competition between urban and rural labourers

---

⁹ For a discussion of the problem of labour shortages in Guangdong, see the contribution of Zheng Zizhen in this book.

¹⁰ For detailed information on women in the informal sector, see Jin Yihong's contribution in this book.

may be one of the reasons why the Chinese government is currently paying increased attention to informal employment. Several local governments have launched projects to support informal workers and to move this kind of employment closer towards the "zone of integration."

Résumé

To conclude, it can be stated that the urban labour market is divided between informal and formal employment and that this kind of segmentation is gradually replacing the traditional, *hukou*-based segmentation of the labour market. On the one hand, this trend blurs the boundaries between urban citizens and rural migrants in the labour market. Migrants and urban workers find themselves in similar jobs and employed under similar working conditions. The dichotomy "urban citizens" vs. "rural migrants" becomes less strict and inequalities are partly lifted. This tendency towards integration is, on the other hand, contrasted by a new split in the urban labour market. The labour market is again divided between a segment of relatively stable and well paid employment and a segment of marginal jobs. The new division has a new quality, however: the segmentation now cuts through the urban society and the precarious segment has expanded significantly in comparison with the "traditional" segmentation of the labour market.

The future will show whether this new kind of labour market segmentation is just a transitional phenomenon during the process of transformation or whether it will lead to a permanent fragmentation of the urban labour market in China. Given the huge extent of informal employment in China, the improvement of the working and living conditions of the workers will be a major challenge for the Chinese government over the next few years. To maintain an adequate level of social security and to secure their leadership, the Chinese government will have to ensure that informal employment moves closer towards the "zone of integration" and that it does not lead to the permanent endangerment of large parts of the population and their exclusion from society.

References

Appleton, Simon; Knight, John; Song, Lina; Xia, Qingjie (2001) *Towards a Competitive Labour Market? Urban Workers, Rural Migrants, Redundancies and Hardships in China*, Nottingham.

Bartelheimer, Peter (2002) *Themenfeld Integration, Gefährdung, Ausgrenzung. Arbeitskonferenz „Berichterstattung zur sozio-ökonomischen Leistungsfähigkeit der Bundesrepublik Deutschland" am 27. und 28. Juni 2002 im Bundesministerium für Bildung und Forschung*, Bonn.

Cai, Fang and Wang, Meiyan (2004) "Irregular employment and the growth of the labor market. An explanation of employment growth in China's cities and towns," in *The Chinese Economy*, 37 (March-April 2004) 2, pp. 16-28.

Castel, Robert (2000) *Die Metamorphosen der sozialen Frage. Eine Chronik der Lohnarbeit*, Konstanz.

Cheng Duoshen (2004) "A preliminary study of the flexible forms of employment in China." Online. Available HTTP: <http://www.kli.re.kr/iira2004/pro/papers/ChengDuosheng.pdf> (accessed: 5 October 2005).

Hebel, Jutta (2004) "Transformation des chinesischen Arbeitsmarktes: Gesellschaftliche Herausforderungen des Beschäftigungswandels," discussion paper, No. 41, Institut für Rurale Entwicklung der Universität Göttingen, Göttingen.

Henneberger, Fred and Kaiser, Christian (n.d.) "Die Auswirkungen der Globalisierung auf die Segmente des Arbeitsmarktes. Welthandel, multinationale Unternehmen und Lohnsetzung," n.p.

Howell, Jude (2002) *Good Practice Study in Shanghai: Employment Services for the Informal Economy*, ILO: Geneva.

Huang, Ping and Pieke, Frank N. (2003) *China Migration Country Study*, Dhaka: DFID.

Hussmanns, Ralf (2004) *Statistical definition of informal employment. Guidelines endorsed by the Seventeenth International Conference of Labour Statisticians (2003)*, Geneva: ILO.

International Labour Office (ILO) (2002) *Decent Work and the Informal Economy*. International Labour Conference, 90th Session, Report VI. Geneva.

Kühnert, Uwe (2003) "One year of socially acceptable temporary employment in Nanjing," in *Women's Way*, 10 (June), pp. 3-8.

Li, Qiang 李强 and Tang, Zhuang 唐壮 (2002) "Chengshi nongmingong yu chengshi zhong de feizhenggui jiuye" 城市农民工与城市中的非正规就业 [Rural migrants and informal employment in the cities], in *Shehuixue yanjiu*, 6, pp. 13-25.

Liu, Qiming and Chan, Kam Wing (1999) "Rural-urban labor migration process in China: Job search, wage determinants and occupational attainment," CSDE working paper, No. 99-16, University of Washington.

Luhmann, Niklas (1995) „Inklusion und Exklusion," in Niclas Luhmann *Die Soziologie und der Mensch. Soziologische Aufklärung 6*, Opladen, pp. 237-264.

Mo, Rong (2003) *2002 nian Zhongguo jiuye baogao – Jingji tizhi gaige he jiegou tiaozheng zhong de jiuye wenti.* 2002年中国就业报告 - 经济体制改革和结构调整中的就业问题 [China employment report 2002 – problems of employment during reform of the economic system and structural adjustment], Beijing: Zhongguo Laodong Shehui Baozhang Chubanshe.

Oschmiansky, Heidi and Oschmiansky, Frank (2003) *Erwerbsformen im Wandel: Integration oder Ausgrenzung durch atypische Beschäftigung? Berlin und die Bundesrepublik Deutschland im Vergleich*, Berlin: WZB.

Research Group of the Department of Training and Employment, Ministry of Labour and Social Security of the PRC (2002) *Skills Training in the Informal Sector in China*, Geneva: ILO.

Schucher, Günter (2005) „Arbeitslosenrate gesunken," in *China aktuell*, 1, p. 63.

Sengenberger, Werner (1987) *Struktur und Funktionsweise von Arbeitsmärkten. Die Bundesrepublik Deutschland im internationalen Vergleich*, Frankfurt a.M./New York: Campus-Verlag.

Solinger, Dorothy J. (2002a) "Economic informalisation by Fiat: China's new growth strategy as solution or crisis?," in Luigi Tomba (ed) *East Asian Capitalism. Conflicts, Growth and Crisis*, Milano, pp. 373-417.

Solinger, Dorothy J. (2002b) "Labour market reform and the plight of the laid-off proletariat," in *The China Quarterly*, 170, pp. 304-326.

Vogel, Berthold (2003) "Leiharbeit und befristete Beschäftigung – Neue Formen sozialer Gefährdung oder Chance auf Arbeitsmarktintegration?," in Gudrun Linne and Berthold Vogel (eds) *Neue Formen sozialer Gefährdung oder Chance auf Arbeitsmarktintegration?*, Arbeitspapiere der Hans-Böckler-Stiftung, Düsseldorf, pp. 53-65.

Wang, Jun 王军 and Tan, Junbo 覃俊波 (2003) "Feizhenggui jiuye: jiuye de xin qudao" 非正规就业 - 就业的新渠道 [Informal employment – a new employment channel], in *Dangdai jingji* [Contemporary Economics], 12, pp. 46-47.

Williams, Colin C. and Windebank, Jan (1998) *Informal employment in the advanced economies. Implications for work and welfare*, London/New York: Routledge.

Wüllner, Claudia (2001) "Laodongli liudong de tedian ji qi dui Shanghai chengshi laodongli shichang de yingxiang" 劳动力流动的特点及其对上海城市劳动力市场的影响 [Labour migragtion in Shanghai – its characteristics and impacts on the urban labour market] in Ke Lanjun and Li Hanlin (eds): *Dushi li de cun-min – Zhongguo da chengshi de liudong renkou* 都市里的村民 - 中国大城市的流动人口 [Villagers in the city – rural migrants in Chinese metropolises], Beijing: Zhongyang Bianyi Chubanshe, pp. 195-218.

Xia, Wang (2004) "Improve wages policy to stimulate flexible employment," Online. Available HTTP: <www.kli.re.kr/iira2004/pro/papers/WangXia.pdf> (accessed: 27 January 2005).

Yang, Yunyan and Chen, Jinyong (2001) "Transitional labor market segmentation and competition – An analysis of Wuhan," in *Social Sciences in China,* Winter, pp. 13-25.

Zhang, Xiaofeng (2003) "Feizhenggui jiuye – ruoshi qunti jiuye de youxiao tujing" 非正规就业 – 弱势群体就业的有效途径 [Informal employment – an effective way for the employment of weak groups], in *Ningxia dangxiao xuebao* 宁夏党校学报 [Journal of Ningxia Communist Party Institute], 5 (July) 4, pp. 46-48.

Zhongguo Guoji Gongcheng Zixun Gongsi 中国国际工程咨询公司 [China International Engineering Consulting Corporation](ed)(2004) *Zhongguo touzi xiangmu. Shehui pingjia zhinan* 中国投资项目社会评价指南 [Social assessment manual of Chinese investment projects], Beijing: Zhongguo jihua chubanshe.

Informal Employment and Labour Market Segmentation – A Gender Perspective

Jin Yihong

Expansion of informalized employment in China

Concept of informal employment

The concept of informal employment (*feizhenggui jiuye* 非正规就业) was first defined by the International Labour Office. "China Statistics" (*Zhongguo tongji* 2002) adopted this concept explaining: "This concept was formally proposed by the International Labour Organization (ILO) in the early 1970s. The informal sector refers to those small-scale enterprises involved with commercialized production, circulation and service, including small enterprises, family-run production and service enterprises and the self-employed." In "The dilemma of the informal sector," a report by the Director-General of the ILO in 1991, it is further defined as referring to the *low-income, low-remuneration, non-organized, non-structured small production or service enterprises*. The labour in the informal sector is taken as informal employment (some scholars refer to informal employment as *decentralized employment*). Based on this definition, the large numbers of persons who are self-employed or employed by private enterprises in the urban and rural areas can be included in the informal employment sector. With the further revitalization of the economy, the numbers of people in informal employment will increase greatly and this segment will become an important component of the employment market.

At present, the concepts of elastic (*danxing* 弹性) employment and flexible (*linghuo* 灵活) employment are both used in connection with informal employment in China; these terms therefore need to be clarified. It was the Department of Labour and Social Security, Shanghai, which first offered a definition of flexible labour: in a document dated January 2001, it was stated that flexible employment is diversified employment, mainly the staggered employment of workers by the hour, with flexible working hours, multiple employment methods and verified employment contracts.

In 2002, "China Statistics" defined flexible employment as diversified employment without the limitations of time, income and place. In contrast to full-time employment, flexible employment includes part-time employment, temporary employment (such as short-term employment, seasonal employment, contracted employment, job by call, independent employment), dispatched employment (employed dispatch and registered dispatch) and employment by the hour."(Zhongguo tongji 2002) This is a more extensive definition than that of the Labour and Social Security Bureau of Shanghai.

What is the relation between flexible employment and informal employment? There are similar and overlapping sections as well as differences between the two concepts. For example, informal working methods are adopted in informal employment (such as employment by the hour, temporary employment, seasonal employment and self-employed work). Employment with flexible working time also comes under flexible employment, but the employment in informal economic organizations is not always flexible employment; small enterprises in cities may not adopt the flexible job system.

Figure 1. Informal employment

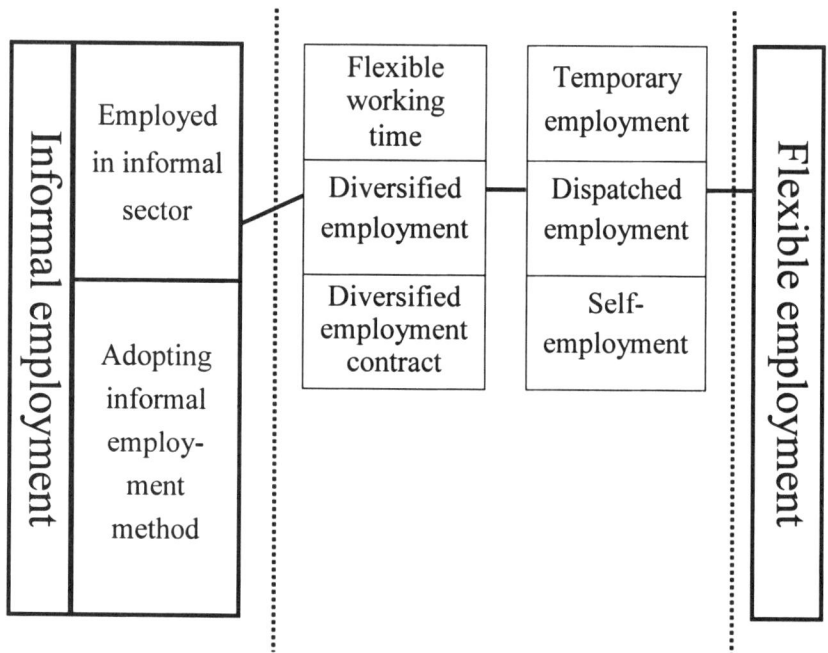

There is also "inadequate employment" (also called employment inadequacy) which overlaps with the concept of informal employment. In 1995, China Statistics defined "inadequate employment" as referring to those individuals who, for non-personal reasons, can not work for half the standard weekly working hours (20 hours) but would like to be able to work more. In practice, three conditions are used to define people with inadequate employment: the first is that they cannot work for half the weekly standard working hours of 20 hours per week; the second is that the short working hours do not arise from personal reasons; the third is that the people would like to do more work. The three conditions must exist simultaneously for people to be included in the category of inadequate employment. At present, some foreign scholars maintain that only the condition of wishing to do more work should be used to define those people who have inadequate employment (Zhongguo tongji 2002).

Some people (Yuan 2002: 13) have indicated that "informal employment" is a concept already accepted and applied extensively all over the world. The concepts of flexible employment, non-full-time employment, temporary employment currently used in our country hardly cover the complete field. "Informal employment" is, however, a very general term comprising many different areas of employment.

There is an overlapping and intercrossing section between informal employment, flexible employment and inadequate employment, they are not all exactly the same. For example, a worker employed by the hour could be described as having flexible employment from the point of view of temporality and changing work places, or as having informal employment from the point of view of having a non-permanent labour contract, or as having inadequate employment from the perspective of amount of work and income. It could also be described as adequate employment because the worker could take on several jobs so that the working hours could exceed eight hours by far.

There is another category, "staggered employment" (*jieduanxing jiuye* 阶段性就业), where labourers give up their jobs voluntarily during their careers and return to employment after a certain period. This is referred to as a type of flexible employment. For some people, "staggered employment" shows a strong gender bias towards women, who give up their jobs during the child-bearing period and infant growth stage to feed and take care of their children at home, and then return to employment after their children start to go to kindergarten or primary school. Staggered employment is often considered by some mainstream economists as a means of solving the problems of employment in China.

There are similarities and differences between the concepts of informal employment, elastic employment and flexible employment. They are usually mixed and used alternately in some situations. Internationally, the concept of informal employment is in general use. In recent years, the Chinese government has been inclined to encourage the use of this concept and usually considers it in terms of flexible employment.

Trend of labour informalization

Since the 1990s, there have been remarkable changes in the labour market in China. The number of people employed in state enterprises has decreased distinctly. There are more people taking up flexible employment. From 1998 to the end of 2002, the number of people employed in state enterprises in China fell by 40 million. Just in the three years from 1997 to 2000, the people employed in state enterprises as a proportion of all employed people dropped by 19.8 per cent from 74.4 per cent to 54.6 per cent. The proportion of flexible employment such as self-employment and community service, etc., increased to 45.4 per cent. By 2002, the proportion of non-state enterprise employment compared with township employment had further increased to 55.67 per cent (Guojia tongji ju 2001). In other words, 75 per cent of the people used to be employed by certain state enterprises, but over half (55.67 per cent) of the urban employed by that time were not employed by state enterprises.

The proportion dropped by 30.7 per cent in five years. This is a remarkable shift to occur in such a short period. Informal employment is expanding rapidly in China. According to data provided by the Department of Labour and Social Security, by the end of 2002, 30 per cent of 248 million township state enterprise employed people (75 million people) had taken up flexible employment. With the 70 per cent of migrant labourers who have taken up flexible employment, this makes, at present, around 145 million urban employed in informal employment in China (Wang 2003).

Impetus of labour informalization

The next step is to analyse what gives impetus to the rapid expansion of the informalization of the labour market.

The situation that the labour force supply outreaches demand has existed for a long time

This fact, that the labour force supply outreaches demand, is what we have to face: it could produce two results in the labour market: Firstly, stable employment will be a rarity for a long time. Some people will be excluded or suffer discrimination and become the disadvantaged group in the labour market. This disadvantaged group will be comprised of those who will be the first to become unemployed when the tide of unemployment rises and the last to benefit when the employment situation improves. The disadvantaged group will have to scrape the bottom of the barrel to try to find some sort of employment, under conditions of low stability, low income, low welfare and low accessibility. Secondly, the combined pressure of trying to avoid high unemployment rates and increasing international competition is a huge inner impetus to the flexibility of the labour market. With increasing economic integration and competition worldwide, enterprises are inclined to increase flexible employment to diversify capital risk. In addition, enterprises adopt "core-periphery" employment to increase competition.

Restructuring expedites diversification of the labour market

On the one hand, enterprise restructuring promotes the popularity of "non-standard" (*fei biaozhun* 非标准) employment, such as part-time jobs and temporary jobs. On the other hand, industrial restructuring also promotes the popularity of non-standard employment. While the second industry is shrinking, the third industry is expanding. Formal full-time employment is a product of the dominant manufacturing age. The various service requirements of customers decide the characteristics of the tertiary sector, that is, the employees must provide flexible and elastic services.

During the process of restructuring, the elements of production accelerate the circulation and the employment competition become intensified. The labour force market is segmented distinctly into the formal labour market and the informal labour market. Some labourers with disadvantages in terms of age, skills, gender, identity (residence permits), including people who have been laid off, young urban people without work experience and skills and large numbers of migrant workers from the countryside, have to enter the informal labour market. It is estimated by the Ministry of Labour and Social Security that 70 per cent of migrant labour takes up flexible employment (ibid.). Both these factors affect women's employment.

Impetus of globalization

At present, China is being integrated into the world economy at an unprecedented speed. Under the influence of globalization, and in order to diversify capital risk and increase the competition, enterprises require:

- More flexibility in the labour market, which means the possibility of lower labour standards in enterprises;
- New employment modes, such as sub-contracting, transferred contracts and labour dispatch, etc.
- New working modes, such as part-time, temporary, workers employed by the hour, which are all non-standard working modes.

Informalization of labour in China has distinct characteristics of restructuring

Since the middle of the 1990s, there has been a large structural alteration in the labour market of China. The pressure of rural labour force urbanization, the tide of large scale migration, the existence of both the labour concentration and capital concentration and the three adjustments between industries are all reasons for this structural alteration. It could be said that the increase in informal employment in China is the result of market reform, economic restructuring and employment pressure. Especially in recent years, there has been less employment in state and collective enterprises. Most of the people who have been laid off and are at the disadvantaged stage in the employment competition have to choose informal employment.

What is the structure of the informal employment segment? Let us take the survey in Xuzhou, Jiangsu Province in 1999 as an example. Among the 15 thousand people in private employment (only covered part of informal employment), there are 6,400 people who had been laid off by state enterprises, 1,380 unemployed people, 1,300 people on leave without pay and 2,000 migrant workers. The remainders are retired people and people with a second occupation.[1] The above data reveals that the people who had been laid off (including those from non-state enterprises) account for 60 per cent. The informalization of labour in China has distinct characteristics of restructuring.

Informalization of women labour

Informalization of women labour

Analysis of the labour structure of the Organisation of Economic Co-operation and Development (OECD) countries in the 1990s, revealed the feminization of the

---

[1] This material was provided by Mr. Song Xiaowu, Vice President of China Academy of Labour, quoted from Cai 2002a: 103.

informal sector and the informalization of women's employment. The ILO also indicated:

> With the process of globalization, technology innovation and the occurrence of new employment modes, women's status changed significantly. They were taking more and more informal employment (temporary jobs, occasional employment, part time jobs, employment as home-workers or contracted work. (...) Enterprise restructuring promotes the popularity of "non-standard" working modes, such as part time jobs and temporary jobs. More women than men took up informal employment.(Guoji laodong ju 2001: 1, 119)

Has there been such a feminization of the informal sector and an informalization of women's employment during the process of labour force market segmentation in China? At present, there are neither accurate statistics on informal employment nor statistics on the gender distribution, but we can still analyze the informalization of labour based on the increase in the number of people employed in non-state enterprises.

During the five years from 1995 to 2000, the total number of women employed in urban state enterprises was reduced by 14.777 million. The number of women employed in state enterprises was reduced by 1.5 per cent (Without author 2002: 268f.). This reveals that more women than men transferred from state enterprise employment to flexible employment during the restructuring. And this trend continued, because the number of women employed in urban state enterprises went down from 38.0 per cent in 2000 to 37.8 per cent in 2002 (Laodong baozhang bu peixun jiuyesi n.d.).

Some scholars do not think that the feminization of flexible employment has been taking place. For example, Li Qiang indicated there is no feminization of workers by the hour according to the results of a "workers by the hour employment" investigation. According to this investigation, the proportion of men workers employed by the hours is 53.9 per cent and that of women workers employed by the hour is 46.1 per cent in China. It must be pointed out, however, that in this investigation, of the "working content," private tutoring accounts for 21.5 per cent, sales promotion accounts for 44.5 per cent in addition to students' part-time jobs of typesetting, document translation and fast food service (multiple choice of work content). It is not indicated whether the samples selected meet the structure of current workers employed by the hour (Li et al. 2001: 96). In addition, "housekeeping service" makes up a large proportion of the work. In the housekeeping service, as many as 85.1 per cent of those employed are women (Guojia tongji ju renkou yu shehui keji tongji si 2004: 39). However, this investigation did not analyze by gender the numbers of those people employed in the housekeeping service (the blue collar workers in flexible employment). Li Qiang's conclusion that there is no feminization in the employment of workers by the hour in China cannot therefore be justified.

Now let us analyze the employment differences between men and women based on the second investigation into the status of women made by the Women's Federation in 2000 (see Zhonghua quanguo funü lianhehui 2000).

Table 1. Gender structure of employment (in per cent)

	Men	Women	Men's employment structure	Women's employment structure
State enterprise employment	62.0	38.0	59.8	47.8
Non-state enterprise employment	50.1	49.9	40.2	52.2
Urban employment	56.6	43.4	100.0	100.0

Source: Zhonghua quanguo funü lianhehui 2000.

The above analysis is based on the relevant investigation data from 2000.[2] We can see that the number of women employed in non-state enterprises amounted to 52.22 per cent in 2000, while the number of men amounted to 40.19 per cent. The number of women is 12 per cent higher than that of men, and that number exceeds half of women employment. Even if there is still dispute about the feminization of informal employment in China, the informalization of women's employment is an obvious trend.

We have to face the fact that the change in working modes has a different influence on men and women. The change in working modes always results in more women taking up informal employment.

Reasons for the informalization of women's labour
Women are likely to be excluded from formal employment

One of the direct results of unemployment rate increase is the intensified exclusion of the disadvantaged group from the labour market. This exclusion becomes more obvious especially when the integrated economic sector can not offer adequate employment opportunities.

A universal phenomenon can be seen during the social structure transition in China: a large number of women are replaced by fresh a labour force from the employment sector. The women's labour force that is replaced is getting younger.

Women are the first to be affected by the tide of unemployment in our country. It is an undisputable fact that women are more likely to lose their jobs than men. According to the labour market survey in Beijing and other five cities, the proportion of woman is 13 per cent higher than that of men among the people being laid off (Cai 2002a: 187). Hu Angang indicated that contrary to the view that women find jobs more easily than men, the age of "reducing women staff" has arrived in urban areas of China. Most sectors are "reducing women staff". The women who are laid off have fewer employment opportunities in the formal sector. There are also

---

[2] I would like to thank Ms. Jiang Yongping for providing the data of the National women status survey of 2000, see Zhonghua quanguo funü lianhehui 2000.

more "destroyed vocations" than "creative vocations." Hu stated: "Women are the group who face the most pressure in the competition for employment" (Hu 2002: 6, 8-11).

In 2002, the Women's Federation conducted a questionnaire on women's re-employment in eight cities, Chongqing, Wuhan, Harbin, Shenyang, Xi'an, Hohehot, Taiyuan and Nanjing, and found that 25.4 per cent of those people who have been laid off can never be reemployed and 15.8 per cent of them are reemployed after three years. According to another survey on urban families carried out by the National Bureau of Statistics in 45 cities (including Beijing, Tianjin, Chongqing and other 15 provincial capital cities) in December 2003, it was found that among the people surveyed, the number of women who had experienced unemployment was 17 per cent higher than that of men, that the average unemployment period for women was two months longer than that of men and that the number of women unemployed at that time was 20 per cent higher than that of men.[3] All these surveys show that once a woman is unemployed, she is more likely to stagnate in the labour market. Usually, the only option for a woman is to "go down" to the informal labour force market. The formal labour market is inclined to exclude older labourers and the age of the women excluded is falling. Many investigations reveal that the age of 35 has become a threshold of women's employment. Once women over 35 leave their posts, they can rarely be reemployed in the formal sector.

Re-employment after being laid off is one of the labour restructuring modes. A large number of women change their jobs after dismissal, post alteration and reemployment during restructuring, but we can see that a large number of women who have been laid off go "down line" in reemployment. Most of them cannot return to the formal labour market and have to take up informal employment.

State and non-state enterprise gender preference on employment

Most women went to the non-state enterprises during restructuring. In 2000, the Department of Sociology of Beijing University, the Institute of Population of CASS, the Australian National University, and Bates College worked together on a labour market survey in six cities.[4] The survey revealed that different ownership enterprises had different gender inclinations on employment. In state enterprises, the number of men in the labour force is pretty high, with an employee sex ratio of 120 (women=100). In non-state enterprises, the number of women in the labour force is higher than that of men with a sex ratio of 75. The state enterprises offering formal employment are inclined to employ men, while the non-state enterprises, together with a large number of private economic istitutions offering informal employment, prefer to hire women (Chinese Academy of Social Sciences 2002: 274).

---

[3] See data presented in Chapter "Gender Disparities in Unemployment Duration in Urban China" by Du Fenglian and Dong Xiaoyuan.
[4] The author was involved in carrying out this survey in Nanjing City.

Trend towards a concentration of women in the tertiary sector

The survey on the status of women in China carried out by the Women's Federation in 1990 and 2000 revealed that the number of women in the tertiary sector increased by 7.1 per cent in ten years. In 2000, around one third of urban woman labourers were concentrated in the tertiary sector. This figure is nine per cent higher than that of men. The data from the Shanghai Bureau of Statistics revealed that the concentration of women in the tertiary sector is as high as 60.9 per cent. In the short period from 1998 to 2000, the figure increased by four per cent.

The transfer of the labour force from the primary and secondary sector to the tertiary sector is in line with the laws of economic development. But if we look at the sectors, we can see that most women are concentrated in the traditional service sectors such as retailing, restaurant and social services. In the new and developing service sectors such as information technology, finance and insurance and scientific consulting services, the numbers of women are low. According to the data obtained from the fifth census, 55.78 per cent of women in the tertiary sector are distributed in wholesales and retailing, restaurant and social services. Only 11.96 per cent of women are in the new and developing sectors such as finance and insurance, transportation, telecommunication and scientific and technological services. The number of men in the traditional service department is 13 per cent lower than that of woman, but 13.5 per cent higher than woman in new and developing sectors. The traditional tertiary sector fields such as tourism and service are inclined to offer informal employment due to the fact that they are likely be affected by seasonal factors and the international situation (Zhongguo Renmin Gongheguo guojia tongji ju 2002: 909-934).

Threat to low-skilled jobs by advanced technology

Why is there an informalization trend in women's labour? Women are more likely to be affected by globalization, market reform and economic restructuring. Any change will bring about a re-distribution of resources and the change to the law of distribution. If there is no special policy support, the status of original disadvantaged group on resource possession will become worse through the change. It is usually these people who pay the cost of reform.

For instance, if there are cuts in the public sector, it is usually the female staff, such as secretaries and clerks who are the first to be affected.

Another reason for the change in the status of women in the labour market is the development of advanced technology; this has resulted in an increase in the demand for highly skilled workers and a decrease in the demand for workers with low skills. The fact that women have been employed to do low-skilled jobs places them in an unfavourable position in the labour market.

Generally speaking, the reason that more women than men have transferred to informal employment is that women are more likely to be discriminated against and excluded from the labour market. The rarity of formal employment opportunities means that the formal sectors exclude older labourers. The especially harsh requirements governing the age of women labourers means that they leave formal employment early. In addition, women of child-bearing age are also likely to be excluded. Some women have to take flexible employment in order to take care of their families.

Influence of labour informalization on women

Informal employment provides more livelihood-oriented employment opportunities for the disadvantaged women

The positive influence of informal employment development on women is obvious. The vulnerability of the disadvantaged group is the result of their being excluded from society on the grounds of age, gender and skills. Informal employment does not have high requirements regarding people's gender, age, education, skills and physical strength. Informal employment with its low entry requirements and flexible mechanism thus provides the disadvantaged women in the labour market with more opportunities. Community employment and livelihood business establishment offer informal modes of employment.

Negative influence of labour informalization on women

Low income and the income gap between the genders increase

According to the survey on the status of women conducted by the Women's Federation, the average annual income of urban employed men in 2000 was 8,272.82 RMB and that of women was 7,073.34 RMB. Women's income was 85.5 per cent of that of men's.

Figure 2. Employment and income (in RMB)

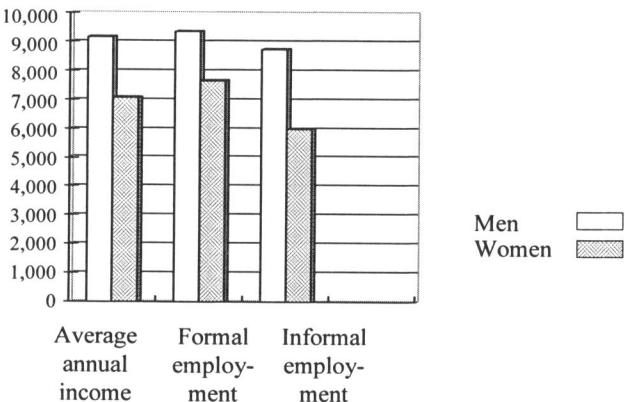

The informalization of women's labour is one of the reasons for the increase in the income gap between men and women (see Figure 2). The income of women in formal employment is 88 per cent of that of men, but the income of women in informal employment is only 80.30 per cent of that of men. For formal employment, the income gap between men and women is 1,684.58 RMB, but for informal employment, the income of men is 2,728.06 RMB more than that of women.

Taking the figures of women alone into account, the income of women in informal employment is 1,665.2 RMB less than that of women in formal employment. The difference in the case of men, however, is only 621.72 RMB. That means when both men's and women's labour is informalized, the reduction in women's income is much greater than that of men's. The average annual income of women in informal employment is only 5,982.15 RMB, less than 500 RMB per month. Most women in informal employment do hard work and earn a low income (Zhonghua quanguo funü lianhehui 2000).

Low and inadequate social welfare and security for women

Table 2 is based on data taken from the survey on the status of women by the Women's federation in 2000. A comparison of the possession of endowment and medical insurance between formal and informal employment and between men and women shows that the informalization of women's labour affects women's social security status.

Table 2. Social insurance conditions according to gender and employment modes, 2000

	Percentage of people with pension insurance		Percentage of people with pension insurance	
Employment	Men	Women	Men	Women
Formal employment	84.7	81.3	73.9	65.5
Informal employment	14.8	10.4	14.4	9.0

Source: Zhonghua quanguo funü lianhehui 2000.

There are clearly great differences in the social security status of men and women. That more and more women are concentrated in informal sector employment will lower job security and social security and the low security of women makes them increasingly reliant on men and family. This is an unbalanced social gender structure. It will not only affect the development of women, but also affect the development of men and society.

Know-how differentiation and "gender segregation" of occupation

Fixed role of gender. Housekeeping services certainly provide the disadvantaged women in the labour market with livelihood employment opportunities, but it is likely that the huge potential abilities of women and their rights to develop these abilities will be overlooked. If informal employment is encouraged to solve the crisis of women's employment, we will be forcing women into the simple, service and family derivative occupation mode.

Could a gap in know-how occur? Just as is indicated in the "World Employment Report," one of the factors that decide the future employment is "globalization, technological development and change of work organization. There is an increasing demand for workers with technical know-how," especially in the manufacturing industry. "With reduced employment opportunity, the increase of employment has transferred to sectors requiring good technical know-how." The "world factory" oriented strategy in China decides the demand for workers with good know-how and the reliance of the nation on technology. This trend will lead to further differentiation among the labourers. The income gap is widening due to differing technical know-how and "total working hours" because of the inadequate employment of workers with poor technical know-how. At the same time, there is the "social exclusion" of workers with poor know-how from the labour market.

The negative influence of women being concentrated in low-skilled technology sectors is obvious. Not only does it widen the income gap between men and women, it also promotes the low technological status of women due to the fact that there are fewer training opportunities in informal sector employment. We were warned that the "digital gap" probably occurred in the network technology age; we should also watch out for the gender specific "know-how gap," which would result in women being excluded from the highly-skilled technological job market. This would mean that blue collar workers among the women would have fewer opportunities to enter formal sector employment. The gender segregation of occupation would thus be further fixed.

Inadequate security for the rights and interests of women in informal employment

Women employed in the informal sector cannot usually get adequate security regarding their rights and interests at work due to the lack of organizational resources.

After carrying out research on housekeeping service workers, Guo Huimin concluded that the problems of security for the rights and interests of housekeeping workers exist as follows:

- Absence of labour security resulted from the separation of contracts of labour and contracts of employment.
- Problems of working hours and the right to be paid
- No sector standard regarding the amount of work due to informal employment
- No protection regarding economic security (salary security) and personal safety (industrial injuries)
- Right to occupational physical and mental health treatment
- Infringement of rights due to nonstandard management of agency (Guo 2005: 316).

In addition, there is the problem of sexual harassment in the working place. The "Rural women's culture development center" introduced several cases which had occurred in rural areas, of sexual harassment of nannies by male employers.[5] Due to the social identity (residence permit), gender and occupation (no authority, only labour relations but no contract of employment) of the victims, they are susceptible to sexual harassment and rarely find anyone to turn to for help; they often find themselves in hot water after their rights have been infringed. This is the vulnerability of women in informal employment. Guo Huimin called them the "marginalized labourers."

In general, the Chinese women labourers are being marginalized during the restructuring, which is reflected in lower employment structures and informalized and unstabilized employment.

The marginalization of women's labour exists in:
- The fact that women become the most susceptible to social exclusion and to employment risks;
- The gender segregation and the low level of women's employment structures, as a result of which women are concentrated in low-income "women's sector" and "women's vocations;"
- The informalization and instability of women's labour.

These three trends are interlinked, but the most significant influence comes from the informalization of women's labour. The informalization of labour has a much more negative influence on women than on men, including lower social welfare and inadequate security.

Discussion about future development trends and policies

Informalization of labour will become a long term worldwide trend

According to the data provided by the ILO, even in the economically developed countries, there is a variety of flexible employment, which accounts for 30 per cent of all employment in the U.S. and 25 per cent in Japan. It is an obvious phenomenon in developing countries. 80 per cent of the new vocations in Latin America, and 93 per cent in Africa were created by the informal sectors between 1990 and 1994. At present, people in flexible employment amount to 57.2 per cent of the people employed in total in Africa and 32.8 per cent in Asia and Pacific area (Guoji laogong ju 2000: 45). In developing countries, the informal sectors are growing rapidly due to the fact that the formal economic sector can not provide adequate employment opportunities. Under the pressure of unemployment and limited formal employment, the state governments have issued a series of policies to promote the development of flexible employment. Therefore, the increasing proportion of flexible employment is not a local and temporary phenomenon, but will be a widespread trend in many countries for a long period in future.

---

[5] Here, I refer to a case presented at the "Seminar of Ethical, Legal and Social Problems against Sexual Harassment at Working Places," hosted by the China Academy of Social Sciences, Institute of Philosophy, 24-25 September 2005.

Informalization of women's labour and feminization of informal labour are worldwide trends

According to the analysis of the individual numbers of men and women in part time employment in 12 OECD countries, the number of women is two to ten times higher than that of men. In Australia and in the U.K., over 40 per cent of women are in the informal employment sector (ibid.: 118).

In Japan, from 1965 to 1999, the number of part-time workers (part time meaning fewer than 35 working hours a week) as a proportion of those in total employment increased 15.6 per cent, from 6.2 per cent to 21.8 per cent, while the number of women workers increased 27.8 per cent from 9.6 per cent to 37.4 per cent (Riben laodongsheng nüxing ju n.d.: 41).

It has become the practice in developed countries to solve the unemployment problems by displacing women to the informal employment sector. According to the labour force statistics of Eurostas, in the Netherlands, where the unemployment problem was solved properly, the informal employment rate of women in the past ten years has increased rapidly. It accounted for 90.7 per cent of women in total employment, up by 24 per cent compared with 66.7 per cent ten years ago. Informal employment has become an important employment mode for women in the EU (Chen 2001).

The trend in developed countries reveals that flexible employment in the labour market affects women the most. It is predicted that informal employment will be taken up by more and more women labourers, in a future period of time, especially those over 35 with low vocational skills.

Policy problems

Government shall reinforce the support for informal employment and criticism of "informal employment misuse"

Should government intervene in the segmented labour market? At present, the opinions of academia stand for reinforced support for the development of the informal employment and informal economic sectors. They have pointed out that the women's labour force "has a bright future in the informal service sector employment, and government should relax their control and create a good environment to improve the working conditions and promote the development of the informal sector" (Hu 1999: 75f.). But a different voice can be heard from the women's circle. For example, Jiang Yongping indicated that informal employment should not be "misused." In China Women NGO Evaluation Report of Chinese Government Performance "Guidance" of 2005 (purple-book), it is also indicated: "While reinforcing support for informal employment, we should prevent the misuse of it" (Jiang 2005: 19). This is, however, a weak voice.

I well understand the intention of Jiang Yongping and others to change the vulnerability of marginalized women labourers, but I cannot agree to use the concept of "misuse". The labour market has its own rules of development. What the government should do is to promote the healthy development of a market with a fair competition mechanism, and to establish a public system aiming at market failure at the same time.

As for the government policy on informal labour, we shall analyze the problems individually. Informal employment can be classified into two types. One can create new vocations but may not lower the production costs. The other can lower the production costs but cannot create, or even reduce vocations. From the standpoint of employment-oriented policies, the government should support the informal employment which creates vocations, such as grassroots business establishments and self-employment through micro enterprises, family enterprises and community employment. The latter are the economic institutions that might adopt formal employment but adopt center-periphery employment, especially those employers who may adopt either formal or informal employment. Must informal employment be adopted? However, even if there is a trend towards "misuse", the government should not intervene directly but induce action through policies, for example, the general minimum wage level, the inclusion of informal employment in the social security system and supervision of contracts of employment, to narrow the gap between labourer security and welfare between the two labour markets.

Design of welfare system

Social security is the core of social policy. At present, the attention of academia with regard to informal employment in our country is also concentrated on low welfare and low security. They think the most important reason for low welfare and low security in informal employment is the absence of system supply and the delay of social insurance management during the social transition.

The original endowment and medical insurance system was designed for people in formal employment and implemented by the state enterprises. Now, people in informal employment have nearly no institutional relation with current social insurance, thus a very huge group is still excluded from the social security system. Therefore, academia has appealed for the establishment of a social insurance system for people in informal employment as soon as possible to protect them and for people on a low-income to be entitled to basic social security. The improved welfare and security policy for people in informal employment will undoubtedly benefit the women in informal employment.

In May, 2003, the Ministry of Labour and Social Security proposed to include the people in flexible employment in the current social security system. Some places and cities issued social insurance policies to protect the people in informal employment. However, due to the fact that the "inclusion" is still based on formal employment, the informalized labour relations, multiple labour relations (for example, temporary worker or worker by hours employed by several enterprises simultaneously), even absence of labour relations, right and obligation counterpart (self-employed flexible employment people, such as self-employed worker and freelancer) of informal employment require the informal employment people to pay the social insurance independently. There are preferential policies in many places, but their low income renders them unable to afford the fee. The high costs still exclude people in informal employment from social insurance system. In Shanghai, there is a comprehensive social insurance system designed for informal employment, including medical, pension, industrial injury and unemployment. But the insurance premium for workers paid by the hour is the same as that of employees in formal enterprises, which hinders many people in informal employment from participating in the insurance plans. Though there are some preferential policies of reducing premiums in the cities investigated (there is the measure of reducing part of the insurance premium in Dalian) (Laodong yu shehui baozhang bu shehui baoxian yanjiusuo kewenzu, unpublished), this is still a long way from the actual demand and affordability of people in informal employment. The preferential policies become lip service.

The reasons for the absence of a system are found in the deficiency of our values in making public policy, that is, the lack of concern about the situation and needs of disadvantaged groups. When we consider establishing a security network covering the people in informal employment, we shall see that what these people need now is stable and "decent work." The term "decent work" refers to, as proposed by the ILO at the 87th International Labour Organization Conference in 1999, the decent, productive continuable work accomplished in conditions of freedom, equity, security and human dignity. The core of this proposal is to promote respect for workers' rights, employment equality, adequate social protection and social dialogue at work. Therefore, when making a public policy aimed at sharing development benefits, attention should be paid to the system in favour of both informal employment development and the rights and interests of people in informal employment, the increase of incomes in the informal sectors and the elimination of the discrimination and social exclusion due to age, sex and health. For instance, we can bring the public resources into play and establish a public training system and vocational guidance in favour of labourers lacking in human capital (including people in informal employment).

Next, we should have the concept of "due" and pertinent security standards. In fact, the disadvantaged groups in the labour force market need social security more than anyone else. One of the purposes of the global "Strategy and approach against social exclusion and poverty" project carried out by the ILO is to extend the scope of social protection, especially to informal sectors. There is some difficulty in including informal employment in the social security system, but it is possible as long as the security standard is pertinently designed and operable. Some countries are seeking approaches in this respect. In Hong Kong, for example, from 2001, all employees, including white-collar, blue-collar, half-time or part-time workers, workers employed by the hour and casual workers, however much they earn, must buy compulsory insurance, as long as they work for the same employer for more than 30 days and no less than 18 hours per week. Basically, employees pay five per cent of their wages and employers pay another five per cent. If the employee's monthly income is less than 4,000 HK$, they are exempt from payment, but the employers must pay their five per cent. This provides essential security for people in informal employment and on a low-income. We may adopt this mode and provide the necessary social aid to people in informal employment by reducing their insurance premiums, or even exempting them from paying the insurance premiums.

We should accept that both our researchers and public policy maker have a blind spot regarding female gender. It should not be doubted that women are reduced to working in the informal sector because there is discrimination against women and they are subject to social exclusion. One of the serious results of the feminization of informal employment and the informalization of women's employment is that women are rapidly marginalized. The current social security policies aimed at people in flexible employment are usually designed for free-lancers and those employed informally in formal sectors, but are not applicable to housekeeping workers and workers employed by the hour, both areas which are dominated by women. The public policy makers in future should pay attention to the problem of how to include these people in the social security system. In addition, there is something else which is worth our consideration.

Can we establish a labour market which is not only flexible but also stable?

If we concentrated on increasing the stability of informal employment and the security and welfare of informal labourers, we would increase labour rigidity and reduce the flexibility of the labour force market. These would probably affect the interests of those disadvantaged groups.

Interflow between two labour force markets

It is impossible to eliminate the ranks in the labour market, but the institutional segregation (the labour force from rural areas cannot enter the formal labour force market due to residence permit restrictions) should be eliminated. The labour should be able to flow between the two types of market freely. It is not a one-way downward flow, but a two-way interflow.

Strategy

From a long-term viewpoint, a strategy to eliminate the marginalization of women should include:
- Making a law of equal employment against discrimination and exclusion.
- Providing necessary social protection for the disadvantaged groups in the labour market, especially those informally employed people who, with unstable work, have multiple labour relations or are hardly able to establish labour relations with employers, and the establishment of a widespread social security network;
- Making public training available for people in informal employment to increase their human capital by public investment after providing them with livelihood employment, offering people in informal employment "promotion" opportunities and enhancing their employment ability;
- Offering special encouragement policies to women when cultivating "grey collar" and "senior blue collar" workers. The "grey collar" strategy for women

should also be included in a women's development guidance and program made by the government;
- Changing the outdated gender concept that underestimates women's occupational development and the potential ability of high tech, and reduces women's occupation space (for instance, the opinion that woman can only do service jobs and take care of others, that a woman has nothing to do with high tech, that married women shall take account of their job and families at same time, etc.), especially of those public policy makers and implementers.

References

Cai, Fang 蔡昉 (ed.) (2002a) Zhongguo renkou yu laodong wenti baogao 中国人口与劳动问题报告 [China population and labour report], Beijing: Shehui kexue wenjian chubanshe 社会科学文献出版社 [Social Sciences Academic Press], 2002, pp. 103, 187.

Cai, Fang 蔡昉 (ed.) (2002b) *2000 nian: Zhongguo renkou yu laodong wenti baogao – chengxiang jiuye wenti yu duice* 2002年：中国人口与劳动问题报告——城乡就业问题与对策 [China population and labour report 2002 - urban and rural employment problem and strategy], Beijing: Beijing: Shehui kexue wenjian chubanshe 社会科学文献出版社 [Social Sciences Academic Press].

Chen, Yuexin 陈月新 (2001) Oumeng guojia funü feizhenggui jiuye de fazhan yiqi de woguo funü jiuye de qishi 欧盟国家妇女非正规就业的发展及其对我国妇女就业的启示 [Illuminating remarks on women informal employment development of EU countries and the employment of Chinese women], in *Funü yanjiu luncong*妇女研究论丛 [Women Study] 1.

Chinese Academy of Social Sciences (2002) "'6 chengshi zhigong xiagang qingkuang diaocha' kewenzu" 《6城市职工下岗情况调查》课题组 [,Lay-off Survey in 6 cities' group], in Cai, Fang 蔡昉 (Ed.) (2002b) *2000 nian: Zhongguo renkou yu laodong wenti baogao – chengxiang jiuye wenti yu duice* 2002年：中国人口与劳动问题报告——城乡就业问题与对策 [China population and labour report 2002 - urban and rural employment problem and strategy], Beijing: Shehui kexue wenjian chubanshe社会科学文献出版社 [Social Sciences Academic Press], pp. 274.

Hu, Angang 胡鞍钢 (ed.) (1999) Kuaru xin shijie de zuida tiaozhan: woguo jinru gao shiye jieduan 跨入新世界的最大挑战：我国进入高失业阶段 [Biggest challenge in the new century: We are entering high unemployment stage], in *Zhongguo zouxiang*中国走向 [China Trend], Hangzhou: Zhejiang Renmin Chubanshe 浙江人民出版社 [Zhejiang People's Press], p. 75-76.

Hu, Angang 胡鞍钢 (2002) "Woguo jiuye xingshi" 我国就业形势[Employment situation in our country], in *Zhongguo laodong* 中国劳动 [China Labour], p. 6, 8-11.

Guo, Huimin 郭慧敏 (2005) Qugongyehua, fangyuanhua, nüxinghua he ququanyihua – yige jiazheng gongqunben de quanli bansheng xianxiang fenxi 去工业化、边缘化、女性化和去权益化——一个家政工群体的权利伴生现象分析 [Deindustrialization, marginalization, feminization, and de-rightization—right associated phenomena analysis of housekeeping workers], in *Shehui xingbie yu laodong quanyi*社会性别与劳动权益

[Social gender and labor rights and interests], Xi'an: 西北工业大学出版社 [Northwest University Press], p. 316.

Guoji laogong ju 国际劳工局 [International Labour Bureau](2000) *Shijie jiuye baogao* 世界就业报告, 1998-1999 [World employment report, 1998-1999], Beijing: Zhongguo laogong yu shehui baozhang chubanshe 中国劳动与社会保障出版社 [China Labour and Social Security Publishing House], p. 1, 45, 119.

Guojia tongji ju 国家统计局 [National Bureau of Statistics] (Eds) (2001) *Zhongguo tongji nianjian* 中国统计年鉴 [China statistical yearbook], Beijing: Zhongguo tongji chubanshe 中国统计出版社[China Statistics Press].

Guojia tongji ju renkou yu shehui keji tongji si 国家统计局人口与社会科技统计司[National Bureau of Statistics of China, Department of Population Social Science and Technology Statistics] (eds) (2004) *Zhongguo shehui zhong de nüren he nanren – shishi he shuju* 中国社会中的女人和男人——事实和数据 [Women and men in Chinese society – facts and figures], Beijing: Zhongguo tongji chubanshe 中国统计出版社[China Statistics Press] p. 39.

Jiang, Yongping 蒋永萍 (2005) "95+10, Zhongguo funü jingji luntan" 95+10，中国妇女经济论坛[95+10, China Women Economic Forum], in Zhongguo feizhengfu funü zuzhi dui Zhonguo zhengfu zhixing (xingdong gangling) he (chengli wenjian) de pinggu baogao (zipi shu) 中国非政府妇女组织对中国政府执行"行动纲领"和"成果文件"的评估报告（紫皮书）[China women NGO evaluation report of Chinese government performance "guidance" and "achievement" (purple book)], p.19.

Laodong baozhangbu peixun jiuyesi, Zhongguo jiuye peixun jishu zhidao zhongxin 劳动保障部培训就业司，中国就业培训技术指导中心 [Ministry of Labor and Social Security, Vocational Training Technical Instruction Center, Department of Training and Employment] (n.d.) *Jiazheng fuwu baipi shu* 家政服务白皮书 [Housekeeping Service White-book].

Laodong yu shehui baozhangbu shehui baoxian yanjiusuo kewenzu 劳动与社会保障部社会保险研究所课题组 [Institute of Social Security, Ministry of Labour and Social Security] (unpublished) Linghuo jiuye qunti shehui baoxian yanjiu baogao 灵活就业群体社会保险研究报告 [Research report on social security of flexible employment group].

Li, Qiang 李强; Hu, Junsheng 胡俊生; Hong, Dayong 洪大用 (2001) *Shiye xiagang wenti duibi yanjiu* 失业下岗问题对比研究 [Comparative study of lay-off problems], Beijing: Qinghua daxue chubanshe清华大学出版社[Tsinghua University Press].

Riben laodongsheng nüxingju 日本劳动省女性局 [Bureau of Women, Ministry of Labor, Japan] (Eds) (n.d.) Nüxing laodong baipi shu 女性劳动白皮书 [White book on women labour].

Wang, Dongjin 王东进 (2003) in *Zhongguo laodong* 中国劳动[China labour], 13 November 2003.

Without author (2002) "Laodongli shichang de xingbie shijiao" 劳动力市场的性别视角 [Gender view of labour force market], in Cai (2002b) pp. 268-269.

Yuan, Yunpeng 袁运鹏 (2002) in *Zhongguo laodong*中国劳动[China Labour] (2002) 9, p. 13.

Zhonghua quanguo funü lianhehui 中华全国妇女联合会 [China Women's Federation] (2000) *2000 nian quanguo funü diwei diaocha shuju* 2000年全国妇女地位调查数据 [National women status survey of 2000].

Zhongguo tongji 中国统计 [China Statistics] (2002) 4.

Zhonghua Renmin Gongheguo guojia tongji ju 中华人民共和国国家统计局 [Statistical Office of the People's Republic of China] (2002) Zhongguo 2000 nian renkou pucha ziliao 中国2000年人口普查资料 [Material 2000 national population census in China], Beijing: Zhongguo Tongji Chubanshe 中国统计出版社 [China Statistics Press], p. 909-934.

Social Protection for Migrant Workers in the Informal Economy – Issues and Options

Peng Xizhe and Yao Yu

Introduction

The large-scale rural-to-urban migration has not only changed the spatial distribution of China's population, but has also affected the pattern and path of urbanization and slowed down the urban aging process. Its contribution to economic growth is the provision of an unlimited and flexible supply of cheap labour which has resulted in the restructuring of urban labour markets. Employing rural migrant workers leads to reductions in labour costs because they are paid low salaries and because they are excluded from social security systems. However, while migration helps to enhance the flow of money and information from the cities to the countryside, it also creates a number of problems, such as social tension between the regular city dwellers and the temporary migrant residents. Tackling the needs of migrant workers is not only an issue of urban poverty reduction but also of enhancing social stability.

The Chinese leadership under Hu Jintao has implemented a series of regulations aimed at the migrant workers in particular. The "Regulation on the Detention and Deportation of Vagrants and Beggars in Urban Areas," for example, was replaced by a new "Regulation on Adminstration and Aid for Vagrants and Beggars in Urban Areas" by the Ministry of Civil Affairs in August 2003. Another important measure is the gradual liberalization of the household registration system (*hukou zhidu*). However, the *hukou* system is both an essential tool of political and social control in China and also the basis for social segregation in terms of social welfare and other entitlements, so that changes to the system, if they are to be carried out in an orderly and comprehensive manner, will take time.

The Chinese government has acknowledged the huge gap in social security and social protection between different population groups, including formal and informal workers. Local governments have launched various initiatives to reduce these discrepancies. The government of Shanghai municipality, for example, has undertaken efforts to extend the coverage of the urban social security system by financial subsidies and thus to include workers in the informal sector. Among the registered informal workers in Shanghai, 84 per cent have basic social insurance (including pension insurance, healthcare insurance, unemployment insurance), and 80 per cent of them have taken part in risk insurance (a special institutional arrangement for informal workers and migrant workers). In addition, a new social security system, the "Comprehensive Insurance Scheme," which was specifically designed for migrant workers, has been operating since 2003.

At present, the system is fully independent of the existing social security system, in terms of fund management and benefits' arrangements. It is clear that the Shanghai government is hoping that the series of reform measures they have implemented to pursue the goals of "poverty reduction and decent work" will bring more and more migrant workers into the social security system.

This paper starts with a short description of the main characteristics of Shanghai's migrant population with regard to gender, age, education, employment and wages. It then discusses the challenges of establishing social protection measures for migrant workers in Shanghai.

Demographic and social characteristics of migrant workers in Shanghai

Gender and age

Most of the temporary migrants are young (between 16 and 30 years of age), and there are slightly more males than females (Guojia tongji ju 2005). In 2000, there were 3.87 million temporary migrants in Shanghai, which amounted to about one quarter of the city's total population. Among them, men accounted for 57.6 per cent while women made up 42.4 per cent, the sex ratio being 135.9. The age structure of migrants is shown in Figure 1.

Figure 1. Age pyramid of temporary migrants in Shanghai, 2000

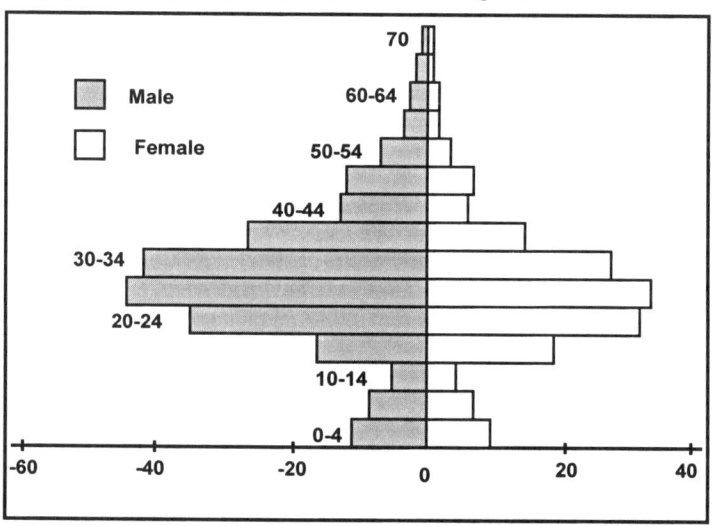

Source: Shanghai shi tongjiju, 2002.

Education

Those who migrate from rural to urban areas normally have higher than average educational levels. Data from Shanghai shows that about half of all migrants have been educated to junior high school level, and thus to a lower level than that of the local urban population (see Figure 2) but to a higher level than that of China's rural population.

Figure 2. Education level of local population and migrants in Shanghai, 2000

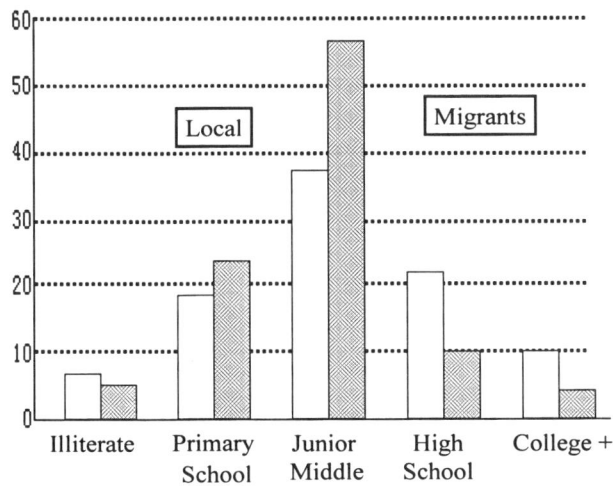

Source: Shanghai shi tongjiju, 2002.

Employment

Migrant workers usually take up the so-called 3-d (dirty, demanding and dangerous) jobs that urban workers are no longer willing to do. This can be seen clearly in Table 1 which shows the job distribution of the urban labour force and migrant workers in Shanghai. Female migrants are mainly engaged in household services, waste collection and small-scale trade, while a large number of male migrants work on construction sites, in factories, etc. Their activities are normally outside the supervision of the government. Few of them obtain either certificates issued by the Labour Administration Department, or individual business licenses. Only those with a higher education are formally employed. This is to say that migrant workers are highly concentrated in informal sectors and employed in an informal manner.[1]

Many Chinese cities now depend on migrant women to maintain sanitation. Domestic work is another kind of job, which is typically taken up by migrant women. It can be said that the economic participation of local urban women is partly supported by these migrant women who have become an indispensable part of the

---

[1] The definition of informal employment used in this paper is based on ILO documents. It is also called flexible employment by the Chinese Labour and Social Security authority.

urban support structure. It is interesting to note that maids working in a given city district often, through chain migration, come from the same village or region; they establish social networks in the cities to protect themselves and these allow them to bargain for better pay from their employers.

Table 1. Job distribution of Shanghai's labour force (in per cent)

Job Type	Local Labour Force	Migrant Worker
Managerial and officials	3.4	0.6
Professionals	12.8	3.8
Office staff	11.8	n.a.
Agricultural workers	11.3	7.3
Sales and service personnel	22.4	13.9
Food service	n.a.	6.6
Household service	n.a.	6.9
Industrial workers	38.2	2.9
Manufacturing Industry		25.8
Building & Construction		19.5
Recycling & waste collection		1.6
Others	0.1	11.1
Total	100.0	100.0

Source: Authors' compilation based on data from various population statistics.

Approximately 25 per cent of migrant women engage in various commercial activities. Migrant women with families are more likely to become peddlers, snack-bar owners, vegetable sellers, etc. These types of work are more flexible and thus can be more easily combined with family duties. These activities of migrant women have resulted in the rapid development of street markets, which have made urban life much more convenient – a factor which is certainly welcomed by urban residents (Yao 2004).

Wages

The wages of migrant workers are low, only slightly higher than the minimum salary for local inhabitants. Nationwide, the income level of migrant workers is only 58 per cent of that of formal workers in cities (Guojia tongji ju 2005). In addition, the female migrant workers' income is even lower than that of male migrants'.[2] And very often migrant workers are unable to get their full salary on time. Although the central government has issued many regulations, some migrant workers still have to struggle to get their full salary paid by their employers.[3]

---

[2] No exact data is available, but many employers say that they pay migrant women workers only 70 per cent of the amount paid to male migrant workers.
[3] See also contribution by Yang Wenjian et al. on "The Problem of Overdue Migrant Wages" in this volume.

Table 2. Monthly income of migrant workers (RMB)

	2004	2003	2002
Whole country	780	702	659
Eastern region	798	709	669
Central region	724	643	623
Western region	701	644	589

Source: Guojia tongji ju 2005.

Data obtained from the National Bureau of Statistics show that the average income of migrants is RMB 780 per month, the living costs amount to RMB 291. The income level of the urban residents is 599, not including subsidies for housing, health care and education, etc. In order to be able to maintain a basic standard of living and to save some money, most migrant workers are forced to float between urban and rural areas.

Social protection for male and female migrant workers in Shanghai

After years of discussion and investigation, a basic social security system has been set up, consisting of social insurance, social relief, social welfare, social mutual help and special care for disabled ex-servicemen and family members of revolutionary martyrs, featuring the raising of funds through various channels and the gradual socialization of management and services. After efforts spanning more than a decade, basic social insurance policies have been formulated, successively promulgated and implemented, which now cover the vast majority of urban staff and retirees. In some regions, even rural people working in cities are included. However, informal employees, particularly migrant workers, are often excluded from the system either by the institutional arrangements or by the migrants themselves. In addition, there is a salient gender difference in terms of social protection.

Social protection in China is mainly channelled via work units and residential status. Migrant women, especially those who work in factories and institutions, are often employed through organized arrangements involving administrative organs responsible for recruiting them from their original place of residence and receiving them at their urban employment destination. They are in a relatively good position to protect their rights for higher pay and better living conditions. However, a large number of individual female migrants have no access to these two channels of support, since they are usually not formally employed and have no stable place of residence. On the one hand, they have left their homeland and entered a more risky and unfamiliar urban environment; on the other hand, they have lost their former contacts, i.e. kinship networks, through which they used to get legal and social protection. This situation makes them extremely vulnerable.

Table 3 demonstrates that while people engaged in informal employment are generally much less likely to be covered by a pension system, the coverage for female informal workers is even lower. In 2004, more than 88 per cent of the migrant workers were not covered by the pension system (Guojia tongjiju 2005). A similar situation is observable with regard to health care insurance (see Table 4).

Table 3. Coverage of pension insurance by gender and employment (in per cent), 2000

Type of employment	Coverage	Male	Female	Total
Informal employment	Covered	14.8	10.4	12.6
	Not covered	83.9	88.3	86.2
	Not clear	1.3	1.2	1.3
Formal employment	Covered	84.7	81.3	83.3
	Not covered	12.2	16.2	13.8
	Not clear	3.0	2.6	2.8

Source: Zhonghua quanguo funü lianhehui 2002.

Table 4. Coverage of health care insurance by gender and employment (in per cent), 2000

Type of employment	Coverage	Male	Female	Total
Informal employment	Covered	14.4	9.0	11.6
	Not covered	84.0	90.5	87.4
	Not clear	1.6	0.5	1.0
Formal employment	Covered	73.9	65.5	70.6
	Not covered	24.6	32.5	27.7
	Not clear	1.5	2.0	1.7

Source: Zhonghua quanguo funü lianhehui 2002.

Reproductive health is a field in which protection is especially vital for migrant workers. A survey in Shanghai showed that while the majority of women interviewed are aware of the major forms of sexually transmitted diseases (STDs), confusion about the transmission of the most publicized STD or AIDS still exist (Peng/Chen 2002). However, female migrants with at least a junior high school education or longer duration of residence in Shanghai seem to have a much lower level of ignorance. In general, female migrants reported good health status. About one in seven respondents reported that they had had at least one symptom of reproductive tract infection (RTI), but did not seek treatment. A fairly large number of pregnant migrant women wait until very late for the first prenatal exam, and many pregnant women either go back to their place of origin or simply deliver outside of a hospital. The city health authority has taken note of the health problems of female migrants and has tried to remove the institutional barriers to obtaining health care in urban areas. However, without any form of medical insurance coverage, more than 90 percent of female migrants need to pay all health expenses out of their own pockets (ibid.). The expenses they incur in hospitals also tend to be several times higher than those of local residents who benefit from the reduced rates charged by insurance network providers. As a result, health care costs are exorbitant for most migrant women and their families, who are living on low and uncertain earnings. In addition to these institutional barriers, some migrants do not trust the urban health system and fear unfair treatment by doctors.

We can use the following graph to illustrate, approximately, the differences in network reachability for social protection between urban formal workers and informal workers. Figure 3 shows clearly the different coverage of social protection for different groups of employees, namely, formally employed workers, informally employed workers and the group of workers who fall between formal and informal employment arrangements. The latter group is those workers formerly employed in state-owned enterprises who used to have perfect social security coverage but have gradually been excluded from the mainstream system over time.

Figure 3. Access to social protection by employment types

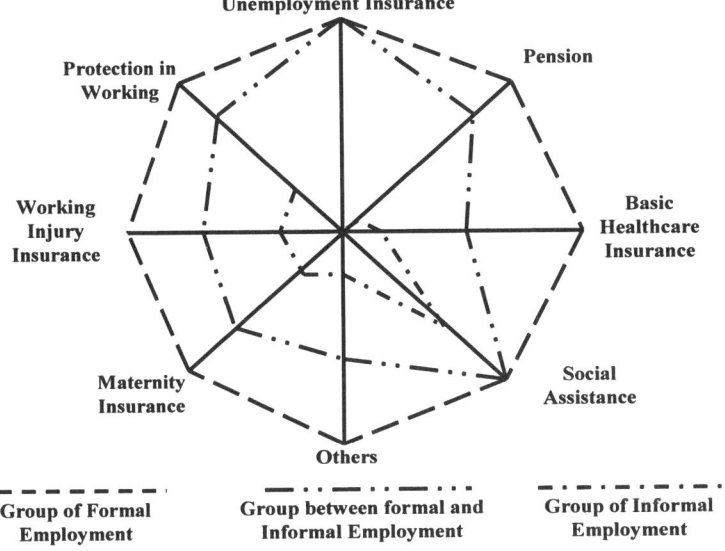

Source: Authors' own compilation.

As can be seen from the figure, the coverage of social protection measures is relatively complete for people working in the formal sector; for the group between formal and informal employment, measures include mainly unemployment insurance and social assistance, but much less coverage regarding health care and other components of the social protection system. In comparison with these two groups, the coverage of social protection measures for people employed in the informal sector is very limited; they have some access to social assistance, but are entirely without basic employment, pension and health insurance.

China's urban sector has received fruits of reforms disproportionate to its contribution. It is estimated by the World Bank that rural-urban labour mobility contributed to about 16-20 per cent of China's GDP increase (Project Team on Rural

Labour Migration 2001). As large scale rural-to-urban migration will inevitably continue in the future, more efforts should be made to include rural migrants in the urban "formal" labour market. One specific measure would be to include migrants in the urban social security system. On the one hand, this could extend the contribution base of urban social security funds, which will partially solve the problem of an increasing deficit that is mainly caused by rapid population aging. Meanwhile, this is also a way of providing Chinese farmers with some kind of social security, and it will help to reduce the gap in labour costs between local urban and migrant workers that in turn may help to resolve the urban unemployment problem.

There are several options with regard to providing social protection for informal workers in China:

1) Extending government-sponsored programmes to cover migrant workers.

2) Establishing protection programmes run by migrant workers or organisations. Local government can direct and sponsor them.

3) Relying on market mechanisms, commercial insurance.

4) Organising protection programs to be run, like charities, for example, by NGOs.

5) Encouraging female migrant workers to obtain more rights.

6) Instituting a multi-pillar integrated system, to make best use of existing social resources through mainstreaming approaches.

To date, there is no consensus in this field. In our opinion, the struggle for the provision of social protection for migrant workers may learn from the strategy of gender mainstreaming. There is a so-called "three-legged equality stool," including the perspective of equal treatment, the women's perspective and the gender perspective (Booth/Bennett n.d.). While the perspective of equal treatment emphasizes statutory and mandatory legal instruments, the women's perspective inspires initiatives which recognise women as a disadvantaged group in society deserving of particular treatment and special provisions. The gender perspective promotes actions that aim at transforming the organisation of society by a fairer distribution of human responsibilities through new tools for gender sensitive policy-making. Social protection for informal workers, especially migrant workers, in China should progress in all three fields: equal treatment through legal and institutional arrangements, special programmes to meet the particular needs of informal employees and, finally, the mainstreaming policy instruments. To this end, we should launch a dialogue between different social groups. Meanwhile, China can also learn a lot from other developing countries.

Concluding remarks and discussion

On 18 January 2006, China's State Council passed a motion concerned with migrant workers' social welfare. This is one of the most recent series of efforts undertaken by the Chinese government to provide social protection for migrant workers. Shanghai is one of the forerunners in this regard.

By the end of 2005, according to official reports, about two million (or two thirds) of all migrant workers in Shanghai had joined the comprehensive insurance system, including industrial accident, hospital treatment and old-age subsidy. Although the benefits are much lower than those of other urban social security arrangements, the system has been well accepted by migrant workers. Out of 300,000 migrant children, 60 per cent are enrolled in special schools for migrant children, while most of the others are studying at local urban schools. Shanghai's government has tried to improve the quality of those schools, while also trying to allow more migrant children to enrol in normal local schools. Female migrants are covered by free family planning services as well.

There is, however, some concern about Shanghai's experiment. At present, most other cities in the country have not taken measures to bring migrant labourers into their own social security systems. If Shanghai alone undertakes the reform, its enterprises will be in an inferior position regarding labour costs, when competing with companies in other parts of China. Thus, the local government is faced with a dilemma: they have to choose between equity and efficiency when constructing a social security system to cover informal workers of the migrant labour force.

Furthermore, Shanghai's experiment may encounter special difficulties in collecting social security payment from informal workers, because the practices of payment calculation and collection under formal employment conditions will be of no use under informal employment conditions. The basic measure for the collection of contributions is similar to that in the urban social security system, but has much lower premiums and benefits. The money collected will be passed on to commercial insurance institutions with the aim of supplying basic social security treatment for immigrated workers. The major obstacle to the new system for migrant workers is the reluctance of both the employers and the migrant workers themselves. Increased labour costs for employers and a lower immediate cash income for workers are the main concerns.

In fact, because of the uncertainties in labour contracts and income under informal labour market conditions, it is hardly possible for employers and employees to pay for social insurance in accordance with regulations that depend on constant salaries. Thus, if migrant informal workers are to be brought into the city's formal social security system, an efficient social security administration system needs to be established which is based upon an individual credit system, a relatively complete revenue system, and coordinated efforts by related bureaus such as the Labour and Social Security Administration, Public Security and Civil Administration (Zhou et al.: n.d.).

References

Booth, Christine and Bennett, Cinnamon (n.d.) *Gender Mainstreaming in the European Union: Toward a New Conception and Practice of Equal Opportunities?*, unpublished manuscript.

Cai, Fang 蔡昉 (2002) *Zhongguo renkou yu laodong wenti baogao: chengxiang jiuye wenti yu duice* 中国人口与劳动问题报告：城乡就业问题与对策 [Report of Chinese population and labour: employment in rural and urban China: issues and options], Beijing: Shehui kexue wenxian chubanshe 社会科学文献出版社 [Social Sciences Academic Press].

Guojia tongji ju 国家统计局 [National Bureau of Statistics of China] (2005) *Guojia tongjiju tongji baogao* 国家统计局统计报告 [Statistics report of National Bureau of Statistics of China], Beijing 2005.6.

International Labour Organisation (ILO) (2002) "Decent work and the informal eco-nomy," paper presented to the Committee on the Informal Economy at the International Labour Conference, Geneva.

Lund, Frances and Srinivas, Smita (2001) *Learning from experience: A gendered approach to social protection for workers in the informal economy*, Geneva: International Labour Organization.

Ministry of Civil Affairs (2003) "Chengshi shenghuo wuzhi de liuliang qitao renyuan jiuzhu guanli banfa" 城市生活无着的流浪乞讨人员救助管理办法 [Regulation on adminstration and aid for vagrants and beggars in urban areas], PRC State Council Circular No.381, August 2003.

Peng, Xizhe and Chen, Yuexin (2002) "Quality reproductive health service to migrant women in Shanghai," Survey report, submitted to United Nations Food Program Association (UNFPA).

Peng, Xizhe 彭希哲 and Yao, Yu 姚宇 (2004) "Liqing feizhenggui jiuye gainian, tuidong feizhenggui jiuye fazhan" 厘清非正规就业概念,推动非正规就业发展[Clarify the concept of informal employment, promote the development of informal employment], Shanghai: Journal of Social Sciences, Issue 7, pp. 63-73.

Project Team on Rural Labour Migration 2001 (2001) "Rural labour migration in China: retrospect and prospect," in *Beijing: A Review of Ford Foundation Grant Making 1997-2001*.

Shanghai shi renkou pucha bangongshi 上海市人口普查办公室 [Shanghai 2000 Census Office] (2000) *Shanghai Population Development Report* 上海人口发展报告 2000. Shanghai: Shanghai Statistics Publishing House.

Shanghai shi tongjiju 上海市统计局[Shanghai Bureau of Statistics] (2002) *Shanghai renkou pucha baogao* 上海市人口普查报告 [Population census report, Shanghai], Beijing: Chinese Statistics Press.

Yao, Yu 姚宇 (2004) "Jiating gongren, xingbie chayi burong hushi" 家庭工人,性别差异不容忽视 [Homeworker: we can't ignore the gender difference], in: *Zhong-guo funü bao* 中国妇女报 [China Woman News, Beijing], Issue 8, 13 July 2004.

Zhonghua quanguo funü lianhehui 中华全国妇女联合会 [All-Chinese Women's Federation] (ed.) (2002) *Di'erci Zhongguo funü shehui diwei diaocha* 第二次中国妇女社会地位调查 [2nd Women's condition survey], Beijing.

Zhou, Guoliang; Yang, Te; Chen, Gang; Ge, Jingfeng (n.d.) "Social security of informal employment in Shanghai," abstract of internal report.

Active Empoyment Policies

Labour Market Policy – Conflict of Aims Between Quantity and Quality

Michaela Baur

The following paper will cover a broad range of labour market issues, which characterize the overall labour market situation in contemporary China. The specific perspective of the paper is based on the experiences of the Chinese-German cooperation project, "Reintegration of Unemployed Women in the Labour Force," which is nearing completion after seven years of successful implementation. In addition to such practical experiences, this paper also presents the various findings, impressions and conclusions of the author.

The first section gives details of the most important background information about the Chinese-German cooperation project, with its major fields of operation and activities. The second section classifies the meaning and tasks of labour market policy in general. It can be widely observed, internationally as well as in China, that labour market policy has frequently not been appraised in a reasonable way and that, therefore, the ranking of labour market policy in the wide set of other policy fields has to be clarified.

The labour market situation in China is unique. Chinese society faces the typical problems of a transforming economy, but there are certain additional problems and challenges which make the Chinese example a special one. The third section covers the most important aspects of these. The fourth section discusses the question of whether the Chinese government's answer to these challenges is appropriate and will be able to reduce the pressure on the labour market. There are certain strengths and weaknesses, but one of the major problems is the mainly quantitative approach of Chinese labour market policy, which very often lacks the urgently needed quality aspect. The fifth section draws some conclusions, basically with reference to the question of whether an integrated labour market is in the making.

Background: The German-Chinese project for the reintegration of women

In the middle of the 1990s, the transformation of the economic system in China also brought huge changes to the labour market. Most of the state-owned enterprises had to lay off redundant workers, this being their only chance to become profitable and competitive. Whereas unemployment was somewhat unknown before this time in China, it now became more and more common. Similar processes took place in other countries during transformation. These processes usually appear in a way which makes the labour market status of women worse: not only do they more frequently lose their jobs, they also have difficulty in finding new jobs. In fact, it is not only a quantitative problem. Women are finding themselves more and more often in odd and badly paid jobs with low career opportunities and weak social security. In different ways, they are facing discrimination in the labour market.

This was the current situation, when the German and the Chinese government agreed on a project for the reintegration of unemployed women. After the general agreement, a fact-finding mission with Chinese and German experts had to choose between five different cities. Finally, they took Nanjing as a pilot city for the first phase and Nanjing and Benxi as pilot cities for the second phase. The project started in 1999 and will come to an end in 2006. On the Chinese side, the Ministry of Labour and Social Security is responsible for the project; on the German side, it is the Deutsche Gesellschaft für Technische Zusammenarbeit (GTZ). The responsible institutions in the pilot cities are the Municipal Labour Administrations in Benxi and Nanjing, but in fact, there are a lot more stakeholders: the Women's Federation, the trade unions, private and state-owned training institutes and other labour market service suppliers, employers' federations and so on. The project objective is to help the unemployed women who asked for support from the labour administration to find new jobs or to start up their own businesses. This objective sounds rather operational; in fact the basic idea was to create a reasonable structure in the labour market policy, to build a strong network of related institutions, to develop efficient labour market tools, to qualify the multipliers and to strengthen the female position. As described below, the project consists mainly of four issues and three crosscutting subjects.

Job Counseling

When the project started in 1999, the concept of job counseling was very new. In addition to the methods of group counseling, we also introduced individual counseling, which was basically unknown in China. In the past, under the rules of the planned economy, matching processes on the labour market worked completely differently. At this time, a lifelong working relationship with one employer was the common pattern. In the market economy, new requirements came up for the placement staff in labour administration as well as for the job seekers themselves. First, we conducted several training sessions for job counselors, introduced different methods, opened some counseling rooms, developed working procedures and did a lot of PR work for the public. Step by step, we improved the services, qualified more counselors and expanded the services to district level. After the start of the project activities in Benxi, colleagues from Nanjing became involved in the transfer of experience. Currently, we are working on the JobLab software. This is a computer-based tool to support job counseling processes. It was originally invented, and very successfully used, in Germany and both developers are working hard to get an adapted version for the Chinese labour market.

Training

Before the project started, training for the reintegration of the unemployed was conducted by the labour administration and others. This was one main focus of the governmental reintegration policy. Nevertheless, the impact was often not sufficient. Our project emphasized quality rather than quantity in its training activities. That is to say, we established a comprehensive training circle which included all the steps, such as market surveys, trainee selection, curriculum development, interactive training methods, integrated placement, evaluation and improvement. In Nanjing and Benxi we have conducted, to date, 9 pilot training sessions in very different fields. On the one hand, we aimed to prove, that jobless women are also able to do qualified jobs, if the training is good enough. On the other hand, the main impetus of the pilot schemes was to learn, to analyze and to transfer the good experience into common practice. Whereas the market orientation of training, at that time, was something new for the colleagues of the administrative staff and the multipliers, today, it has become a matter of routine for many of them. The new methods being applied attracted their interest and the trainees became much more active. A huge improvement can also be seen in statistical terms: the placement rate was, on average, around 80 per cent, the "old styled" training could only achieve 50 per cent.

Additionally, we tried to diversify the training modes: in the past, it was mainly up to the labour administration and neighbouring institutions to organize the training themselves. Today, there is a broad mixture of training institutes; some are private, some are state-owned. The tasks of the labour administration now focus on tendering, evaluation and controlling. This new pattern has brought not only more variety, but also more competition, which in turn has led to more quality.

Business creation start-up

Not every unemployed person is a naturally born business man or woman. However, even if only 10 to 20 per cent had the potential to create their own jobs and perhaps some jobs for others too, it would be useful to support this group. Our project interprets this support in a very comprehensive way. It involves counseling as well as training, follow-up activities, networking, access to micro-credits and so on. In the year of 2000, we started to build a group of voluntary counselors in the field of business creation who are available every day. The project also supported a private service supplier, who has a very broad range of different services and is, in this form, rather unique in China. In the field of business creation promotion we emphasized quality: training classes are small; the counseling is intensive and continues to be available after the founding of the enterprise. As in the other fields, the project was not satisfied with the improvement of services alone. The mechanism and the structure between the joint stakeholders was considered to be more important. With regard to the upcoming market economy, we had to think about reasonable procedures and an efficient institutional mix. In the newly-founded business creation service center, under the umbrella of the labour administration, a bundle of service suppliers are now offering their services as a one-stop agency. There is still a long way to go towards the establishment of a diversified, high quality and sustainable service center, but it is on its way.

Temping work

The introduction of temping work in China could be viewed as the most innovative idea. We had a very special concept, which originally came from the Netherlands. It emphasized a labour market orientation and targeted vulnerable groups. From the very beginning, there was agreement that a special temping agency for women would not make too much sense, because this would seriously restrict the market opportunities of this company. The figure of 60 per cent involvement for women, working at all levels of qualification, was decided upon, In the beginning, we worked mainly with two temping agencies, one private and one state-owned, which soon exceeded the agreed indicators and took on a very healthy development. These helped to create some more temping agencies and either with or without their support, 200 companies have mushroomed in Nanjing to date. It became quite clear that a temping work federation was urgently needed. In the year of 2004, the federation was founded and it is now working on the basic standards and working principles which are necessary for temping work to avoid the exploitation of workers and ruinous competition between the companies. The temping work experience was also transferred from Nanjing to Benxi; we could see that the pattern would work well under different economic circumstances.

Crosscutting subjects

There are three of these and all should be applied to all activities. The first is a *business-friendly labour market policy*. That means all methods, structures and policies should be in line with the needs of the economy. Companies are required for job creation and should be given room for healthy development, which also takes the interests of the workers into account. The second is the importance of accurate and easily accessible *labour market data*. How can labour market actors make the right decisions, if they lack basic and detailed information about the current situation and trends in the labour market? Last but not least, there was a very strong emphasis on *gender balance and gender equality*. The new economic system includes opportunities as well as risks for women. Many of the new developments have given rise to concern over how the position of women can be strengthened in the labour market and in society in general.

Labour market policy – sometimes overestimated, sometimes underestimated

The term "labour market policy" often leads to the misconception that this policy area might be mainly responsible for the development and creation of jobs. This is in fact an exaggeration, because there are many other policy areas which, directly or indirectly, affect the level and structure of employment in a given economy. Here I should like to name just a few:

- Fiscal policy: decisions on public spending and creating public debt have a clear impact on the labour market. There are direct and indirect effects. For

example, there might be a public spending program which aims to improve the infrastructure in a particular region. This will lead to an increase in the demand for construction workers, will improve the investment climate in general and will be followed by different multiplicatory effects.
- Financial Policy: the level of interest rates and the whole issue of inflation and deflation have a direct impact on the investment climate and consumer spending, all of which have various effects on the labour market.
- Business Promotion Policy/Economic Policy: a government can implement a variety of measures to improve the business climate and to give a clear economic order. A transparent and sustainable framework is important for business actors to build confidence and give them a logical background for their economic decisions.
- Pension Policy: some countries tend to react to their labour market troubles by instituting a very early retirement age. By this means, they reduce the workforce in order to ease the tensions. There are, however, a lot of side effects, especially with regard to the financing of the pension system and to the structure of the workforce, which may have a negative long term impact.
- Protection against dismissal: this has a direct impact on the labour market, but the force of this depends on the tightness of the regulations for dismissals. Some people maintain that the level of employment is also affected; there is certainly an impact on the employment structure and the mobility of the labour supply.
- Technology Policy: to improve the economic structure, a government can promote the direct or indirect application of technology and the establishment of new industries; this might lead to a general change in the industrial structure, with losses in the labour intensive branches.

All these examples, and they are certainly not a complete list, show that labour market policy itself is just one of the policy fields which influences the labour market. The specific task of labour market policy is to improve the structure of the labour supply according to demand, and to smooth and improve the matching processes. Only in a very indirect way does it have an effect on the level of employment. In countries with labour market imbalances, such as China and Germany, the decision-makers have to consider the coherence of the different policy fields. A government, which gives the issue of employment a high priority, should follow a policy of growth, with positive effects on employment.

Labour market policy, itself, has strong specific interactions with economic policy and with social policy. Depending on whether labour market policy is more economically-oriented or socially-oriented, it has to live with various conflicts of aims. In the majority of cases, an economically-oriented labour market policy will emphasize long-term effects but will also sometimes interfere with short-term social requirements and vice versa. We want to imagine a situation, where labour market policy goes hand in hand with economic structural transformation. An economically-oriented labour market concept would help to induce innovations, would turn around a part of the workforce and would accept friction on the workers' side. Compared with this, a socially-oriented labour market policy would smooth the changes for the people, stabilize income and try to maintain the level of social security. There is, unfortunately, no universal remedy for this conflict of aims.

The specifics of the Chinese labour market in transformation

China is a huge country and the labour market challenges are equally huge. The current unemployment rate has little to do with good or bad labour market policy; it is simply the result of the transformation process in the economic sector and society as a whole. With problems like this, China does not stand alone in the world. There are, however, other aspects, which make the Chinese labour market quite unique. This applies, at least, to the specific combination of labour market relevant factors, the most important of which are as follows:

In China, the *conditions in the cities and in the countryside* are completely different. This has a very long history and even today, after the relaxing of some regulations, the differences remain quite high. The distinctions concern the institutional system as well as certain regulations and policies. If the social security system is taken as an example, it is easy to recognize that the current reforms in this policy field refer mainly to the urban population. The government has also made several attempts to expand the social security system to the rural population. The differences, nevertheless, remain high. The differing regulations have led, at the same time, to restricted mobility between the cities and the countryside. The so-called *hukou* system makes it very difficult, for example, for rural-to-urban migrants to change their places of permanent residence. They can move to the fast-developing centers of the east coast in order to work there, but it remains a very complicated business for them to obtain their full rights as urban inhabitants. Thus, although the boomtowns in China have had a strong influx of new residents, these are still not being treated fairly. The saying, "one country, two systems" refers to the relationship of the mainland with Hong Kong, but it could equally well be applied to the differing terms and conditions which exist between the cities and rural areas. All of these have important and relevant impacts on the labour market in general and the coherence of labour market policy. The goal of achieving one integrated labour market in China is still a long way off.

Regional disparities are quite common in most national economies. In China, they are gigantic and with the impressive development of the economy over the last 25 years, the regional disparities have actually grown. Compared with the glittering cities on the east coast belt, development in the central and western regions has been much slower. There is also the rust belt in the north east, which has been confronted with huge challenges in the transformation process. In addition to the regional disparities, the growing gap between the rich and the poor has become a special headache for economists and politicians. The so called Gini coefficient has now reached the frightening level of 0.47 per cent and is increasing from year to year.[1] Ten per cent of the richest people enjoy 45 per cent of the country's wealth, whereas ten per cent of the poorest people possess only 1.4 per cent. This development seems to be the main reason and background for the government's strategic policy of developing a "harmonious society" and "modest wealth." If the economic developments fail to offer opportunities for everybody in all groups and regions, social stability will be jeopardized. One important part of the development strategy for the poorer regions is related to urbanization. According to estimates, the urbanization rate has increased from 20 per cent to 40 per cent in the last ten years. This development will continue and could, if it takes place in a socially and environmentally acceptable way, form one part of a comprehensive development solution.

The issue of *reform in the social security system* has already been mentioned. Here, too, lies a huge challenge for the overall reform agenda. The social system has to be adapted concurrently with the transformation of the economic system from a planned to a market oriented economy. In the past, it was up to the state-owned enterprises to take care of the social security needs of their employees. From kindergarten to medical treatment, from social life to pensions, everything was covered by the operational social system. Simultaneously with the privatization of the SOEs, an autonomous system of social security had to be founded. Today, the government and other public institutions have to handle the constitution of a functional and cost-effective social security system, which, while providing cover for more and more people, at the same time has to improve individual insurance benefits. Nowadays, most of the urban workers in the formal sector are covered by a basic social security system, mainly in the fields of retirement and unemployment insurance. Health insurance remains a problem and an adequate solution has not yet been found. Another important issue is the inadequate coverage offered by the social security system for people from rural areas and urban inhabitant working in the informal sector. The task of extending the system to reach more beneficiaries and also improving the benefits cannot be overestimated.

China is still an agrarian country. The primary sector holds a share of 14.8 per cent (figures for 2003) of the overall GDP, but employs 50 per cent of the national labour force. This means that productivity in the agricultural sector is rather low and that a lot of further structural changes can be expected in the future.[2] The tertiary sector, the services, holds shares of 32.3 per cent and 28 per cent of the GDP. A typical industrialized country presents a quite different picture: in France, for example, the primary sector holds a GDP share of 2.7 per cent (4.1 per cent work in this sector), whereas the tertiary sector holds a share of 72 per cent of the GDP (71.5

---

[1] In the year of 2001, China had, according to the World Fact Book, a Gini coefficient of 0.4 per cent: The Gini coefficient refers to a statistical rate for measuring the income disparities in a country. With the current Gini coefficient of 0.47per cent, China ranks 90th internationally, in a similar position to countries such as, Mongolia, Kenya, Cameroon and Bolivia.
[2] Government estimates refer to 150 million redundant workers in rural areas.

per cent work here). China still has a long way to go on the road to becoming a modern and developed economy. There is also an imbalance in the structure within the second sector. Meanwhile, with regard to increased industrial output, heavy industry accounted for 60.9 per cent, 64.3 per cent, 67.6 per cent, and 70 per cent in 2002, 2003, 2004, and in the first half of 2005, respectively. Heavy industry occupies two-thirds of the secondary industries as a whole, which in itself accounts for more than half of the overall economy, indicating that economic structure is over-reliant on heavy industry.(China Daily 10 October 2005)

After 20 years of state-owned enterprises (SOE) reform, their importance regarding their share of the GDP and employment has decreased significantly. In 1978, nearly all companies were state-owned or collectively-owned. They were of correspondingly high importance for the labour market. In these days of the "iron rice bowl," only 0.16 per cent of the working people, all of them self-employed, were not covered by state-owned or collectively-owned employers. In 2002, it was the other way round: only 32 per cent belonged to the state and collective sector. Nevertheless, the reform of SOEs remains an important and difficult issue. One task is to promote other sectors, mainly the private sector, in order to boost job opportunities and to modernize and diversify the economic structure. Another challenge, however, is the further transformation of the remaining SOEs. Some of these will have to be privatized, others will remain state-owned but should become much more competitive. In particular, in the old industrial base in the north-east, the importance of SOEs for the regional economy is still very high. In Jilin, for example, the state sector contributes nearly 80 per cent of the province's GDP, but most of the enterprises are plagued by high debt, redundant personnel, and, in particular, out-of-date equipment and technology. This exceptional situation calls for further action in order to promote the private sector. The non-public economy has become an important driving force for the Chinese economy. Since the opening-up of the country, the non-public economy has been growing at a rate several times higher than the national economy. The proportion of the non-public economy in the GDP has exceeded one third. The non-public economy has become a main channel for employment and reemployment. The private enterprises have offered five to six million new jobs annually since the 1990s, representing three-quarters of all newly created jobs in cities and townships. Currently, the majority of employees in cities and townships are working in private enterprises and foreign enterprises (China Daily 1 March 2005) but there are still obstacles to the companies' gaining fair and reasonable access to credit and promotion policies. Not all the discriminating practices have yet been abolished.

The Chinese labour market faces a mismatch problem. This means that the structure and profile of the jobseekers do not correspondent with the requirements of the vacancies. Thus there is a growing number of jobseekers who are difficult to place and to integrate in the labour process. This development has been seen now for more than ten consecutive years; at the same time, the phenomenon of long term unemployment has occured more and more frequently. According to figures obtained from the Ministry of Labour and Social Security (MOLSS), from the 1990s to 2002, 31 million workers in SOEs were affected by lay-offs; 18 million of them were successful in finding new jobs. Currently, there are around eight million officially unemployed (without being laid off) and ten million further job seekers in China. Every year sees a surge of six million additional job seekers onto the labour market. On the demand side of the labour market; there are eight to ten million new vacancies every year. The mismatch leads, on the demand side, in the enterprises, to a growing problem in finding suitable persons for their vacancies. Compared with developed countries, China has a shortage of qualified people. The vocational training system is also undergoing reform and is trying hard to catch up with international standards. A demand-oriented vocational training system is still not yet in sight. This mainly concerns jobs with higher technical requirements and other specific qualifications. More and more companies, especially in prosperous cities, are confronted with an obvious bottleneck, which might lead to an underperformance in the companies' development. Salaries in certain professions are also rising at a relatively high rate, which affects their competitive positions. No matter which side of the labour market is examined, the same degree of pressure can be observed.

China is in respectable company, with regard to the *demographic factor*. It is mainly the highly industrialized countries which are facing the remarkable challenge of an aging population and China is probably one of the very few developing countries with the same problem. This is one of the side effects of the "one child policy," and the governmental population policies in the 1950s, which encouraged women to give birth to a lot of children. The median age is 31.8, but there is a increasing number of people over 60, which means that the huge challenges of the social security reform are endorsed by a further problem. China has tried to ease labour market tensions in previous years through an "early retirement policy" which has been somewhat extreme, compared with strategies in other countries. Particularly in the public sector, people were retired very early; in the case of women, even at the age of 45. Time will show more and more clearly that this was a short-term strategy which only succeeded in shifting the problems into the future, where they will lay a heavy burden on the social policy system.

One significant feature of the Chinese labour market is the fact that particular groups are confronted with placement difficulties or are offered fewer opportunities for secure jobs in the formal sector at fair wages. This is certainly the case for migrant workers who are generally offered unattractive jobs. The urban population with few qualifications is also affected, especially as this group has to compete with rural migrants for the same jobs. The migrants generally have better chances of obtaining these jobs, since they are willing to accept lower wages and less labour security. The older unemployed are also difficult to place. Here it should be noted that "old age" is relative: in some vocations, persons over the age of 30 have almost no chance of finding jobs. Newcomers to the labour market are also increasingly confronted with obstacles. Until recently, graduates of high school and universities had few problems finding jobs but now there is a surplus of job seekers among this group, which is also perceived as having low entrance wages. Finally, women, in addition to all these obstacles, face further difficulties as a result of gender inequality in the labour market.

Structural problems and challenges of Chinese labour market policy

The previous section of the article has dealt with the characteristics of the Chinese labour market and the scope of the problems; the many different layers were also identified. Most of the stated phenomena are connected and can be seen, to some extent, as mutually impacting on each other. Labour market policy and policy fields relevant to employment are thus extremely challenging. On a positive note, the Chinese government is aware of the problem of unemployment and has given employment promotion a high priority. Due to these measures, a substantial number of laid off people have been reintegrated into the labour market, but many have experienced wage cuts, poorer working conditions, fewer career opportunities and less prestigious work. Despite the efforts of political and social institutions, labour market policy measures have produced losses due to friction caused by their imperfect design. The main aspects of these are as follows:

As noted before, labour market policy is only one of the policy fields relevant to employment. The demand for coherence in these policy fields is of great importance but is rarely realized. This is not only the situation in China, but also in other countries, where operations based on harmonized employment promotion are often inadequate. In China, several ministries are in charge of tasks related to labour market policy. In addition to the Ministry of Labour and Social Security, the Ministry of Education plays a significant role in vocational education and has substantial influence on the supply side of the labour market. The Ministry of Personnel is responsible for a special target group, higher public officials, who form an individual impervious labour market. Finally, the Ministry of Agriculture is responsible for the labour market questions concerning the rural population. The institutional overlapping would not be problematic, if responsibilities were clearly defined and fewer barriers existed between them.

As early as the 1990s, shortly after the first wave of dismissals, the government reacted with a massive reduction in the supply of labourers. Particularly in the public service sector, and especially for women, it was possible to retire as early as the age of 45. This strategy had three main disadvantages. One group of employees was systematically cut off, although it was rich in experience; thus the employment structure was homogenized, which with regard to a "healthy" age structure is a disadvantage. The second disadvantage was that the pension system was in the midst of restructuring and the new pension system faced a massive challenge due to the sudden increase in potential beneficiaries. Finally, the demographic situation in China does not really allow for early retirement; the opposite is the case. The number of persons paying into the pension fund is disproportionate to the number of beneficiaries.

A further problem is that labour market participants have an inaccurate idea of the real situation on the labour market. Statistics only include some of the groups of job seekers. In addition, the statistics are almost entirely based on absolute numbers and do not take changes into consideration. This means that developments and changes, which are possibly relevant, escape detection, unless they are clearly perceivable in numbers. Thus it is very difficult to achieve a target-oriented labour market policy.

Consequently, monitoring of labour market measures is not possible. Financial resources for labour market policy are always scarce and should be used for those measures which are most promising and those where the demand is greatest. This includes target groups, as well as the regional distribution of resources and a sensible mix of measures. This can result in resources being used at the wrong end, but this goes unnoticed because of the lack of monitoring.

Labour market policy in China is currently following and implementing a quantitative, top-down approach. This means that the responsible ministry annually publishes quotas with regard to the unemployment rates, to the trained persons and to the required business creations, etc. that must be met. These quotas are then broken down into the districts and streets levels in the municipalities. There are also campaigns and competitions between cities for the lowest unemployment rates, comparable with similar competitions in other policy fields concerning growth rates. The responsible institutions are thus judged on the extent to which they meet the quantitative requirements. This approach leads to the neglect of the qualitative and sustainability aspects and, combined with the problem of monitoring the various measures and calculating success in placement, leads to further difficulties in employing a qualitative approach.

Even though the fulfillment of quantitative requirements is a strict order from higher levels and there is little leverage for individual regional characteristics in labour market policy levels, the methods employed can vary with the implementing agencies. Thus measures and instruments with similar names may lead to very different methods of implementation in the different regions, which renders a comparative analysis of labour market policy in the different provinces almost impossible.

Several years ago, it was still common for the labour administration itself to organize all the training courses financed by the labour departments within the context of re-employment programs. Step by step, these services have been outsourced leading to new challenges and tasks for the labour departments. Mechanisms for tendering (submitting tenders, transparent criteria etc.), financing and the development of a substantial monitoring and evaluation (M&E) system are at this point essential. Especially with regard to the M&E system, there is much room for improvement; the labour administrations should be enabled to transfer resources to successful implementation agencies, thus increasing efficiency.

Corresponding with the different levels of economic development in Chinese provinces, the financial input for employment promotion varies. Financial resources for employment promotion mainly stem from the respective public budgets. Municipal employment promotion is financed by the municipal budgets; district employment promotion by the district budgets. Vertical redistribution from the higher to the lower level hardly exists; horizontal revenue equalization between financially poor and rich regions does not exist at all. This means that poor provinces, which generally have a higher need for employment promotion, have much less financial scope. This leads to a hardening of the differences between the rich and poor provinces.

Finally, it should be noted that the positive experiences gained in pilot projects and through regional innovation are rarely injected systematically into the mainstream. There is no reliable mechanism that promotes experience transfer. Experience transfer does exist, but it is often left to coincidence whether it occurs or not and thus, it does not come up to its actual potential. Particularly due to the huge challenge facing labour market policy and the relatively scarce financial resources, the responsible institutions cannot afford to disregard ways of improving efficiency. Chinese projects with foreign partners can help with the identification of instruments and structures, but there are often difficulties in transferring this knowledge. This requires the commitment and authority of the central decision-makers.

Conclusion

When the project described above comes to an end, we ourselves and a lot of interested stakeholders will ask: "What was the impact of the project? How sustainable will the impact be? And how can the project experiences contribute to a general improvement in labour market policy?" Certainly, for the inner circle of the project, these questions have long been a subject of discussion; from the very beginning, we have tried hard to achieve a qualitative and quantitative impact as well as sustainability.

The most important aspects we have introduced are the qualitative approach and the individual approach. Up to now, many of the labour market decision-makers have been addicted to the quantitative approach. Certainly, the Chinese population is huge; the labour force seems to be never-ending. But inclusion in the world market and the desire to play an important role in the more developed industrial branches, have made it increasingly clear that there is an important mismatch in the labour market, which can only be improved through a common effort at human resource "upgrade". Our project delivers a whole toolbox of labour market policies, which aim to improve qualifications in a sustainable way. At the same time, we have managed to decrease prejudices against women in general and also against unemployed people. Certainly, such prejudices are deeply rooted in society, but the opening leads also here to a more diverse opinion. There are more and more women and formerly unemployed individuals who can provide us with perfect examples. Another outcome of the project is that there has been more reliable experience with an institutional mix in labour market policy. In the past, only state-owned institutions and administrations played an important role in the implementation of labour market policy. Now they are concentrating more and more on the policy-making and controlling, and entrusting others with the implementation. This burden-sharing is far from working smoothly and in a really customer-oriented way, but it is a step in the right direction. Last but not least, I would like to mention the shrinking of barriers between rural and urban areas. Also here, the institutions are now more able to handle "trans-boundary" problems and impacts. The issue of migration is politically of great importance and the rights of migrants are nowadays seen as a stabilizing factor in society.

So an integrated labour market is in the making indeed, but not finished yet. There is still a long way to go. It is hard to estimate, how long this process will take. Normally, the speed at which the Chinese work is internationally admired, but setbacks or delays may occur which hardly can be foreseen. It is more than relevant, that the government keeps the feeling, that a continuous move in this direction serves the harmonious society and the modest wealth.

Small Business Start-up Models by Chinese Women – Introduction to the Research Report

Chen Xiaojiang and Dang Tianhu

In recent years, laid-off and unemployed women workers have been the subjects of much debate in China, as the country has experienced a period of social transformation and adjustment of its economic structure. The issue has attracted attention throughout society in China, because of its crucial links to the lives and development of individuals and families. For a number of reasons, Chinese urban women workers who have been made redundant or are unemployed, have exceeded more than 50 per cent of the total numbers of the laid-offs and the unemployed workers. Such high levels of unemployment among women may have a serious negative impact on both their own welfare, and also on their marriages and families. Because society can only provide a limited number of new job opportunities, setting up a business has become a major avenue of re-employment, and a popular choice both for laid-off workers and those newly entering the labour market. As a result, job creation and re-employment through women's business start-ups has come to be seen by private individuals, society and government as an important economic reform strategy.

The Chinese government began its policy of creating jobs through business start-ups in 1998, attracting widespread interest in China. Implementation of this policy has been of great significance: it's seen as epitomizing a positive attitude towards economic globalization, as well as helping to reduce the tensions created by unemployment and encourage the establishment of individual businesses and the development of small and medium-sized enterprises (SMEs). The Ministry of Labour and Social Security has focused on setting up an integrated business start-up service system, incorporating advice, training, and gathering of project proposals, micro-finance and follow-up activities. Local governments and non-governmental organizations have accumulated a wealth of data and practical experience in using a range of flexible approaches to support and assist laid-off and unemployed women in setting up small businesses. This has provided us with very important source materials for understanding and studying laid-off and unemployed women, as they face up to the tremendous changes and difficulties they encounter in setting up small businesses in the midst of the transition to a socialist market economy, and the challenges involved in overcoming such difficulties.

The research focuses on the use of women's small business start-up models in the non-state sector, as a means of tackling redundancy and unemployment. With the focus specifically on women, the research aims to supplement a general understanding of the background and development of the growing awareness of business start-ups in China, and the trends witnessed. It also aims to attract the attention of society and government, and encourage the implementation of effective policies to provide better basic living conditions for vulnerable laid-off and unemployed women, along with equal opportunities, and also to motivate a greater number of capable women to set up businesses which will give them greater space for self-development, and - through becoming self-employed and taking control of their own lives – will enable them to fulfill their true potential.

The research reveals that women involved in small business start-ups differ in many respects from those working in large or medium sized enterprises; there are also differences resulting from the social and economic situation in different cities.

The challenges faced by Chinese women in setting up businesses

For women, setting up their own businesses marks a great change from their traditional types of employment. To be employed is simply to seek a "rice bowl," an income, whereas setting up a business implies managing of one's own life. For women who have been laid-off or made unemployed from the state sector, waiting for an opportunity for re-employment is very hard to accept; but taking control of their lives by starting up a business is even more difficult. Most laid-off and unemployed workers are used to working in the state system, where everything was planned for them; managing their own life is something new. For many laid-off women, setting up their own business is the only way to make a living and improve their livelihoods, but it also means a tremendous change in their lives; most significantly, it means that they must learn to make their own plans, and learn about finance and marketing, as well as how to compete in the world of business.

The four major models of small businesses set up by Chinese women in the non-state sector

China is a large country where development of society and the economy remains uneven. The practical models of business start-ups by laid-off and unemployed women have developed in response to different conditions in the various project areas, and vary depending on the scale of the city and its level of economic and social development.

The study group devised questionnaires and carried out surveys on common types of business start-up models initiated by local governments, institutions or individual women themselves. By studying the different models of women's business start-ups in four cities, we were able to assess the capacity and potential of vulnerable women to manage their own lives and run their own businesses.

MODEL 1: Business start-up model with incubation and assistance initiated by local women's federations (Tianjin model)
Initiated by the Tianjin Municipal Women's Federation, this model of incubation and assistance provides micro-credit loans and business incubation services to laid-off women who are setting up businesses. Its funding, totaling 900,000 US$ comes jointly from UNDP, Aus-Aid, and the Tianjin Municipal Government. It is an international cooperation project under the administration of MOFTEC (Ministry of Foreign Technological & Economic Cooperation; meanwhile replaced by the newly established Ministry of Commerce), as well as supported by the All-China Women's Federation.

The project, "Assisting laid-off women workers in reemployment and setting up businesses," takes a gender-focused approach, and aims to provide targeted and long-term services to women who are establishing businesses. The significance of this model lies in the pioneering work done to support laid-off and unemployed urban women by providing micro-credit loans, and in the introduction of the foreign concept of the "business incubator" as part of the follow-up assistance provided to women-run small and medium sized enterprises (SME's). (Some alterations have been made to fit in with the local situation in Tianjin.)

This approach not only regards laid-off women as labourers who have a right to work, but also considers them as human resources that their potential must be developed. The services established through this project are based on the network of Women's Federation organizations at different levels, with backing from the local government and logistical support from the local financial sector. However, government recognition and authorization of the service agency as a formal financial service agency remains an issue, since national regulations on the subject are unclear. This uncertainty could lead to the marginalization of this type of micro-credit loan service for women, and therefore limit the numbers of urban laid-off women who can benefit from it.

MODEL 2: Business start-up model supported by micro-credit loans, mainly administered by local government and in cooperation with its employment agencies (Shangluo model)
This is a project implemented by the local government, backed by micro-credit loans. Laid-off women are among the beneficiaries of the project, and the concept of gender equality has been gradually introduced into the project implementation. The number of female beneficiaries rose during the two years after the project began in 1998. In this model, the majority of financial support received by women beneficiaries comes from relatives, with government financial aid in second place. While the amount of micro-credit is low - between 2,000 and 3,000 Chinese RMB – and is only sufficient to help women establish small businesses such as small grocery or food stores, it has nevertheless helped women to achieve greater equality in the

obtaining and control of financial resources, and has thus given laid-off women a greater degree of economic independence.

MODEL 3: *Informal employment organization model implemented by local government (Shanghai model)*

This is known as the "Shanghai model" because it has been widely promoted by the Shanghai Municipal Government. In recognition of the difficulties faced by laid-off women workers, the Shanghai government has placed great emphasis on the question of women's re-employment. The government provides many preferential conditions for those setting up this type of business, which must include women among its beneficiaries. Gender-awareness is incorporated into the implementation of this model – and women run more than 50 per cent of the informal employment organizations established. In order to tackle the problem of older laid-off women and men, the Shanghai government has established the "40, 50 Project," which focuses on promoting re-employment for women over 40, and men older than 50. This has now become a part of the government's social and economic development programme. Participants in the "40, 50 Project" are mainly involved in setting up businesses in the informal employment sector.

MODEL 4: *Self-supporting business start-up model (Xi'an model)*

The "Xi'an model" is a model in which individual laid-off and unemployed women establish businesses by themselves. This model has provided a successful route for many women to go into business in the socialist market economy, and has been a major avenue for laid-off and unemployed women to attain re-employment and overcome financial problems. Self-supporting business start-ups imply that the women involved rely largely on their own resources (including support from relatives and friends as their social resources) to establish their businesses. They rarely receive support from service institutions or other external sources. This has made them more adaptable to the market system once they could persist in their business for the first two years. Women who have established their own businesses in this way in Xi'an are optimistic about their future. Their model of self-supporting business start-ups has already made some impact in society, and could provide an example for laid-off and unemployed women to set up their own businesses in other large cities in China.

Results from the Shaanxi Study Group survey in Tianjin, Shangluo and Xi'an

The Shaanxi Study Group carried out a survey on models of women's small business start-ups in Tianjin, Shangluo and Xi'an. A total number of 450 questionaires were sent out of which 400 returned back and were valid. The results are as follows:

Motivation for setting up one's own business

66.9 per cent of women started a business in order to make a living; 31.51 per cent in order to achieve fulfillment in their lives; 4.46 per cent were following the example of relatives or friends who were already in business; 3.2 per cent started a business for other reasons.

Funding and assistance for women setting up businesses

56.82 per cent of women received support from relatives and friends; 26.8 per cent received support from governments and local communities; 32 per cent of women received assistance from organizations such as Women's Federations or Trade Unions; 26.55 per cent of women made the decision to set up their own business entirely by themselves.

The scale of small business investment

42.08 per cent of women invested less than 5,000 RMB; 26.73 per cent women put in between 5,000 and 10,000 RMB; 10.04 per cent women between 10,000 and 15,000 RMB; 7.92 per cent invested more than 30,000 RMB.

Monthly income of women who have set up their own business

42.18 per cent of women made less than 500 RMB per month; the same proportion earned 500 – 1,000 RMB. Just 9.18 per cent of women earned between 1,001 and 2,000 RMB; while 3.72 per cent made between 2,000 and 3,000 RMB. These figures show the relatively low incomes earned by laid-off and unemployed women who set up businesses. However, setting up these businesses nonetheless enabled them to emerge from poverty.

Satisfaction and achievement of expectations by women who set up businesses

78.16 per cent of the women surveyed stated that they had not yet achieved their objectives in business. Just 17.62 per cent were satisfied with the current performance of their business.

Respondents' future business plans

54.84 per cent of women planned to expand their business; 24.18 per cent said they would maintain their current level of business; 14.64 per cent said they intended to invest in other projects; 4.21 per cent planned to give up their current business; 5.46 per cent chose the category "other;" 0.99 per cent did not respond.

Age of women going into business

20 – 30 years old: 15.38 per cent; 31 – 40: 57.07 per cent; 41 – 50: 24.32 per cent; only 3.23 per cent of women who set up their own business are 51 or above.

Educational level

34 per cent of the women surveyed were graduates of junior high school; 49.38 per cent graduated from senior high school; 9.18 per cent were graduates of institutions of higher education; 1.24 per cent had higher qualifications. Just 6.2 per cent of the women surveyed had only primary school education.

These results from three typical cities give a general picture of the situation of women who start businesses in China, and in particular of women who have been laid-off or unemployed, and who, by their own efforts, have achieved greater self-reliance and a greater ability to fend for themselves.

Characteristics of models of small business established by Chinese women

Businesses set up by women on their own - and businesses set up with assistance

There are relatively few studies of models of business start-ups by women. Our recently completed research suggests that models of small businesses set up by Chinese women can be divided into two categories: businesses set up by women on their own, and those set up with assistance.

Businesses set up by women on their own

Many women decide to set up a business in order to survive. Self-supported business start-ups have four characteristics: fund-raising carried out by the women themselves; type of project self-determined; marketing also carried out by women themselves; risks also assumed by women themselves.

Businesses set up by women with assistance

As China undergoes a process of economic transformation, governments at different levels have offered favourable conditions and policies for people involved in setting up businesses. Some local and international organizations and foreign government agencies also provide funds and technical assistance to support women who are setting up their own businesses.

Businesses set up by women with assistance have the following features:
- External financial aid + support from relatives and friends;
- Self-determination of project + outside consultancy and guidance;
- Self-conducted marketing + joint promotion;
- Establishment of networks and support groups + capacity building for change.

Survival-type business start-up: A major characteristic of Chinese women's small business start-ups

From our study of the four different models of women's business start-ups in China, survival (making a living) can be identified as a common characteristic, and the number one motivation for laid-off and unemployed women to set up their own businesses. This is in contrast to the characteristics of business start-ups in other countries - a survey conducted in 37 countries and regions revealed that opportunity-type business start-ups ranked first, with survival-type in second place. The percentage of businesses start-ups involving women is also higher in China compared to other countries (8.2 per cent). The proportion of Chinese women whose business start-ups are for subsistence reasons indicates the hardship of many women's living conditions, as well as the challenges they face in business development.

Setting up a business: A route to a decent job for laid-off and unemployed women

Employment is not only a means of making a living, but also an important indicator of the level of an individual's participation in society, and of that individual's fulfillment of his/her personal potential. The employment circumstances of women reveal the degree of women's participation in the economy, and the degree to which men and women enjoy equal opportunities in achieving economic status. Though there are many obstacles, setting up a business remains a path to a decent job for laid-off and unemployed women. According to the data we have collected in our study, most women who established a business have been able to make a living, and almost half of them have an income equal to or higher than the average wage in the cities where they live.

Suggestions for government decision makers on policies to promote employment and business start-ups

Given the growing demand and the increasingly large number of workers interested in setting up their own business, there is a need to establish an integrated Business Start-up Guidance and Service System, with government backing and financial support, participation from civil society, investment from private companies, and training and intermediate services provided by NGOs. This can be established in line with the growing trend for socialized implementation of government objectives, and market-based operation of social services.

Explore integrated models of promoting instruction on business start-ups. A better environment must be created for laid-off and unemployed workers who want to establish their own businesses. This requires a combined approach incorporating the promotion of business start-up projects, training and guidance from experts, and the provision of financial services.

Gender mainstreaming should be emphasized in government decision-making on job creation and policy on business start-ups. Its aim is to promote gender equality in the establishment of business start-ups.

Training programs such as the SYB (Start Your Business) established by the International Labour Organization should be introduced, in order to explore which business start-up models are appropriate for the situation in China.

A voluntary support group of experts should be established, providing individual advices and services to meet the needs of different people involved in business start-ups.

A national support system for the establishment of private business should be set up. This system would provide reference information, financial support, and instruction in setting up a business, as well as social welfare benefits, to facilitate the establishment of a market-based individual business start-up platform.

Recommendations to women involved in small business start-ups

Women involved in small businesses are living in a rapidly changing society. Our study identified the following major issues, which could play a part in helping women to develop their businesses – in particular women who have experienced redundancy or unemployment.

1. Try to find opportunities to take part in business start-up training.
2. Carry out a self-evaluation if you intend to take part in a business start-up.
3. Ensure that you have thought carefully about your concept for the business you intend to set up.
4. Make a careful evaluation of the market situation in your chosen line of business.
5. Ensure that the roles and responsibilities of your employees are clearly defined.
6. Ensure that your business has a correct and appropriate legal status.
7. Fulfill your responsibilities as owner of the business.
8. Do your best to predict the financial requirements of your business.
9. Make a plan of predicted revenues/profits.
10. Make a thorough business start-up plan, and realistically assess the prospects of survival for your business.
11. Start your business. Be self-confident; face the challenge of starting up your own business boldly.
12. Keep in close contact with professional business associations and other groups in civil society, including women's organizations, trade unions etc.

In recent years more and more Chinese women have set up their own businesses. The transformation and adjustments in the social and economic system have given them a great deal of space for personal development. However, the true "springtime" for women setting up businesses can only come when more and more women choose to go into business not just to survive, but in order better to fulfill their potential in life.

Note: An earlier version of this paper appeared as "A Research Report on Small Business Start-up Models by Chinese Women." It has been revised and reprinted: © 2004 by Konrad Adenauer Foundation, Germany, by permission of Konrad Adenauer Foundation.

Business Development Services for Migrant Workers in China

Andreas Klemmer

Introduction

In China, migrants have become an attractive target group for entrepreneurship development and the efforts of the government in this direction could pave the way for the successful integration of the migrants into their local host society. According to the findings of a market research survey, however, which was carried out on domestic migrants in China in 2005 under the institutional umbrella of the Start and Improve Your Business (SIYB) China programme, the current demand of the target group for business support services is limited, partly due to their ignorance of their own training needs and partly due to a lack of knowledge on the part of training suppliers.

In the context of the Start and Improve Your Business China programme, the survey presented in this paper covered 3,000 migrants working in the urban construction industry and the gastronomy sector in Sichuan Province. The purpose of the research was to assess the intrinsic demand of these domestic migrants for entrepreneurship development services.

The conclusion is that the demand of migrants for business support services needs to be stimulated in order to unlock their entrepreneurial development potential. To this end, it is recommended that a policy should be developed to promote the concept of entrepreneurship among migrant workers by way of the mass-media, and then that classroom-based training and related business support services should be offered as a concrete follow-up.

Background of the Start and Improve Your Business China programme

The Start and Improve Your Business China programme has been implemented by the Ministry of Labour and Social Security as part of the active labour market policy of the Chinese Government. The overall objective of the SIYB China programme is to reduce poverty and promote employment by way of small enterprise development. The immediate objective of the programme is to enable the urban unemployed to start and run their own businesses and to create quality jobs for others in the process.

The SIYB China programme was launched in 2004 and receives technical support from the International Labour Organization (ILO).[1] ILO support is based on three strategic initiatives: training capacity development, quality control services and

---

[1] ILO technical support services are funded by the British Department for International Development and the Japanese Ministry of Health, Welfare and Labour.

brand support for local business support service organizations in the public and private sector. As regards training capacity development, these business support service organizations are offered access to the product family of ILO-SIYB training packages.[2] More particularly, trainers and consultants working for these business support service organizations are coached by programme experts on how to train potential entrepreneurs using the SIYB course materials and the SIYB action-oriented and participatory learning approach.

With regard to quality control, the programme has established a national monitoring and evaluation system to ensure that the training services for entrepreneurs meet international standards. The national programme coordination unit at the Ministry of Labour and Social Security monitors and evaluates the training activities of the business support organizations at local level and uses the information to fine-tune the service processes for the benefit of the end users.

For brand support, the programme has developed a unified brand identity for the SIYB training product family and has also designed a wide range of support materials to promote the brand throughout the country. The programme also sponsors research on the market for small and medium sized enterprises (SME) training, disseminates the market research data among stakeholders and assists them in developing their own marketing strategies. The market research on migrants described in detail below refers to this strategic initiative.[3]

Description of the research framework

The aim of the market research on migrants was to furnish the SIYB China programme with the market intelligence required to adapt its range of business start-up and management training products to the needs of migrant workers, in line with the so-called guiding principles for the development of business support service markets. These guiding principles were developed by the global donor committee on enterprise development and promote the development of vibrant private sector driven markets where many business support service organizations compete in the delivery of cost-effective services that are paid for by the actual clients.[4]

In line with the aim of the research, the scope of the research was limited to sub-groups in the migrant universe who, it was considered, had both an intrinsic demand for SIYB training services and would also be willing and able to pay at least part of the service costs. The findings are thus not necessarily representative of the

---

[2] The SIYB product family comprises four material-based, modular training packages, namely the "Generate Your Business Idea" (GYB) package, the "Start Your Business" (SYB) package, the "Improve Your Business" (IYB) package and the "Expand Your Business" (EYB) package. For more information, see <http://www.ilo.org>.

[3] More information can be found on the SIYB China programme website <http://www.siyb.com.cn>.

[4] For more information on the guiding principles, see <http://www.sedonors.org>.

migrant universe and mainly refer to migrant sub-groups with comparatively high entrepreneurial potential.

The dialectic tension resulting from the development objective of the SIYB China programme to reach the urban poor and the research focus on sub-groups willing and able to pay at least partly for business support services is given explicit acknowledgement here. In order to reconcile the two, the decision was taken to focus on relatively vulnerable migrants who have some resources to start their own business.

The research was thus focused on segments which were thought to have:
- a need for external technical and financial support, that is, vulnerability characteristics which would justify government intervention
- the resources or skills required to set up their own businesses
- the comprehension capacity to benefit from SIYB training
- a comparatively strong inclination to return-migrate[5]
- the willingness to consider self-employment as a realistic option

The list of segmentation variables given in Table 1 reflects these selection parameters. The variables chosen were based on empirical evidence from other migrant surveys carried out in China (see also bibliographical references).

With reference to these variables, two segments were identified for detailed profiling:
- Registered migrants employed by large-scale companies on construction sites in Chengdu. To be eligible for the sample, these construction workers had to be males between 20-30 years of age and had to have completed at least junior middle school. The target group was also supposed to have arrived in Chengdu after 1997.
- Registered migrants employed in local restaurants. To be eligible for the survey, these workers had to be females between 20-30 years of age and had to have had at least a junior middle school education. These restaurant employees were also supposed to also have arrived in Chengdu after 1997.

---

[5] The original intention of the Ministry of Labour and Social Security (MOLSS) had been to focus SIYB China programme support on return-migrants, to help them to reintegrate into their places of origin. This intention was dropped when it emerged that notwithstanding the segmentation effort, the majority of migrants covered by the survey indicated their determination to settle permanently in the place of destination. In view of the research results, it was decided to focus on the permanent integration of migrant workers into the host society by way of business start-ups.

Table 1. Variables used to identify prospective target segments for SIYB

Parameter	Variable	Explanatory remarks
Vulnerability	Gender	Women face gender discrimination that makes them relatively more vulnerable than men (i.e. they are paid less).
	Occupational profile	Certain sectors are especially hazardous; labour regimes particularly severe.
Resources to start a small business	Occupational profile	Occupations offering migrants good opportunities to acquire practical skills which can be exploited to start a business.
	Income situation	Certain occupations pay better, so the savings rate of migrants and their capacity to invest in their own business and skills development is presumably higher.
	Size of firm employing the migrant	Large organizations pay higher wages.
Comprehension capacity for functional skills training	Education	Numeracy and literacy skills indispensable in order to derive full benefit from standard SIYB training.
Inclination to return migrate	Age	Women between 20-25 and men between 25-30 most likely to return-migrate.
	Family status	Single migrants more likely to return migrate.
	Duration of migration period	Migrants are most likely to return migrate after at least four years and not more than seven years away from their place of origin.
Inclination to start a business after return migration	Political pull on the macro-level	Business start-up in selected occupations actively promoted by local authorities in place of origin ("sunrise" industries, i.e. small-scale construction and social services).

The segment profiles highlight the fact that the survey focused on registered migrants. Illegal migrants were excluded since the target group had to be eligible for support services offered by the local labour labour and employment bureaus. Furthermore, the segment profiles indicate the research emphasis on those migrants who were actually holding jobs – a factor not necessarily to be expected in a programme targeting the urban unemployed. As already mentioned above, the intention was to identify (legal) migrants who would be highly vulnerable but at the same time have at least some of the resources and skills required to set up their own businesses. Migrant workers in the construction industry and the gastronomy sector were selected since they were thought to have comparatively good resource bases to start businesses but also to hold precarious employment. For example, construction workers are known to earn comparatively higher salaries than other migrant groups, but in turn they also face harsh labour regimes and low job security since their industry is highly exposed to economic cycles.

The actual market survey was carried out in May 2005 and June 2005 in close collaboration with the Chengdu Labour Bureau. The set-up of the collaborative effort was as follows:

- Ministry of Labour and Social Security (MOLSS) supervised the research work
- The project experts developed the research framework and analyzed the market data with advice from the Institute of Labour Studies.
- The Chengdu Labour Bureau collected the data from 3,058 migrants (1,581 construction workers and 1,477 restaurant workers) with the help of local enumerators.

To identify individual migrants for the survey, the Chengdu Labour Bureau, with technical support from the project, compiled a list of registered businesses and organizations in the construction industry and the restaurant sector in the six urban districts of Chengdu. Next, after obtaining the consent of the respective managers/directors, the enumerators were sent to these businesses and selected migrant workers at random for the interviews. At the beginning of each interview, the enumerators made sure the interviewee would fit the segmentation profile. Between July 2005 and September 2005, the project computed and analyzed the research findings.[6]

Research findings

The research findings for both market segments are described within the following parameters: Demographics, occupational profiles, financial situation, other assets, personal entrepreneurial characteristics, mid-term settlement strategies, information sources, support networks, and effective demand for business support services.

As will be explained below, each of these parameters has a direct bearing on the marketing mix for business support services.

Demographics

The vast majority of migrant workers in the construction industry are young: 22.5 years of age on average in the case of restaurant workers and 25 years of age in the case of construction workers. Most construction workers cluster in the age cohort of 24-26 years, while most restaurant employees are below 23 years of age.

---

[6] A full version of the final research report is also available from the NPO or the ILO Beijing office.

Just one in every six construction workers and a mere one per cent of all restaurant workers belong to the age cohort of 28-30 years.[7] This means that an entrepreneurship development programme targeting these migrants would need to be geared towards young people in their mid-twenties.

All migrant workers have a relatively advanced comprehension capacity for material-based business start-up, management training and related services. The survey results show that beyond the minimum threshold of completing junior middle school, one in three construction workers has moved on to complete senior middle school and one in ten construction workers has moved on to complete some form of tertiary education. In the case of restaurant employees, 28 per cent have completed senior middle school and 18 per cent have moved on to complete some form of tertiary education.

The majority of construction workers are married while most restaurant employees are single. The family status of a prospective client is another relevant factor for the marketing mix of a business support service since married people tend to have different priorities, planning horizons and resulting service needs than singles. 54 per cent of all construction workers in the sample register as married, while 44 per cent claim to be single and two per cent have divorced their wives. For their part, 78 per cent of all restaurant employees are single, while 20 per cent are married and one per cent is divorced. The family status of the migrants seems to be largely a function of gender and age, not the occupational profile: Older male migrants are far more likely to be married than younger female migrants.

The main migration flows are intra-provincial, that is to say, the migrants have moved within Sichuan Province; this observation has ramifications for the curriculum of an enterprise development programme since the target group seems to be familiar with the "local way of making business" – a major bonus for any entrepreneur. Nine in ten migrants covered by the survey originate either from areas within the administrative boundaries of Greater Chengdu or from areas within the surrounding Sichuan Province.[8] The remaining migrants originate from neighbouring provinces in South-West China.

Only few migrants belong to ethnic minorities. The ethnic affiliation of a migrant worker is important since it determines whether there is a need to develop highly differentiated niche products. The survey shows that 99 per cent of all construction workers and 98 per cent of all restaurant employees in the sample belong to the Han ethnicity. Keeping in mind that ethnic minorities in Sichuan Province make up for an estimated five per cent of the population, this means that

---

[7] See below under "mid-term settlement strategies" of migrant workers for more details about where these migrants plan to go and what they intend to do when they are older.
[8] For example, in case workers from the Greater Chengdu area would be classified as migrants, they would have to hold a rural *hukou* but live and work in one of the six urban districts of the city. Also refer the housing arrangements and monthly transport costs of migrants to verify compliance with these selection criteria.

ethnic minorities are under-represented in the domestic migration stream. This observation confirms findings from earlier surveys according to which members of ethnic minorities in China show a comparatively low propensity for out-migration.

Many but certainly not all, migrant workers have opted for group accommodation. The housing arrangements of migrants are important for the marketing mix of a business support service because they are indicative of the longer-term settlement plans and resulting business support service needs of the target group. These housing arrangements are also indicative of distinctive buying behaviour (i.e. increased demand for white goods), which in turn can be relevant information for prospective commercial sponsors for a business support service.

The survey results indicate that 70 per cent of the construction workers stay in dormitories provided by their employers. About 20 per cent of them rent their own rooms, eight per cent rent their own small apartments, occupied a room in a guesthouse or settle for other housing arrangements. In cases where construction workers have opted for private housing arrangements off the construction site, they typically share a room or flat with a group of colleagues, and in few cases with their families. In turn, 60 per cent of all service staff stays in dormitories and another 35 per cent either rent their own rooms or their own apartments together with friends or family members.

Occupational profiles

Information about the occupational profiles of migrants is crucial for determining their practical work skills and the extent to which these skills might be mobilized for the benefit of a small business. The survey findings indicate that many construction workers but few restaurant employees perform work tasks that require specialized technical and vocational skills. About half of the construction workers perform work tasks that require specialized technical and vocational skills while the other half registers as general construction helpers. Among the construction workers with specialized work tasks, almost one fifth register as bricklayers and around eight per cent register as welders. Other types of construction work performed by smaller groups of migrants are working with reinforced steel, cement works, carpentry, molding and electrical work. With regard to restaurant workers, the majority of them (86 per cent) perform tasks that require limited specialized skills – they mostly work as waitresses and receptionists, and in some cases as cleaners. The few restaurant workers with more specialized work tasks are employed as supervisors and cashiers and in back-office administration.

Most of the migrants have acquired their work skills on-the-job and without formal vocational or technical training. More than two in three construction workers and most of the restaurant employees have acquired their occupational skills on-the-job by learning from others; the remainder have either completed some form of formal training or done self-studies after work.

Some of the migrants have had exposure to experience in running a business but few of them have undergone formal skills training in business management.

Further to technical and vocational skills, about one third of all migrants seem to have had some practical exposure experience of the functional skills needed to start and run a small enterprise, either because they have run or are still running (side) business activities or because one of their family members was an entrepreneur. However, hardly any of them have participated in formal small business management training.[9]

Financial situation

Income is a key determinant of the financial resources at the command of migrant workers, and by extension, their capacity and willingness to invest in a small business. The survey shows that construction workers and restaurant employees earn average monthly salaries of 766 RMB (95US$) and 669 RMB (83US$) respectively – pegging both groups firmly above the national poverty line and also above the minimum wage levels set by the government for both sectors. The income spread, however, is wide in both sectors: for example, while almost one third of all construction workers and nine per cent of all restaurant employees earn more than 1,000 RMB, 30 per cent of all construction workers and more than 50 per cent of all restaurant employees receive a monthly pay-check of less than 600 RMB.

The survey also confirms the observation made in other surveys that gender is an important criterion for determining the pay of migrants. In brief, male migrants earn higher incomes than female migrants even if they share similar work experience and occupational skills. The gender specific income differential becomes obvious when looking at the higher-income earners in both samples – men are three times more likely than women to earn more than 1,000 RMB although both sub-groups hold sector-relevant specialized occupational skills.

Some construction workers and a few restaurant employees earn a side income from letting houses and farm plots back in their place of origin. One in six construction workers and one in ten restaurant employees earn an additional income from renting out a house or from leasing out a farm plot in their place of origin. Other sources of additional income for a few migrants are side jobs, financial aid from relatives (typically for migrants recently arrived in the city) and side businesses – six per cent of construction workers and restaurant employees respectively claim to have a side income from running side-business activities, and often also from trading in agricultural products.

In addition to their income, the savings, remittances and spending patterns of migrants provide further insight into their investment capacity. Statistically, construction workers spend about 100 RMB and restaurant employees spend about 75 RMB to meet their basic needs for food, shelter, clothing, communication and transport. They spend another 30 RMB on entertainment and, where applicable, education. The relatively low expenditure on food, accommodation and transport

---

[9] See also below under "effective demand for business support services" for more details on the service take-up rate of the target group.

should be understood in light of the fact that the majority of the migrants are provided with food and shelter at their workplace at a nominal cost or free of charge. Migrants who have opted for accommodation off the construction site often share rooms and apartments with colleagues to keep their rent expenditure low, and also receive free meals during working hours.

On average, a construction worker holds personal savings amounting to 1,980 RMB while a restaurant employee holds savings amounting to 1,814 RMB. About half of all construction workers and close to two thirds of all restaurant employees (62 per cent) claim that they have savings of up to 5,000 RMB. 12 per cent of all construction workers and 10 per cent of all restaurant employees report savings of between 5,000 and 10,000 RMB. This leaves about one third or all construction workers and one fourth of all restaurant employees with no reported savings. The figures indicate that restaurant employees are more likely to save part of their income than construction workers, and that they save a higher portion of their salary – an observation supported by evidence from other surveys that points towards higher saving rates for female migrants.

Construction workers remit on average about 300 RMB per month while restaurant employees remit on average 150 RMB.[10] The overwhelming majority of construction workers remit between 200-500 RMB while two in three restaurant employees remit up to 100 RMB and the other third remits up to 1,000 RMB – this is partly a reflection of the lower base salary and the higher income spread among restaurant employees but is possibly also explained by the fact that the young and mostly single women making up this segment have fewer family responsibilities back in their place of origin than construction workers.

Other assets

Another key factor for determining the business investment capacity of individuals is their ownership of fixed assets that might be used as collateral. The market survey indicates that more than two in three construction workers and half of all restaurant employees own property in their place of origin. More than 70 per cent of all construction workers and 51 per cent of all restaurant employees claim to own fixed assets in their place of origin – typically a farm plot or a house. The property seems to be typically occupied (by family members) since only a few migrants generate a side income from rents or leases. This also indicates that a few migrants will be willing to trade their homesteads as collateral for a business loan.

In addition to assets, information about the personal belongings of migrant workers in their places of destination is the key to a better understanding of their consumer preferences; knowledge of these consumer preferences, in turn, is essential for attracting commercial sponsors of business support services. Among the personal belongings of migrants in Chengdu, the most frequently registered

---

[10] All data about remittances should be read as merely "indicative" of the situation since many migrants failed to specify their monthly transfers during the survey.

goods for both men and women are bicycles, TV sets and mobile phones. More than 50 per cent of all construction workers and 47 per cent of all restaurant employees own a bicycle, 44 per cent and 33 per cent of both samples respectively, own a television set and 40 per cent of both samples own a mobile phone. The ownership of other goods seems to be more gender-specific: for example, female migrants are more likely to own selected white goods, an MP3/CD player and a computer, while male migrants are more likely to own a motorbike and a radio.

Personal entrepreneurial characteristics

Personal entrepreneurial characteristics are the "soft underbelly" of the research on the entrepreneurship development potential of migrants, since these characteristics are considered to be instrumental for a successful business start-up but very difficult to qualify. To gauge the personal entrepreneurial characteristics of migrant workers, the survey focused on an analysis of their life goals, career aspirations, locus of control, willingness to use their own initiative and take risks.

A clear majority of all migrants rank health and material wealth as priority life goals, followed by a harmonious family life and happiness. They most frequently rank social prestige and a high salary as important aspects of their work. Many migrants also consider "being their own boss" as another important aspect in their career aspirations. Furthermore, a large proportion of the construction workers (80 per cent) and restaurant employees (88 per cent) claim to be eager to use their own initiative and to strive for a higher level of personal independence.

Mid-term plans for permanent settlement

The mid-term settlement strategies of migrants have a strong bearing on the marketing mix of a business support service, in particular on the contents of the training course and the focus of the promotional message. The survey findings clearly show that most construction workers and restaurant employees are determined to stay permanently in their place of destination. More than two in three migrants are clearly determined to settle permanently in Chengdu while the remainder plans to either return migrate or on-migrate.

The main pull factors for migrants determined to settle permanently in Chengdu are better employment opportunities and more attractive living conditions. In order to be able to continue to support themselves, the majority of them plan to stay on in their current jobs. Seven per cent of the construction workers and four per cent of the restaurant employees plan to start their own businesses. Only very few migrants (all of them women) plan to focus exclusively on family life in the future.

Three out of four potential return migrants are not yet able to specify the timing of their planned return migration. Among the few workers that actually do plan to return-migrate within the next two years, again only a small minority has actually started concrete preparations for the return move. The main pull factors that motivate both construction workers and restaurant employees to return migrate are family (responsibilities) and friends back in the place of origin. In order to earn a living after their return-migration, half of them plan to go back to work in agriculture. The other half of the respondents would prefer to take up wage-paid employment and one in ten cases would like to start up their own businesses. Only very few potential return-migrants (all of them women) plan to focus exclusively on family life in the future.

Migrants planning to on-migrate are primarily driven by economic pull, and more precisely by expectations of more attractive work and better pay. However, like potential return-migrants, most would-be on-migrants among the construction workers are fairly vague about when such an on-migration move would take place. Overall, potential on-migrants among the construction workers seem more attracted to move to places "closer" to Chengdu, starting by on-migrating to other Chengdu districts and moving on to places within the province. Restaurant employees, for their part, are more open to the idea of on-migrating to cities in the Pearl River Delta or the East Coast.

In order to earn a living, the majority of construction workers and restaurant employees plan to once again take up wage-paid employment, either within or outside their current industry. Restaurant employees are clearly more inclined to exit their current occupation in the new place of destination. One in five potential on-migrants has thought about starting a small business. 18 per cent of the potential on-migrants among construction workers and 22 per cent of the potential on-migrants among the restaurant employees have thought about starting their own businesses in the new place of destination.

Information sources

Knowledge about the main information sources of migrant workers (where, when and how the target group communicates, and to whom they listen) is important for determining the distribution variable, the promotion variable and the product variable of the service marketing mix. In a nutshell, the survey indicates that the **most powerful media to reach migrants in the city is television, trailed by the** print media; radio is the least popular.

Most migrants claim to watch TV on a daily basis and for between one and two hours. The overwhelming majority watch TV in the evenings after work and/or at weekends, and mostly for entertainment purposes or to seek news. Very few workers watch TV for educational purposes. The most popular TV broadcasting station is the national CCTV network, but regional channels also enjoy some popularity. When asked for their favorite ingredient for a good TV series, most migrants feel that it should depict a story from real life and have an element of fun. Construction workers also more frequently stress "action" as another important element of a good TV series while restaurant employees prefer "romance" and a shot of "illusion." Soap operas enjoy high popularity with all migrants.

Only few migrants listen frequently to the radio: just 21 per cent of all construction workers and 17 per cent of all restaurant employees frequently listen to the radio, mostly for about an hour per day either in the morning before work or in the evening after work. They listen to the radio for news and entertainment; very few migrants listen in for educational purposes.

Newspapers are read frequently by most migrants but magazines are more likely to be read only by restaurant employees. About one third of all construction workers read newspapers on a daily basis. One in five construction workers claim to buy newspapers more than once and up to three times a week, a further 15 per cent buy a newspaper at least once a week and the remaining 28 per cent do not read newspapers at all. As far as restaurant employees are concerned, 42 per cent read newspapers on a daily basis, a further one in five restaurant employees read a newspaper more than once and up to three times a week and 14 per cent buy newspapers at least once a week. 25 per cent of these respondents said that they do not read newspapers. Magazines are significantly more popular with restaurant employees than with construction workers. Only one in five construction workers but 39 per cent of all restaurant employees read magazines.

Support networks

Semi-formal and formal migrant support networks can be important for communicating with prospective clients and also for delivering business support services. In the case of the construction workers and restaurant workers, however, it would appear that these support networks are rather weak: few of the migrants patronize self-help organizations or are associated with national mass organizations which lobby, among other things, for the rights of migrants. Three per cent of all construction workers and four per cent of all restaurant employees have taken up membership with such organizations. In the case of the construction workers, their affiliation is mostly with the All-China Youth League or the All-China Federation of Trade Unions (ACFTU); in the case of the restaurant employees, the affiliation is mostly with the ACFTU and the All-China Women's Federation. Only one in ten construction workers and a mere four per cent of restaurant employees claim to patronize migrant clubs or other self-help organizations set up by migrants or for migrants. In cases where they do, construction workers say they go there to seek information about employment opportunities, for entertainment and to socialize with others.

Effective demand for business support services

The specific demand of migrants for business support services can be measured by various means, for example, by asking them to specify their service needs, by analyzing their past service take-up rate, by assessing their understanding of the spectrum and the capacity of service suppliers, by reviewing their past service experiences and by checking on their willingness to pay. The survey findings indicate that there is some demand among migrant workers for business support services and particularly for vocational training; the current demand for start-up training is, however, rather limited. Few migrants have actually taken up services in the past and few of them know of any local suppliers.

Relatively speaking, the training service in highest demand among migrants is vocational training; almost half of all construction workers and restaurant employees express a demand for vocational skills training, with restaurant employees in particular, (20 per cent of all respondents) specifying a demand for computer training.

The specific demands of migrants for business start-up and management training vary from sector to sector; 20 per cent of all restaurant employees and about 15 per cent of all construction workers expressing an interest in business start-up training.

Migrants seem to be quality conscious and price-sensitive customers. When asked to specify the most important aspect of a training service, 28 per cent of the construction workers and 29 per cent of the restaurant employees rank the training content as the most important aspect of a training offer, while 23 per cent of all the workers feel that the qualifications of the trainers and the training costs would be the decisive aspects.

The majority of migrants are seemingly ignorant about the spectrum of service providers in the local market. Almost 90 per cent of all construction workers and restaurant employees failed to specify a single training organization. The few migrants who are aware of an individual provider typically cite the names of public sector training institutes.

The overwhelming majority of migrants have never participated in a self-selected training course before. Only one in ten construction workers claim to have participated in a self-selected skills training programme. Almost one third of them seem to have participated in occupational health and safety training. Only five workers claim to have participated in management training. As regards restaurant employees, the few workers who have participated in self-selected training have mostly taken part in computer courses. Very few of them have registered for beauty treatment training and not one of them has participated in business management training.

The construction workers who have taken up training services in the past mostly participated in short courses while the restaurant employees who have taken up training have participated more frequently in courses lasting anywhere between one week and six months.

Most migrants who have taken up training in the past have been either satisfied or very satisfied with the service: two thirds of all construction workers and restaurant employees who have participated in a training course were either satisfied or very satisfied. A further 29 per cent of these workers were at least satisfied with how they were treated.

Finally, almost half of all construction workers and two in three restaurant employees who did receive training in the past seem to have paid at least part of the service costs, which could possibly serve as a useful factor in assessing their willingness to pay (again) for future services. 42 per cent of all construction workers who have previously received training actually paid (part of) the service delivery costs and the fees paid varied from under 200 Yuan to over 4,000 RMB. For restaurant employees, 63 per cent paid (part of) the service delivery costs and here the fees paid varied from 200 RMB up to 4,000 RMB.

Conclusions and recommendations

In conclusion, the mix of segmentation variables is thought to have been very effective in identifying sub-groups among migrants with good potential to start their own business. As shown in the case in point, many of those construction workers and restaurant employees who have been identified with the assistance of this mix of segmentation variables can comprehend material-based business start-up and management training, hold work experience, command some savings that could be mobilized as equity and own property that could be used as collateral for a loan. In addition, many construction workers, at least, hold specialized occupational skills that might be useful for setting up a small construction company.

Furthermore, these migrants are young, highly mobile and flexible, often have strong personal entrepreneurial characteristics, and, in particular, an internal locus of control, the willingness to use their own initiative, the ambition to work independently and to accept responsibility. In many cases, these migrants have already thought about starting a business or have already run some side-business activities. Also, quite a number of these migrants come from families with a history of running income-generating activities of some sort and, as a result, feel that they could count on moral support from their families if they should start their own small businesses.

In turn, the market segmentation variables have proven to be a less effective tool for identifying those migrants who have a high propensity to return-migrate. It is a matter of debate whether this outcome is due to the poor choice of segmentation variables or is rather a reflection of the fact that the overwhelming majority of men and women in the local migrant universe de facto prefer to settle permanently in their places of destination. If the latter were shown to be the case, any mix of segmentation variables would have resulted in the same outcome.

From the perspective of market development, migrant workers form a challenging customer segment because their specific demands for business support services other than vocational training are rather weak, and they seem largely ignorant about local service providers. Looking at the segment from the angle of the SIYB programme, very few of the prospective clients have ever taken up classroom-based training before and it should thus not be assumed that migrants are readily willing to register and pay for SIYB courses.

It is also debatable whether targeted government-sponsored entrepreneurship development support for these migrants is justified since they are already in employment and also earn a comparatively higher income than many other blue-collar workers.

However, the survey also proves that work on construction sites and in restaurants is indeed a transitory livelihood strategy for most migrants. Most migrants, construction workers and restaurant workers alike, are determined to continue working in the city, and remain in their current jobs as they grow older. Here, targeted support through a business start-up training programme can build a bridge to enable migrants aged 25 years and over to move from an increasingly precarious employment status to a more sustainable livelihood. As a welcome spin-off, the same programme might open a door for younger migrants to enter into comparatively more attractive and *legal* employment in the construction and restaurant sector

The survey shows quite clearly that the majority of migrant workers is determined to stay in the place of destination and to continue working even after leaving their current job. Here, access to business start-up training programmes can enable these migrants to permanently integrate as business people into their host society and to create new jobs for others in the process, and thus act as an effective barrier against the raising tide of urban unemployment.

In any case, if attempts to attract large numbers of migrants to start-up training are to be successful and financially sustainable, the focus of an entrepreneurship development programme might have to shift at least initially from classroom-based training to mass-media based training. The most effective mass media to reach these migrants is TV.

To deliver an entrepreneurship promotion message via TV, learning content would best be packaged in an entertaining format since very few construction workers and restaurant employees watch TV for educational purposes. One possible format would be a television drama since many construction workers enjoy this type of programme. The emphasis of any such television drama should be on realism, that is to say, it should depict the real life story of a migrant. Furthermore, migrants – men and women alike – would appreciate an element of fun in learning.

The main message of the entrepreneurship promotion programme should be focused on entrepreneurial self-assessment and business idea generation techniques, enabling the migrant audience to find out whether they are "the right persons" to start businesses and to create innovative business ideas on their own. In order to attract the attention of the audience, there should be a specific focus on the link between business start-up and permanent socio-economic integration into the host society.

Structurally, the mass media entrepreneurship programme should be closely linked to classroom based business start-up training. More particularly, the programme could be used as a channel to promote classroom-based SIYB training as a fee-based follow-up service for migrants who are attracted by the idea of starting their own businesses. Start-up training would need to be bundled with vocational training, legal support and credit in order to significantly increase the value of the service proposition.

To develop the television drama and to pilot it in Sichuan Province, a partnership could be established between the Ministry of Labour and Social Security and a regional channel popular with migrants. The production costs should be born partly by the service facilitator, in this case the SIYB China programme, in order for the facilitator to retain public co-ownership over the format and to be able to replicate it later in other provinces.[11]

References

Ash, Robert (2004) "Rural Underemployment and Social Welfare in China," in DSG Asia, 11/2004.

Atkinson, J. (2000) *Employment Options and Labour Market Participation*, European Foundation for the Improvement of Living and Working Conditions, Office for Official Publications of the European Communities, Luxembourg.

Banister, Judith and Wiemer, Calla (2005) "Labour demographics in China: long boom slow bust," in *China Economic Quarterly*, Q3, pp. 20-22.

Battasali, Deepak; Lee Shantong; Will, Martin (eds) (2004) *China and the WTO. Accession, Policy Reform, and Poverty Reduction Strategies*, The International Bank for Reconstruction and Development/The World Bank, Washington D.C.

Biao, Xiang (2005) "Migration and health in China: problems, obstacles and solutions," Asian Metacentre Research Paper Series no.17, Asian Metacentre for Population and Sustainable Development Analysis.

Boyd, Mary (2005) "Migrant Labour Mechanisms: The Down and Dirty," in *China Economic Quarterly*, Q3, pp. 29-33.

Cai, Fang (2003) *Migration and Socio-economic Insecurity: Patterns, Processes and Policies*, ILO, Geneva.

Claude, Aubert and Li, Xiande (2002) "Agricultural Underemployment and Rural Migration in China: Facts and Figures," in *Perspectives Chinoises*, 41/2002, May-June, p.47. Online. Available HTTP: <http://www.cefc.com.hk/uk/pc/articles/art_ligne.php?num_art_ligne=4105>, accessed 9 January 2006.

Chan, Anita (2002) "Labor in waiting. the international trade union movement and China," in *New Labor Forum*, Fall/Winter 2002, pp.54-59.

Chen, Tao (2004) "The determinants of temporary labor migration in rural China: a Tobit analysis," Paper, Department of Economics, Tulane University, New Orleans.

Deshingkar, Priar (2005) "Maximizing the benefits of internal migration for development," Background Paper, Regional Conference on Migration and Development in Asia, Lanzhou 14-16 March 2005, International Organization for Migration (IOM), Department for International Development (DFID), China.

---

[11] These recommendations were submitted to the Ministry of Labour and Social Security (MOLSS) in September 2005. When this article was compiled in November 2005, negotiations between the Ministry and the Sichuan TV broadcasting network for the physical production of the entrepreneurship promotion programme were underway. One recommendation, which could help to recoup the costs for transmitting the entrepreneurship promotion programme and thus to build up a financially self-sustaining market exchange for entrepreneurship promotion services, would be to win a commercial sponsor to run advertisements during the television drama. In view of the purchasing trends of the migrants, one field of corporate business which might have a potential interest in sponsoring such a programme could be, for example, mobile phone companies.

Hokenson, Richard (2005) "Migrant labour flows: measuring the tide," in *China Economic Quarterly*, Q3, pp. 23-28.

Li, Minghuan (2004) *Labor Brokerage in China Today: Formal and Informal Dimensions*, Duisburg Working Papers on East Asian Studies, 58, 2004.

Lilja, Reija and Haemaelaeinen, Ulla (2001) *Working Time Preferences at Different Phases of Life*, European Foundation for the Improvement of Living and Working Conditions, Office for Official Publications of the European Communities, Luxembourg.

Fleisher, Belton M. and Yang, Dennis Tao (2004) "China's labor market," Stanford Center For International Development, Working Paper 203/2004, Stanford.

Garcia, Beatriz Carillo (2004) "Rural-urban migration in China: temporary migrants in search of permanent settlement," in *Portal*, Vol.1, 2/2004.

Ghai, Dharam (2002) *Decent Work: Concepts, Models and Indicators*, DP/139/ 2002, ILO, Geneva.

Hayes, Anna (2004) "Human insecurity in twenty-first century China: the vulnerability of women to HIV/Aids," Paper for the 15th Biennial Conference of the Asian Studies Association of Australia (ACESA), June 29 - July 2, 2004.

Hussain, Athar (2003) *Urban Poverty in China: Measurement, Patterns and Policies*, ILO, Geneva.

ILO Committee on Employment and Social Policy (ESP) (2003) *A Review of the ILO Decent Work Pilot Programme*, Geneva: ILO.

Iredale, Robyn and Fei, Guo (2003) *Unemployed among Migrant Population in Chinese Cities: Case Study of Beijing*, Proceedings of the 15th Annual Conference of the Association for Chinese Economics Studies Australia (ACESA), June 29 - July 2, 2004.

Iredale Robyn; Zheng, Zhenzhen; Ghosh, Swati (2005) "Health and social protection in South and Northeast Asia: case study of HIV/AIDS," Regional Conference on Migration and Development in Asia, Lanzhou, March14-16, 2004, International Organization for Migration (IOM), Department for International Development (DFID), China.

Knight, John and Yueh, Linda (2003) "Job mobility and migrants in urban China," Department of Economics, Discussion Paper Series, 163, 2003, Oxford.

Knight, John; Song, Lina; Jia, Huaibin (1999) "Chinese rural migrants in urban enterprises: three perspectives," in *The Journal of Development Studies*, 35/3, pp. 73-104.

Martin, Philip (2005) *Merchants of Labour: Agents of the Evolving Migration Infrastructure*, International Institute for Labour Studies Geneva.

Miller, Tom (2005) "Hukou reform: one step forward," in *China Economic Quarterly*, Q3, pp. 34-37.

Murphy, Rachel (2002) *How Migrant Labor is Changing Rural China*, Cambridge: University Press.

National Bureau of Statistics of China (2004) *China Labour Statistical Yearbook 2004*, Beijing.

Ngai, Pun Dr. (2004) "A new practice of labour organizing: community-based organization of migrant women workers in South China," Paper for the International Conference on Membership based Organization of the Poor, Hong Kong University of Science and Technology.

Nielsen, Ingrid; Smyth, Russel; Zhang, Mingqiong (2004) "Unemployment within China's floating population: empirical evidence from Jiangsu survey data," Paper, Monash University.

Li, Minghuan (2004) "Labour brokerage in China today: formal and informal dimensions," Duisburg Working Papers on East Asian Studies, 58, 2004.3.

Miehlbradt, Alexandra Overy (2001) *Guide to Assessment for BDS Program Design. A Fit Manual*, Geneva: ILO.

Miehlbradt, Alexandra Overy (2004) *BDS Update, Seminar Reader - Developing Markets for Business Development Services: Pioneering Systemic Approaches, Small Enterprise Development Program of the ILO*, Swiss Agency for Development and Cooperation, Chiang Mai, Thailand, September 2004.

Park, Albert; Yang, Du; Wang, Sangui (2004) "Is migration helping China's poor?" Paper for the Conference on Poverty, Inequality, Labor Market and Welfare Reform in China, Australia National University, August 25-27, 2004.

Pieke, Frank and Ping, Huang (2003) "China migration country study," in *Migration Development Pro-Poor Policy Choices in Asia*, The Refugee and Migratory Movements Research Unit (RMMRU) at the University of Dhaka, Department for International Development (DFID), Dhaka and London.

Roberts, Kenneth (2001) "The determinants of job choice by rural migrants," in *Shanghai, China Economic Review*, 12/1, pp. 15-39.

Rozelle, Scott; Huang, Jikun; Zhang, Linxiu (2002) "Emerging Markets, Evolving Institutions, and the New Opportunities for Growth in China's Rural Economy," in *China Economic Review*, 13/2002, pp. 345-353.

Tuan, Francis; Somwaru, Agapi; Diao, Xinshen (2000) *Rural Labour Migration, Characteristics, and Employment Patterns: A Study Based on China's Agricultural Census*, Trade and Macroeconomics Division, International Food Policy Research Institute, Washington D.C.

Xiang, Biao (2004) "Transcending boundaries: Zhejiangcun: the story of a migrant village in Beijing," Leiden : Brill (China Studies).

Zhang, Mei (2003) *China's Poor Regions: Rural Urban Migration, Poverty, Economic Reform and Urbanisation*, London and New York: RoutledgeCurzon Studies on the Chinese Economy.

Zhao, Zhong (2003) "Migration, labor market flexibility wage determination in China - a review," paper, The World Bank, Washington D.C.

Zheng, Zhenzhen and Qiang, Ren (2005) "People's Republic of China," Background Paper, Regional Conference on Migration and Development in Asia, Lanzhou, March 14-16, 2005, IOM, PRCh, DFID China.

Active Employment Policies – The Case of the Nanjing Labour and Social Security Bureau

Zhong Xiaoyun

The Nanjing Party committee and the government are focusing much attention on the migration of the rural labour force. In 2005, they issued the "Opinion on accelerating the integrated rural and urban development in Nanjing" and the "Implementation regulations on the integrated management of the rural and urban employment and the improvement of the rural social security system" and made the integrated management of urban and rural employment a priority of the labour and social security departments. The documents called for more support for and less demand from the rural areas, peasants and agricultural development; production facilities should be concentrated in industrial zones, peasants should be concentrated in towns and cities, and land should be concentrated and operated according to scale. The rural economic restructuring should be combined with the adjusted migration of the rural labour force. The ultimate goals are to develop the economy, increase farmers' income and develop a harmonious society.

The city government is planning to develop the so-called "five systems" (*wu ge tixi* 五个体系) in five years' time: firstly, an industrial system based on the development of advanced manufacturing industries; secondly, an urbanized system driven by centralized population and industries; thirdly, a collective land use system based on the protection of benefit rights of the rural lands; fourthly, a secondary distribution system of the national revenue to benefit the peasants, and fifthly, an employment system with equal treatment for all people in the same city.

When the labour and social security plan was formulated for the equal treatment of all people in the same city, concrete objectives and measures were worked out in order to establish an integrated rural and urban labour market system.

Scope and fields of the work of the labour and social security departments will also undertake great changes in the future. There are still, however, many policy bottlenecks that need to be eliminated in developing an integrated urban and rural labour market, for instance, the residence permit, etc.

Our first step was to abolish the boundary between urban and rural areas and regional areas. The differentiation between urban people and rural people no longer exists in the management of residence permits; residents can seek for work in any employment information station with their Identification Card and be employed according to their qualifications through equal competition. We have done a lot in this field in Nanjing. As far as we know, secondary markets still exist in other cities but not in our city.

Secondly, an employment service network has been established in suburban areas and counties. Such a network covering 70 per cent of the city has been established in each town or township and community with a proper institutional structure, staff, funding, working places, regulations and tasks. The network links urban areas with suburban areas and counties to ensure quicker transmission of more comprehensive employment information of various kinds.

Thirdly, various employment information organizations are being fostered. Employment information units under different ownership, such as the temporary work companies and private employment information centers have managed to combine the migration of the labour force with the development of the labour service economy. At the same time, there are plans to classify and register the employed peasants in the countryside and provide them with "Employment Registration Cards" just like unemployed urban people.

Fourthly, an allowance is paid to those employment information centers that have successfully found jobs for the migrant workers. In order to promote the migration of the rural labour force, the government will pay an amount of 30 RMB to the employment information centers that have successfully found jobs for rural labourers, after a contract for longer than one year has been signed and insurance paid.

Fifthly, training is strengthened for the migration of the rural labour force. In the process of promoting the migration of the rural labour force, the government has allocated a huge amount of funding for the training of no less than 30,000 people each year. The annual financial budget is seven million RMB for training on employment consultancy, for vocational skills training and business start-up training. Up to September 2005, 29,000 people had been trained in Nanjing and a higher employment rate is seen among these trainees.

Training is organized in two ways: first, each district and county can directly organize training for peasants; second, they can choose training institutions and training courses, themselves, according to their needs, and their training fees will be reimbursed in their district, county or neighbourhood committee.

Sixthly, migrant workers are encouraged to go back to their hometowns to set up their own businesses. The government provides free business start-up training and services and a bonus of 500 RMB per person for those who successfully start up their own businesses.

Seventhly, the various rights of the migrant workers are protected. Activities are organized to select credible projects with labour security, improve the long-term management mechanism of labour security in the working units and to intensify inspection and law enforcement so as to prevent and stop phenomena such as the delayed payment of migrant workers.

Eighthly, experiments are being carried out on formulating policies for rural pension insurance and other policies. Last year, relevant policies and measures were promulgated. There are mainly three forms: rural insurance, the participation of migrants in urban pension insurance schemes, and pension security for peasants who lost their land. In addition, the government is organizing research and studies on how to transfer these three forms and to see whether the cooperative medical system should be adopted for medical insurance.

In general, the integration of urban and rural employment and the implementation of an active employment policy are important measures in carrying out the concept of human-oriented and scientific development and developing a harmonious society. It is also an inevitable demand of promoting agriculture with industries and rural areas with urban areas as well as a key task in realizing the "two firsts" (*liang ge lüxian* 两个率先). Today, the bottleneck for the "two firsts" in Nanjing is in rural areas, and the bottleneck in the rural areas is to increase the income of the farmers in the rural areas. To realize the goal of the "two firsts," we need to focus on increasing the peasants' income, and employment improvement is an important means of increasing their income. Therefore, to push forward the migration of the rural labour force is the foremost task of the labour and social security departments in this new historical period and we shall do our best to fulfill this task.

Vulnerable Groups
in the Urban Labour Market

Gender Disparities in Unemployment Duration in Urban China[1]

Du Fenglian and Dong Xiaoyuan

Introduction

In the past decade, China's public enterprises have undergone dramatic ownership reforms and labour retrenchment. The deepening of public sector reforms has brought an end to the era of "cradle-to-grave" socialism and lifetime employment for state workers. While industrial restructuring is an inevitable feature of market transition, it has affected men and women differently. Studies show that women have borne a disproportionate share of the costs of adjustment. Women are more likely to be unemployed[2] than men and have more difficulty finding re-employment in the private sector (Appleton et al. 2002). In consequence, women endure higher unemployment rates and their unemployment spells are longer (Du 2004). The deterioration of the employment status of women makes the feminization of urban poverty a real possibility in post-restructuring China. The rising gender inequality in paid employment affects the well-being not only of women themselves but also of their families, given the evidence from a diverse set of countries that increasing a woman's share of household income significantly increases the share of the household budget allocated to children's education, health and nutrition-related expenditures (World Bank 2001). Despite the significant impact, the gender implications of industrial restructuring have not received adequate attention from economists and policy-makers in China.

The purpose of this paper is to study the determinants of gender differences in unemployment spells in urban China using a nation-wide household survey undertaken in 2003. We will apply a duration regression model to investigate the main reasons as to why women's unemployment spells are longer than those of men. We will next evaluate the extent to which the gender disparity in unemployment duration is attributable to structural and institutional factors of the labour market and to observed individual characteristics. A better understanding of the causes of gender disparities in unemployment is of critical importance in designing gender-

---

[1] The authors acknowledge Poverty and Economic Policy (PEP) gender challenge fund for its financial support, the grant No. is 05-RG-10348. The authors also thank the Ford Foundation for its support for the post-graduate economic research and mentoring program for Chinese young women economists. They are also grateful to Professor Yaohui Zhao (China Center of Economic Research (CCER), Beijing University), Professor Swapna Mukhopadhyay (India), Professor H. Djebbari (Canada) and Dileni Gunewardena (Sri Lanka) for their valuable comments. They also thank Anne J. Braun for her valuable suggestions.
[2] We define unemployment in this paper according to ILO, which is different from the registered unemployment by the government.

sensitive public policies and seeking gender equitable solutions for urban unemployment.

The paper is organized as follows: the data and descriptive statistics are introduced in the next section. Section 3 analyzes the empirical framework. Section 4 discusses the regression results of unemployment duration determination. Section 5 presents the findings from a decomposition analysis of unemployment duration by gender. The final section summarizes the main results and discusses their policy implications.

Data and descriptive statistics

The data used in this paper is derived from a household survey for urban unemployment conducted by the Chinese National Bureau of Statistics in December 2003. The survey covered 17 major municipalities and provinces selected from six geographic regions, namely, Beijing, Tianjin, Hebei, Shanxi, Liaoning, Jilin, Heilongjiang, Jiangsu, Anhui, Henan, Guangdong, Hubei, Chongqing, Sichuan, Yunnan, Guizhou and Gansu. Except for Beijing, Tianjin and Chongqing, three cities in each province were covered by the survey, including the capital of the province, a medium and a small-size city. Within each city, urban-registered households were selected using stratified random sampling methods.[3] A total of 11,422 households across 45 cities were included in the survey. Among the urban residents who were covered by the survey (men aged between 16 and 60 and women aged between 16 and 50[4]), there were 2,573 people who had experienced involuntary unemployment in the past 3 years, of whom 1008 were re-employed and 1,565 remained unemployed at the time the survey was undertaken. Excluding those observations with missing information on unemployment duration and excluding those who were laid-off before 1998[5] we had a sample of 2,102 unemployed men and women for the analysis.

We derived the dependent variable of unemployment spells[6] and the explanatory variables for personal characteristics, such as gender, age, marital status,

---

[3] In each city, the surveyed households are the same as those in the annual urban household survey by the Urban Household Survey Team of the National Bureau of Statistics.

[4] We took women up to the age of 50 into our survey (despite the official retirement age being 55), because women are likely to be retired before the age of 55. Of course, the fact that there is a 10 year difference between the retirement ages of males and females might lead to an underestimate of the difficulties faced by women who have been laid-off. It should be added that urban registered unemployment refers to those within a certain working age range (16-50 for male and 16-45 for female) (China National Bureau of Statistics 2004: 652).

[5] The retrospective data includes those samples with long unemployment spells; in order to reduce the selection bias, we drop these samples.

[6] Those who were unemployed more than once reported their latest unemployment spells, and the observed unemployment spells for the currently unemployed are not the real ones because of the censoring.

education, health, party membership, income and demographic characteristics of households, unemployment benefits (UB) and job search channels directly from the survey. Variables for economic growth and share of tertiary sector in GDP by city were obtained from the China Statistical Yearbook 2003 and the China City Statistical Yearbook 2003. Unemployment rates by province were calculated using information obtained from the Urban Household Survey (China National Bureau of Statistics 2003a).[7]

Table 1. Unemployment durations in urban China by gender, 2003

Unemployed in past 3 years (1)	Total	Male	Female
No. Obs.	2,102	865	1,236
Percentage	100	41.17	58.83
Unempl. duration	17.67	16.22	18.68
(month)	(15.82)	(15.42)	(16.03)
Re-employed (2)			
No. Obs.	881	386	495
Percentage	41.91	43.81	56.19
Unempl. duration	13.29	11.88	14.39
(month)	(12.42)	(11.89)	(12.72)
Remain unemployed (3)			
No. Obs.	1,221	479	741
Percentage	58.09	39.26	60.74
Unempl. duration	20.82	19.72	21.55
(month)	(17.21)	(16.98)	(17.33)

Note: Standard deviations are in parentheses.

Table 1 presents descriptive statistics of the unemployment and re-employment of the sample. From this table, we noted that women make up a disproportionately large share of the unemployed and a small share of the re-employed, that unemployment durations for men and women are long and women's are even longer. Specifically, of the 2,102 unemployed, only 881 (41.8 per cent) are re-employed and the average unemployment durations are about 18 months for the entire sample, 13 months for the re-employed and 21 months for those still unemployed. With regard to gender differences, we found that female workers make up about 59 per cent of the unemployed, 18 percentage points higher than the share for men, whereas their share in re-employment is only 56 per cent. Moreover, the mean length of unemployment spells for women is more than two months longer than that of men. These results confirm that unemployed women have experienced more difficulty in re-entering the labour market.

---

[7] We define those who worked fewer than 4 hours in November 2003 as unemployed.

Table 2. Summary statistics of personal characteristics of the sample, by gender

	Male		Female		F/M
	Mean	Std. Dev.	Mean	Std. Dev.	
Continuous variables					
Years of schooling[1]	11.16	2.32	11.26	2.10	1.01
Spouses' years of schooling[2]	10.54	2.83	11.36	2.84	1.08
Experience[3]	21.65	11.27	19.72	8.34	0.91
Pre-displacement earnings (RMB/month)	702.33	496.44	541.50	260.92	0.77
Income of other members (RMB/month)	632.05	677.62	981.84	775.42	1.55
Property income (RMB/month)	360.77	642.14	250.57	696.04	0.69
UB (RMB/month)	82.22	82.42	77.62	78.07	0.94
Discrete variables					
Party[4]	0.142	0.350	0.089	0.285	0.83
Marriage	0.776	0.418	0.884	0.320	1.14
Health	0.877	0.328	0.889	0.314	1.01
Household demographic[5]					
No children	0.109		0.129		1.18
Child aged 0-6	0.034		0.078		2.29
Child aged 7-18	0.284		0.399		1.40
Child aged 19-22	0.183		0.184		1.00
Child aged 23-28	0.215		0.096		0.44
Child aged over 28	0.176		0.115		0.65
Job search channels (%)					
Government	0.170		0.175		1.01
Market	0.027		0.028		1.04
Relatives and friends	0.438		0.437		0.99
Themselves	0.311		0.318		1.022
Other	0.054		0.045		0.833

Notes: 1. Years of Schooling are calculated from levels of education attainment with 6 years for primary school, 9 for junior school, 12 for high school, 15 for college graduates (*dazhuan*), 16 for university graduates and 19 for postgraduates. 2. As far as the 16 per cent of individuals who have no spouses are concerned, the household heads' education levels are used. 3. Years of pre-displacement experience are derived by subtracting the sum of 6, years of schooling and years of unemployment. 4. Party is a dummy variable for communist party membership; Marriage is a binary indicator of marriage status; and Health is a dummy which is equal to one if the person is reported to have good health. 5. Household demographic and job search channels are binary indicators of respective categories.

Table 2 presents a summary of the statistics of observed personal and household characteristics of men and women in the sample. The statistics on education, experience and health show no striking disparity in human capital endowment between men and women. Women have, on average, slightly more years of schooling, better health, and fewer years of work experience than men. The job search channels are also fairly similar between men and women. However, marked gender gaps are found in pre-displacement earnings, unemployment benefits, and income from other household members. The ratio of women to men is 0.77 for pre-displacement wages, 0.69 for property income, and 0.94 for unemployment benefits, whereas income earned by other household members is 55 per cent higher for women than for men. Moreover, women are less likely to be party members, indicating that women may have less social capital than men. Compared with men, the distribution of women with no children or younger children is higher. The differences in income, social capital, and household demographics are likely to affect incentives for and constraints on men and women to re-enter the labour market. Lower pre-unemployment wages, property income and unemployment benefits for women tend to reduce women's reservation wages relative to men's and consequently women's probability of regaining employment, whereas higher income from other household members (mainly husbands) for women has the opposite effect. The lack of access to a social network may represent an important obstacle for women in undertaking a job search. The fact that a larger proportion of unemployed female workers have young children may raise their opportunity costs of working relative to men or put more pressure on women to work in order to support their families.

In addition to the differences in individual and household characteristics, the sector distributions are different between male and female workers before unemployment, see Tables 3 to 6. The data shows that before being unemployed, more women worked in the enterprises that suffered loss, had collective ownership and were in the service sector. This means that the women's workplaces are inferior to those of men. In order to see how the unemployed workers in the sample changed with time, we calculated the inflow rates and outflow rates[8] from the survey data, see Table 7.

Table 3. The financial situation of the units by gender (pre-unemployment)

Status quo	Male			Female			F/M
	Freq.	%	Cum.	Freq.	%	Cum.	
Bankrupt	176	38.18	38.18	276	38.07	38.07	1.00
Loss	130	28.20	66.38	210	28.97	67.03	1.03
Profit	55	11.93	78.31	64	8.83	75.86	0.74
Government agency	8	1.74	80.04	4	0.55	76.41	0.32
Institution	13	2.82	82.86	23	3.17	79.59	1.12
Others	79	17.14	100.0	148	20.41	100.0	1.19

Source: China National Bureau of Statistics 2003a.

---

[8] Average annual rates of the number flowing into unemployment divided by the number employed and multiplied by 100; average annual rates of the number flowing out of unemployment divided by the number unemployed, multiplied by 100.

Table 4. Ownership distribution by gender (pre-unemployment)

Ownership	Male			Female			F/M
	Freq.	%	Cum.	Freq.	%	Cum.	
Central SOE	94	10.87	10.87	102	8.26	8.26	0.76
Local SOE	309	35.72	46.59	381	30.85	39.11	0.86
Collective	109	12.60	59.19	273	22.11	61.21	1.75
Private and self-employed	125	14.45	73.64	189	15.30	76.52	1.06
Joint venture	21	2.43	76.07	15	1.21	77.73	0.50
Share holding	48	5.55	81.62	60	4.86	82.59	0.88
Others	159	18.38	100.0	215	17.41	100.0	0.95

Table 5. Industry distribution by gender (pre-unemployment)

	Male			Female			F/M
	Freq.	%	Cum.	Freq.	%	Cum.	
Agriculture	7	0.81	0.81	11	0.89	0.89	1.10
Mining	18	2.08	2.89	16	1.29	2.18	0.62
Manufacturing	352	40.69	43.58	453	36.65	38.83	0.90
Energy	14	1.62	45.20	13	1.05	39.89	0.65
Construction	42	4.86	50.06	43	3.48	43.37	0.72
Geology and water conservancy	1	0.12	50.17	5	0.40	43.77	3.33
Communication, transportation	89	10.29	60.46	50	4.05	47.82	0.39
Trade	139	16.07	76.53	301	24.35	72.17	1.52
Financial	8	0.92	77.46	14	1.13	73.30	1.23
Housing	6	0.69	78.15	10	0.81	74.11	1.17
Non-financial Services	71	8.21	86.36	168	13.59	87.70	1.66
Government Agencies	40	4.62	90.98	66	5.34	93.04	1.16
Others	78	9.02	100.0	86	6.96	100.0	0.77

Table 6. Occupation distribution by gender (pre-unemployment)

	Male			Female			F/M
	Freq.	%	Cum.	Freq.	%	Cum.	
Managerial personnel	60	6.94	6.94	26	2.10	2.10	0.30
Technicians & engineers	143	16.53	23.47	171	13.83	15.94	0.84
Staff	107	12.37	35.84	209	16.91	32.85	1.37
Trade	91	10.52	46.36	214	17.31	50.16	1.65
Service	107	12.37	58.73	112	9.06	59.22	0.73
Manufacturing	263	30.40	89.13	334	27.02	86.25	0.89
Others	94	10.87	100.0	170	13.75	100.0	1.26

Table 7 shows that although inflow rates and outflow rates keep increasing for both men and women, women's inflow rates are higher and their outflow rates are relatively lower. This means that women who have been laid-off face a tougher environment in the labour market.

Table 7. Average inflow rates and outflow rates by year and by gender

	Male		Female	
	Inflow rates	**Outflow rates**	**Inflow rates**	**Outflow rates**
1998	4.86	4.76	5.42	4.48
1999	7.52	4.90	9.13	3.51
2000	14.99	10.85	19.33	8.33
2001	26.81	21.35	28.27	17.00
2002	37.87	21.26	37.55	18.52
2003	53.23	25.97	53.21	22.16

In the following sections we will examine how gender differences in those observed characteristics influence the re-employment outcomes of men and women.

Empirical framework

We use a duration model commonly applied in labour literature to analyze the determinants of unemployment spells (for references, see Nickell 1979, Lancaster 1979, Narendranathan et al. 1985; Meyer 1990). Let us denote $h(t)dt$ the hazard function in period t of the unemployment spell, which is the probability that individual i will leave unemployment during the period $(t, t+dt)$ conditional on the person having been unemployed for t periods. The conditional probability of regaining employment is the product of the probability that individual i receives a job offer during $(t, t+dt)$ and the probability that such an offer is accepted.

The probability of receiving a job offer during $(t, t+dt)$ is determined by three factors. The first involves individual characteristics such as gender, experience, educational attainment and health status, which are indicative of the expected productivity of the individual for employers. The second factor includes those affecting the general level of labour demand faced by the individual, such as the regional rate of growth, industrial structure and unemployment rates. The third variable reflects the nature of job search mechanisms.

The probability that the individual will accept a job offer is determined by a comparison of the wage offer and the reservation wage. While the wage offer shares the same determinant of the probability of receiving a job offer, the reservation wage is affected by such factors as the pre-displacement wage, income from other sources, unemployment benefits, and demographic characteristics of the household associated with the opportunity cost of employment. Thus, the hazard function of leaving unemployment is written as $h(t) = h(X(t), t)$, where X is a vector of explanatory variables, which include the productive attributes of individuals, local labour demand conditions, job search channels, pre-displacement wage, household income, unemployment benefits, the and demographic characteristics of the household.

Following Narendranathan et al. (1985), we assume the Weibull distribution and write the regression model of unemployment duration as:

$$h(X(t),t) = \exp[X(t)'\beta]\alpha t^{\alpha-1}, \alpha > 0 \qquad (1)$$

Where β is a vector of regression parameters and α is the indicator of how the hazard function is changing with respect to duration, that is, in the cases where $\alpha > 1$, $\alpha < 1$, and $\alpha = 1$, the conditional probability of re-employment is increasing, decreasing or independent of unemployment duration.

In this model, the expected mean duration of unemployment for time invariant explanatory variables X is given by:

$$ED = \Gamma(1+\frac{1}{\alpha})\exp(-\frac{X'\beta}{\alpha}) \qquad (2)$$

Where $\Gamma(\ )$ is the standard Gamma distribution function. The elasticity of expected duration with respect to a variable which enters the hazard function in logs is the negative of the corresponding element of β divided by α.

Using equations (1) and (2), we will analyze the patterns of regaining employment for men and women in urban China and explore the determinants of gender differences in unemployment spells in the remainder of the paper.

Results

To depict the difference of re-employment probabilities between men and women, we will first present the Kaplan-Meier survival curves by gender using the nonparametric method.

Figure 1. Kaplan-Meier survival estimates by gender

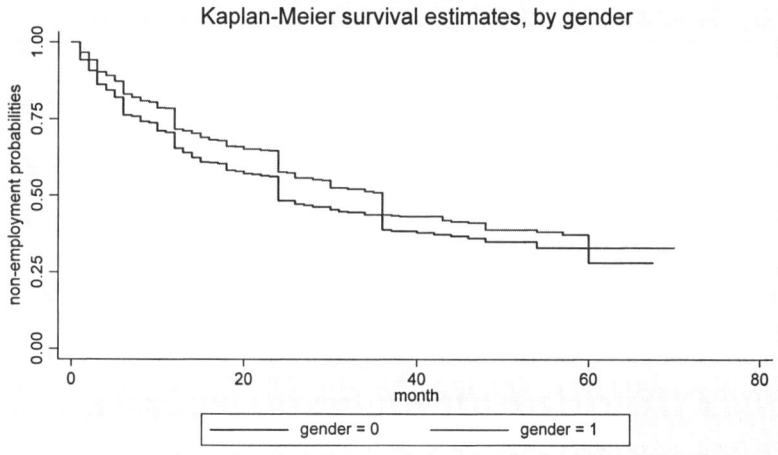

Note: male is represented by the above curve, e.g. gender=0, and female by the bottom curve, e.g. gender=1.

Figure 1 shows that the non-employment probability of females is always higher than that of males. In order to identify the determinants of the difference, we estimate the hazard function of unemployment spells in (1) by Maximum Likelihood Estimation techniques using the STATA computer software package. The regression is first applied for a pooled sample of men and women and then for men and women separately. The estimates are presented in Table 3. Based on the likelihood ratio tests reported at the bottom of Table 3, all three regressions are statistically significant at the one per cent level.

We will now take a look at the regression estimates. The estimates of the pooled regression show a significant gender gap in unemployment duration, as the probability of being re-employed for women is only 62.2 per cent of the probability for men. As expected, experience, education, good health and a party membership have significant positive effects on the probability of being reemployed. Also consistent with economic intuition, pre-displacement wages, income from other members and unemployment benefits are found to decrease the hazard ratio of re-employment and the effects are significant at the one per cent level. In addition, the results show that those unemployed workers whose spouse or other household members are also unemployed are significantly less likely to find re-employment. Moreover, compared with those who rely on governments for their job searches, the hazard ratio of employment for those who rely on relatives and friends or themselves for their job searches is significantly higher. This result indicates that private social networks are more effective than public job replacement services in helping laid off workers re-enter the labour market. Interestingly, in contrast to our result, using data gathered in the spring of 2000, Appleton et al. (2002) found that job replacement services provided by governments are more effective than private job search mechanisms. Given that our analysis uses data obtained in December 2003, the contrast between our results and Appleton's is indicative of the deepening of labour market reforms in urban China.

The factors associated with local labour demand do not appear to have any significant impact on re-employment. Surprisingly, we find that workers with children aged between 0 and 6 are more likely to find re-employment than the workers with no children, but the estimate is significant only at the 10 per cent level. This result may be attributable to the fact that unemployment rates are higher for the younger age group, given that workers with no children are most likely to be young people.

We will now examine the estimates by gender. These estimates reveal that there are noticeable gender differences in the marginal effects of observed characteristics on unemployment durations. We will first take a look at the impact of human capital. Men are found to benefit from experience more than women in that the estimates for experience and its squared terms are significant for men but insignificant for women. The fact that pre-displacement work experience does not help women as much as men is perhaps because women received less on-the-job training than men prior to being laid off as a result of gender segmentation in the workplace.

Table 8. Regression estimates of unemployment duration

Variables	Pooled regression		Male		Female	
	Hazard ratio	t-ratio	Hazard ratio	t-ratio	Hazard ratio	t-ratio
Gender	0.622***	-4.87	--	--	--	--
Experience	1.103***	3.96	1.100***	3.28	1.037	1.17
Experience square	0.998***	-3.24	0.998***	-3.07	1.000	-0.16
Education	1.119***	4.83	1.041	1.58	1.161***	5.61
Health	1.754***	3.62	2.034***	3.53	1.505**	2.23
Party	1.494***	3.13	1.196	1.12	1.587***	3.26
Marriage	0.807	-1.25	1.023	0.10	0.745	-1.46
Log(Pre-displacement earnings)	0.766***	-5.50	0.828***	-3.95	0.739***	-5.90
Log(Income of other members)	0.971*	-1.70	0.980	-1.01	0.964*	-1.61
Child aged 0-6	1.429	1.62	1.097	0.28	1.514*	1.75
Child aged 7-18	1.182	1.16	1.297	1.35	1.174	0.98
Child aged 19-22	0.989	-0.07	0.936	-0.31	1.077	0.43
Child aged 23-27	0.800	-1.26	0.982	-0.08	0.733	-1.35
Child aged over 28	0.788	-1.34	0.923	-0.37	0.814	-0.93
Other household member unempl.	0.106***	-4.81	0.126***	-2.90	0.107***	-3.80
Log(Property income)	0.987	-0.83	0.967*	-1.73	1.008	0.47
Local unemployment rates	0.980	-1.20	0.984	-0.75	0.981	-0.97
Share of tertiary	0.996	-0.56	0.979**	-2.26	1.006	0.69
Local economic growth	1.002	0.08	0.999	-0.02	1.004	0.13
Market	1.245	0.75	1.597	1.17	1.118	0.32
Relatives& friends	1.873***	4.57	2.319***	4.34	1.402**	2.14
Themselves	2.176***	5.41	1.971***	3.36	1.864***	3.93
Others	1.335	1.25	1.557	1.46	0.972	-0.10
Log(UB)	0.886***	-6.05	0.892***	-4.85	0.899***	-4.75
α	1.0390*	-1.75	0.8997**	-2.55	0.993	-0.20
Log likelihood	-2138.79		-918.11		-1196.39	
LR chi2 (.)	322.34		178.52		203.83	
P value	0.00		0.00		0.00	
Number of obs.	2,071		850		1,221	

Notes: ***,** and* indicate 1, 5 and 10 per cent levels of significance, respectively. Based on the log likelihood tests, there is unobserved heterogeneity in pooled regression and no significant evidence for this problem in regressions by gender. For dummy variables, reference groups include those who have no children, rely on governments for finding reemployment, and have no other family member unemployed.

In contrast to experience, education appears to be more important for women than men; one additional year of schooling increases the hazard ratio by 16.1 per cent for women and only 4.1 per cent for men, and the estimate is significant only for women. Health status affects the prospect of re-employment for men more positively than for women, perhaps because jobs for men are more physically demanding.

Striking gender differences are also found in the marginal effects of social capital endowments. Holding party membership makes a significant difference in unemployment duration for women but has no effect for men. Quantitatively, a woman's probability of re-entering the workforce is 58.7 per cent higher for a party member than a non-party member. Moreover, the estimates of dummy variables for job search channels show that help from relatives and friends or self efforts have significant positive effects for both men and women but the estimates are numerically larger for men than for women. Furthermore, unemployment of other family members has a significant negative impact on the re-employment prospects of both men and women but the effect is larger for women than for men. These results suggest that lack of social contacts represents a major handicap for unemployed females in re-entering the labour market.

With respect to re-employment incentives, the estimates show that pre-displacement earnings have a significant negative effect on re-employment for both men and women but the effect is larger for women than for men. Income from other family members also has negative effect for both men and women but the estimate is significant only for women. The stronger negative effect for women is consistent with the social norm that men are considered the bread-winners of the households. However, property income has a significant negative effect on re-employment for men but no effect for women. This may be because women do not have the same degree of control over property income as do men. Despite gender differences in private income, the effects of public income support for unemployment are fairly similar for men and women, unemployment benefits significantly decrease the hazard ratio of re-employment for both sexes and the difference in the magnitude of the effect between men and women is negligible.

To discern the sensitivity of unemployment spells to these re-employment incentives for men and women, we have calculated the elasticities of unemployment duration and reported the results in Table 4. The estimates indicate that a one-per cent increase in pre-displacement wages tends to raise unemployment duration by 0.21 per cent for men and 0.31 per cent for women. However, with respect to unemployment benefits, the male elasticity of 0.13 is only slightly higher than the female elasticity of 0.11. Ham et al. (1998, 1999) estimate that the point elasticity of unemployment spells is 0.21 for women and 0.34 for men in the Czech Republic.

Compared with their estimates, the negative incentive effects of public income support for unemployed workers are weaker in urban China than in the Czech Republic. The sensitivity of unemployment duration with respect to property income and income earned by other household members is also rather small.

Turning to other observable characteristics, marital status appears to have a positive effect for men and a negative effect for women, but none of the estimates are statistically significant. Moreover, none of the dummy variables on children are statistically significant for either men or women. It appears that the responsibility of childcare does not represent a significant impediment for men or women to regain employment. Local unemployment and growth rates also have no significant impact on the re-employment of laid off men or women. However, the share of the tertiary sector has a negative effect on men's re-employment but a positive effect on women's reemployment; only the estimate for men is statistically significant. This finding is consistent with the pattern of gender segmentation in which the service sector is female intensive. The estimates of variables on local labour demand imply that the nature of unemployment in urban China is structural and fictional rather than inadequate general demand for labour.

Table 9. *Elasticities of unemployment duration with reference to income and unemployment benefits, by gender*

Variables	Male			Female		
	Coefficient	t-ratio	Elasticities	Coefficient	t-ratio	Elasticities
Pre-displacement earnings	-0.188***	-3.95	0.209	-0.303***	-5.90	0.305
Income of other members	-0.020	-1.01	0.022	-0.037	-1.61	0.037
Property income	-0.034*	-1.73	0.038	0.008	0.47	-0.008
UB	-0.115***	-4.85	0.127	-0.106***	-4.75	0.107
α	0.900**	-2.55	--	0.993	-0.20	--

Last, but not least, the estimates of α indicate that the probability of re-entering the workforce is decreasing in unemployment duration for men ($\alpha = 0.90$) but is more or less independent of the length of unemployment spells for women ($\alpha = 0.99$).

Decomposition of gender differences in unemployment duration

From the regressions of unemployment spells, we estimate that the expected length of a spell of unemployment is longer for women than for men by about four months. Theoretically, this observed gender gap in unemployment duration can be attributed to: (1) differences in observable characteristics and /or (2) differences in regression coefficients.

To disentangle the sources of the observed gender differences in predicted unemployment spells, the male-female difference in unemployment duration is decomposed by the Oaxaca method:

$$\overline{ED}_F - \overline{ED}_M = [ED(\bar{X}_F, \hat{\beta}_M) - ED(\bar{X}_M, \hat{\beta}_M)] + [ED(\bar{X}_F, \hat{\beta}_F) - ED(\bar{X}_F, \hat{\beta}_M)]^9 \quad (3)$$

Where $\overline{ED}$ is the expected mean length of unemployment duration of males (M) and females (F) at the mean value of X for each sub-sample. The first term on the right-hand side of (3) captures the gender differences in unemployment duration due to the differences in observed characteristics between men and women. In other words, it represents the difference in unemployment duration between men and women if the women respond to changes in observable characteristics in the same manner as do men. The second term measures the gender differences attributable to differences in the estimated coefficients. The implicit assumption underlying the second term is that if the mean characteristics are identical across gender groups, then gender differences in unemployment spells are driven by structural and institutional factors of the labour market. This term also captures the effects of unobservable factors that are not equally distributed among men and women (such as, for example, individual tastes and preferences or quality of productive attributes). It essentially represents the difference between a female's predicted length of unemployment when facing a male labour market structure, and a female's actual predicted unemployment duration at the mean characteristics of the female sample. The Oaxaca decomposition of differences in ED is presented in Table 10.

Table 10. Oaxaca decomposition in unemployment duration by gender

	Month	Percentage
Gender disparities in ED	4.0844	100.00
Difference due to Coefficients	10.5746	259.00
Explanatory variables	-6.4992	-159.00

The first finding in Table 10 is that the difference in unemployment duration between women and men is 4.08 months. Moreover, all of this difference is due to differences in coefficients and none of it arises because of differences in explanatory variables. Specifically, if men and women faced the same market structure as male's, women's predicted mean unemployment spells would be 6.5 months shorter than men's, given the gender differences in observed characteristics. However, when holding the females' observable characteristics constant at the sample average, their actual predicted mean unemployment duration is more than ten months longer than it would be if they were treated differently from men in the labour market. Ham et al.

---

[9] The gender disparities in ED can also be presented by:

$$\overline{ED}_F - \overline{ED}_M = [ED(\bar{X}_F, \hat{\beta}_F) - ED(\bar{X}_M, \hat{\beta}_F)] + [ED(\bar{X}_M, \hat{\beta}_F) - ED(\bar{X}_M, \hat{\beta}_M)]$$

The results presented in Table 5 are the simple average of the two formulas.

(1999) draw a similar conclusion, pointing out that differences between men and women's labour supply behaviour and institutional responses to gender are the major determinants of observed gender differences in unemployment duration in the Czech and Slovak Republics.

Conclusions

In this paper, we have studied the gender patterns of unemployment duration in urban China using data derived from a recent, national representative household survey. We have estimated the determinants of unemployment spells for men and women and have analyzed the sources of gender differences in unemployment duration. The results confirm that laid-off female workers have a lower probability of finding re-employment than their male counterparts and their unemployment spells are longer. Our analysis has shown that most of the gender gap in unemployment duration is explained by male-female differences in the marginal propensity of re-employment (as measured by differences in their parameters) instead of male-female differences in measured demand and individual characteristics. Specifically, we find that pre-displacement experience does not help women find re-employment as much it does for men, whereas pre-displacement wages have a stronger negative effect on reemployment for women than for men. We attribute these results to the existence of gender segmentation in the workplace prior to the lay off and the rising gender wage gap as workers leave the state sector to seek employment in the private sector. Moreover, our analysis indicates that the lack of a social network represents a major handicap for women in regaining employment relative to men.

In addition to the findings on gender disparities, our analysis has also generated several important results regarding the operation of China's urban labour market. Our estimates indicate that the problem of unemployment in post-restructuring urban China is structural and fictional rather than lacking an aggregate demand for labour. The analysis also shows that public income supports for unemployment are having a rather moderate effect on the durations of unemployment of both men and women in urban China.

The results of our analysis have important policy implications. The main message is that to reduce gender inequality in employment, policy measures must be taken to address external constraints and structural features of China's urban labour market. Chief among these are public interventions for reducing gender segmentation in the workplace, narrowing gender wage gap in the emerging private sector, and making active labour policies, such as skill-training and job replacement services more sensitive to the needs of unemployed female workers. Beyond the concern about gender inequality, policies designed to provide a social safety net for unemployed urban workers are also warranted in order to ease the pain borne by these workers in the face of labour market turbulence.

References

Appleton, Simon; Knight, John; Song, Lina; Xia, Qingjie (2002) "Labour retrenchment in China: determinants and consequences," in *China Economic Review* 13, pp. 252-275.

Cai, Fang; Giles, John; Park, Albert (2004) "The impact of institutions, information and demographics on the re-employment of China's laid-off workers," mimeo, RSPAS, Australian National University.

China National Bureau of Statistics (2004) *China Labour Statistical Yearbook*, Beijing, p. 652.

China National Bureau of Statistics (2003a) *Household Survey for Urban Unemployment*.

China National Bureau of Statistics (2003b) *China Statistical Yearbook*.

China National Bureau of Statistics (2003c) *China City Statistical Yearbook*.

Du, Fenglian (2004) "Gender disparities in unemployment durations in urban China," paper presented at the 4th China Economic Annual Conference, Nankai University, Tianjin.

Ham, John C.; Svejnar, Jan; Terrell, Katherine (1998) "Unemployment and the social safety net during transitions to a market Economy: evidence from the Czech and Slovak Republics," in *The American Economic Review*, 88, pp. 1117-1142.

Ham, John C.; Svejnar, Jan; Terrell, Katherine (1999) "Women's unemployment during transition, Evidence from Czech and Slovak micro-data," in *Economics of Transition, 7*, pp. 47-78.

Hu, Angang; Cheng, Yonghong; Yang, Yunxin (2002) *Creating Employment and Meeting the Challenge of Unemployment: Evaluation of China's Employment Policies (1949-2001)*, Beijing: China Labour and Social Security Press.

Kiefer, Nicholas M (1988) "Economic duration data and hazard functions," in *The Journal of Economic Literature* 26, pp. 646-679.

Li, Shi; Zhao, Yaohui; Han, Li (2002) "Unemployment and re-employment in China's economic restructuring," mimeo, paper prepared for ASSA annual meeting in Atlanta.

Narendranathan, Wiji; Nickell, Stephen; Stern, Jon (1985) "Unemployment benefits revisited," in *The Economic Journal* 95, pp. 308-329.

World Bank (2001) *Endagering Development: Through Gender Equality in Rights, Resources, and Voice*, Washington, D.C.: Oxford University Press.

Peasants Who Lost Their Land – Rehabilitation Options from the Perspective of Sustainable Development

Chen Shaojun and Zhang Runsen

Introduction

Along with the comprehensive development of the infrastructure, the process of industrialization and urbanization in China is progressing rapidly and a great deal of agricultural land has been converted into non-agricultural land. A group of people, the peasants who lost their land, have emerged. According to the latest survey by the Ministry of Land and Resources, the area of agricultural land in China shrank from 1.951 billion *mu* (unit of area equals to 0.0667 hectares) in 1996 to 1.889 billion *mu* in 2002, and by an average of 8.85 million *mu* per year during this period. At the speed of current urbanization and infrastructural development, at least 5 million *mu* of cultivated land will be expropriated each year. If each peasant occupies 0.7 *mu* of land in the suburbs, more than seven million peasants will lose their land every year (Song/Jing 2004: 54).

Jiangning District in the south of Nanjing City, Jiangsu, can be taken as an example: there are many land-less peasants in this District due to the engineering construction work which has occupied a large amount of land. The total area of Jiangning District is 1566 square km. Up to now, the Economic and Technological Development Zone, the Science Park, the Chinese Merchandise Science Park and the Binjiang Economic and Technological Development Zone have been developed. The total allocated area is 800 square km, accounting for over half of the district area. More than 100 thousand households in the district have been relocated in recent years. The area of demolished houses is spread over more than 10 million square metres. Due to their involuntary and forced displacement, the peasants face a huge risk of impoverishment after their original economic and social system has been changed, with the ensuing landlessness, joblessness, homelessness, marginalization, food insecurity, increased morbidity and mortality, inaccessibility to public facilities and services and social disassembly (Cernea 2002: 7-9). One of the key measures to avoid the risks of impoverishment for land-less peasants is to resettle them according to methods of sustainable development to enable them to support themselves.

The perspective of sustainable development was set out by the World Commission of Environment and Development (WCED) in the book entitled "Our Future," which mentions three factors: to maintain the overall quality of life, to maintain the sustainable utilization of natural resources and to avoid continuous environmental deterioration (Wang 2000: 2). Sustainability means the continual and permanent ability to sustain and support an objective matter (Ye 2001: 64). During the process of relocating and resettling the land-less peasants, it should be considered whether the peasants have the ability to continue improving their livelihoods, whether their living standards can be improved steadily and whether the development of the land-less peasants can be harmonized with the local economy, society, resources and environment.

Analysis of the resettlement of the land-less peasants in Jiangning

Scientific and rational resettlement is important for land-less peasants. However, the traditional administrative measures usually place more emphasis on relocation rather than on resettlement and do not plan and design the resettlement of land-less peasants as an important component of engineering construction. The land-less peasants are often left impoverished after relocation. At present, there are many theoretical proposals about the resettlement of land-less peasants, such as land for land resettlement, non-agricultural resettlement, resettlement through running township enterprises, resettlement through private ownership production, resettlement through joint-investment production, resettlement through retirement pensions, etc. (Shi 1996: 60). Generally speaking, the land for land resettlement, non-agricultural resettlement and resettlement through retirement pensions are three typical modes. In November, 2004, the authors conducted a survey among the peasants in Jiangning District of Nanjing City, Jiangsu Province. We carried out a systematic analysis of the internal and external conditions as well as the controllable and uncontrollable factors faced by different groups of land-less peasants under different types of resettlement based on the data collected through household interviews and questionnaires.

Impacts of different types of resettlement on elders

Table 1 reveals that different resettlements have different impacts on different groups of people. For the elders, the land for land resettlement gives them stability and security and a social network. Although agricultural production is a traditional industry with a high input and a low output, the elders can make a low-cost living as before based on this resettlement. The non-agricultural resettlement, however, brings them more negative impacts than positive impacts. An old man resettled through the non-agricultural resettlement in Jiangning said:

After relocation, the overall environmental conditions, traffic conditions and public facilities were improved a lot. But we lost our original close relations with neighbours. We are not native city residents of Nanjing. The city residents have social security but we do not. When we lived in the countryside in the past, however, we could make a living by farming. At least, we never worried about a shortage of food. Now most of the households maintain a basic living standard with their savings and the government compensation. I'm afraid we will have to go begging in a few years' time.

This shows that the convenient traffic conditions and the new environment can not eliminate the loneliness resulting from the disruption of the original social network. The employment opportunities from non-agricultural resettlement do not make any sense to the elders. When they are rejected by employers because of their age and health, they have the risk of impoverishment following on their heels. In contrast, the exclusive resettlement through retirement pensions for this group of people is worth considering. The compensation for land expropriation would be used to buy pension insurance. The elders would be able to draw the pension regularly. This type of resettlement gives them relative stability and security. Nevertheless, the problem still remains whether the retirement pension would be sufficient to maintain the elders.

Table 1. SWOT analysis of the impact of different types of resettlement on different groups of land-less peasants in Jiangning

	Strengths	Weaknesses	Opportunities	Threats
Type 1: Land for land resettlement				
Elders	Land can be treated as a guarantee; good relations with neighbourhood; familiarization with the livelihood	Low income of agricultural production	Low living expenses; availability for sideline production	Hard work in agricultural production; low income; risks of relative impoverishment
Youngsters	Land can be treated as a guarantee; good relations with neighborhood	Low income of agricultural production; traffic discomfort; inconvenient communication	Low living expenses; availability for sideline production	Losing opportunity of urbanization; risks of relative impoverishment
Women	Land can be treated as a guarantee; good relations with neighborhood	Low income of agricultural production; traffic discomfort; inconvenient communication	Low living expenses; availability for sideline production	Hard work in agricultural production; poor natural environment
Children	Land can be treated as a guarantee; good relations with neighborhood	Low income of agricultural production; traffic discomfort; inconvenient communication	Low living expenses	Poor educational conditions
Type 2: Non-agricultural resettlement				
Elders	Convenient traffic and communication; good environment	High living expenses; losing the original reciprocal ralations with neighbourhood; loneliness	Opportunity of living in cities; avoiding agricultural activity	Losing security from land; low compensation for land expro-priation; impending risks of impoverish-ment

	Strengths	Weaknesses	Opportunities	Threats
Youngsters	Convenient traffic and communication; good environment; elimination of discrimination due to the change of status	High living expenses; losing the original reciprocal relations with neighbourhood; lack of non-agricultural production skill	Opportunity of living in cities; avoiding agricultural activity; employment opportunities	Losing security from land; low compensation for land expropria-tion; impending risks of impover-ishment; less education; much difficulty to find a job, 37.7% unemployed
Women	Convenient traffic and communication; good environment	High living expenses; losing the original reciprocal relations with neighbourhood; lack of non-agricultural production skill	Opportunity of living in cities; avoiding agricultural activity; employment opportunities	Losing security from land; low compensation for land expropria-tion; impending risks of impover-ishment; less education; much difficulty to find a job
Children	Convenient traffic and communication; good environment in favor of future development	High living expenses; losing the original reciprocal relations with neighbourhood, not in favor of their socialization	Opportunity of living in cities; more opportunities of education	Losing security from land; low compensation for land expropria-tion; impending risks of dropout
Type 3: Retirement pensions				
	Strengths	**Weaknesses**	**Opportunities**	**Threats**
Elders	Regular pensions as a stable security	High living expenses; hardly subsisting on pensions	Avoiding agricultural activity	Losing security from land; low compensation for land expropriation; impending risks of impoverishment

Note: The term "elders" refers to men of 60 and over; women of 55 and over. The term "youngsters" refers to men between 18 and 60 and women between 18 and 55. The term "children" refers to those under 18. The retirement pension is available only for the elders, so only the elders are involved in the analysis.

Impacts of different types of resettlement on youngsters

In contrast to the elders, the youngsters expect more opportunities from development. They do not want to be tied to the land all their lives. Therefore, the land for land resettlement gives them the same benefits although the negative influence is equally very great.

Non-agricultural resettlement brings us opportunities. We need not to do hard farm work any more and we can live in cities as well.

However, difficulty in finding employment is one problem which lurks behind this opportunity, as a result of their low standard of education. The survey in Jiangning revealed that 37.7 per cent of the youngsters are unemployed.

The compensation fund is low and cannot be provided in time. It can barely maintain us. We hope that the government can help us with employment, so that we can have some security.

Impacts of different types of resettlement on women

Women belong to a disadvantaged group. They expect to lead a low-cost life with stability and security through the land for land resettlement, but they also want to develop their own human resources by taking up the opportunity offered by non-agricultural resettlement to participate in employment in cities and to lead new lives. A grocery owner said:

We did hard farming work before, so we want to take this opportunity to find a job. But it is difficult for women to get a job. Even positions as community cleaners are fully occupied. The compensation fee is not sufficient to maintain us. We can but run a grocery store to make ends meet.

The impacts of different types of resettlement on women are complicated. Unlike the elders and the youngsters which are an extreme case, the optimum resettlement option for women is a realistic problem worth further discussion.

Impacts of different types of resettlement on children

Children, highly similar to the youngsters, need opportunities for development. Non-agricultural resettlement is suitable for them. They are very flexible and can quickly adapt to urban civilization. Non-agricultural resettlement would give them a better education. Most of the parents interviewed said,

The education conditions are poor in the countryside. With non-agricultural resettlement, the children can go to school nearby.

But children also have some similarities with the elders. Once the children leave the original living environment, they will suffer from loneliness. In addition, they might encounter discrimination when they start to live in the cities. This would not favour their socialization and long-term development.

Sustainable development evaluation of the land-less peasants in Jiangning

Indicator system for the sustainable development evaluation of Jiangning land-less peasants

In the previous section, the impacts of different types of resettlement on different groups of people were analyzed in the SWOT matrix. Each type of resettlement has both positive and negative impacts. In order to select the optimum type of resettlement for the different groups, there should be an indicator system for the sustainable development evaluation of the Jiangning land-less peasants. Only a scientific indicator system can clearly define and measure which resettlement option meets the target for the sustainable development of land-less peasants.

The sustainable development of resettlement for the land-less peasants is not decided by a single factor, but by a complicated system consisting of different hierarchies and factors. According to the relations between them, the sustainable development of resettlement can be divided into four sub-systems of economy, society, resources and environment. In other words, in order to analyze sustainable development, an indicator system must be established. (As shown in Figure 1)

Figure 1. Indicator system for the sustainable development evaluation of resettlement for the land-less peasants in Jiangning

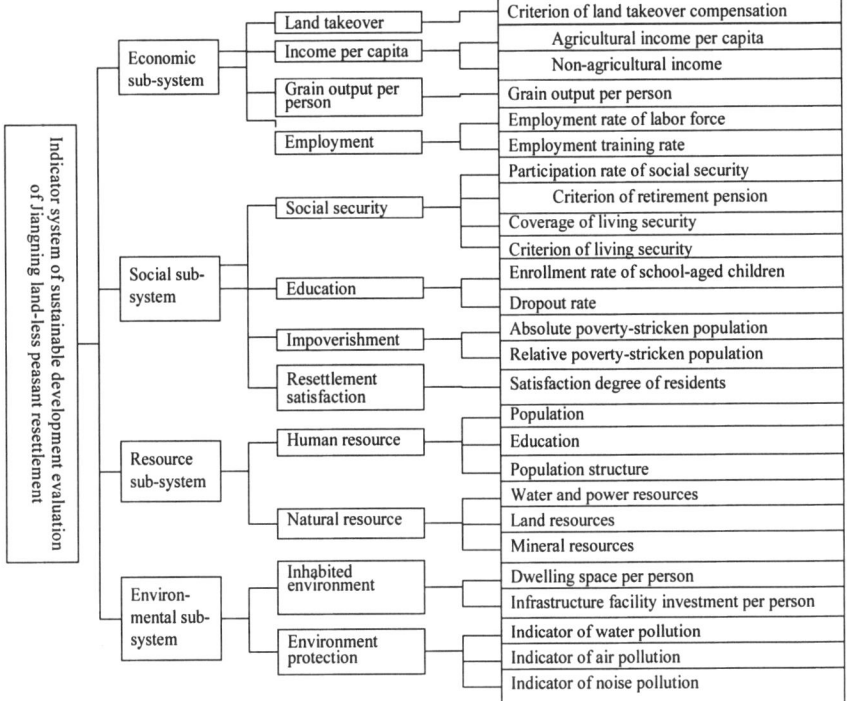

Economic sub-system

Indicators of land expropriation compensation. For land-less peasants, the first realistic problem after their land is expropriated is economic compensation. According to the survey in Jiangning, the compensation criterion for land expropriation is 18000 RMB/*mu*. Most land-less peasants think this is too low for them to able to maintain themselves. During the process of losing land, their status is changed. If non-agricultural resettlement is adopted, they will have to shift from the first industry to the second or the third industry. In a situation where the landless peasants lack relevant skills, the compensation becomes their keenly needed investment capital. Therefore, whether they can maintain themselves after losing their land depends, to a great extent, on the criterion of compensation.

Indicators of income per capita. The sustainable development of the production and livelihoods of land-less peasants depends not only on reasonable levels of compensation, but also on whether they have any other income. These indicators include the agricultural income per capita and the non-agricultural income per capita.

Indicators of grain output per person. If the agricultural resettlement option is adopted, the land-less peasants will remain engaged in agricultural production. Due to the weak agricultural base in the resettlement area, the restoration of the agricultural production system faces some risks. In addition, agricultural production is a traditional industry with a low profit and a low output. The grain output per person thus becomes one of the important indicators of the economic sub-system. The grain output per person is used as a specific evaluation indicator.

Indicators of employment. Land provides the basic employment for peasants. Losing land results in the peasants becoming unemployed and impoverished. The employment of land-less peasants is therefore an important indicator of social stability, which includes the employment rate and, especially, the training rate. Most land-less peasants do not have any vocational skills. Those peasants who have been re-employed are engaged in physical labour which does not require high vocational skills. With the increase in economic development, the labor market is changing from the physical types of labour to the professional and technological types of labour. The peasants with low vocational skills will find it more difficult to find jobs. It is important to carry out re-employment training for the land-less peasants and increase the input of their human resources deposits.

Social sub-system

Indicators of social security. Under the existing urban and rural dual structure in China, the social security system has a dual character. Peasants have never been included in the social security system of city dwellers. In this situation, the land has the dual functions of providing a means of production and providing social security for the peasants. When they lose their land, they also lose their stability and security and are confronted with huge risks. If the retirement pension is adopted as the resettlement option for the elders, an analysis must be carried out on the social security indicators, such as the participation rate in social security, the criteria for social insurance, the rate of the lowest social security coverage and the criteria for the lowest social security provisions.

Indicators of education. Whether the land-less peasants can plan and realise their long-term development also depends on their literacy levels; education is thus an important factor, especially for their offspring. It is necessary to assess the education status of peasants, i.e. the enrollment rate and the dropout rate of school-aged children.

Indicators of impoverishment. After relocation, the land-less peasants are susceptible to the risk of impoverishment. They may even be plunged into poverty as a result of improper resettlement. In order to evaluate whether a resettlement option meets the requirements of sustainable development, it is essential to understand the status of the absolute poor in the population and the relatively poor population in the group.

Indicators of resettlement satisfaction. From a subjective viewpoint, whether the land-less peasants are satisfied with their relocation, whether they identify with the process and the results of resettlement, is also an indispensable component of the sustainable development evaluation of resettlement.

Resource sub-system

Indicators of human resources. The engineering construction works have taken up a large amount of land resources. Meanwhile, a large number of land-less peasants has been displaced. This has resulted in a high population density in migrant relocation areas. Furthermore, the population is still increasing. It is an ordeal for the resettlement areas to accommodate an extra large population with limited environmental capacity. The indicator of population size becomes the key to evaluating whether the resettlement option meets the requirements of sustainable development. In addition, whether the literacy levels of the inhabitants and the population structure meet the requirements of the optimum human resources quality and structure is also an important component of human resource indicators. In general, these indicators include the population size, the literacy level and the population structure.

Indicators of natural resources. Sustainable development is based on the sustainable utilization of natural resources. The resettlement of land-less peasants must meet the prerequisites of water resources carrying capacity and land resources carrying capacity. The water, land and mineral resources must also be protected and exploited efficiently. According to the situation of the land-less peasant resettlement area, the water and power resources, land resources and mineral resources are adopted as evaluation indicators for natural resources.

Environmental sub-system

Indicators of residential environment. Economic compensation and secured employment and education for land-less peasants do not guarantee sustainable resettlement. Another type of factor which needs to be considered is, whether the land-less peasants have a secure place of residence. The living space per capita and the infrastructure input per capita can be taken as evaluation indicators.

Indicators of environment protection. At the core of sustainable development lies the harmonized development of the economy, society and environment. Sustainable development cannot exist without environment protection. The water pollution index, air pollution index and noise pollution index obtained from environmental monitoring can be used as evaluation indicators.

Conclusion

The impacts of three typical resettlement types on land-less peasants were analyzed and the indicator system of sustainable development evaluation was proposed previously. In this way, two optimum resettlement concepts presented themselves:

Concept I is to carry out sustainable development evaluation of all the Jiangning land-less peasants and to select the resettlement option with the optimum value according to the evaluation results of the different resettlements. Concept II is to carry out the evaluation of different groups, one by one, under different resettlement conditions, to select the optimum resettlement type for each group, and finally to adopt combined resettlement options for different groups, i.e. the resettlement option for elders, youngsters, women and children are selected. This sustainable development concept can be applied to the planning, monitoring and evaluation of the land-less peasants' resettlement in general engineering construction projects.

References

Bao, Haijun 鲍海君 and Wu, Cifang 吴次芳 (2002) "Lun shidi nongmin shehui baozhang tixi jianshe" 论失地农民社会保障体系建设 [Study on construction of social security of land-less peasants], in *Guanli shijie* 管理世界 [Management World]. 2002 (10), pp. 37-42.

Cernea, Michael M. (1998) *Yimin – chongjian – fazhan: shijie yinhang yimin zhengce yu jingyan yanjiu* 移民·重建·发展——世界银行移民政策与经验研究（二）[Resettlement, reconstruction and development: study on resettlement policy and experience of World Bank (2)], Nanjing: Hehai daxue chubanshe 河海大学出版社 [Hohai University Press].

Cernea, Michael M. (2002) "Fengxian, baozhang he chongjian: yizhong yimin anzhi moxing" 风险、保障和重建：一种移民安置模型 [Risk, security and reconstuction: a resettlement option], in *Hehai daxue xuebao* 河海大学学报（哲学社会科学版）[Hohai University Transaction (Philosophy and Social Science Edition)], 2002 (6), pp. 3-17.

Chang, Jinxiong 常进雄 (2004) „Chengshihua jincheng zhong shidi nongmin heli liyi baozhang yanjiu" 城市化进程中失地农民合理利益保障研究 [Reasonable security of rights of land-less peasants in the course of urbanization], in *Zhongguo ruan kexue* 中国软科学 [China Soft Science], 2004 (3), pp. 5-10.

Deng, Peiquan 邓培全; Tan, Caitian 谈采田; Shao, Dongguo 邵东国 (2003) Shuiku yimin kechixu fazhan moshi yu shijian 水库移民可持续发展模式与实践 [Sustainable development option and practice of reservoir resettlement], Zhengzhou: Huanghe shuili chubanshe 黄河水利出版社 [Yellow River Water Conservancy Press].

Fang, Quanyao 方泉尧; Xu, Hesen 徐和森; Shi, Guoqing 施国庆 (2004) *Gongcheng yimin zheng hetong lun* 工程移民整合通论 [Summarization of integration of project resettlers], Beijing: Renmin chubanshe 人民出版社 [People's Press].

Gao, Yong 高勇 (2004) "Chengshihua jincheng zhong shidi nongmin wenti tantao" 城市化进程中失地农民问题探讨 [Study on land-less peasants in the course of urbanization], in *Jingji xuejia* 经济学家 [Economist], 2004 (1), pp. 47-51.

Hu, Zuoliang 户作亮; Chen, Shaojun 陈绍军; Zhang, Junsheng 张俊生; Xu Jiajun 许佳君 et al. (2004) *Shuiku yimin anzhi yu guanli* 水库移民安置与管理 [Rehabilitation and management of reservoir resettlement], Yinchuan: Ningxia Renmin Chubanshe 宁夏人民出版社 [Ningxia People's Press].

Ji, Mingfeng 冀名峰 (2004) "Guanyu jiejue nongmin shidi shiye wenti de jidian sikao" 关于解决农民失地失业问题的几点思考 [Thinking about resolving the problem of losing the land and unemployment of peasants], in *Nongye jingji Wenti* 农业经济问题 [Agricultural Economy Problem], 2004 (5), pp. 13-16.

Li, Yahua 李亚华 (2004) "Jiejue shidi nongmin baozhang wenti de jidian sikao" 解决失地农民保障问题的几点思考 [Thinking about resolving the problem of security of land-less peasants], in *Wuhan daxue xuebao (zhexue shehui kexue bian)* 武汉大学学报（哲学社会科学版） [Wuhan University Transaction (Philosophy and Social Science Edition)], 2004(3), pp. 358-363.

Ma, Chi 马驰 and Zhang, Rong 张荣 (2004) „Chengshihua jincheng zhong shidi nongmin de quanyi baohu" 城市化进程中失地农民的权益保护 [Right protection of land-less peasants in the course of urbanization], in *Nongye jingji* 农业经济 [Agricultural Economy], 2004 (3), pp. 48-49.

Shi, Guoqing 施国庆 (1996) *Shuiku yimin xitong guihua lilun yu yingyong* 水库移民系统规划理论与应用 [Programming theory and application of reservoir resettlement system], Nanjing: Hehai daxue chubanshe 河海大学出版社 [Hohai University Press].

Shi, Guoqing 施国庆; Chen, Shaojun 陈绍军; Yuan, Ruhua 袁汝华; Hu, Weisong 胡维松 (1996) "Shuiku yimin shengchan shenghuo shuiping fenjin yu pingjia fangfa" 水库移民生产生活水平分析与评价方法 [The analysis method for productivity and living standards of immigrant in settlement], in *Shuili xuebao* 水利学报 [Water Conservancy Transaction], 1996 (2), pp. 51-55.

Song, Binwen 宋斌文 and Jing, Wei 荆玮 (2004) "Chengshihua jincheng zhong shidi nongmin shehui baozhang wenti yanjiu" 城市化进程中失地农民社会保障问题研究 [Study on the social security of land-less peasants in the course of urbanization], in *Lilun tantao* 理论探讨 [Theoretic Discussion], 2004 (3), pp. 51-52.

Tang, Chuanli 唐传利 and Shi, Guoqing 施国庆 (2002) *Yimin yu shehui fazhan guoji yantaohui lunwen ji* 移民与社会发展国际研讨会论文集 [A collection of theses of workshop of resettlement and social development], Nanjing: Hehai daxue chubanshe 河海大学出版社 [Hohai University Press].

Wang, Huimin 王慧敏 (2000) "Liuyu kechixu fazhan xitong lilun yu fangfa" 流域可持续发展系统理论与方法 [Theory and method of sustainable development of drainage area], Nanjing: Hehai daxue chubanshe河海大学出版社 [Hohai University Press].

Yang, Wenjian 杨文健 (2004) *Zhongguo shuiku nongcun yimin anzhi moshi yanjiu.*中国水库农村移民安置模式研究 [Study on the rehabilitation option of reservoir rural resettlers in China], Kunming: Yunnan meishu chubanshe 云南美术出版社 [Yunnan Art Press].

Ye, Wenhu 叶文虎 (2001) *Kechixu fazhan yinlun* 可持续发展引论 [Introduction of Sustainable Development], Beijing: Gaodeng jiaoyu chubanshe 高等教育出版社 [Advanced Education Press].

Zhang, Shouzheng 张寿正 (2004) "Guangyu chengshihua guocheng zhong nongmin shidi wenti de sikao" 关于城市化过程中农民失地问题的思考 [Thinking about the problems of peasants loosing their land in the course of urbanization], in *Zhongguo nongcun jingji* 中国农村经济 [China Rural Economy], 2004 (2), pp. 44-49.

Involuntary Resettlement in Urban Areas – Development of Human Capital

Han Zhenyan, Dong Liyi and Zhou Ying

Human capital theory

Formation of human capital theory

The concept of human capital was derived from economics as a theory in the 1950s and has been evolving continuously since that time. Schultz (1990[1960]: 234)[1] indicated that the source of economic growth should rely more on an increase in human capabilities, rather than only on an increase in material investment in the labour force. Human capital is the integration of health, knowledge, experience, skills and intelligence reflected in human beings through investment in education, training, health care, etc. It emphasizes the use of human resources in the productive process. When human resources are used as means of profit-making, there is a connotation with human capital, and the carrier, in this case, the labour force, is the real owner of the human capital. That is to say that "human capital" is defined from the perspective of the "value" of economic activities, and the emphasis is placed on the "value" and "society."

The characteristics of human capital

The human capital theory, as Schultz perceives, is something unique in labourers themselves; it differs from material capital and is "seen as the result of investment"(ibid.). Human capital is formed through acquiring external "investment" in education, training and healthcare. Apart from sharing the basic characteristics of human resources such as initiative, time effectiveness, intelligence, and reproducability, human capital has the following characteristics as a kind of "capital:"

Human capital is the current value generated by a particular investment. The form of capital that exists in the human body as capability and knowledge is the real labour force, and the labour force does not appear initially in the form of capital. The focus is on "repayment" for the capability obtained.

Human capital is naturally "inseparable" from its owner. Human capital always belongs to the owner, and the "ownership is unique." The excess profit of human capital must be realized through giving full play to the subjective initiative of human beings themselves. Once the property rights of human capital are damaged, the capital may be devalued or vanish immediately. Human capital must have an

---

[1] Originally, the American economist and Nobel Prize winner, Theodore W. Schultz, introduced the concept of "human capital investment" at the American Economics Academic Society Annual Meeting in 1960; published as: Schultz, Theodore W. (1961) "Investment in Human Capital," in *American Economic Review* 51, pp. 1-17.

owner and the owner can only be the individual. It is naturally embedded in the bodies of individual labourers and is always seeking market opportunities for self-realization. Theodore W. Schultz also pointed out that the distinguishable symbol of human capital is that it belongs to human beings, and that no one can separate human capital from its owner. The owner will always carry his own human capital, no matter whether it is used for production or consumption. It is exactly this distinguishable characteristic which separates the right of utilization of human capital and the right of its ownership, and results in bringing about its commercial reputation. This reflects the private nature of human capital.

Human capital has the characteristic of increasing capital in terms of value. This is the key to turning the labour force into human capital. People invest in labourers because human capital, like material capital, is expected to bring profits. To use human capital is to make use of its knowledge and skills, and a value beyond itself can be created through its use. The value of the labour force can be increased through accumulated labour experience or self-improvement. This is described in detail in Marx's "On Capital."

Labour force itself is not capital, and can only be transformed into capital as a kind of economic resource when combined with the means of production and turned into the "life body" that executes the value-adding function. (Yan/Xu 1999)

Human capital does not only have the characteristic of increasing profits by itself; it can also lead to a progressive increase in the profit of money capital and other essential factors of production.

The time effectiveness of human capital. The value of human capital lies in the time effectiveness of the knowledge and skills contained in its owner, that is, the effectiveness of human capital is strictly limited by time. Normally, intellectual achievement and technical expertise can only be brought into full play within a certain period, and the effectiveness will be reduced by the replacement of the product life cycle itself, the general improvement of social science and technology and competitors' involvement. Some human capital will lose the ability to gain profit at a certain stage.

The variability and reproducability of human capital. Human capital, in the first place, is a kind of capability embedded in the labourers themselves. After being educated and trained, the degree of improvement in capabilities, intelligence and skills in different labourers will be different, because they vary in quality, working capabilities, skills and proficiency. In a different social environment and psychological state, the extent to which the capabilities of human capital can be brought into play may vary greatly. Meanwhile, human capital can renew its knowledge and continue innovating through the accumulation of labour experience and self-improvement, thus acquiring reproducibility and overcoming the constraints and limits resulting from its time effectiveness.

Human capital has its savings and increments. The human capital deposit is the knowledge, skills, experience and intelligence at a certain point in time; and the increments are the knowledge, skills, experience and intelligence increased over a certain period. The deposit of human capital determines the qualification for gaining employment, and the increments of human capital determine the qualification for starting businesses and being promoted.

Type of human capital required for economic growth

Today, with the market economy and the ever-changing environment of the New Economy, human capital exceeds other types of capital in its role of promoting the economic growth. In economic activities, human beings continuously make huge investments of resources in production in order to manufacture various goods to meet market demands; they also develop and improve their intelligence, physical strength and moral character, by various means, in order to achieve higher productive capabilities. Combined with material capital, human capital becomes a kind of prerequisite for development and the production of wealth. Human capital is important because material capital cannot produce any wealth without human capital. Without good human capital, material capital is a pile of dead machines and factory buildings, no matter how good these are. For economic growth, the role of human capital is more important than that of material capital. Investment in human capital is in direct proportion to national income and increases more rapidly than material capital. In the 1960s, famous economists, such as Schultz and Baker, used human capital to explain the reasons for America's economic growth, concluding that human capital played an important role in promoting economic growth; this initiated the human capital revolution. More and more people are now paying attention to the quality improvement of human capital and the role it plays.

Generally speaking, human capital can be divided into three types according to its different functions in economic growth, i.e. common human capital, professional human capital and entrepreneur human capital, in view of the conditions of its formation, capabilities and corresponding role in the social labour division.

Common human capital. This refers to the human capital possessed by individuals before they start work. It is acquired through common living experience and education, which enables them to master simple, day-to-day, standard and routine operations, and complete work which is ordinary, less innovative and relatively easy to measure. Generally speaking, the more education people receive the more common human capital they can obtain. The relevant common knowledge which a labour force possesses is applicable to any profession anywhere. Represented as homogeneity, it reflects the commonality of human capital. It mainly consists of physical or normal work with no risks taken and its results and performance can be observed and measured. Scattered through all kinds of enterprises and professions, this type of human capital is the basic force to promote social and economic development.

Professional human capital. This refers to the special skills obtained by individuals in their work through an increase in working experience, which varies greatly in different jobs. So the special knowledge a labour force possesses can only play its role in the corresponding job or type of work. The education and training involved takes much longer, as does the acquisition of special knowledge and the practice of different technical skills and abilities to become innovative.

In the knowledge society, with the development of the Internet, computer technology and biotechnology, all kinds of new creations are speeding up economic development. The common and special types of knowledge are constantly chosen by each and every industry and profession, and people with high levels of technical capabilities are preferred.

Entrepreneur human capital. The main function of entrepreneur human capital is to innovate in the fields of organization, marketing, institutions and products, etc. People with entrepreneur human capital have relatively outstanding capabilities regarding the disposition of resources, the discovery of new opportunities, and insights into the development of enterprises, management and coordination. With their strong will to succeed in business start-ups, a hard-working spirit, good interpersonal communication skills and extraordinary capabilities in the fields of organization and management, these individuals are the main initiators and the driving force of social and economic development and change. As a special human capital, entrepreneur human capital can integrate the other two types of human capital and promote economic and social development.

Current situation and changes in human capital in involuntary resettlement

As a kind of resettlement, involuntary resettlement (*fei ziyuan yimin* 非自愿移民)[2] has the characteristics of forcibility, irreversibility, thoroughness, and compensation and concentration in regions and time. In China involuntary resettlement occurs mainly in rural areas, for example, the resettlers from the Shanxi key water control project area in Wenzhou, Zhejiang Province mainly came from a mountainous area, which is economically backward and impoverished, to the coastal flatlands in the east of Wenzhou which has a convenient transportation system, a perfect infrastructure and a relatively well-developed commodity economy. After they had come to the city, the human capital of the resettlers faced challenges and has changed greatly along with the changes in social and economic conditions and environment.

---

[2] Resettlement can be divided into two types: voluntary and involuntary resettlement. Involuntary resettlers have no choice but to move because of project construction, ecological environment protection, social conflict, natural disasters, etc., and the resettled families have no right to choose whether to move or not.

Human capital condition before the resettlers left the reservoir area in Wenzhou

Before resettlement, the involuntary migrants of the Wenzhou reservoir area lived mostly in Wencheng County and Taishun County, which are located in the mountainous area in the south of Wenzhou, Zhejiang Province and the western mountainous area in Rui'an City, which were all national key poverty counties with a backward economy. There was a low household income and people lived in poverty over a long period of time due to the constraints of the natural environment. The dominant sources of production were agriculture and forestry. Their labour experience and skills were simply related to farming, vegetable-growing, tree-planting, sand-excavation, brick-making, bamboo-cutting, mushroom-collecting and tea-picking, etc. The quality of human resources was generally low. With little investment in education, they seldom participated in any technical training or self-study and their educational levels were generally very low. The statistics of the survey on the Wenzhou resettlement show that 12.7 per cent of the resettlers were illiterate; 10.7 per cent did not finish primary school; 24.7 per cent were primary school graduates; 11.45 per cent did not finish junior middle school; 23.4 per cent were junior middle school graduates; 2.3 per cent did not finish senior high school; 12 per cent were senior high school graduates; 2.3 per cent were secondary specialized school graduates and 0.3 per cent were college graduates. They have fewer opportunities and scope for self-development. The value of their human capital is low.

Changes in human capital after the involuntary resettlement from the Wenzhou reservoir

The market economy has been developing rapidly in Wenzhou in recent years. It is highly urbanized and has developed a brisk business life. The proportion of the tertiary industry is increasing progressively and the three industries are developing in a coordinated manner. The income of urban and rural residents has increased rapidly and their living conditions are continuously improving. The involuntary resettlers have faced differences in the economic environment, market conditions, production modes and life styles since migrating to the city. In order to orient themselves in the city as quickly as possible, their human capital has seen huge changes, which are detailed below:

The basis on which the resettlers rely for their survival has shifted from land to human capital. Although they have settled down on the coastal flatlands in the east of Wenzhou where a commodity economy and prosperous market have developed, quite a lot of resettled families from the reservoir area in Wenzhou have lost the land on which they relied to make a living. The developed urban economy has made it necessary for them to change their ideas regarding production and making a living. They have had to study new technical skills and become actively engaged in the secondary and tertiary sectors, seeking ways and means to earn a livelihood through bringing human capital into play.

The labour experience and skills of the resettlers have changed a lot. With the complete change in the sources of livelihood and in the nature of their work as a result of their resettlement, the labour experiences and technical skills of many resettlers have become useless, and reality has forced them to gain new life knowledge and labour skills. The survey has revealed that 16 per cent of the resettlers think the original techniques they had are of a little help in their current work; 25.5 per cent think they are basically of little help and 13.2 per cent think they are of no help at all. The previous production skills and experience gained from sand-excavating, brick-making, bamboo-cutting, mushroom-collecting, tea-picking, farming, vegetable-growing and tree-planting are now basically useless. In the meantime, the resettlers need to study new living and production skills, such as computer technology, electrical home appliance repairing, sweater and bag knitting, transportation, construction and doing business. This clearly demonstrates the differences in human capital required by different modes of production and life styles before and since resettlement.

The investment in human capital by the resettlers has greatly increased. The real economic life requires them to learn new knowledge of life and labour skills as soon as possible to guarantee their earning a basic livelihood. They have to seek opportunities for development on the basis of their common human capital, and this has forced some resettlers to begin focusing on investment in human capital by actively participating in all kinds of training courses held by the government or by taking the initiative to study, in order to improve their professional capital and develop production through improving their own quality and relying on science and technology. The investment in education by the resettlers has increased remarkably. Monitoring the statistics on the expenditure of the resettlers from the Shanxi Reservoir on cultural education, medical care and consumption in April, 2004, showed that expenditure on cultural education accounted for 2.3 per cent to 13.85 per cent of the total net income, and that per capita expenditure on education was 288.90 RMB per year (eight per cent of the total expenditure), of which the minimum was 111.11 RMB per capita per year and the maximum was 668.53 RMB per capita per year. This increase in expenditure on education implies that the educational and cultural level of the resettlers will improve in line with the increase in investment on education and that they have realized the importance of knowledge which can help them to improve the value of human capital. Another change indicated by the statistics from the questionnaire survey was that the resettlers have also taken an active part in various kinds of training. The survey conducted by the authors of this paper in 2004 revealed that, in answer to the question "How much time would you like to spend on training, if you had the opportunity?," 19.3 per cent of the resettlers surveyed said that they would spend much time and 66.1 per cent said that they would spend a little time. In answer to the question, "How much money would you like to spend on training, if you had the opportunity to receive training?," 6.4 per cent said that they would spend a lot of money and 71.6 per cent said that they would spend a little money.

The resettlers have more opportunities and rooms for individual development now, since their resettlement. They have more opportunities for employment and development, because the city they have moved to has a highly developed commodity economy with secondary and tertiary sectors, and the government has provided favourable policies and strong support for the resettlers to develop the economy. The questionnaire on the resettlers in Wenzhou showed that 11.2 per cent agreed that they currently have many more opportunities for re-education and training compared with the situation before they were resettled, and 30.5 per cent thought that the opportunities have increased just a little bit. Their individual value will be increased along with the increase in opportunities for re-education and training. In answer to the question, "Are there more or fewer opportunities for making money than before the resettlement?," 5.8 per cent of the interviewees said that there are many more opportunities and 28.5 per cent said that there are some more. In answer to the question, "Are there more or fewer opportunities for employment than before the migration?," 3.6 per cent said that they have many more opportunities, while 28.8 per cent said that they have some more and 14.4 per cent said that the situation is roughly the same.

The value of women has increased to some extent, compared with the investment value of men. There were 18,559 women among the resettlers from the Shanxi key water control project area, among them 7,794 were the female labour force, which made up 42 per cent of the total labour force. The questionnaire revealed that 76.6 per cent of the interviewees were male while 23.4 per cent were female. When asked what changes had occurred in their own current production and living conditions, most of the females answered that they were not only an important part of the labour force in their households, but also the main sources of their family income. There were 18 resettlers among the workers in the Hongji Plastic-Spinning Craft Co., Ltd in Cangnan County; 80 to 90 per cent of the workers were women with a monthly salary of 900 – 1000 RMB . In Yongjia County, the female labour force can earn more than ten RMB per day by processing materials provided by their customers at home. This never happened to them when they were living in the mountainous area before they were resettled. In addition, the female resettlers have become more conscious of themselves since they were moved and have begun to focus on improving their self-values and starting their own businesses in order to explore a way of their own.

The human capital in different groups of resettlers has changed. The numbers of the resettlers from Shanxi are large and their age span is wide. There are big differences in economic conditions and technical skills among them as well.[3] The changes in human capital will thus differ among different groups of resettlers.

---

[3] See also the contribution of Chen Shaojun and Zhang Runsen in this volume on resettlement impacts on different demographic groups of involuntary resettlers.

Human capital also changes differently at different ages. With regard to the age structure of the interviewees, 13.5 per cent were aged under 30; 29 per cent were aged between 30 and 40; 31.8 per cent were aged between 40 and 50, 12.8 per cent were aged between 50 and 60; 7.5 per cent were aged between 60 and 70 and 5.4 per cent were aged over. Young people, with their strong social adaptability, find it easier to accept advanced technology and ideas, and to master all kinds of skills in order to gain employment and the means to earn a living; their human capital has relatively more opportunities for change and has shown a greater increase in value since they were resettled. Middle-aged people are in the next best position and the elderly come last. As for the children, their human capital has the greatest scope for increase, since they are receiving education in school. There were 6,134 people aged under 16 (minors) among the resettlers from the Shanxi key water control project area, amounting to 16.49 per cent of the total population. Today, the studying and living conditions of minors (those under 16) have been greatly changed and improved. In 2003, the per capita net income among the resettlers from the Shanxi key water control project area reached 4,851 RMB. In comparison, the national rural per capita net income of that year was 2,622 RMB.

The original difference in economic conditions, knowledge and skills among the resettlers has had a direct impact on the changes in their human capital. Before they were resettled, some of the resettlers already had better economic conditions and stable jobs, while others who had relatively lower cultural and technical levels and a weak economic basis did not know what to do. Their professional capital has changed since they migrated as a result of the changes in production modes and their jobs. For the former, resettlement has had little impact on the changes in their human capital, but for the latter, resettlement has had a fundamental impact on the changes in their human capital. Among them, most of the resettlers have been able to increase their human capital through training and study and have adapted themselves to the local social and economic situation since settling down, but there are still some disadvantaged groups (the special groups of resettlers, who are less capable of taking part in the competitive market and gaining employment, and, have a lower or unsteady income due to the economic, cultural and age factors since resettlement), whose human capital has relatively fewer opportunities for increase.

Development and exploration of involuntary resettlers' human capital in urban areas

Today's society is characterized by knowledge globalization. Knowledge has become the productive force, the competitive power and the key factor for economic development. Human capital, with investment in education as its key, has become the core of social and economic development as physical labour is replaced by mental labour. The development and accumulation of the human capital of the resettlers must be emphasized and scaled up in order to increase the reproduction of their human capital as soon as possible and to get the most out of it.

The key to developing the human capital of the migrants is to invest in their intelligence development. According to the human capital theory, it is known that any activities to improve the quality and capabilities of the individual and increase the knowledge deposit, skills and health of the individual can be seen as an investment in human capital. The investment covers many aspects, including education and training, medical care, the mobilization of the labour force, etc. Among these, investment in education and training is the main aspect and the most important means of human investment. Investment in education should not treat the reproduction of human capital as a kind of consumption but as a kind of investment, since the economic benefits from this investment are far more than those deriving from material investment. It can improve the overall labour force quality, and the skills and proficiency of the resettlers, so that economic growth can be promoted and the resettlers can really be merged into local social and economic activities. Investment in medical care is also an important aspect of human capital. This can lower mortality rates and increase the number of future labourers; it can strengthen the physique of the labourers and improve their labour capabilities.

To improve the planning for the post-resettlement support and to strengthen the implementation of human capital development. With the arrival of the knowledge economy, the industrial structure and consumption patterns in the city have been changed thoroughly; the quality of the resettled labourers cannot meet the standards of knowledge and skills required for the current status of sustainable economic development. Quite a lot of migrant labourers have become unemployed, because they cannot meet the requirements of modern careers that require more and more skills. At the same time, there is a shortage of personnel with the special skills required for local economic development and there are not enough skilled labourers to meet the needs of the economic structure adjustment. The current situation of a low human capital deposit has therefore become a "bottleneck" in the further oriented resettlement development and it is imperative that the development of human capital should be intensified.

To adopt diversified means for the development and accumulation of resettlers' human capital. According to the human capital theory, human capital accumulation is the process of obtaining and increasing the storage and experience of skills, information and knowledge and improving the quality of the individual. Human capital is generated by human investment through investment mainly in education, training, healthcare and labour force mobilization. We must therefore make overall plans and arrangements and take all factors into consideration for the development and accumulation of resettlers' human capital. Multidimensional and diversified investment in the education, training, medical healthcare, and mobilization of the resettlers must be made in order to increase the human capital accumulation, so that their knowledge deposit, skills and health can be increased, their comprehensive quality and capabilities can be improved and the value of their human capital can be raised. Investment in education is an essential aspect of human capital investment. The process of human capital accumulation is the process of the labour force receiving education and training. If other factors remain unchanged, the longer and higher the education received, the greater will be the human capital deposit gained, and the accumulation of the quantity of human capital will lead to a qualitative leap. The qualitative improvement of human capital is the origin of technological and institutional innovation as well as the sustained driving force for economic growth.

To explore the development and accumulation of resettlers' human capital with multi-access and multi-resources. From the perspective of the socialization degree of human capital, the investment and benefit of human capital is of an integrated, private, organized and social nature. The channels for investment in human capital are diversified and include at least three: investment by individual or family (private); investment by enterprise or organization (e.g. job training, etc.) and investment by society (various sources provided by government or public institutions). Since the resettlers in Wenzhou are involuntary resettlers and have generally low economic capabilities, outdated ideas and backward cultural and technical standards, the present source for the development and accumulation of their human capital should rely mainly on the investment by society and enterprise or organization. The departments responsible need to make full use of the supporting funds for the post-resettlement activities. In addition, society and the recruiting units should be mobilized to invest in the resettlers and provide support and assistance for their education and technical training as well. Meanwhile, propaganda must be strengthened intensively in order to mobilize the initiative and enthusiasm of the resettlers to participate in education and training, to make them "ask for study" instead of "being asked to study" and to develop self-investment and spontaneous study in all their lives.

To provide education and training at diversified levels and with a diversified content according to the different cultural and technical levels of the resettlers. Involuntary resettlement is a huge and complicated system, and most of the migrants, consisting of people of different levels with generally low cultural and technical levels, come from backward (mountainous) rural areas. The development of human capital must therefore be conducted in accordance with the characteristics of the different levels and structures of the resettlers. There are three main areas: the first is to focus on providing basic technical training for the resettlers labour force with low cultural and technical levels; the second is to focus on skills training, for the development of the secondary and tertiary sectors, for the resettlement labour force with medium cultural and technical levels; and the third is to focus on the systematic training of professional productive skills and social and economic management for the resettlement labour force with high cultural and technical levels to make them the leaders of economic development in the areas of resettlement.

To encourage diversified types of investment in education and training. Diversified types of investment in education and training will be adopted to meet the needs of the characteristics of the resettlers and economic development. One of the types is formal education and training and the other is informal education and training. The former mainly includes long or short-term education and training in colleges and secondary specialized schools; the establishment of well-equipped educational and training bases; technical training conducted by enterprises, organizations and the employing units themselves. The latter mainly refers to the spare-time education and training organized by society; "learning by doing;" on-the-spot operations and coaching; experience exchange and self-training, etc. Training modes of combining technical training with professional training, quality training with pre-job training, vocational training with training to increase employment opportunities, and the training mode of combining long with short-term training at high, medium and low levels will be developed gradually.

To improve the managerial system for the development of resettlers' human capital. Perfecting and improving the managerial system can ensure the effective development and accumulation of the resettlers' human capital. Based on the Migration Settlement Office of the government, relevant internal agencies have been established in the departments of labour, education and health to support and cooperate with each other and make overall planning for balanced development. Efficient market operating mechanisms will be established and implemented with transparent policies, standardised systems, accessible information, funds open to the public, reduced intermediate links, timely feedback and orderly management. The resources will be organized and allocated in accordance with the employment information and the needs of the migrants themselves, and regular or non-regular education and training will be organized for the resettlers.

The female labour force among the resettled people is also precious human capital and they are becoming the main force in the resettlers' economic development. To increase investment in the human capital of female resettlers, to improve their overall qualities, to increase the level of their human capital deposit and accumulation and to solve various problems related to family, child care and health that prevent them from gaining employment are priority issues which need to be addressed urgently.

References

Henan Huashui Zixun Fuwu Gongsi 河南华水咨询服务公司 [Huashui consulting service company of Henan] (2004) *Zhongguo – Zhejiang – Wenzhou – Shanxi shuili shuniu gongcheng yimin jiance pinggu baogao* 中国·浙江温州珊溪水利枢纽工程移民监测评估报告（第12期）[The monitoring and accessing report of the water control project Shanxi, Wenzhou, Zhejiang (12th edition)], March 2004.

Hu, Angang et al. 胡鞍钢等 (2003) "Daguo xingshuai renli ziyuan kaifa 大国兴衰与人力资源开发 [The rise and decline of big country and human resources development], in *Jiaoyu Fazhan Yanjiu* 教育发展研究 [Research on Educational Development], 2003(4-5), p. 5.

Schultz, Theodore W. (1990[1960]) *The Investment in Human Capital,* translated by Xu Guojun et al., Beijing: Bejing Economic College Publishing House.

Yan, Wuda 阎五达 and Xu, Guojun 徐国君 (1999) "Renli ziben de lilun yu yingyong de ji ge wenti" 人力资本的理论与应用的几个问题 [Some problems of the theory of human capital and application], in *Kuaiji yanjiu* 会计研究 [Accounting Research], 1999 (6).

Zhang, Jijiao 张继焦 (2004) *Chengshi de shiying - qianyizhe de jiuye yu chuangye* 城市的适应—迁移者的就业与创业 [Adaptation to the city – employment and business start-ups of resettlers], Beijing: Shangwu yin shuguan商务印书馆[Commercial Press], May 2004.

Zhang, Yili 张一力 (2005) "Cong renli ziben jiegou kan quyu jingji fazhan moshi de xuanze" 从人力资本结构看区域经济发展模式的选择 [The choice of the development model of regional economy from the perspective of the human capital structure], in *Jingjixue dongtai* 经济学动态 [Economic tendency], 2005(7).

Zhejiang sheng Wenzhou shi yimin anzhi bangongshi 浙江省温州市移民安置办公室 [Resettlement and Allocation Office of Wenzhou in Zhejiang Province] (2004) *Zhongguo – Zhejiang – Wenzhou – Shanxi shuili shuniu gongcheng yimin gongzuo zuidong baogao* 中国·浙江·温州珊溪水利枢纽工程移民工作最终报告 [The final working report on resettlement in water control project of Shanxi in Wenzhou,·Zhejiang, China], April 2004.

Zhejiang sheng Wenzhou shi yimin anzhi bangongshi 浙江省温州市移民安置办公室 [Resettlement and Allocation Office of Wenzhou in Zhejiang Province] (n.d.) *Zhongguo – Zhejiang – Wenzhou – Shanxi shuili shuniu gongcheng yimin houqi fuchi jihua* 中国·浙江·温州珊溪水利枢纽工程移民后期扶持规划 [Post supporting plan the water control project Shanxi ,Wenzhou of Zhejiang, China].

Index

Page references in bold indicate figures and tables.

"40, 50s" 34, 60, 223
"2003-2010 National Migrant Workers' Training Plan" 102
accidents 75, 158, 202; *see also* injuries
accommodation 66, 123, 141-2, 236
adaptation 22; cultural 142, 146; economic 13, 142; level of 146; psychological 13, 146; social 13
adaptability 24, 140-1; *see also* migrants
administration 100, 103; *see also* government, system
Administrative Criminal Law (HK) 157
advertisement 82, 150
advertising 150
Africa 187
age: and retirement 25; *see also* elderly, employment, migration, youngsters
agenda: political 97
agriculture 38, 78, 100, 281
AIDS 200
All-China Federation of Trade Unions 106, 168, 239
All-China Women's Federation 106-7, 148, 181-2, 184, 208, 222, 239
All-China Youth League 106, 148, 239
allocation: administrative 27; planned 26; of resources 82; *see also* labour, job
allowance(s) 39, 100
Anhui Province 72, 91-2, 252; Fuyang District 90, 93-4
Appleton, Simon 169, 259
areas: labour demand 103, 105; labour supply 102-3; rural 26-7, 30, 32, 38, 65, 68, 70, 100, 103, 113-15, 120, 175, 199, 219, 246; underdeveloped 90; urban 10, 12, 30, 65, 101, 115, 175, 199, 219, 246
Asia Pacific region 187
Asia Foundation 107
assimilation 137, 146
Aus-Aid 222
Australia 188
Australian National University 182

balance 10, 19, 59-60; of work and family life 41
Bartelheimer, Peter 163
Bates College 182
behaviour 22
Beijing 84, 114, 146, 166, 181-2
Beijing University 182
Benxi 208-10
benefit 25; economic 72; environmental 66; social 13, 66; of peasants workers 60; short-term 113; *see also* cost-benefit of migration
Beynon, Louise 79
Blau, Peter 129
brain: drain 89; re-drain 90, 96
bread-winner 40, 119, 261
brokerage 84
business: development 94; development services 14, 228-42; incubation 222; individual 14; opportunity 78; small 123; start 73, 89-90, 92; start-ups 11, 14, 209-10, 220-7, 247, 280; start-up models 222-5; support services 15

cadres 94, 107
Cai, Fang 114, 169
campaign: "competent worker" 147
capital 59, 170; concentration 179; constraints 93; financial 93; intensive 57, 93; and labour relationships 60; shortage of 104; social 93, 255; usage 103; *see also* human capital
capitalism 22
career: development 113, 123-4
"cash cows" 94-5
Castel, Robert 163
CCTV 238
change: demographic 37, 40; institutional 19; pathway to 24; technological 20
charity supermarket 149
Cheng, Duosheng 41
Chengdu 116, 123, 230, 232, 236-8; Labour Bureau 232

290

children 15, 120, 255, 270, 272, 274; see also education, migrants
China Statistical Yearbook 253
China City Statistical Yearbook 253
China's People's Political Consultative Conference 140
Chinese Academy of Social Sciences (CASS) 34, 182
Chinese Communist Party: 16th National Congress 105, 154; Central Committee 153
Chinese Criminal Law 157
Chinese leadership 24, 30, 33; see also leadership
Chinese National Bureau of Statistics 33, 182, 199, 252
Chinese National Labour Law 28, 39, 42
Chongqing 182, 252
cities 14, 58, 60, 65, 67, 90, 140, 150
citizens 97, 148: Chinese 11; "First Class" 150; "Second Class" 150; urban 61, 146, 155, 161, 168, 172
citizenship 126: urban 43
civil society see society
civilization 158
class: working 140, 148
clothing 153
commune 26, 27
communication: problems 72; ways of 146
community 146-8; situation 122
Community Training Project for Young Migrant Workers 106
competition 38, 58, 94, 178
competitiveness 60, 106
competitor 43, 278: global 44
conditions: of employment 25, 30, 165; of living 16, 72, 81, **117**, 118, 158, 168, 172, 199, 226; local 93; working 19, 75, 81, 84, 117, 172; see also labour conditions
consumption 142-4; level of 44, 71; pattern of 285
contractors 82
contracts: temporary 75; see also work
control 100: of population mobility 25; socio-political 20, 22, 25-8, 44
cooperation: foreign 105; international 101
cooperatives: producers' 162
coordination 24

cost-benefit see migration
costs 10, 126, 145, 189; of adjustment 15; cultural 72; of energy fuels 58; -free 144; hidden 144; of land 58; monetary 66; non-economic 72; non-monetary 66; opportunity 66, 126, 257; psychological 66, 72, 126; of raw material 58; reducing 157; social 72; subsistence 69, 71; for training 240; for transportation 68; see also expenditure, fees, labour, migrant worker, migration, production
countryside see rural areas
credibility: lack of 83
credit 90; micro- 209, 222; see also market, loans
cultural: elements 25; see also migrants, life
Czech Republic 261-4

Dalian 190
danwei see work unit
decentralization 95: political 94
demand: intrinsic 14
demographics 11, 31, 60, 91-2, 232-4; see also change
Deng Xiaoping 10
Deutsche Gesellschaft für Technische Zusammenarbeit (GTZ) 208
development 57: economic 59-61, 65, 71, 95, 104, 140, 217, 284; export-driven 10; individual 76; interventions 16; level 71; opportunities 76; personal 227; rural 89, 93, 95; scientific 60; social 60, 71; strategy of 38, 96, 213; technical 186; see also business
developing countries 58-9
digital gap 186
directives 95
discrimination 190-1, 208, 270; see also peasant worker, social exclusion
dismissal see workers
divide: rural-urban 10, 25
Dongguan 55-6, 65
donors 149
dual economic structure 66, 68, 71
dual-sector model 59

East Asia 58
Eastern European countries 21

291

economic: growth 10, 19, 89, 277, 279; information 72; restructuring 13, 65; structure 14, 53; reform 30, 43; stability 119; status 66; system 43; theories 21; *see also* development, productivity
economy 43: Chinese 59, 153; global 43; informal 82, 162, 195-203; local 104, 106; modernising 19; planned 21, 24; private 32, 168; restructuring of 20; "shadow" 162; transition 20; urban 43
education 11, 15, 25, 38, 58, 60, 73, 75-6, 93, 123-4, 126, 130, 132-4, 137, 142-3, 145, 154, **197**, 242, 254, 287; children's 100, 115, 128, 251; cultural 147, 282; elementary 130; high school 33, 43, 123, 132, 146, 281; higher 29; investment in 38, 282, 285; level of 59, 93, 130, 144, 224; lifelong 38; standard of 67; system 22, 26, 29, 43, 51, 102; tertiary 26, 38, 233; *see also* policy, training
efficiency 25, 61, 158
elderly 15, 23, 26, 116, 127, 268-70, 272, 274
employability 24
employees 38, 55, 101, 154, 157, 162, 214; blue-collar 180, 190-1; formal 39; grey-collar 191; qualified 37; rights of 148; white-collar 82, 190-1; young 37; *see also* workers
employers 24, 38, 82, 86, 145, 154, 157, 162
employment 10, 13, 20, 28, **35**, 38, 51, 60, 65, 67, 81, 86, 100, 119, 145, 226, 228; and age 178; agencies 34, 37; attitude 113; atypical 24, 37, 41 172, 43; change 27; channel 13; decentralized 175; dispatched 175; diversified 175; duration 164; elastic 175, 177; and endangerment 162-3; external 81; flexible 30, 41, 175-8, 180, 184; formal 11, 40, 43, **166**, 185, 187, 201; full 23, 155; full-time 178; gender structure of **181**; growth rate 31; hardship 53, 55; inadequate 176-7; industrial 75; informal 10-12, 27, 41, 75, 161-5, **166**, 167-72, 175, **176**, 177-91, 197, 199, 201; information 136; information release system 72; legal 241; life long 19, 39, 251; non-agricultural 55; non-planned 27; non-standard 41, 178; opportunity 51-5, 134, 155, 181, 183, 239, 287; "other" 37; paid 15; part-time 23, 175; permanent 23; planned 27; population 31; rate 20; re- 13-15, 34, 40, 42, 161, 169, 182, 220-1, 251, 253, 257-9, 262; regime 11, 22, 25, 30; registration 83, 247; relations 23; relationship 39, 163-4; restrictions on 37; rights 155; risk 75; rural 37, 248; seasonal 175-6; security 24, 163; self- 23, 27-8; 32, 37, 41, 75, 81, 119, 166, 175-7, 189, 221, 230; shocks 40; staggered 177; standards 163; status 20, 162, 169; strategy 44; structure 43, 210, 216; system 26, 58, 246; temporary 41, 123, 175-7; "three-zone" concept of **163**; transfer 58; typical 43; under- 33, 55; urban 31-2, 37, 161, 168, 248; *see also* conditions, fee, gender, labour, ownership, policy, unemployment, work
endangerment *see* employment
enterprises 26, 37-8, 40, 43, 57, 58, 60, 101, 145, 147, 158, 189: collective-owned 32, 41, 85, 95; foreign funded 38, 85, 214; individually-owned 85, 162, 221, 230; large and medium sized 14, 42, 166; micro- 81, 166, 189; public 15, 251; private-owned 32, 37, 39, 93, 148, 162, 214, 226; in rural areas 32; small and medium sized 14, 42, 175, 220, 222, 229; state-owned (SOE) 21, 25, 30, 32-3, 38-9, 42, 43, 54, 75, 85, 94-5, 177-80, 182, 207, 213-14; town and village (TVE) 32, 37, 41, 73, 90, 94-6
entertainment 94, 144, 238-9
entrepreneurs 12, 66; *see also* migrant returnees
entrepreneurship 15, 228, 237, 241-2; "myth" of 89, 96; returnee 90, 93-5; stars of 90
environment 273: unfamiliar urban 72
equality 157-8
etnic minorities 234
Europe 19
European Union 188
Eurostats 188
exclusion 11, 162-3, 172; social 12, 24; *see also* employment, workforce

expenditure 66, 128; of migration journey 68; of production and living 67-70; *see also* costs, fees
export: processing industries 10

factors: institutional 15
fairness 61; *see also* social fairness
family 14, 22, 40, 60, 182, 251; barycentre 115; composition 93; decisions 116; dual earner 26, 28; ethics 115; extended 117; of husband 80, 86; law 26; leaving the 71; and marriage system 79; members 81, 115, 117, 120, 153; modes **118**, 119; net 26, 80; nuclear 29, 117, 137; order 43; relation 79; separation 116; size of 117; stem 117; strategies 86; system 25; ties 86; unwritten agreements of 115; *see also* kin, migrants, policy
farming 70, 93, 281-2
fees 82, 94, 155, 165, 189, 241; certification 68-9; communication 68; employment information 67, 69; flat 81; management 103; regulation 67; training 67, 69, 240; tuition 102, 105
feminization 15, 180, 251; *see also* informal employment, poverty
filial piety 26
financial: aid 134; situation **255**; transfer 89
flexibility 11, 19, 23, 25, 27-8, 43; *see also* labour market
flexicurity 11, 24
food 66, 123, 142, 153, 235; insecurity 266
foreign: direct investment 10; investment 19; investors 30; trade 10; *see also* enterprises
forestry 281
fragmentation *see* labour market
France 213
freelancer 41, 165
Fujian Province 11
funds 100

Gansu Province 252
GDP: of China 201, 213-14; of France 213
gender 76, 85, 93, 126-8, 178, 184-6, 192, 196, 210, 233; determents of differences 15, 251, 258; dimension 11; disparities 15, 251-64; inequality 15, 216; order 22; perspective 13, 79, 175-91, 202, segregation 185; structure of employment **181**; *see also* informal employment, female migrants, unemployment, women
German Criminal Code 157
Germany 157, 167, 208, 211
Giles, John 33-4, 40
Gini coefficient 213, 214
globalization 10, 14, 22, 27, 44, 57, 179-80, 183, 186, 284
governance 156
government 34, 39, 59, 71, 95, 100-2, 106, 146-8, 156-7, 187, 197, 198, 207-8, 212-13, 220-1, 246-7, 282-3, 287; administration 75, 100, 155; agencies 82, 287; capacity 158; central 43, 71, 89-90, 100, 102, 105, 140; Chinese 14, 19, 38, 58, 97, 172, 195, 208, 216, 228; departments 52, 100; fiscal budget of 100; hotlines 104; intentions 41; local 13-14, 39, 43, 57, 89, 90, 94, 100, 103, 105, 195, 220; policy 12, 83, 145, 189; services 100; township 95
Granovetter, Marc 80, 127, 129
groups: disadvantaged 157, 181, 184, 191, 284; internal 143; "marginal" 23; pressure 149; relieve 149; standards of 141; stronger 24; weak(er) 24, 31, 42-44; vulnerable 11
growth 57; *see also* economic growth
Gu, Edward 39, 44
Guangdong Province 11, 50, 53-8, 61, 104, 107-8, 170, 252; Department of Public Security 56
Guangzhou 55, 84
guanxi: networks 37
Guizhou Province 252
Guo, Hiumin 186, 187

Ham, John C. 261
Harbin 182
harmonious (socialist) society 41, 57, 151
hardships 78
health 15, 158, 254; system 201
Hebei Province 252
Heidenreich, Martin 23
Heilongjiang Province 252
Henan Province 68-9, 72; Xinyang City 107
hinterland 90
HK Amity Foundation 150

Hohehot 182
homelessness 266
homesickness 72
Hong Kong 10, 157, 212;
Hotline: "12333" for labour security 101; "12351" for assistance on workers' rights 106
household 76, 78, 92, 251; budget 15, 251; decision 115; helpers 41; registration system 13, 22, 25, 28, 37-8, 75, 79, 96-7, 114, 126, 155, 161, 166-9, 172, 195, 233; private 22; strategy 79, 85; *see also* income, workers
housing 25, 128, 234
Hu, Angang 31-2, 181
Hu, Jintao 40, 153, 195; *see also* leadership
Huang, Guangguo 129
Huang, Huahua 56
Hubei Province 252
hukou-system *see* household registration system
human: capital 21, 42, 89, 147, 190, 254, 277-87; resources 21, 155, 270

identity *see* labour, migration
illiteracy 281
ILO *see* International Labour Organization
image: political 106
immobility 26
impoverishment: risk of 15-16
inclusion *see* welfare programs, population, women, work
income 24, 38, 42, 65, 68-9, 127-8, 132-4, 141-2, 153, 165, 175, **199**, 203, 224, 235, 248, 257, 272; gap 75, 184-6; household 15, 251; level 70, 198; and migration decision 71; national 279; non-monetary 68; property 255; rural 19, 38, 43; side 235; tax 41, 162; urban 38
individualism 127
individuals 14, 42, 76-7, 86, 285; and responsibility 158
industrial relations 43
industrialization 19, 27, 44, 89; pathway 31
industry 57-8, **256**; catering 75; coal mining 92; commerce 75; construction 11, 14, 75, 228-42; consultancy 165; finance 32, 183, 221; food processing 93; gastronomy 14, 228-42; insurance 32; knowledge 41; labour intensive 19; manufacturing 75, 186; mining 32; quarrying 32; private 27; production 11; public 27; real estate trade 32; restructuring 57; retail 93, 183; service 75, 93, 183; state 75; telecommunications 183; textile 171; tourism 183; traditional 32, transport 93
inequality 25
informal employment *see* employment
informal sector *see* sector
informal work *see* work
information 11, 27, 73, 86, 90, 144; channel 76, 82-3; legal 148; publicly available 84; technology 165; *see also* economic, social
infrastructure 90, 94
injuries 71, 92
Inner Mongolia: Chifeng City 107
innovations 21
Institue for Labour Studies 232
institutional: arrangements 22; change 156; legacies 21; innovations 286; patterns 22; set 30; vacuum 21
institutions 11, 19-20, 25; informal 37; interplay of 22; political 26, set of 21, 43; social 27; types of 84; *see also* job placement, labour market
insurance 41, 75, 191, 203; health or medical 40, 57, 128, 185, 189, **200**, 201; pension 40, 57, **200**, 201, 247; private 26; social 60, 105, 165, **185**, 189; work injury 57; unemployment 40, 57; *see also* industry, reform
integration *see* labour market, migrants
International Labour Organization (ILO) 101, 162, 175, 179-80, 187, 190, 197, 226, 229, 251
Internet 82, 280; bars 144
investment 94, 148, 224; capacity 235; environment 106; *see also* education
"iron rice bowl" 25, 154, 221

Japan 187-8
Jiangsu Province 16, 68, 69, 72, 73, 252; Hual'an City 90, Xuzhou 179
Jiangxi Province 94
Jilin Province 214, 252
Jinhua City 150

job: allocation 32; atypical 31, 42-3; career 80; changing of 37, 42, 83; counselling 208; creation 14; distribution **198**; duration 38; entry 37, 168; first 38, 80, 85, 86, 136; full-time 23; high-tech 43; hunting 68, 82; information 11, 75; initial 76; lifelong job tenure 27; mobility 28; opportunities 14, **80**; part-time 178; placement 80-1; placement institutions 37; precarious 163; prestige 164; searching strategy 75-6, **80**, 82, 84-5; security 13, 24, 75, 232; seekers 34, 215-16; selection 68; subsequent 76; temporary 178; transitions 23; *see also* employment, training, work

Kaplan-Meier survival estimates **258**
kin: networks 26, 28; order 22; reciprocity 26; -ship 25, 199; -smen 81
Knight, John 33, 37-8, 169
knowledge 14, 147, 277-9, 282, 284-5
Konrad Adenauer Foundation 227

labour: allocation 28, 39, 57, 78; bureaus 25, 203; conditions 12, 42; consuming production 25; concentration 179; contract system 39; contracts 39, 165, 177, 186, 203; costs 10, 58, 60, 106, 202-3; demand 10, 257, 259; division of 86; exchange 42; flexible form of 75; flow 38, **257**; force 11, 20, 23, 33-4, **36**, 37, 41, 44, 51, 54-8, 60, 65, 67, 91, 100, 179, 248, 286; household 92; and identity 178; intensive 23, 44, 57-8, 72; -to-land-ratio 76; laws 83, 162; mobility 10-11, 13, 37-8, 81, 89, 201; new ways of 60; optimization 39; participation 21; prices 58; problems 54; process 25, 28; recruitment 56; redistribution of 30, 31; redundancy 25, 53; relations 12, 24, 34, 39-41, 189; retain peasant 96; retrenchment 15, 251; risk 76; security 100, 247; services 100; shortage 57-8, 170; shortfall of 11; situation 53; skilled 94; standards 75, 179; state 32; supply 10, 58-9, 102, 104; surplus 11, 65; system 10, 19, 21, 37, 58; transfer 44; turnover 38; unions 22, 106, 107; *see also* area, labour market, labour regime; migration, population, reform, women, workforce

labour market 10, 14, 21, 31, 40-2, 58, 82, 113, 117, 191, 195, 251, 257; binary 126; changes 22; demand 29, 82, 215; diversification of 89; dual 42; effectiveness of 20; emerging 75; entering the 14; entrants 36, 43; expansion 37; external 24, 27, 43; first 164; flexibility 20, 41, 179; fluctuations 58; fragmentation 13, 172; in China 10, 24, 27, 37; inclusion 20; innovation of 104; institutions 22, 30; integrated 10, 207, 219; integration of urban and local 15, 161-72; internal 24, 27; management of 104; monopolization 70; parameters 19; policy 13, 15, 19, 83, 207-19; process 20; regime 19; regulated 156; research 21, 41; "retro strategy" 19; security 20; segmentation 13, 38, 75, 161, 164-6, **167**, 169, **170**, 171-2, 175-91, 241; segments 21, 42; segregation 161-172; self-adjustment of 59; single 22; standardization of 59, 104, 156; structure 15, 164; supply 82; systemization of 104; theories 20; theorists 20; unified 11, 40; urban 10, 113-14, 168; *see also* gender, reform, women
labour regime 11, 20, 22, **23**, 25, **29**, 42, 232; socialist (SLR) 20, 24-7, 43, 44; "socialist" market (SMLR) 19, 28, 30, 43-4; *see also* labour market
laid-off *see* workers, unemployment, *xiagang*-concept
landlessness 16, 266
land 95: acquisition 90; collectivisation of 27; cultivation 113; farm- 10; industrial use of 10, 246; shortage 78
Latin America 187
law 156
leader 81
leadership 195; Hu-Wen 41; secure of 172
Lee, Everett S. 65
legal: framework 108, 153; protection 42, 199; rights 97; system 83, 156
legislation: lack of positive 75
Lewis, W. Arthur 59
Li, Minghuan 81-2, 84
Li, Peng 90
Li, Qiang 166, 180
Liaoning Province 252

liberalization 44, 169; *see also* household registration system
libaries 149
life: cultural 142, 145-6; planning 79; quality of 145; style 140-3; social 143; urban 73, 76, 151, 198
livelihoods 59, 282; secure of 16; strategy 241; sustainable 16
living standard 44, 267
loans 94-5; *see also* credit
Luhmann, Niklas 163
Lutz, Burkart 21
luxury 142, 144

Mallee, Hein 78
management: experience 93; positions 43; service-oriented 155; techniques 90; *see also* fees, labour market, (social) risk
manufacturing 10
market 76: credit 94-5; dual 22; economy 11, 21, 30, 156, 281; external 37; forces 38; imperfections 26; information 94, 136; opportunity 73; order 153; system 10; transition 15, 251; world 30, 218; *see also* reform, socialist market economy
marketing 221, 225, 280
marriage 14, 115, 220; plans 86; patrilocal system of 80, 86; *see also* migrants
Marx, Karl 35, 278
media 106, 128, 150; mass- 35, 228, 242
medical treatment 153; system 247
metropolises 81
migrant workers 11, 15, 57, 69, 72-3, 75, 97, 100, 105, 120, 147, 166, 179, 195-203, 228-42; benefit level of 71; demands 103; family modes of 116, **118**, 119, 122, 123; flow of 66, 69-71; floating experience of 119, 121-2; generations 77; rights 11, 100, 154; services for 12, 102-3, 146, 150; shortage 65, 70, 105, 147; "task force" for 116; temporary 41; tide 65, 96, 115; *see also* family, migrants, peasant worker
migrants 10-11, 13-14, 19, 28, 33-5, 37-9, 41-3, 75-6, 82, 96, 172: and acquaintances 129, 134; and children 12, 92, 119-121, 136, 203; choices 76, 83; couples 114; cultural life of 140-150; families 12, 82, 85, 91, 114, 116, 143-4, 153-4; and family pattern 113; female 76-7, 79-80, 84, 92, 143, 149, 198-202, 236, 283, 287; flow of 89-90; and friends 82, 129, 134; groups of 81; and husbands 79; integration of 14, 140; leaving hometowns 81-2; male 81, 84, 92; and marriage 79-80, 91; and parents 79, 83, 92, 120; residential quarters for 104; returnees 12, 89, 93, 95, 237-8; returning to hometowns 65, 71, 73, 83, 90-1, 115-16, 121, 123, 153; and relatives 80, 82, 129, 133-4, 144; rights 11, 219; single 143; skilled 90; social activities of 136; and spare time activities 142-6; and spouse 79, 83, 115, 119-20, 122, 129, 136; and "townspeople" 129; 132-5, 137; unmarried 119; and wives 79, 120; *see also* family, life(style), migrant workers, networks, payment, (re)settlement, wages
Migrants Options Theory 65
migration 43, 56, 84, 86, 179, 219, 248: and adaptation 66, 141; and age **77**, 92, 118, **120**, 127-8, 132, **195**; benefits 65-7, 70; chain- 37, 94, 198; choices 113, **121**; control 26; cost-benefit analysis of 65-73; cost-benefit rate 67-71; costs 65-7, 70; cross-provincial flow of 65, 105; cross-regional flow of 65; "cultural" 140; and culture 66, decision 65, 76, 78, **79**, 83, 115-16; family 124; and family modes **120**; and family strategy 78; flow and volume of 91; "free space" for 126; "free resources" for 126; and future planning 121, 123; and hometowns 67; and identity 66, 187; individual 126; international mass 10; involuntary 280-1, 284; labour 79; and martial status 118; model 115; motivation 69-70, 76, **77**, 79; phases 91; process 113, 123; quantitative estimates 37; re- 93, 96; regional 28; research 115, 122, 127; return 12-13, 89-92, 96, 238; reverse chain- 94; and sending region 89; spatial 140; strategies 10; rural-to-urban 28, 36-7, 113, 126, 166, 202; target destination of 83; *see also* family, gender, job, population, pull factors, push factors, settlement
Migration Settlement Office 287
mini firms 23
Ministry of Agriculture 65, 92, 216

Ministry of Civil Affairs 195
Ministry of Commerce 222
Ministry of Construction 101
Ministry of Education 101, 216
Ministry of Finance 101
Ministry of Foreign Trade & Economic Cooperation (MOFTEC) 222
Ministry of Labour and Social Security (MOLSS) 14, 33, 39-40, 53, 101, 168, 178-9, 189, 208, 214-15, 220, 228-30, 232, 242
Ministry of Land and Resources 266
Ministry of Personnel 216
Ministry of Science and Technology 101
mismatches 20, 28
mobility 20, 23, 25, 28, 38, 43, 78, 83-4; barriers to 38; cross-regional 40; initial 84; inter-enterprise 36; subsequent 84; *see also* job, social mobility
modernity: adapt to 128
modernization 44; agents of 90; rural 90; theory 89; urban 146
money: sending back home of 114; *see also* remittance
monitoring and evaluation system (M&E) 217
mortality 266
Muffels, Ruud 23
multi-national corporations 12, 100

Nanjing 13, 68, 129, 134-7, 182, 208-10, 246, 248; Jiangning County/District 16, 266-74, Labour and Social Security Bureau 15, 246-8
Nanjing University 142-5
Narendranathan, Wiji 258
National People's Congress 90, 104, 140, 148
neighbourhood committee 247
Netherlands 188, 210
networks: personal 75, 81-2, 86; social 13, 72-3, 75, 80, 83, 122, 126-9, **129-30**, 132-3, 136-7, 198, 255, 259; social relations 71; structures 127; ties 129, 135, **136**, 137
networking activities 81
new institutionalists 21
newspapers 82, 238-9

non-governmental organizations (NGOs) 12, 14, 100, 106, 108, 150, 202, 220, 226

occupation 187, **256**
Organisation of Economic Co-operation and Development (OECD) 179; countries 188
organizations 104; formal 104; people's 148; social 148
Oschmianski: Frank 163; Heidi 163
overtime 57; rate 72
ownership 15, 32, 37, 236, 255, **256**, 278; *see also* enterprises, reform
Oxfam HK 150

participation 156, 197
party 148; membership 255, 261; policies 145; responsibility of 37; state 39
past-dependency 39
payment 190; delayed 13, 70-1, 84, 153-8; legal guarantee of 13; overdue 140; *see also* income, prices, wages
"Peaceful Working" Campaign for Migrant Workers 106
Pearl River Delta 11, 65, 70, 104, 147, 238
peasant worker 50, 56, 60; discrimination of 71-2, 92, 167; scarcity of 50; self-discrimination of 71; shortage 50-1, 53, 55-6, 59; surplus 57; tide 55-6, 96; *see also* benefits, (migrant) workers
peasants 66-7, 70, 100-1, 103, 113; mentality 113; psychology 113; who lost their land 11, 15, 247, 266-74, **268-9, 271**; *see also* unemployment
pensions 26, 168, 268; system 40, 216; *see also* insurance, policy, reform
perceptions 22
personnel: decisions 39; lack of 170; policies 25
performance: individual 38
"phoenixes returning home to their nests" 89, 93, 95
placement 11; agencies 34; *see also* services
policy 15, 153, 187; design of 86; economic 20, 211; educational 11, 20; employment 11, 246-8; family 11, 20, 28, 37; family planning 53; financial 32; fiscal 210; implementation 71; industrial 32; macro-100, 105; one-child 37, 215; opening up

44; pension 211; public 15; social 11, 140; technology 211; *see also* labour market
political: correctness 108; protection 44
Political Consultative Committee 148
pollution 94
population 20, 37, 44, 61, 273; aging 40; of China 50, 59; density 140; development 53; floating 50, 114-16, 140; inclusion of 26; inflow 56; labour 58; migration 105; mortality rate model 50; registered 53; rural 51, 212; structure 50; urban 19, 26, 215; urbanization of rural 51, 53, 55, 60-1; *see also* working age population
poverty: anti- schemes 95; in countryside 78; feminization of urban 15, 251; reduction 89, 228; (new) urban 19, 33
prices: income 21; real estate 10; of wages 21; for work 21
privatization 27-8
product: life cycle 278; quality 94
production: brigades 25; costs 189; factors 65; modern 42; planning 25; process 41; regime 21-2, 43; rural 67; strategies 21, 26, 44; structure 58
productive: competitor 42; forces 19
productivity 23, 44; control of 113; high 30-1; low 31, 94; sectors 31; *see also* social
profitability 58
profits 58, 69-70
Project Hope 106
promotion 113
propaganda 286
pull factors 78-9, 92
push factors 78-9, 92
"putting people first" concept 57, 60, 105

qualification 21, 38, 76, 167; demand 29: level of 20, 38, 42; type 20

rationalisation 20
recreation 144
recruitment 57; agencies 82; conditions 83; notices 84; programs 82; *see also* job
reform: of administrative system 154; economic 30, 37, 113; fiscal 94-5; of health system 40; of labour market 11, 13, 19, 30, 38, 44, 259; of labour system 10, 40; market 179, 183; and opening period 54, 65;

of ownership 15, 251; of pension system 40; period 27; policy 95; price 97; rural 32; tax 97; wage 38; of welfare regime 40
regime 23; change 28; performance 23; trajectory 27; *see also* employment, labour, production, productivity, welfare
regions 59
regulations: of state 21
relations: non-government 104
relocation 16
remittance 236
resettlement 267, **268-9**, 270, **271**, 274, 277-287; involuntary 11, 16, 277-87; willingness 13; *see also* settlement
residence 12; duration 132-4, 136; marginal 126; permanent 34, 104-5; permits 178, 187; temporary 34, 129; urban 38, 40, 114, 144, 154; *see also* household registration
resources 26-7, 95, 127; financial 218, 223, 235; natural 273
restructuring 43, 126, 178-9, 182-3, 246; industrial 36, 251; of public sector 28; of state-owned enterprises 33-4
retirees 168, 169, 179
retirement 272; age 40, 51; benefits 25; early 40, 216; regular 25; regulations 43
return migration *see* migration
revenue 94, 218
rights *see* employment, migrant workers, women, workers
risk(s) 26, 28, 83, 93, 71, 225; individual 26, 83; protection 82, 86; *see also* employment, impoverishment, labour, social risk management
rural "aristocrats" 93
rural migrants *see* migrants
rural workers *see* migrant workers

safety: net 75; *see also* work
salary 101, 140, 195, 198, 215, 231; *see also* payment
SARS epidemic 108
savings 235-6
schooling 12, 26, 120, 149, 261
Schultz, Theodore W. 65-6, 277-9
sector: agricultural 65; commercial 81; formal 13, 32, 34, 75, 161, 183, 186; highly productive 32, 44; industrial 158; informal

13, 27, 41-2, 75, 161-2, 175, 186, 195; non-agricultural 102; non-state 14; primary 32, 183; private 15, 28, 37-8, 84-5, 95, 214, 229, 264; public 25, 27-8, 183; rural 51; secondary 32, 65, 96, 183, 282-3, 286; service 19, 41, 81, 183; state 32, 38, 166, 168; technologically advanced 44; tertiary 32, 65, 96, 182-3, 213, 253, 282-3, 286; urban 51

security 11, 19, 23, 24, 31, 42-3, 187, 270; contract 21; land-based 158; legal 44; *see also* employment, labour market, social security

segmentation: indicators of 37; process 21; *see also* labour market

segments 38: primary 21; secondary 21; *see also* labour market, sector

Sengenberger, Werner 21

seniority 38

separation 137

service(s) *see* business development, industry, migrant workers, sector

settlement: choices 126-7; plans 234; strategies 237; willingness 127, 129, **131**, 132-3, **134**, 135-7; *see also* resettlement

settling down 12, 113, 123, 241; in cities 116; in rural areas

sexual harassment 186-7

Shaanxi Study Group 223

Shandong Province: Huantai County 90

Shanghai 40, 79, 84, 114, 164, 171, 175, 195-203, 223; Bureau of Statistics 183; Department of Labour and Social Security 175, 178, 197; model 222, 224-5; Trade Union 148

Shangluo 223-4; model 222, 224-5

Shanxi Province 252; key water control project 280-284, 286

Shenyang 182

Shenzhen 55-6

Sichuan Province 14, 90-2, 228-42; Jintang County 107

"Sino-US Labour Legal Cooperation Project" 101

skills 37, 40, 93-4, 167, 171, 188, 235, 272, 277-8, 280- 2, 285

Slovac Republic 264

social: advancement 37; barriers 165; exclusion 114, 186, 190; fairness 60; harmony 20; information 72; instability 43; intercourse 141, 143; mobility 84, 96; mobilization 107; order 154; position 84; prestige 25, 165, 167, 237; productivity 141; protection 41, 162, 190, 195-202, **201**, 202-3; psychology 141; relations 141; regulations 72; responsibility 147; risk 86; risk management 75-86, ; role 141; safety net 10-11, 264; stability 104, 153-4, 178; status 66; structure 65, 122-3, 127; system 114; ties 86, 128, **135**; *see also* benefits, insurance, life, network, policy, organization; social security

social security 19, 42, 44, 60, 68, 157, 172, 190-1, 203, 272; reform of 40, 213; regulations 43; system 26, 57, 86, 105, 195-6, 199, 202, 212

socialism 251

socialist: countries 27; elements 25; ideology 25-6; market economy 28, 44, 60, 155; normal work pattern (SNWP) 25, 27, 39, 43; *see also* harmonious society; labour regime, society

socialization 141, 270

society 14, 59, 65, 76, 220, 226-7, 277; Chinese 97, 207; circles of 107; civil 106, 227; legal 156; market 10; planned 10; processes in 21; socialist 150; urban 123; Western 21, 41; *see also* harmonious society

sociological approaches 21

Solinger, Dorothy 166, 171

Song, Lina 37, 38, 169

Southeast Asia 58

special economic zones 97

sponsorship 90, 94, 95

sports 147, 149

Spring Festival 72, 121, 154

"Spring Wind Action" 100

"Start and Improve Your Business" (SIYB) program 101, 228-30, **231**, 232-42

"Start Your Business" program (SYB) 226

state 28, 76, 86; agencies 95; central 95; local 94

State Council 102, 153, 168, 202

status: economic 128; in employment 13, 15; of floaters 114; marital 93, 134, 252, 262; socio-economic 126-28, 130, 132-3, 136-7; residential 199; structures 127; *see also* social status
stigmatization 167
street vendor 165
structuralist school 89
students 26
subsidies 25, 40, 103, 195, 199, 202
Sunshine Project 101-3
support: communication 135; emotional 135
sustainable development 16, 60, 153, 266-70, **271**, 272-4; *see also* livelihood
synchronisation 24
system: administrative 154-5; local political 90; planning 11, 30, 40, 44; state-support 39; urban 60; *see also* economic, education, employment, family, legal, labour, labour market, pension, welfare

Taiwan 10
Taiyuan 182
talent 90
tax 90, 95; *see also* reform, income
teams 25
technology 94, 278; *see also* information
tendering 217
"territoriality principle": in social administration 104
think-tanks: Chinese 19
"three agricultural/rural problems" 97, 154
Tianjin 182; model 222, 224, 225
Todaro, M.P. 65; Population Migration Model 65, 126
"townspeople" *see* migrants
trade unions 26, 28, 43-4, 148, 227
tradition 25: patterns of 22
traditional mechanisms 37; *see also guanxi*
trainees 102
training 14-15, 24-5, 29, 51, 58, 60, 90, 100, 103, 107, 147, 191, 203, 208-9, 226, 228, 234, 240, 247, 259, 272; computer 240; certificates 102; expenses for 101; external 27; job preparatory 26; programs 208, 226; re- 27, 102; subsidized 102; technical 145, 286-7; vocational 140, 215, 239-40, 287; *see also* fees, costs

Training Program for Labour Transfer in Poverty-Stricken Areas 101
transformation 10; of China 42; economy 13, 207, 211, 227; social 14, 227; *see also* market, society
transition 11, 21, 23, 36; countries 21; process 44; *see also* economy, market
transportation 66, 235; *see also* costs
Tros, Frank 24
trust: breach of 157; lack of 82
tuition *see* fees

unemployment 11, 13,-14, 20, 23-4, 27, 30, 35, 42-4, 161, 178, 187, 251; and age 33; definition 33; duration 15, 251-2, **253**, 254-9, **260**, 261, **262-3**, 264; formal 40; hidden 33; long-term 36; of peasants 11; rate 33, 212, 217; reduction 33; registered 33-4, 54-5; statistics 33; urban 15, 19, 37, 242; of women 11, 14, 36, 182, 220, 223, 251, 253, 264, ; *see also* employment, insurance, *xiagang*-concept
United Kingdom 188
United Nations Development Program 222
United States 187; Department of Labour 101
unqualified *see* workers
urbanites 25
urbanization 10, 57, 89, 123, 140-1, 146, 195, 213; policy 10; process 51; *see also* population

value(s) 21, 89, 141, 277, 278; of labour force 66
Vogel, Berthold 163
volunteers 107
"voting with their feet" 11

wage(s) 12, 21, 23, 25, 38, 42-4, 68-9, 75, 81, 84, 94, 169, 171, 198, 226, 255, 264; competitiveness of 58; level of 83; dumping 170; minimum rules for 43; reduced 70; overdue/withheld 13; 57, 153-8; *see also* payment
Wang, Chunguang 77
Wang, Meiyan 169
website: for rural women 107

welfare 14, 178, 187; arrangements 26; benefits 75; corporation 68; funds 94; programs: inclusion in 37, 75; provision 38, 44; public- 108; regime 22-3; state 27; system 24, 28, 40, 68, 126, 189; West European model 41; *see also* reform

"well-off society" 97, 146

Wen, Jiabao 40, 153; *see also* leadership

Wenzhou 280-4, 286; model 95

Wilthagen, Ton 24

women 11, 15, 85, 171, 207, 215, 220-7, 274, 283; employment of 175-92; emancipation 43; federations 106-7; inclusion of 23; married 116, 192; participation 43; reintegration of 207-10; rights 156, 186-7; rural 79, 107; services for 107; single 236; urban 14, 197; *see also* groups, migrants, unemployment, website

work: allocation monopoly 25; assignment 25; atypical 11, 20, 30, 34; contract 164, 175; contracted 28; demand 21; dependent 29; experience 93, 255; flexible 10, 24, 30; full-time 33; inclusion 22; informal 10, 20, 28, 34, 171; intensity 143; organization 185; normal pattern of 41; part-time 33; -place 41; precarious 23; permit 83; relationship 25; safety 21, 57; temping 210; unit (*danwei*) 25-7, 31, 38, 40, 43-4, 83, 144, 166, 199; *see also* employment, monopoly, training

workers: co- 84; contract-system- 39; dismissed 34, 43; factory 82; family 162; female 27, 30; flow of 11; flexible 41; formal 32; household 33; industrial 153; informal 37, 166, 202-3; laid-off 33-4, 40-3, 54, 60, 75, 161, 168-70, 207, 215-6, 252, 257; male 27; mentality 113; newly employed 39; older 30; permanent 39; reallocation 39; retrenched 13, 161; representation of 28; rights of 12, 19, 60, 84, 154, 157, 190; rural 101; shortage of (skilled) 57, surplus of 67; 59, 71; tele- 42; township enterprise 113; "-turned-peasants" 91; unqualified 30; urban 27, 32, 38; *see also* migrant workers, peasant worker

workforce 11, 26-7; exclusion 30; formal 28; immobile 44; mobile 43

working conditions *see* conditions

working: attitude 113; hours 41, 84, 144, 164, 176-7, 186, 235; process 103; purpose 113; "sisters" 96; "sons" 96-7; time 143; *see also* working age population

working age population 50-1, **52**, 53, **54**; annual 50; demand 52; indicator 51; ingoing 50-1, 53; net increase 50, 54; outgoing 50-3; registered 55; supply 51

World Bank 201

World Commission of Environment and Development 266

World Trade Organization 10

Wuhan 182

Wuxi 114, 115

Xi'an: model 223-5

xiagang-concept 39-40

Xia, Qingjie 169

Xin, Meng 83

Xue, Jinjun 33

Yang, Yiyong 22, 34, 36

Yang, Yunxin 31-3

Yangtze River Delta 65, 70

youngsters 15, 23, 26, 42, 116, 145, 269-70, 284

Zhao, Shukai 81

Zhejiang Province 11, 281

Zhong, Xiaoyun 170

Zhuhai 114-15

Berliner China-Studien
hrsg. von Prof. Dr. Mechthild Leutner
(Freie Universität Berlin)

Heike Frick
"Rettet die Kinder!"
Kinderliteratur und kulturelle Erneuerung in China, 1902–1946
In der Neuen Kulturbewegung erlebten die Debatten zu Kind und Kinderliteratur einen in der Geschichte Chinas einmaligen Höhepunkt. Kinder wurden als zentrale Ressource entdeckt, von deren Entwicklung das zukünftige Wohl der Gesellschaft abhing. Darüber hinaus diskutierten Literaten und Intellektuelle auch „Eigenrecht", „Wesen" und Bedeutung von Kindheit für das Individuum. Die dabei entwickelten Auffassungen hatten weitreichende Auswirkungen auf die zeitgenössischen Reformen der vorschulischen und schulischen Erziehung, auf das Verfassen von Kinderliteratur und auf die Überlegungen zu den kulturellen Grundlagen einer neuen Gesellschaftsordnung. Der in der Chinaforschung bislang unberücksichtigte Diskurs zu Kindheit und Kinderliteratur wird in vorliegendem Buch anhand ausgewählter theoretischer Texte von Zhou Zuoren (1885–1967), Ye Shengtao (1894–1988) und Tao Xingzhi (1891–1946) rekonstruiert.
Bd. 37, 2002, 288 S., 25,90 €, br.,
ISBN 3-8258-5166-4

Mechthild Leutner; Klaus Mühlhahn (Hg.)
Deutsch-chinesische Beziehungen im 19. Jahrhundert
Mission und Wirtschaft in interkultureller Perspektive
Im Kontext der neueren Imperialismusforschung kommt den Grundzügen und Charakteristika der Beziehungen zwischen europäischen und überseeischen Gesellschaften eine zentrale Rolle zu. Die Interaktionen zwischen indigener Bevölkerung und Vertretern fremder Mächte werden in dem vorliegenden Band am Beispiel deutscher Kaufleute und Missionare in China am Ende des neunzehnten Jahrhunderts untersucht. Die Deutschen standen im beruflichen wie auch im privaten Leben stets in Kontakt mit der sie umgebenden chinesischen Gesellschaft. Unabhängig von ihren spezifischen Interessen trafen sie auf eine Gesellschaft, deren soziale Ordnung und kulturelle Orientierung ihnen fremd war. Im Verlauf des imperialistischen Vordringens aber musste die deutsche Seite lernen, dass der Erfolg ihrer Tätigkeit in China davon abhing, ob es gelang, eine Möglichkeit zu Verhandlungen und Kompromissen mit der anderen Seite zu finden. Auch auf chinesischer Seite wurde danach gesucht, den Handlungsspielraum aktiv zu erweitern und eigene Prioritäten zu setzen. Der Band enthält sechs Studien zu den Interaktionen zwischen Deutschen und Chinesen, 1890–1910, die auf zugrunde liegende interkulturelle Handlungsmuster hin analysiert werden und ein neues Konzept zur Analyse interkultureller Beziehungen entwickeln.
Bd. 38, 2001, 408 S., 35,90 €, br.,
ISBN 3-8258-5736-0

Heike Schmidbauer
Aufbruch aus den Dörfern
Chinesische Migrantinnen zwischen Modernisierung und Marginalisierung
Eine schwerwiegende Folge der chinesischen Reformpolitik ist der bislang beispiellose Massenexodus vom Land in die Städte. Nicht nur männliche Migranten, sondern auch Millionen von jungen Frauen und Mädchen haben in den 80er und 90er Jahren ihre Heimatdörfer verlassen, um in den urbanen Zentren Chinas nach neuen Erwerbsmöglichkeiten Ausschau zu halten. Im Mittelpunkt der Untersuchung steht die Analyse der veränderten Beschäftigungs- und Lebenssituation dieser sogenannten "Arbeitsmädchen" oder *dagong mei*. Die Voraussetzungen für die massenhafte Abwanderung werden ebenso beleuchtet wie die Konsequenzen im Hinblick auf die soziale, ökonomische, familiäre und persönliche Stellung junger Landfrauen. Es zeigt sich, daß die Position von Migrantinnen im gegenwärtigen Transformationsprozeß in der

LIT Verlag Münster – Berlin – Hamburg – London   Wien
Fresnostr. 2 48159 Münster
Tel.: 0251 – 62 03 22 – Fax: 0251 – 23 19 72
e-Mail: vertrieb@lit-verlag.de – http://www.lit-verlag.de

VR China von tiefgreifenden Ambivalenzen und Widersprüchen geprägt ist.
Bd. 39, 2001, 200 S., 20,90 €, br.,
ISBN 3-8258-5385-3

Jens Hürter
Tang Caichang (1867 – 1900)
Reformer, Denker und Rebell in China an der Schwelle zur Moderne
Diese Monographie zur Lebens- und Gedankenwelt von Tang Caichang (1867 – 1900) stellt die erste gründlich recherchierte Studie zum Wirken dieser zentralen Persönlichkeit innerhalb der Reformbewegung des ausgehenden 19. Jahrhunderts in China dar. Tang Caichang – traditionell gebildet, interessiert an neuen Ideen, vielfältig aktiv und bemüht um angemessene Reformmöglichkeiten und deren Umsetzung – hat bisher in der sinologischen Literatur (im Osten und Westen) kaum Beachtung gefunden. Die Studie beinhaltet nicht nur eine erste und detaillierte Gesamtdarstellung von Tangs Leben und Wirken, sondern bietet zudem eine übersichtliche Diskussion seines komplexen und sich wandelnden Gedankengebäudes im historischen und persönlichen Kontext (Welt-und Geschichtsbild, Kritik an der chinesischen Gesellschaft, Einstellung zum Ausland), eine Werkanalyse sowie ein kritisches Werkverzeichnis. Das Buch liefert damit einen wichtigen Beitrag zu einem vertieften Verständnis des Reformprozesses in China im späten 19. Jahrhundert.
Bd. 40, 2002, 344 S., 17,90 €, br.,
ISBN 3-8258-5857-x

Joachim Krüger (Hg.)
Beiträge zur Geschichte der Beziehungen der DDR – VR China
Erinnerungen und Untersuchungen
Die Sammlung von Erinnerungen und Untersuchungen umfasst ein breites Spektrum der Beziehungen zwischen der DDR und der VR China über vier Jahrzehnte. In dieser Zeit „deutsch-chinesischer Beziehungen unter roter Fahne" war die DDR beinahe 25 Jahre lang alleiniger staatlicher Vertreter Deutschlands gegenüber der Volksrepublik. Mehrere Autoren beschreiben ihre Erlebnisse aus den fünfziger Jahren als Diplomaten oder Studenten. Untersuchungen zu den fünfziger und sechziger Jahren vermitteln ein Bild von der Breite und Intensität der Zusammenarbeit auf politischem, wirtschaftlichem und kulturellem Gebiet. Bisher kaum bekannte Probleme aus der Anfangsphase der Beziehungen werden behandelt. Die spezifische Position der DDR angesichts des sowjetisch-chinesischen Gegensatzes erfährt eine detaillierte Untersuchung. Sprachforschung, linguistische Ausbildung sowie Ausstellungsaktivitäten in der DDR zeugen von der Ausstrahlung und den bleibenden Ergebnissen der Zusammenarbeit auf staatlichem und nichtstaatlichem Gebiet.
Bd. 41, 2002, 264 S., 25,90 €, br.,
ISBN 3-8258-6149-x

Jens Damm
Homosexualität und Gesellschaft in Taiwan
1945 bis 1995
Diese Arbeit präsentiert erstmalig die sich rasch verändernde Sicht von gleichgeschlechtlicher Sexualität, Liebe und Partnerschaft in Taiwan von 1945 bis 1995. Der Diskurs der Homosexualität in den verschiedensten Medien wird vor dem Hintergrund traditioneller und moderner Sichtweisen erörtert. Medizinische Zeitschriften, literarische Werke und die Massenmedien werden ebenso einbezogen wie die „Untergrund"-Zeitschriften einer Homosexuellenbewegung, die sich in den Neunzigerjahren formierte. Die Ergebnisse zeigen, welche dramatischen Wandlungen sich in einem Zeitraum von nur einem halben Jahrhundert abspielten. Nach Zeiten der Dämonisierung und Kriminalisierung von Homosexualität entwickelte sich in der demokratischen Phase der Insel nach 1987 eine vollkommen neue Sicht: Toleranz gegenüber anderen Lebensformen wurde zu einem Maßstab für die „Freiheit" und „Moderne" der Insel, und das Genre der *queer literature* galt als Symbol für eine neue gesellschaftliche Offenheit. Exemplarisch wird verdeutlicht, dass Taiwan einen sehr eigenen Weg als „glokale" Gesellschaft geht.
Bd. 42, 2003, 288 S., 25,90 €, br.,
ISBN 3-8258-6674-2

LIT Verlag Münster – Berlin – Hamburg – London – Wien
Fresnostr. 2 48159 Münster
Tel.: 0251 – 62 032 22 – Fax: 0251 – 23 19 72
e-Mail: vertrieb@lit-verlag.de – http://www.lit-verlag.de

Martina Wobst
Die Kulturbeziehungen zwischen der DDR und der VR China 1949–1990
Kulturelle Diversität und politische Positionierung
Das Kaleidoskop des kulturellen Austauschs zwischen der DDR und der VR China weist trotz des starken politischen Einflusses ein breites Spektrum auf, das von der klassischen Kunst bis zu zeitgenössischen Tendenzen reicht, die mit der Tradition brachen und modernen Strömungen folgten. Wie sich der Kulturaustausch im Netzwerk der deutsch-chinesischen Beziehungen und im Spannungsfeld zwischen einer alten wechselseitigen Faszination, der Projektion von kommunistischen Zukunftshoffnungen und der zeitweise äußerst kritischen Sicht auf die politischen Entwicklungen im jeweils anderen Land entwickelte, zeigt diese erste größere Studie der Kulturbeziehungen zwischen der DDR und der VR China, die sich neben publizistischen und literarischen Quellen auf umfangreiches Archivmaterial stützt.
Bd. 43, 2004, 280 S., 29,90 €, br.,
ISBN 3-8258-7422-2

Mechthild Leutner;
Nicola Spakowski (Eds.)
Women in China
The Republican Period in Historical Perspective
The Chinese Republican period, often seen as representing a continuum between Imperial China and the People's Republic of China, was shaped by profound upheavals which also impacted strongly on gender relations. This volume presents the latest research on the situation of women during the Republican period, placing it in a historical perspective. In addition to contributions dealing with theoretical and methodological approaches to China-related women's research, a broad spectrum of experiences and discourses related to women in China is also considered: women and the state/women and the nation, political women and their posthumous careers, little traditions and discourses of otherness, women in social and economic life and women's education.
Bd. 44, 2005, 512 S., 59,90 €, br.,
ISBN 3-8258-8147-4

Susanne Kuß
Der Völkerbund und China
Technische Kooperation und deutsche Berater 1928–34
Als staatenübergreifende Organisation war der Völkerbund nicht nur auf dem Gebiet der Friedenssicherung tätig, sondern engagierte sich auch als „technische Arbeitsgemeinschaft" im sozioökonomischen, kulturellen und humanitären Bereich. Das mit Abstand ehrgeizigste Programm dieser Art war die technische Kooperation mit China, die in den Jahren zwischen 1928 und 1934 ihren Höhepunkt erreichte. Es handelte sich dabei um eine bis dahin unbekannte Form internationaler Zusammenarbeit, die im Rahmen einer Institution von staatlichen und individuellen Akteuren gestaltet wurde.
Bd. 45, 2005, 456 S., 39,90 €, br.,
ISBN 3-8258-8391-4

Berliner China-Hefte
Chinese History and Society
Edited by Mechthild Leutner (FU Berlin)

China and Modern Historiography
Bd. 26, 2004, 112 S., Jahresabonnement (2 Hefte) 25,00€ plus Versandkosten, Einzelheft 20,90€ plus Versandkosten, br.

Chinesische Literatur
Zum siebzigsten Geburtstag von Eva Müller. Herausgegeben von Mechthild Leutner und Jens Damm
Irmtraud Fessen-Henjes: *Laudatio zum 70. Geburtstag von Eva Müller*; Lutz Bieg: *Schriftenverzeichnis Eva Müller*; Wolfgang Kubin: *Ding Lings Yan'aner Erzählung „Die Nacht" (1940)*; Hans Kühner: *Von der (Un)Produktivität des Ressentiments in der Literatur. Einige aktuelle chinesische Beispiele*; Raoul Findeisen: *„Cherchez la femme": Eine kritische Hommage an die Schriftstellerin Zhang Zhaohe (1910–2003)*, Nach-

LIT Verlag Münster – Berlin – Hamburg – London – Wien
Fresnostr. 2 48159 Münster
Tel.: 0251 – 62 032 22 – Fax: 0251 – 23 19 72
e-Mail: vertrieb@lit-verlag.de – http://www.lit-verlag.de

lassverwalterin von Shen Congwen (1902–1988); Dorothee Dauber: *Blumen und Blüten als Spiegel der Frau in der klassischen chinesischen Lyrik*; Kathleen Wittek: *Chen Ran und Kafka – eine unilaterale freundschaftliche Beziehung*; Mechthild Leutner: *Richard Wilhelms chinesische Netzwerke: Von kolonialen Abhängigkeiten zur Gleichrangigkeit*; Andreas Steen: *„Im Frühjahr kehrt Lei Feng zurück!" – Zur gesellschaftlichen und politischen Relevanz eines „Mustersoldaten" in der Postmoderne*
Bd. 27, 2005, 144 S., Jahresabonnement (2 Hefte) 25,00€ plus Versandkosten, Einzelheft 20,90€ plus Versandkosten €, br., ISBN 3-8258-8434-1, ISSN 1860-2290

Bettina Gransow; Pál Nyíri; Shiaw-Chian Fong (Eds.)
China
New Faces of Ethnography
Twenty years ago, foreign researchers were just (or to be more exact: again) beginning to venture into China for fieldwork. Today, „the field" itself has become mobile, ephemeral and virtual as more research focuses on human mobility and communication. This issue of the Berliner China-Hefte takes a look at some of the trends and problems of fieldwork in and about China today, touching on issues that range from Internet research to sexual harassment in the field, foreign investors in China and Chinese tourists abroad as research subjects, and the role of social and poverty assessment in development.
Bd. 28, 2005, 168 S., 20,90 €, br.,
ISBN 3-8258-8806-1

Nicola Spakowski;
Cecilia Milwertz (Eds.)
Women and Gender in Chinese Studies
Women and gender studies increasingly contribute to a more differentiated knowledge of China. This issue presents research on a variety of topics related to women and gender in modern and contemporary China including the question of women's citizenship in the Republican period, health issues of women soldiers on the Long March, the problem of and activities against domestic violence and the revision of the marriage law. By exploring how gender interacts with other categories and how processes of modernization and transformation are gendered the articles shed new light on the structures of Chinese society.
Bd. 29, 2006, 168 S., 20,90 €, br.,
ISBN 3-8258-9304-9

William C. Kirby; Mechthild Leutner;
Klaus Mühlhahn (Eds.)
Global Conjectures: China in Transnational Perspective
This issue deals with the integration of modern China into processes of global exchange and cross-border interaction. The articles explore the broader theme in different ways and in different subfields, ranging from the history of political ideas to the history of institutions, from global migration of people to the transmigration of academic discourses. Focusing on modern as well as contemporary periods, the studies demonstrate that China in the course of the twentieth century became an ever more important nodal point in a complex set of worldwide networks and engagements. The integration into global networks, together with the global consciousness that corresponded with it, made possible significant connections transcending national borders. The essays also show that the effects could be homogenizing (or globalizing), but at the same time the growing interactions also produced opposition and fragmentation.
Bd. 30, 2006, 168 S., 20,90 €, br.,
ISBN 3-8258-9481-9

LIT Verlag Münster – Berlin – Hamburg – London – Wien
Fresnostr. 2 48159 Münster
Tel.: 0251 – 62 032 22 – Fax: 0251 – 23 19 72
e-Mail: vertrieb@lit-verlag.de – http://www.lit-verlag.de